T0215057

Communications
in Computer and Information Science 803

Commenced Publication in 2007
Founding and Former Series Editors:
Alfredo Cuzzocrea, Xiaoyong Du, Orhun Kara, Ting Liu, Dominik Ślęzak,
and Xiaokang Yang

More information about this series at http://www.springer.com/series/7899

Quan Yu (Ed.)

Space Information Networks

Second International Conference, SINC 2017
Yinchuan, China, August 10–11, 2017
Revised Selected Papers

 Springer

Editor
Quan Yu
Institute of China Electronic Equipment
Beijing
China

ISSN 1865-0929   ISSN 1865-0937   (electronic)
Communications in Computer and Information Science
ISBN 978-981-10-7876-7   ISBN 978-981-10-7877-4   (eBook)
https://doi.org/10.1007/978-981-10-7877-4

Library of Congress Control Number: 2017963754

This Springer imprint is published by Springer Nature
The registered company is Springer Nature Singapore Pte Ltd.
The registered company address is: 152 Beach Road, #21-01/04 Gateway East, Singapore 189721, Singapore

Preface

The Space Information Networks Conference (SINC) is the annual conference of the Department of Information Science, National Natural Science Foundation of China. SINC is supported by the key research project on the basic theory and key technology of space information networks of the National Natural Science Foundation of China, and organized by the Space Information Networks major research program guidance group. The conference aims to explore new progress and developments in space information networks and related fields, to show the latest technological and academic achievements in space information networks, to build an academic exchange platform for researchers at home and abroad working on space information networks and industry sectors, to share their achievements and experiences in research and applications, and to discuss the new theory and new technology of space information networks. SINC 2017 was the second conference in the series. There are three sections in these proceedings including models of space information networks and mechanisms of high-performance networking, theory and method of high-speed transmission in space dynamic networks, and sparse representation and fusion processes in space information.

This year, we received 145 submissions, including 96 English papers and 49 Chinese papers. After a thorough reviewing process, 30 outstanding English papers were selected for this volume (retrieved by EI), accounting for 31.3% of the total number of English papers, with an acceptance rate of 26.9%. This volume contains the 27 English full papers and three short papers presented at SINC 2017.

The high-quality program would not have been possible without the authors who chose SINC 2017 as a venue for their publications. We are also very grateful to the Program Committee members and Organizing Committee members, who put a tremendous amount of effort into soliciting and selecting research papers with a balance of high quality and new ideas and new applications.

We hope that you enjoy reading and benefit from the proceedings of SINC 2017.

November 2017   Quan Yu

Organization

SINC 2017 was organized by the panel of guiding experts of the "Spatial Information Network" Major Research Plan, Department of Information Science, National Natural Science Foundation of China, Posts and Telecom Press, *Journal of Communications and Information Networks* Periodical Office, Ningxia University, and the Beijing Institute of Remote Sensing Information.

General Chairs

Jianya Gong	Wuhan University, China
Jianhua Lu	Tsinghua University, China
Quan Yu	Institute of China Electronic Equipment System Engineering Corporation, China

Steering Committee

Chang Wen Chen	The State University of New York at Buffalo, USA
Hsiao-Hwa Chen	National Cheng Kung University, Taiwan, China
Ning Ge	Tsinghua University, China
Ronghong Jin	Shanghai Jiao Tong University, China
George K. Karagiannidis	Aristotle University of Thessaloniki, Greece
Feng Liu	Beihang University, China
Jianwei Liu	Beihang University, China
Zhaohui Song	National Nature Science Foundation of China, China
Dongjin Wang	University of Science and Technology of China, China
Mi Wang	Wuhan University, China
Haitao Wu	Chinese Academy of Sciences, China
Xiaoyun Xiong	National Nature Science Foundation of China, China
Xiaohu You	Southeast University, China
Jun Zhang	Beihang University, China
Zhaotian Zhang	National Nature Science Foundation of China, China
Zhixin Zhou	Beijing Institute of Remote Sensing Information, China

Technical Program Committee

Xianbin Cao	Beihang University, China
Yingkui Gong	University of Chinese Academy of Sciences, China
Depeng Jin	Tsinghua University, China
Hongyan Li	Xidian University, China
Lixiang Liu	Chinese Academy of Sciences, China

Chengsheng Pan	Dalian University, China
Yong Ren	Tsinghua University, China
Chundong She	Beijing University of Posts and Telecommunications, China
Min Sheng	Xidian University, China
Qingyang Song	Northeastern University, China
Xiaoming Tao	Tsinghua University, China
Junfeng Wang	Sichuan University, China
Weidong Wang	Beijing University of Posts and Telecommunications, China
Jian Yan	Tsinghua University, China
Shuyuan Yang	Xidian University, China
Zhihua Yang	Harbin Institute of Technology, Shenzhen, China
Qinyu Zhang	Harbin Institute of Technology, China
Minjian Zhao	Zhejiang University, China

Organizing Committee

Lin Bai	Beihang University, China
Jinho Choi	Gwangju Institute of Science and Technology, South Korea
Jun Fang	University of Electronic Science and Technology of China, China
Yuguang Fang	University of Florida, USA
Lin Gao	Harbin Institute of Technology, Shenzhen, China
Lajos Hanzo	University of Southampton, UK
Jianhua He	Aston University, UK
Chunxiao Jiang	Tsinghua University, China
Ahmed Kamal	Iowa State University, USA
Nei Kato	Tohoku University, Japan
Geoffrey Ye Li	Georgia Institute of Technology, USA
Jiandong Li	Xidian University, China
Shaoqian Li	University of Electronic Science and Technology of China, China
Wenjing Li	Beijing University of Posts and Telecommunications, China
Changjun Liu	Sichuan University, China
Jianfeng Ma	Xidian University, China
Xiao Ma	Sun Yat-sen University, China
Shiwen Mao	Auburn University, USA
Luoming Meng	Beijing University of Posts and Telecommunications, China
Joseph Mitola	Stevens Institute of Technology, USA
Chunhong Pan	Chinese Academy of Sciences, China
Mugen Peng	Beijing University of Posts and Telecommunications, China
Sherman Shen	University of Waterloo, Canada
Zhongxiang Shen	Nanyang Technological University, Singapore
William Shieh	University of Melbourne, Australia
Meixia Tao	Shanghai Jiao Tong University, China
Xiaoming Tao	Tsinghua University, China
Y. Thomas Hou	Virginia Polytechnic Institute and State University, USA

Xinbing Wang	Shanghai Jiao Tong University, China
Feng Wu	University of Science and Technology of China, China
Jianping Wu	Tsinghua University, China
Qi Wu	Beihang University, China
Gang Wu	University of Electronic Science and Technology of China, China
Xiang-Gen Xia	University of Delaware, USA
Shaoqiu Xiao	University of Electronic Science and Technology of China, China
Liuguo Yin	Tsinghua University, China
Shaohua Yu	FiberHome Technologies Group, China
Guanglin Zhang	Donghua University, China
Honggang Zhang	Zhejiang University, China
Hongke Zhang	Beijing Jiaotong University, China
Yafeng Zhan	Tsinghua University, China
Youping Zhao	Beijing Jiaotong University, China
Hongbo Zhu	Nanjing University of Posts and Telecommunications, China
Weiping Zhu	Concordia University, Canada

Contents

Theory and Method of High Speed Transmission

System Architecture and Efficient Networking Mechanism

Multi-dimensional Resource Management for Satellite Network

Wei Ma[(⊠)], Zhe Zhao, Hanwen Sun, Leifang Hui, and Zhou Tian

Xi'an Institute of Space Radio Technology, Xi'an, China
mawei_mail@sina.com

Abstract. The satellite network includes various resource types, involved space, frequency, time and other resource dimensions, and the resources are distributed in different heterogeneous autonomous systems. How to realize the uniform representation of diversified satellite network resources, how to find the resource discovery mechanism suitable for satellite network, how to have the expansibility of the Satellite network resource management architecture, and to combine the efficiency of resource utilization and the flexibility of use are the main contents of this paper.

Keywords: Satellite network · Resource characterization
Resource discovery · Resource management

1 Introduction

As a whole, the satellite network resources are characterized by wide-area distribution, multiform and heterogeneous autonomy, including: antenna, beam, spectrum, power, transparent transponder, operation, storage and other resource types, involving space, frequency, time and other dimensions. The satellite system is a typical limited system, the resources of satellite network are very valuable because of the long period of resource construction and the difficulty of rapid expansion. How to find and make full use of the network resources dispersed in different satellite systems is a problem that the satellite network must study and solve. This paper is based on the above considerations, from the three aspects of satellite network resource characterizations, resource discovery and resources management mechanism, carried out related research work.

2 Resource Characterization

The unified representation of resources is the basis of the unified management and deployment of the network resources of different discrete heterogeneous systems in satellite networks, including the research contents of resource classification standards and resource description methods.

From different perspective, the network resources can be divided into different kinds, and the overly refined classification is easy to increase the cost of resource mapping and management, but also loses the meaning of classification, and the

© Springer Nature Singapore Pte Ltd. 2018
Q. Yu (Ed.): SINC 2017, CCIS 803, pp. 3–12, 2018.
https://doi.org/10.1007/978-981-10-7877-4_1

improper selection of classification criterion is easily divorced from practical application, and it is difficult to embody the practicality and value of resource classification.

Satellite networks are usually wireless networks, taking into account resource entities and network features in the network, dividing resources from satellite networks into four categories: access resources, spectrum resources, link resources and processing forwarding resources. The distribution of these resources in satellite networks is illustrated as follows (Fig. 1):

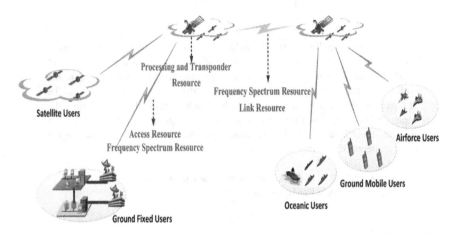

Fig. 1. Resource classification in satellite network

The resource description method is a hot topic in the current academic field, according to the characteristics of various kinds of network and the task demand, the corresponding resource description method is put forward by many institutions.

In the Internet of Things (IoT), some researchers defined that the things are classified into data (sensors), events (accentures) and services (actuators) according to the type of action. In the IoT, data refers to attribute values such as variables and to integer values; events refer to when certain conditions are met or when certain states are reached. Services allow certain functions to be carried out through a predefined interface [1, 2].

In the Internet Searching Based on Resource Description (ISBORD), the structure of resource description is starting with BEGIN and ending with END, part of the description consists of one or more keywords. The keyword, being the basic element, is organized by the Type-Length-Value (TLV) field [3].

In the Geospatial Resource Description Framework (GRDF), some researchers use the following sections: feature, geometry, topology, value, observation, Coordinate Reference System (CRS), TimeObject and coverage to provide a detailed description of the types defined in the ontology [4].

Resource description method in IoT paid more attention to the description of node resource capabilities, and ISBORD is more concerned about the description of the data content. The GRDF only gives a descriptive framework, but does not define a specific implementation mechanism.

The above mechanism cannot cover the resource types of satellite network, and it is difficult to meet the resource description requirement of satellite network, so it is necessary to study and propose a resource description method suitable for satellite network.

In the aspect of satellite network resource characterization, we used attribute parameters and state parameters to reflect the intrinsic and dynamic characteristics of satellite network resources.

Attribute parameter: describes the inherent attributes or attributes of various resources in the network, such as: available time, frequency, power, etc.

State parameters: describe the specific state of various resources in the network, such as: availability, occupancy rate, allowance, etc.

Based on the above-mentioned resource classification criterion and the resource characterization method, the four kinds of satellite network resources are characterized as follows:

2.1 Access Resources

Property parameters	Resource ID
	Resource entity type (antenna type, etc.)
	Network attribution
	Beam number
	Coverage range
	Transmitting frequency
	Transmitting power range
	Antenna gain
	Loss of feeding
	EIRP
	Receive antenna gain
	Receive feeder loss
	Receive signal level
	Receive thermal noise
	Noise coefficient
	G/T
	Noise power spectral density
	C/N0
	Information rate
	Eb/N0
	Coding gain
	Available time
State parameters	Current position
	Transmitting power
	Receiving power
	Resource availability status
	Resource occupancy status
	Current period

2.2 Spectrum Resources

Property parameters	Resource ID
	Resource entity type (frequency bands, wavelength, etc.)
	Network attribution
	Frequency range
	Frequency subdivision particle size
	Location range
	Available time
	Power range
State parameters	Working frequency
	Current position
	Current period
	Current power
	Spectrum quality
	Spectrum occupancy Status

2.3 Link Resources

Property parameters	Resource ID
	Resource entity types (Wireless Link, wired link, laser link, etc.)
	Network attribution
	Total link bandwidth
	Link bandwidth subdivision granularity
	Location range
	Available time
State parameters	Current position
	Current period
	Available status
	Link quality (link-breaking, BER, transmission delay, etc.)
	Link overhead (expense, etc.)
	Link bandwidth occupancy Status

2.4 Processing Forwarding Resources

Property parameters	Resource ID
	Resource entity types (transparent transponder, regenerated forwarders/routing switching devices/operational storage devices, etc.)
	Network attribution
	Transparent transponder/transparent transponder band range
	Transparent transponder/transparent transponder number
	Flexible forwarding/sub band granularity
	Flexible forwarding/sub band switching capacity

	Processing forwarding/data throughput
	Processing forwarding/switching latency
	Processing forwarding/switching delay jitter
	Processing forwarding/packet loss rates
	Forwarding paths
	Logical resources
	Storage resources
	Operational resources
	Location range
	Available time
State parameters	Current position
	Current period
	Available status
	Move rate
	Resource occupancy rate
	Congestion status

3 Resource Discovery

The resource discovery architecture can be classified into two categories: peer-to-peer architectures and directory-based architectures [5].

Peer-to-peer (P2P) architectures: use fully distributed mechanisms for resource discovery, where networks entities (providers and clients) negotiate one-to-one with each other to discover the available resource. Two basics mechanisms can be used to resource discovery in peer-to-peer systems: query mechanisms and advertising mechanisms.

Directory-based architectures: use a centralized or distributed repository, which aggregates and indexes the information about resources offered in the network. Providers register their resources with this directory, and clients query the directory to obtain information about resources. There are three different general schemes of directory-based systems: centralized directory (CD), distributed flat directory (DFD), distributed hierarchical directory (DHD).

Table 1 summarizes the main pros and cons of the different resource/service discovery architectures in terms of suitability for changing conditions, scalability, bandwidth consumption, discovery delay, and management complexity.

Compared to directory-based architectures, peer-to-peer architectures are useful for fast and dynamic changing network environment, where network infrastructure is unpredictable, and the presence of permanent dedicated directories cannot be guaranteed. For satellite networks, the topological structure is relatively stable and periodic change, directory-based resource discovery architectures is more suitable.

From the point of view of control mode, the resource discovery mechanism of directory-based architectures mainly includes: centralized discovery mechanism, distributed discovery mechanism and the combination of the former two, the Hybrid resource discovery mechanism [6].

Table 1. Main features of discovery mechanisms

	P2P-Query	P2P-Adv	CD	DFD	DHD
Suitability for changing conditions	High	High	Low	Low	Low
Scalability	Low	Low	Low	High	High
Bandwidth consumption	Medium	High	Low	Low	Low
Discovery delay	High	Low	Low	Low	Low
Management complexity	Low	Low	Medium	High	High

Centralized resource discovery mode, the system needs to set up a unified resource information registration management node, which grasps the global resource state information (resource category, distribution, etc.) and provides resource retrieval service to the resource requester, each time the resource request accesses the resource information registration management node. In this way, there are some problems for the resource information registration management node, such as: a certain probability of single point failure, root node access bottlenecks, and so on. Once the failure, will cause the whole system to crash, system scalability is poor. The advantages are easy to manage, update, and maintain.

In distributed resource discovery, each participant node in the system stores a subspace of the entire resource ID space, and is responsible for maintaining the mapping of the subspace resource IDs to the corresponding physical entities, and the query request forwarding and state maintenance are realized by using a specific protocol between the nodes. This approach has strong scalability, but the routing process of requesting resources cannot effectively narrow the search scope of target resources, there is some blindness, and the resources of network communication will consume more when searching.

The combination of centralization and distribution is the combination and supplement of the first two resource discovery ways, and the hybrid resource lookup balances the efficiency of centralized search and the autonomy of distributed search, which is beneficial to the load balancing and robustness of the system. In the hybrid resource discovery mechanism, the nodes are divided into resource service nodes and index registration nodes according to the ability of nodes, and the resources are registered on any service node. And the service node also has its own index information registered on the registered node of the organization, and the registration node becomes the proxy of the service node, which constructs the upper-level distributed index network, and the registered node and the service node of the proxy form the lower-level centralized index network together.

The nodes in the satellite network are far smaller than the terrestrial network, the spatial information network consist of terrestrial network, near-space network, satellite network and so on, the role of satellite network is more of a space segment information infrastructure than an information service provider, and satellite network users are more concerned with the choice of access networks and the availability of satellite network resources. In view of the role of satellite network and the above reasons, the satellite network can use centralized resource discovery mode, but for the spatial information network using hybrid resource discovery mechanism is a better choice.

In satellite networks, the function of the resource information registration management node is usually implemented by Satellite Network Operator or NCC (Network Control Center) [7].

Satellite resources are usually held in the hands of different holders, which can be divided into private (totally private), protected (restricted access) and public (fully open) three classes according to the level of openness of the resource. Different satellites need to register all resource information at the Satellite Network Operator or NCC in the planning and deployment phases. After the satellite has served on the orbit, it can notify the other resource index registration nodes in the system voluntarily by notifying or registering protected and public category resource information as needed. As shown in the illustration (Fig. 2):

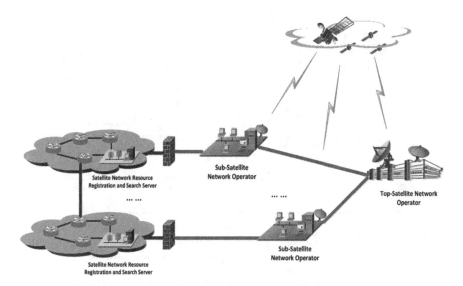

Fig. 2. The organization structure of satellite network resource registration and retrieval

4 Resource Management

As an integrated network, spatial information network is a kind of intelligent network composed of land, sea, air and satellite information processing system, which is characterized by the high complexity, heterogeneity and dynamic characteristics of the network, which repels the completely centralized and completely distributed network resource organization and management.

In view of the above characteristics, this paper presents a hierarchical network resource management structure, which consists of control agent, Sub-Satellite Network Operator, Top-Satellite Network Operator, satellite network access provider, and so on, illustrated as follows (Fig. 3):

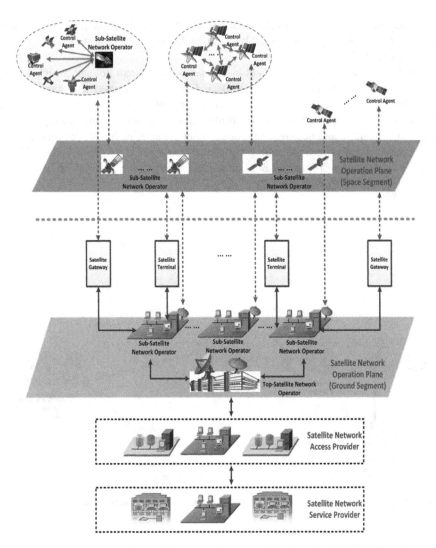

Fig. 3. Hierarchical satellite network resource management architecture

Control Agent: Responsible for the implementation of specific resource entities to control, collect and broadcast related resource status information, including: resource allocation, resource deployment, status monitoring, and resource statistics.

Sub-Satellite Network Operator: Responsible for completing the user management, admission Control, resource allocation and other functions of the sub admin domain, simultaneously receiving and executing the control strategy and processing rules issued by the higher level managers, completing the processing functions of network resource fragmentation and virtual plane mapping.

Top-Satellite Network Operator: Master the state information of the different sub management domains of the whole network, and can control the Sub-Satellite

Network Operators distributed in different domains, and complete the maintenance, management, deployment and operation of the satellite network infrastructure.

Satellite Network Access Provider: Responsible for managing and manipulating satellite network access elements (satellite terminals, gateways, and so on), at the same time, based on the specific task requirements of different service providers for service description, function description, capability description and resource requirements description mapping, according to the mapping results planning and matching network resource fragmentation, policies and rules, and complete the configuration of the operation manager of satellite network, This provides a chunk of transport resources for different service providers.

The management level and business functions of the above-mentioned managers are as shown in the illustration (Fig. 4):

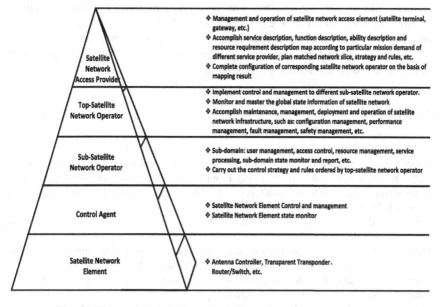

Fig. 4. Hierarchical definition of satellite network resource managers

The satellite network is facing various kinds of service providers and user terminals, in order to meet the resource's effective utilization and flexible management, which must provide multiple levels of resource management granularity and realize the hierarchical management of resources. Satellite network access providers can allocate the dedicated bandwidth of large granularity to the relatively independent service provider network based on the bandwidth requirements of different service providers, so that the service provider can manage and deploy the bandwidth by itself, and the satellite network focuses on the service quality assurance of the users in the network based on the level of agreement (SLA).

The private type resources in different systems of satellite network are managed and assigned by the sub-satellite network operator in the respective management domain; The protected type resources are joined by sub-satellite network operator, top-satellite network operator, and satellite network access provider to complete management and allocation; The public type resource is fully allocated by satellite network access provider and service provider.

5 Conclusions

This paper focuses on the research of satellite network resource characterization method, resource discovery mechanism and resource management framework. Combined with the resource characteristics of satellite network, this paper puts forward the classification standard of satellite network resources and the method of resource representation, meanwhile summarizes the resource discovery mechanism suitable for satellite network based on the existing resources discovery research results. In view of the development demand of the spatial information network, this paper puts forward a kind of satellite network resource management structure which takes into account the efficiency of resource utilization and flexibility.

References

1. ITU-T SG13, Y.2060: Overview of the Internet of Things (2012)
2. Mattern, F., Floerkemeier, C.: From the internet of computers to the Internet of Things. In: Sachs, K., Petrov, I., Guerrero, P. (eds.) From Active Data Management to Event-Based Systems and More. LNCS, vol. 6462, pp. 242–259. Springer, Heidelberg (2010). https://doi.org/10.1007/978-3-642-17226-7_15
3. Yan, Z., Zeadally, S., Geng, G.: ISBORD: internet searching based on resource description. ICT Express **3**, 48–51 (2017)
4. Alam, A., Khan, L., Thuraisingham, B.: Geospatial Resource Description Framework (GRDF) and security constructs. Comput. Stand. Interfaces **33**, 35–41 (2011)
5. Moreno-Vozmediano, R.: A hybrid mechanism for resource/service discovery in ad-hoc grids. Future Gener. Comput. Syst. **25**, 717–727 (2009)
6. Cheng, J., Jiang, Y., Zhang, W.: Research on dynamic discovery model of service resource based on information grid. In: ICICT-2012 (2012)
7. Ferrús, R., Koumaras, H., Sallent, O., Agapiou, G., Rasheed, T., Kourtis, M.-A., Boustie, C., Gélard, P., Ahmed, T.: SDN/NFV-enabled satellite communications networks: opportunities, scenarios and challenges. Phys. Commun. **18**, 95–112 (2016)

The Security Threat and Strategy Analysis of Space Information Network

She Chundong, Jia Luting[(⊠)], Ma Yaqi, and Liu Shaohua

Beijing University of Posts and Telecommunications, Beijing 100876, China
799930600@qq.com

Abstract. According to the characteristics of space information network, this paper introduces a security threat model, and then makes a detailed threat analysis for network system from five levels, physical device, platform system, network security, data security and management security. At last, this paper offers a brief analysis of security strategy of the five levels, these results will serve as a theoretical underpinning for creating a security defense architecture for space information network roundly and dynamically.

Keywords: Network security · Space information network · Security threats
Security strategy

1 Introduction

Space information network is a kind of network system which obtains, transfers and processes space information in real time, based on a variety of space platform (synchronous satellites, middle or low orbit satellites, stratospheric balloons, and manned or unmanned aircrafts, etc.) [1–3]. The system composition is shown in Fig. 1.

As one country's important infrastructure construction, space information network could support high dynamic, broadband real-time transmission in earth observation on the ground [4], and very-long-range, large-time-delay and reliable transmission in deep space exploration [5], when serving significant applications such as emergency rescue, navigation, air transport and aerospace measurement and control, etc. [6]. Thus it could expand human science, culture, production activity to the space, ocean, and even deep space [7, 8].

Compared with other networks, space information network has several characteristics:

(1) A three-dimensional, multiple-layer and global network [9].
(2) Many different kinds of node types, huge differences of links, heterogeneity network [10, 11].
(3) Nodes and links vary with space-time, and the topology is dynamical [12].
(4) Many different kinds of businesses, wide distribution range, huge differences of needs [13].
(5) Limited resources of space, low platform ability, limited ground station [14].

© Springer Nature Singapore Pte Ltd. 2018
Q. Yu (Ed.): SINC 2017, CCIS 803, pp. 13–23, 2018.
https://doi.org/10.1007/978-981-10-7877-4_2

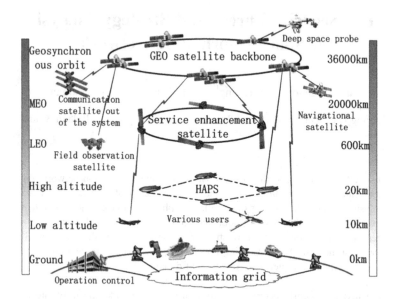

Fig. 1. Satellite system composition

Space information network can achieve the connectivity of space and ground network. But because of the lack of physical isolation, and in view of the above-mentioned characteristics, space information network has more threats than ground [15]. Therefore, in order to provide security for space information network, develop independent and effective security defense architecture, making a detailed security threats analysis is the prerequisite for all research.

2   The Threat Analysis Model of Space Information Network

First, we should define a kind of potential security threat and determine whether it exists in space information network, if not, we don't need to analyze this kind of security threat; else, we should analyze its characteristics and expression, and determine the level of threat (in our paper, we divided network into five levels, physical device, platform system, network, data and management, respectively). Next, we should discuss whether there exist effective safety measures against this kind of threat in system. If there really exists, we don't need to develop safety measures again; else, we need to develop the corresponding safety measures, in terms of the characteristics and expression of the threat. Finally, we should back to the beginning and redefine new security threats after ensuring that the network could protect against the attack effectively. Repeat the cycle as above, it can finally form the whole security analysis threats system of space information network (Fig. 2).

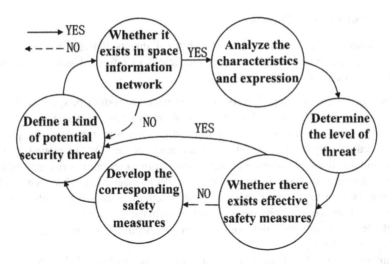

Fig. 2. The threat analysis model

3 Hierarchical Security Threat Analysis of Space Information Network

We can see the threats of space information network and the threat network components in Fig. 3.

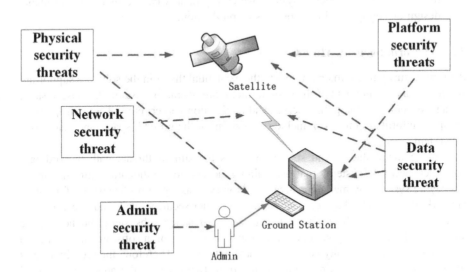

Fig. 3. The security threats architecture

3.1 Physical Security Threats

Physical security threat mainly refers to physical threats that the hardware which constitutes the space information network physical device faces. Usually the cause of the physical security threat has three aspects:

(1) The natural environment factors. The hardware of system in space and on the ground are directly exposed in the external environment, and system is likely to perform tasks in various natural environments. Therefore, the physical equipment is tested directly by the ground and space environment. On the ground, there are earthquake, flood, thunderstorm, sandstorm, tropical storm, corrosive substances, air pollution and so on. In space, complex electromagnetic environment [16] can cause damage to electronic equipment of satellites, a growing number of space junk and meteorites will cause physical damage to satellites or other space vehicles, and influence the normal work of electronic equipment, even cause irreparable damage.

(2) Human factors. The human secure threats of space physical device are mainly caused by weapons which cause destruction and attack to hardware based on the energy flow, such as various space offensive laser weapon, the kinetic energy, etc. In addition to external attacks, incorrect manipulation to the system by internal personnel or artificial damage which cause equipment stolen or communication, power supply circuit or system paralyzed because of the lack of effective physical protection, is also one of the factors that constitutes the system threats.

(3) Self factors of the device. The fault of the device is also an important reason causing the hardware device under threat. The fault is mainly determined by the reliability of the product or system, which is probably caused by the unreasonable design or negligence in the process of production.

3.2 Platform Security Threat

Platform security threat mainly refers to the existential threat in the software supporting system of each component of the system (including operating system, database system, storage system, the computing server and application server, etc.). The main parts of the space information network include subsystem of the ground, space, and near space subsystem.

Among them, the ground subsystem faces the similar threats with the ordinary computer network system, that is, gaining access to confidential information or destroying systems by malicious invasion. However, as a part of the space information network, the ground subsystem should have a higher security level; and because of its universality, it is much easier to be attacked. For space subsystem and near space subsystem, because computer operating system and application software on the satellite nodes have certain specialty and concealment externally. Therefore, the security threats of space subsystem platform mainly come from two aspects: the attack from illegal users and illegal use of legitimate users.

Attacks from illegal users include active attack and passive attack [17]. Active attack might include: the illegal invasion, malicious code hazards, system defect attack, illegal modification and replacement of the system software, etc. These attacks often cause leakage of inside information, data contamination, or the quality decrease of the service and even paralysis. The typical cases include invading command and control system on the ground, intercepting satellite remote control instruction and capturing satellite control, etc. Passive attack might include: scanning the external interface of the system, monitoring and feature analysis. These attacks may lead to mutual information leakage and exposure of system configuration, vulnerability, and service type information, etc. [18].

Illegal use of legitimate users is an internal attack from the system. These users may be forced or voluntary to use internal system services abnormally, surrender internal information, or fake other users' identity to use system services and access information illegally, etc. System service interruptions and information leakage caused by misuse of internal legitimate users might provide convenience to break system for illegal users. For example, users plant computer viruses into the system accidentally.

3.3 Network Security Threat

Network security threat mainly refers to the security threats aimed at the network and related facilities. At the network level, the important assets of system network include: network connection which compose the ground survey control network and command control network, and links from satellites to satellites or satellites to ground. These threats cause potential consequences such as: network congestion, high network transmission delay, low transmission rate, even information transmission interruption.

Although the interfaces for outside of space information network software and hardware platform are fewer and the kind of network internal interfaces are single, system is still faced with attack threats from network, such as vulnerabilities attack, Trojan horse, virus attack and so on, these attacks which infiltrate directly via network need to pay a high price, but once these attacks are successful, it may bring huge effect to system. The plaintext transmitting on network is faced with information leakage. And the data access from external system to internal system via network is faced with identity cheats and unauthorized access. The security threats aimed at communication links include: electronic interference, information flow analysis, truncation, tampering, inserting or resetting information flows, and intrusion or DoS attack aimed at fault of communication protocol.

As for the vulnerability of system network, the ground network has a relatively fixed topological structure and a mature network technology. Therefore, its vulnerability mainly shows in the configuration of communication protocol and network facilities. The space network belongs to wireless network, and its vulnerability mainly shows in several aspects: the topological structure of space information network, configuration of space nodes, wireless communication protocol etc. Space satellite nodes are in constant motion and the network topological structure is in a state of change at any moment, which makes the physical boundary of space information network fuzzy, so it's not suitable for space network to use traditional network boundary protection technologies. In addition, space communication link is an important component of space information network, uses wireless communication, and has several features, such as, unique transmission medium, new communication protocol, wide signal coverage, complex external environment, etc. And these features have a big impact on the security of space information network. Communication quality of wireless transmission is easier to be interfered; defects of new communication protocols are easy to be analyzed and used by enemies, leading to all sorts of network attacks against agreement; large coverage of signal is likely to leak sensitive information; big spatial span, complex external environment, inter-satellite links and satellite-ground links in space, are easily affected by external environment, such as solar activity and geomagnetic storm, which leads to high bit error rate and difficult network maintenance; limited by space vehicle payload, satellites have limited transmission power, size of receiving antenna and the inherent ability of anti-electromagnetic interference of inter-satellite links and satellite-ground links, which might lead to large possibility of the potential safety hazard. Therefore, we should analyze security threats of communication link of the space information network from four aspects, which are satellite uplink (user link), satellite downlink (feeder link), inter-satellite link and terrestrial link.

(1) Threats of satellite uplink

The communication interference station interferes with the satellite uplink by acquiring and analyzing the characteristic parameters of the link at first, and then tracking and aiming the satellite, and launching strong jamming signal to it in order to destroy the satellite receivers, and make it not work properly. Such interference makes the SNR of the uplink greatly worsen, or makes the satellite receiver saturate or blocking and unable to work. At the same time, it also can use the communication link to fake identity, invade the system to steal confidential information, data, etc.

(2) Threats of satellite downlink

Ground station and ground network are the main targets of downlink interruption, and the usually used mean is using interference stations which are carried in space platform, such as unmanned plane and balloon. Such interruptions deteriorate SNR of satellite downlink, and influence the normal communication of satellite ground receiving system. The beam of satellite downlink is wide, and the communication mode is based more on broadcast, so some attackers may use the ground satellite receiving equipment to intercept and decipher, to get sensitive information of system.

(3) Threats of inter-satellite link

The threats of inter-satellite links mainly include two aspects. Firstly, routing information is publicly exposed to spatial channel. To enable the communication of inter-satellite links, constellation satellites should have ability to process and exchange, and the data frames format of links must include some routing information to enable the process of switching and routing. Routing information usually reflects some important information, such as channel capacity, time series, communication mode and so on. Once these information is steal by attacker, it may cause huge threats to normal communication of inter-satellite links. Secondly, the satellite orbit parameters and ephemeris are open. The frequency resource of inter-satellite links sticks to rules of International Telecommunication Union, and is fixed and limited. Attackers can search in the same frequency by the companion stars that are close to target satellite. On the one hand, attackers can get the information from other adjacent satellite nodes in the constellation. On the other hand, the satellite which is close to companion stars is easy to get the interruption information from them.

(4) Threats of terrestrial link

Terrestrial link, that is the communication links of space information on ground, has the same security threats as traditional ground computer network. The security problem of terrestrial link is not specific, so we don't need to make a special discussion.

3.4 Data Security Threat

Data security threat mainly refers to the potential threat which can damage the confidentiality, integrity and availability of data information. Data security is especially important. At the data level, remote and telemetry data from satellites and aircrafts, a large number of investigation data from reconnaissance satellite, military communication data and command control data which will be sent from space information network, all belong to the protected objects of data security.

Data security threat mainly includes two aspects: one is already-stored data, the other is transmitting data. The data stored in computer system or database is in danger of computer virus, illegal invaders and system accidental failures, and is easy to be destroyed. As for general users, computer platform of satellite is unfamiliar, so the data stored in space nodes is less likely to be attacked. Therefore, the data stored in space nodes has high security; but the data stored in the ground subsystem is faced with more threats. The threats of such data include: malicious intrusions by external staffs, accessing system resources illegal, stealing sensitive information, damaging data confidentiality; adding or tampering stored data, damaging data integrity; deleting data, damaging data usability; and it may also cause the important information lost or stolen by enemy when the insiders do misoperation or let out on purpose. As for the inartificial threats, system trouble and natural environment always damage data security. The security of transmitting data is directly related to the security of network. The threats include: enemy stealing unencrypted confidential information by electromagnetic leakage or wiretapped, or guessing the purpose of others and obtaining useful information by the analysis of information flow, communication frequency and communication length, damaging confidentiality; tampering or resetting data information, damaging data integrity; truncating data transmitting, damage data usability.

In both space and ground aspects, the ground subsystem which often uses wire transmission, and is mature no matter on communication protocol or communication technology, has high data security; the space subsystem and the data between ground and space subsystem use wireless transmission, which has obvious vulnerable characteristics, is worse than wire communication no matter on communication rate or quality, in addition, the communication protocol is not perfect and the technology is not as mature as wire communication [19], which makes data transmission faces high security risk.

3.5   Administrative Security Threat

Administrative security threat can be viewed from two aspects: technology level, referring primarily to security problems of the network management system; non-technical level, referring primarily to the security problems such as organizational rules and regulations, work standards, the staffs' consciousness of safety.

The network management system can be divided into several parts: center management node, managed node agent and message communication channel. The security threats of center management node mainly include the illegal use from non-administrators, the illegal operation from administrators and so on. Managed node agent runs directly on the managed node, in general, these managed nodes have high system permissions, can collect sensitive information related to manage node, even control nodes' actions. Therefore, it will cause huge losses if manage nodes are controlled by malicious users. The security threats of managed nodes mainly include that illegal users access system resources and legitimate users illegally use resources. There should be a communication channel between center management node and managed node, only in this way system can finish information collecting and administrative work. However, the communication channel may be attacked by physical interference, eavesdrop, filch, etc., which may affect the confidentiality, integrity and availability of data information.

Non-technical level mainly includes rules and regulations, business process management, device management, staff management, document management etc. Such security threats have good invisibility, and are easily overlooked but can lead more serious damage.

The security threats can be summarized in Fig. 4. The central task of whole space information network is processing data information. Therefore, data information

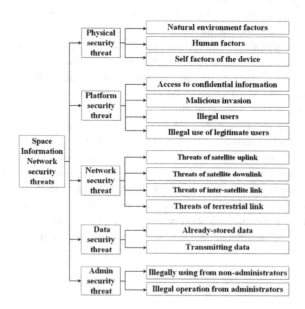

Fig. 4. The security threats of space information network

security is the core of maintaining whole system security; all other layers' security is to ensure data information security. Physical device is the infrastructure construction of whole system, the software system is the platform of processing information system, network is the support of data information transmission, and management is the guarantee of data information security. These five layers' security risks are inter-linking and inter-influencing, single security problem will affect other aspects of security.

4 Space Information Network Security Strategy

In order to ensure safety of space information network, we should create the independent and effective security defense architecture for system. According to the characteristics of space information network, application scene and the security threats analysis of the preceding context, we start with five aspects: physical level, platform system, network, and management, develop the security protection technology and apply to space information network.

(1) Physical security level: We should take the corresponding protective measures according to its trigger factors. In general, it mainly includes several key technologies: reinforcing and defending technologies, monitoring of space junk and enemy weapons, redundant backup for equipment and system.

(2) Platform system level: As for platform system level, on the one hand, we should try to avoid design mistakes of system, ensure the correctness of the software design and implementation, improve the system fault-tolerance ability and reliability; on the other hand, we should detect defects of software support system as timely and early as possible, and make up them in time.

(3) Network security level: We should develop security gateway [20] and communication protocol for space information network. At the same time, aimed at two protocol specifications which are in common use in space businesses at present: SCPS and IP for space, we should put forward the corresponding security protocol or improve security of their basic protocols.

(4) Data security level: We can use symmetric encryption algorithm, Hash algorithm, and asymmetric encryption algorithm to keep the data security [21, 22]. In addition, we should pay attention on data redundancy backup and disaster recovery.

(5) Management security level: For reference of management security threats analysis, we should keep management security in two aspects. First, we should guarantee the security of network management system to a great extent. Second, all the staff who access to sensitive information and operate system should have a high professional quality and professional ethics quality, and strong safety consciousness.

5 Conclusion and Future Work

According to the result of this paper, we made a detailed threat analysis for network system from five levels, physical device, platform system, network security, data security and management security. From the threat analysis we can see, security threats for a system are multi-level, and these five layers' security risks are inter-linking and inter-influencing, single security problem will affect others. Therefore, when we create independent and effective security defense architecture, we should start with multiple layers, create a security defense architecture for whole system roundly and dynamically.

With the development of security threats and security technologies are emerging in an endless stream. We should keep abreast of the times, do more analysis of the newest technologies, and improve our security defense architecture continually; only in this way we can create a safe and effective space information network.

Acknowledgements. This work was supported by the National Natural Science Foundation of China (91438120). And the Foundation of advanced research.

References

1. Li, H., Li, X., Wang, K., et al.: Research on modeling methods of security protocol for space information network. Energy Procedia **13**, 6657–6661 (2011)
2. Lee, J., Sun, K.: Satellite over satellite (SOS) network: a novel architecture for satellite network. In: INFOCOM Nineteenth Joint Conference of the IEEE Computer & Communications Societies, pp. 315–321. IEEE (2000)
3. Zhang, D.Y., Liu, S.S.: Research on mesh-based architecture for space information network. Comput. Technol. Dev. **8**, 020 (2009)
4. Li, X.G.: Design and implement of the wireless real-time data transmission system based on USB. Appl. Mech. Mater. **310**, 596–600 (2013)
5. Pelton, J.N.: Satellite communications. J. Inst. Electr. Eng. **16**(9), 102–103 (2012)
6. Zhou, W., Ao, H., Zhou, Q., et al.: Satellite space information network: application and prospect. In: International Conference on Education, Management and Computer Science (2016)
7. Wang, S., Wu, B., Wang, B.: Research on doppler characteristics of inter-satellite-links in Beidou-based space information network. In: IEEE International Conference on Information and Automation, pp. 2910–2914. IEEE (2015)
8. Zhang, W., Bian, D., Xie, Z., et al.: A novel space information network architecture based on autonomous system. In: International Conference on Wireless Communications & Signal Processing, pp. 1–5. IEEE (2015)
9. Hao, X.W., Ma, J.F., Ren, F., Liu, X.Y., Zhong, Y.T.: A kind of authentication routing protocol based on double satellite network in space information network. Comput. Sci. **38**(2), 79–81 (2011)
10. Shahriar, A.Z.M., Atiquzzaman, M., Ivancic, W.: Network mobility in satellite networks: architecture and the protocol. Int. J. Commun Syst. **26**(2), 177–197 (2013)
11. Long, F., Yang, Z., Sun, F., et al.: A multi-objective optimization based QoS routing algorithm for multi-layered satellite IP networks. In: IEEE International Conference on Networking, Sensing and Control, ICNSC 2010, Chicago, IL, USA, 10–12 April. 2010, pp. 147–152 (2010)
12. Gou, X., Yan, H., Yi, F., et al.: Modeling and simulation of small satellite constellation networking using multi-topology routing. In: International Conference on Computer Application and System Modeling, pp. V12-143–V12-147. IEEE (2010)

13. Zhou, X., Zhang, L., Cheng, Z., et al.: Hypernetwork model and architecture for deep space information networks. Energy Procedia **13**, 8309–8317 (2011)
14. Fang, R., Jiulun, F.: An adaptive distributed certificate management scheme for space information network. IET Inf. Secur. **7**(4), 318–326 (2013)
15. Jiang, C., Wang, X., Wang, J., et al.: Security in space information networks. IEEE Commun. Mag. **53**(8), 82–88 (2015)
16. Zheng, G., Arapoglou, P.D., Ottersten, B.: Physical layer security in multibeam satellite systems. IEEE Trans. Wirel. Commun. **11**(2), 852–863 (2012)
17. Rui, M.P.P.: Security for satellite access to mesh networks (2014)
18. Karadogan, I., Das, R.: Analysis of attack types on TCP/IP based networks via exploiting protocols. In: Signal Processing and Communications Applications Conference, pp. 1785–1788. IEEE (2015)
19. Baek, Y.S., Koo, B.T.: Secure communication method and system in network environment which includes transmitter, receiver, and wiretapper. US9060264 (2015)
20. Hsu, T.S.: Method and apparatus having null-encryption for signaling and media packets between a mobile station and a secure gateway (2015)
21. Wu, H., Preneel, B.: AEGIS: a fast authenticated encryption algorithm. In: Lange, T., Lauter, K., Lisoněk, P. (eds.) SAC 2013. LNCS, vol. 8282, pp. 185–201. Springer, Heidelberg (2014). https://doi.org/10.1007/978-3-662-43414-7_10
22. Lai, J., Deng, R.H., et al.: Fully secure key-policy attribute-based encryption with constant-size ciphertexts and fast decryption (2014)

An Effective Topology Design Based on LEO/GEO Satellite Networks

Jiulong Ma[1(✉)], Xiaogang Qi[1], and Lifang Liu[2]

[1] School of Mathematics and Statistics,
Xidian University, Xi'an 710126, Shaanxi, China
majiulong@163.com
[2] School of Computer Science and Technology, Xidian University,
Xi'an 710071, Shaanxi, China

Abstract. The time-varying topology brings great challenge to the design of the satellite network routing. The key to designing high performance routing is how to handle the time-varying topology. Considering comprehensive advantages of both LEO and GEO satellite networks, a novel double-layered satellite network suitable for space networking is established in this paper. In this model, the ideas of virtual node strategy and satellite grouping are adopted, and the coverage of each LEO satellite is regarded as a virtual node of the network. Different from previous work, the influence of the polar boundary on the division of the satellite footprint is taken into account, such that the upper management satellites are able to accurately acquire the topology of the lower satellites. Using the improved virtual node strategy, the time slices in the network has significant changes, which are better than those in other models in terms of quantity, length and other aspects. The fact is verified by simulation.

Keywords: Satellite networks · Time slices · Coverage unit
Satellite grouping

1 Introduction

Space information network is a network system constructed for acquiring, transmitting and processing spatial information, which plays an important role in communication, navigation, and timing, positioning and monitoring [1]. In the network, all kinds of nodes continue to move, and the links are intermittently connected, such that the whole network has complex time-varying topology. As the backbone of space information network, satellite network, to some extent, affects the overall performance of space information network. Recently, satellite network has attracted more and more attention because of its wide coverage, broadcast capability and high bandwidth service level,

This work is supported by the National Natural Science Foundation of China (Grants No. 6157 2435, 61472305, 61473222); the Natural Science Foundation of Shaanxi Province (Grants No. 20 15JZ002, 2015JM6311); the Natural Science Foundation of Zhejiang; Province (No. LZ16F020 001); Programs Supported by Ningbo Natural Science Foundation (Grant No. 2016A610035); Aerospace T.T. &.C. Innovation Program (KJCK1608).

© Springer Nature Singapore Pte Ltd. 2018
Q. Yu (Ed.): SINC 2017, CCIS 803, pp. 24–33, 2018.
https://doi.org/10.1007/978-981-10-7877-4_3

which will become the bridge of global information transmission and access at a lower cost no matter when and where, so it is an important part of the next generation of Internet [2, 3]. According to the altitude of the satellites, satellite orbits can be divided into geostationary earth orbit (GEO), middle earth orbit (MEO) and low earth orbit (LEO). GEO satellites are about 36 thousand kilometers above the equator, and remain relatively stationary. The longer distance enables the larger coverage, such that only one GEO satellite can cover 40% of the entire earth surface. But it is the distance that leads to larger propagation delay between the GEO satellites and the ground [4]. On the contrary, LEO satellites with orbit altitudes of 500 km to 1500 km have small coverage and shorter distance from the ground. Larger movement speed of LEO satellites results in dramatic topology change over time [5]. An advantage of LEO satellites is that smaller propagation delay is true of real-time transmission service. Thus, the use of only LEO constellation or GEO constellation cannot give full play to their own advantages. In this paper, a novel double-layered satellite network suitable for space networking is established in consideration of the advantages of both LEO and GEO satellites.

Traditional routing schemes cannot be directly applied in satellite networks due to complex topological changes. Routing has become a difficult problem to be resolved in satellite networks and the key is how to deal with the time-varying topology.

Despite those, satellite motion is periodic and predictable, and the nodes and links in network have good symmetry. In order to make it more convenient to design superior routing, many effective methods to deal with the time-varying topology have been proposed and studied. The virtual node strategy proposed in [6] can well deal with the motion of satellite nodes. The idea is to divide the earth surface into several logical regions, each of which is bounded to the satellite that is nearest to it. Each time the satellite leaves a logical area, it is replaced by the next incoming satellite known as the succeeding satellite. For satellite network with a simple and regular structure, the method can shield the mobility of satellites, and what is only considered is logical region instead of mobile satellite nodes. [7] discusses the handover topic between the ground and the satellites, and it enables one ground area served by multiple LEO satellite nodes simultaneously. [8] lowers the complexity of routing computation by utilizing the feature of grid topology, but ignores the survivability of LEO satellite. The virtual node strategy can effectively deal with mobility of nodes, but only aims at the simple and regular topology such as polar LEO constellation. In addition, it is difficult to be extended to general multilayer satellite network.

Another typical approach to handling the time-varying topology is virtual topology strategy. The idea is that the network system cycle is divided into several discrete time slices, in each of which the network topology is regarded as fixed, and then routing can be designed based on these time slices [9]. The method based on dynamic detection [10], in essence, is a typical routing algorithm based on virtual topology strategy, which determines whether the link is normally connected using the periodic detection and confirmation of the number of packets in the queue of the sending satellites. [11], based on virtual topology, solves the problem that the time contact window cannot be fully utilized in the process of downloading data from multiple satellites to the ground station. The virtual topology strategy helps calculate the time slices in advance, but a large number of time slices may require a large amount of storage space.

In satellite networks, the number, length and uniformity of the time slices have significant influence on the network performance. The number of time slices reflects the degree of frequent changes in network topology, and the length reflects the duration of contact between the satellites and the ground or between the satellites and the satellites. The topology performance of the satellite network can be improved by reducing the number of time slices, increasing the length of the time slices and increasing the uniformity of the time slices. According to the traditional way of dividing the time slices, as soon as any link is switched, one new time slice is generated. [12] studies the time slices of satellite network in detail according to the method of virtual topology. And the results show that the number of time slices is large and the length is uneven, which is particularly evident in multilayer networks. For example, for the double-layered network consisting of 7 × 9 polar LEO constellation and 2 × 4 MEO constellation with orbit inclination of 45°, the network topology changes 1892 times, and the maximum length of the time slices is only 29 s in the 7 h of simulation.

Satellite grouping and group management strategy is widely studied in multilayer satellite network. [13] applies virtual nodes into lower layer of multilayer network. Lower-layer satellites that can directly communicate with one upper-layer satellite form one group of this upper-layer satellite. But a large number of discrete time slices are generated because of complex connection relation between lower and upper layer, resulting in huge storage overhead. [14, 15], to some degree, reduce the number of time slices by merging time slices. Similarly, [16] also uses satellite grouping methods. Unfortunately, one of the common defects of these methods is that the lower-layer topology information may not be accurately obtained by the upper-layer management satellites.

In order to further solve the problem of time-varying topology of satellite networks, this paper improves the virtual node strategy in consideration of the influence of the polar boundary on the division of the satellite footprint, and this makes it possible that the upper satellites can get accurate topology of lower-layer network. So it will bring convenience to the design of multilayer satellite network routing. In this way, the network topology has been greatly improved, and produces a small number of uniform time slices, which can further improve the performance of network routing.

The remainder of the paper is organized as follows. Section 2 introduces the double-layered satellite network model and the related definitions, while Sect. 3 is the analysis of the network topology. Performance evaluation is given in Sect. 4. Section 5 summarizes main conclusions.

2   Model and Related Definitions

2.1   Real Network Model

A double-layer satellite network composed of LEO and GEO satellite constellation is shown in Fig. 1. The GEO constellation consists of 3 GEO satellites equally spaced over the equator. The LEO constellation is slightly modified from the Iridium system, a typical LEO constellation widely used [17]. The LEO constellation used in the paper is composed of 72 LEO satellites, uniformly distributed in 6 polar orbit planes. The other parameters of the constellation are the same as those of Iridium system.

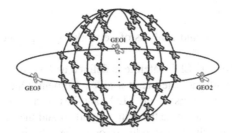

Fig. 1. Real double-layered satellite network model

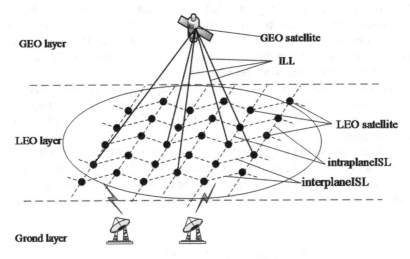

Fig. 2. Network nodes and links

There are several types of nodes and links in the network, as shown in Fig. 2. The network nodes include ground terminals, LEO satellites, and GEO satellites. Links include: (1) The inter-layer links (ILL) consisting of links between LEO and GEO satellites. One LEO satellite can communicate with one GEO satellite if and only if the LEO satellite is in the coverage area of the GEO satellite. (2) The intra-plane links (intra-ISLs) between two adjacent satellites through the same orbital. Clearly, each orbit of LEO layer has intra-ISLs with the same number as satellites through it, while the GEO layer has only 3 intra-ISLs. (3) The inter-plane links (inter-ISLs) between adjacent satellites through adjacent orbits. It should be noted that the motion direction of the satellites through the first LEO orbit is in opposition to those through the last orbit, and so there is no inter-ISLs between these satellites. In addition, there is no inter-ISL in high latitude areas, because the relative angular velocity of satellite motion is larger, and the pointing and tracking of antennas cannot meet the demand. Obviously, inter-ISL does not exist in GEO layer. (4) The user data links (UDLs) connecting terminals and satellites. One ground terminal can communicate with one satellite if and only if the ground terminal is within the minimum elevation angle of the satellite.

2.2 Related Definitions

To facilitate the description and analysis of network topology, the following concepts need to be given.

One coverage unit of one LEO satellite is defined as a set of ground nodes that can directly communicate with the satellite at a given moment. One coverage set is a set consisting of the coverage units of all LEO satellites at a given moment. Standard position refers to the position where the prime meridian and the first orbit of LEO layer are in the same plane, and the first satellite through the orbit is in the same plane with the equator. One standard coverage unit is one element of one coverage set when the LEO layer is in the standard position. Obviously, at any given time point, any LEO satellite has one standard coverage unit that may not belong to itself. In addition, we say one down-satellite link exists between the two standard coverage units of two LEO satellites if one of the following two conditions is satisfied. The conditions are: (1) there is intra-ISL between the two satellites, and (2) the two satellites are not in polar region and there is inter-ISL between them.

A virtual LEO satellite network (VLSN) is a graph G(t) = (V, E(t)), where V and E(t) are the set of coverage units and down-satellite links at time t, respectively. A normal virtual LEO satellite network (NVLSN) is one VLSN where LEO layer is in the standard position.

The NVLSN of the LEO layer in this paper is shown in Fig. 3. The latitude of the polar boundary is 80° and the reason is explained in Sect. 3. In Fig. 3, each vertical line represents a satellite orbit; each dot represents one LEO satellite. The unit in the picture is angular distance. A circle with a radius of 30° represents a standard coverage unit.

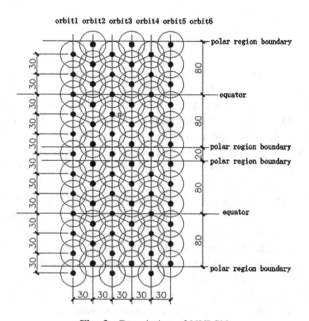

Fig. 3. Description of NVLSN

Orbit 1, orbit 3 and orbit 5 are traversed by the first and seventh satellite above the equator. The satellite directly connected with the first satellite through orbit 1, orbit 3 or orbit 5 is the corresponding first satellites through orbit 2, orbit 4 or orbit 6.

At a certain moment, if the LEO satellite is within the footprint of one GEO satellite, the standard coverage unit below the satellite is a member of the GEO satellite. Obviously, any GEO satellite has many members. A set of all members forms a group of one GEO satellite group manager. It is important to note that the concepts of group member and group manager are different from those in other literatures.

2.3   Virtual Network Model

A virtual terminal-LEO-GEO satellite network system (VTLGN) refers to the network consisting of ground nodes, standard coverage units of LEO layers, GEO satellites, and links between them, which is defined as a graph $G = (V, E)$, where $V = \{v \mid v$ is terminal or standard coverage unit or GEO satellite$\}$, $E = \{e \mid e$ is down-satellite link or ILL or UDL$\}$.

3   Topological Analysis of VTLGN

The VTLGN network model has the advantages over other networks in many ways. The flowing topology analysis is carried out based on VTLGN.

Theorem 1: If $G = (V, E)$ is VTLGN network, G1 is one GEO satellite, and S is one standard coverage unit, then group members of G1 and group manager of S are both uniquely determined at any time point.

Proof: According to the definition of group member, the essence of group member is the standard coverage unit, and the GEO satellite is relatively stationary to ground. So, any GEO satellite and any member of its group remain relatively stationary at any time point, that is, any standard coverage unit and group manager remain relatively stationary at any time point. So group members of G1 and group manager of S are uniquely determined at any time point.

Theorem 1 shows how to use VTLGN to avoid the mobility of actual physical satellite nodes in satellite networks. If one standard coverage unit in VTLGN is regarded as a virtual node, then dynamic property of satellite network is completely shielded. So what needs to be considered is only standard coverage unit when designing routing.

Theorem 2: In VTLGN, when there are some failed LEO satellite nodes, the maximum number of time slices that can accurately reflect the network topology is equal to the number of satellites through one LEO orbit, and the length of the time slices is uniform.

Proof: Each GEO satellite is stationary relative to its members, i.e., there is no link handover, so only LEO layer topology needs to be considered. The time interval required for a LEO satellite to move from the current position to that of the next satellite is noted as dt, then $dt = T/m$ according to the synchronization of satellite motion, where T is the orbital period of LEO satellites, and m is the number of satellites through one orbit. The worst case is that whenever a failed satellite moves to the next position, the standard coverage unit of the next location fails. If the system period of LEO layer is discretized into m time slices [0, dt), [dt, 2dt), ..., [(m−1)dt, mdt], at each time slice, the topology of the network can still be considered as a static topology even when some LEO satellite nodes fail. So the m time slices can reflect the network topology of the LEO layer.

As mentioned in section one, general satellite grouping strategy cannot accurately describe the topology of LEO layer. Figure 4 shows the influence of polar region on the topology of LEO layer. At a certain moment, an inter-ISL exists between LEO satellite S11 and S21, but it disappears after very small time. However, during the small time interval, if the two satellites are still in the same group of one manager, then the change of the link state cannot be captured by the manager.

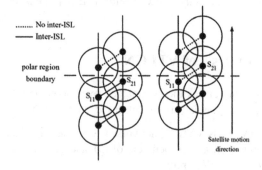

Fig. 4. The influence of polar region on the topology of LEO layer

The VTLGN network proposed in this paper can solve the above problems perfectly. Since any LEO satellite is idealized as a standard coverage unit fixed on the earth, it does not change as the satellite moves. Therefore, as long as a standard coverage unit is affected by a polar region, there is no down-satellite (inter-ISL, in essence) between it

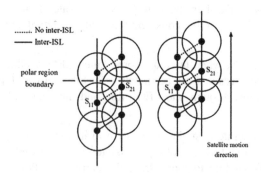

Fig. 5. Polar topology processing in VTLGN

and any other standard coverage unit. As shown in Fig. 5, as long as part of footprint of S21 moves to the polar region, the actual inter-ISL is considered to be absent. One result of this is the decline in the number of inter-satellite links in LEO layers. However, considering the huge routing overhead resulted in dynamic topology, such treatment is suitable. Moreover, by appropriately increasing the latitude value of the polar area boundary, a very small decrease in the number of links cannot significantly affect the performance of the entire network, so the problem is easy to solve.

4 Performance Evaluations

The VTLGN network model proposed in this paper aims to deal with the time-varying topology caused by nodes movement in satellite networks, which is superior to other network topology models in terms of the length and number of time slices. To illustrate this, we carried on the simulation experiment, and the results are compared with those of other classical single-layer and multilayer constellation topologies.

The single-layer constellations mainly include the Walker constellation and the polar orbit constellation. The distribution of time slices in Walker constellation is mainly related to phase factor, while that of polar orbit constellation is only related to the latitude value of polar region boundary [12].

We use Celestri, Teledesic and Iridium constellations for simulation. The results are compared with those in [12] and the simulation parameters are shown in Table 1. The distribution of time slices of several typical single-layer constellations is shown in Table 2, which is obtained by simulation in a complete cycle of each constellation. As can be seen from Table 2, the NVLSN proposed in this paper has the smallest number of time slices, and its time slices are uniform, so it is better than the Celestri, Iridium, and Teledesic constellation.

Table 1. Simulation parameters of single-layer constellations

	Orbit altitude	Orbit inclination	Number of orbit	Satellite number through one orbit
NVLSN	780 km	90°	6	12
Celestri	1400 km	45°	7	9
Iridium	780 km	86.4°	6	11
Teledesic	1375 km	84.7°	12	24

Table 2. Comparison of topological performance of single-layer satellite networks

	Number of time slices	Maximum length of time slices	Minimum length of time slices
NVLSN	12	500 s	500 s
Celestri	252	49.54 s or 29.34 s	6.64 s or 26.84 s
Iridium	44	213.93 s	60.01 s
Teledesic	48	133.77 s	105.78 s

For general multilayer satellite networks, besides the change of LEO layer topology, the links between layers also affect the distribution of time slices. As mentioned earlier, a large number of uneven time slices are generated in satellite grouping method.

We choose the Tr constellation and the LMSN model as a contrast. In addition to the simulation time, the other parameters are the same as those in [14, 15]. Table 3 lists the distribution of time slices of several typical multilayer constellations. Time cycle of 24 h is adopted for reasonable contrast. It can be found that VTLGN proposed in this paper is very suitable for the satellite network, which cannot produce fewer slices but can still guarantee the uniformity of time slices even when some satellites fail. It is convenient for the design of multilayer satellite network routing.

Table 3. Comparison of performance of multilayer satellite network topology

	Number of time slices	Average length of time slices	Time slices uniformity
VTLGN	173	500 s	Uniform
Post-merger Tr	644	133.77	Not uniform
Pre-merger Tr	5340	16.16 s	Not uniform
Post-merger LMSN	644	133.77 s	Not uniform
Pre-merger LMSN	3776	22.81 s	Not uniform

5   Conclusions

In satellite network, the use of only LEO or GEO constellation for space networking cannot give full play to each constellation. The periodic motion of satellite nodes results in time-varying network topology, which makes it difficult to design high performance routing techniques. In order to solve these problems, the paper establishes a new network model and topology based on LEO and GEO constellation, where the advantages of integrated LEO and GEO constellations are considered and the idea of virtual node strategy is improved. The theoretical and experimental results show that the network topology has more advantages than that of other satellite network models.

References

1. Li, D., Shen, X., Gong, J., et al.: On construction of China's space information network. Geomat. Inf. Sci. Wuhan Univ. **40**(6), 711–715 (2015). (in Chinese)
2. Yu, Q., Wang, J., Bai, L.: Architecture and critical technologies of space information networks. J. Commun. Inf. Netw. **1**(3), 1–9 (2016)
3. Qi, X., Ma, J., Wu, D., et al.: A survey of routing techniques for satellite networks. J. Commun. Inf. Netw. **1**(4), 66–85 (2016)
4. Wu, Z., Hu, G., Jin, F., et al.: A novel routing design in the IP-based GEO/LEO hybrid satellite networks. Int. J. Satell. Commun. Network. **35**(3), 179–199 (2017)

5. Wu, Z., Jin, F., Luo, J., et al.: A graph-based satellite handover framework for LEO satellite communication networks. IEEE Commun. Lett. **20**(8), 1547–1550 (2016)
6. Ekici, E., Akyildiz, I., Bender, M.: A distributed routing algorithm for datagram traffic in LEO satellite networks. IEEE/ACM Trans. Network. **9**(2), 137–147 (2001)
7. Korçak, Ö., Alagöz, F.: Virtual topology dynamics and handover mechanisms in Earth-fixed LEO satellite systems. Comput. Netw. **53**(9), 1497–1511 (2009)
8. Liu, X., Jiang, Z., Liu, C., et al.: A low-complexity probabilistic routing algorithm for polar orbits satellite constellation networks. In: IEEE/CEC International Conference on Communications in China, pp. 1–5. IEEE (2016)
9. He, F., Liu, Q., Lv, T., et al.: Delay-bounded and minimal transmission broadcast in LEO satellite networks. In: ICC 2016 - 2016 IEEE International Conference on Communications, pp. 1–7. IEEE (2016)
10. Tan, H., Zhu, L.: A novel routing algorithm based on virtual topology snapshot in LEO satellite networks. In: IEEE International Conference on Computational Science and Engineering, pp. 357–361. IEEE (2014)
11. Jia, X., Lv, T., He, F., et al.: Collaborative data downloading by using inter-satellite links in LEO satellite networks. IEEE Trans. Wirel. Commun. **16**(3), 1523–1532 (2017)
12. Wang, J., Li, L., Zhou, M.: Topological dynamics characterization for LEO satellite networks. Comput. Netw. **51**(1), 43–53 (2007)
13. Chen, C., Ekici, E.: A routing protocol for hierarchical LEO/MEO satellite IP networks. Wirel. Netw. **11**(4), 507–521 (2005)
14. Long, F., Xiong, N., Vasilakos, A., et al.: A sustainable heuristic QoS routing algorithm for pervasive multi-layered satellite wireless network. Wirel. Netw. **16**(6), 1657–1673 (2010)
15. Zhou, Y., Sun, F., Zhang, B.: A hierarchical and distributed QoS routing protocol for two-layered satellite networks. In: IMACS Multiconference on Computational Engineering in Systems Applications, pp. 739–745. IEEE (2006)
16. Wang, Y., Sheng, M., Lui, K., et al.: Tailored load-aware routing for load balance in multilayered satellite networks. In: 2015 IEEE 82nd Vehicular Technology Conference (VTC Fall), pp. 1–5. IEEE (2015)
17. Pratt, S., Raines, R., Fossa, C., et al.: An operational and performance overview of the IRIDIUM low earth orbit satellite system. IEEE Commun. Surv. **2**(2), 2–10 (1999)

An Integrated Framework for Mission Planning in Space Information Network

Fangxiaoqi Yu, Haopeng Chen$^{(\boxtimes)}$, and Lin Gui

School of Electronic Information and Electrical Engineering,
Shanghai Jiao Tong University, Shanghai 200240, China
chen-hp@sjtu.edu.cn

Abstract. With the development of space techniques, more and more missions using both satellite resources and ground cloud resources are being conducted in situations such as sea rescue, earthquake relief or some emergencies. However, lacking of an integrated framework makes this kind of missions inefficient and makes it hard for dynamic adjustment. In this paper, we design an integrated framework, involving demand planning, joint task planning, task assignment, resources allocation and dynamic adjustment. This paper aims to integrate all the relevant techniques and provide a complete framework for rapid space-ground joint mission planning and in-time adjustment in space information networks. We also propose a case study of three investigative missions to help you understand this framework.

Keywords: Space information network · Formal description
Space-ground joint task planning · Demands planning

1 Introduction

With the progress of space information technology, we can use space-ground integrated network to deal with various emergencies to which traditional approaches are not competent, such as anti-terrorism, sea rescue and earthquake relief. Facing with these emergencies, we need the resource of satellites and ground cloud to support joint missions. For example, in disaster rescue, we need the high resolution image captured by the satellites and the rescue plan designed with the computing power of ground cloud. As a result, it is necessary for space-ground joint missions to design a mission planning system based on the space-ground integrated network. However, space-ground joint missions bring great complication to the mission planning system. This complication mainly comes from three aspects:

(1) Large-scale business-oriented planning for users' demand

With the growth of computing ability of space-ground resources, more users will be able to submit joint missions to the mission planning system. The system

© Springer Nature Singapore Pte Ltd. 2018
Q. Yu (Ed.): SINC 2017, CCIS 803, pp. 34–49, 2018.
https://doi.org/10.1007/978-981-10-7877-4_4

needs to perform demand analyzing, decomposing and planning according to the coarse-grained demand described by user. When facing large-scale demands, it becomes a challenge to deal with all this demands.

(2) Management and scheduling of various kinds of space-ground resources and missions

Space-ground resources are of various types, including remote sensing satellites, communications satellites, navigation satellites, receiving resources and ground computing resources. On the other hand, there are also various kinds of missions, such as reconnaissance missions, surveying and mapping missions, early warning missions, communication missions, and navigation missions. In order to allocate resources for tasks, we have to describe the feature of resources accurately and monitor their real-time status. To describe and monitor so many kinds of resources and tasks will inevitably bring extra difficulty to the processing algorithms of mission planning system.

(3) Support of dealing with emergencies rapidly

The mission planning system has to response rapidly to high-priority emergent missions. With many missions to be dealt with simultaneously, it is difficult to re-plan missions and re-schedule resources for emergent missions. The complexity of mission scheduling and resource management will rise sharply if the emergent mission itself has multiple attributes, or a large number of missions are executing simultaneously. It is necessary to solve the three problems above and plan missions rapidly and accurately when facing with large-scale of joint missions.

This paper aims to make use of both satellite resources and cloud computation resources on the ground and give a solution to the problem of how to utilize space-ground resource efficiently to plan missions quickly and automatically when facing with large-scale user demands. We design a framework integrating virtualized resources management, demand-task mapping as well as dynamic task assignment and adjustment, which is able to plan the space-ground missions quickly and automatically while improving resource utilization rate and missions execution efficiency. This framework combines the space-ground resource virtualization management approach based on formalized extensible description mode and on-demand space-ground resource scheduling and reorganization techniques.

Besides the introduction section, there are another five sections in this paper. Section 2 lists the works related to framework of space information network, task assignment and computation offloading. Section 3 describes the design of the framework. Section 4 exhaustively explains the related techniques. Section 5 gives a case study and finally, conclusions are presented in Sect. 6.

2   Related Work

The rapid and automatic planning of joint mission can be accomplished by an integrated control platform, involving multi-task planning and resource allocation, edge plus cloud computation offloading and other techniques. The following describes the related works of the framework and techniques.

2.1 Framework and Control Platform for Space Information Network

The U.S. military's C4ISR system [1] integrated aerospace, air force, ground force, navy and other service information to achieve multi service and multi arm information sharing, resource optimization and collaborative action.

Shi presented a space information network architecture based on OpenFlow which achieved the flexibility of the space information network [2]. Yang introduced a language called STeC to model the observation processes of satellite [3]. In [4], the authors proposed a unified routing framework for space-air network, where realized a HGHR algorithm, improving the performance of message delivery ratio, end-to-end delay, and power consumption. Zhang proposed software defined space-air-ground integrated network architecture to support diverse vehicular services in a seamless, efficient, and cost-effective manner [5].

Almost all of the research focused on some specific aspect while we require an integrated framework for space information network.

2.2 Multi-task Planning and Resource Allocation

Peng presented a near-space multitasking scheme that was implemented by selecting some relatively urgent or special tasks to meet the demands of users with limited resources [6]. In [7,8], the authors gave the different UAV cooperative mission planning approach. Coutinho proposed a distributed resource allocation framework based on autonomic computing, which could be used to expand the virtual machine resources [9]. Amazon EC2's Auto Scaling applied the idea of reactive virtual machine resource provisioning, allowing users to predefine virtual machine resource scaling conditions and carried out the expansion of virtual machine resources in the process of dynamic application of cloud applications based on the actual monitoring of data and pre-defined resource expansion conditions [10]. In [11], a predictive adaptive resource allocation framework was proposed to support the flexibility of cloud applications by estimating future workloads. In fact, it is better to combine the reactive and predictive adjustment strategy for space-ground resource adjustment.

Although there has been little research on space-ground resource adjustment and task planning strategy, we can make use of dynamic resource flexibility strategy in cloud computing which provides a feasible idea to solve the problem.

2.3 Edge Plus Cloud Computation Offloading

Mobile edge computation offloading strategy was presented in [12–14] and many other papers, including offloading strategy to minimize execution delay, to minimize energy consumption while satisfying execution delay constraint and to trade-off between energy consumption and execution delay.

Kosta proposed a framework called ThinkAir which helped to move smartphone applications to the cloud [15]. In [16], the authors presented the first practical implementation of mobile cloud computation for Android called Cuckoo.

Kovachev presented a middleware which helped Android application to extend from a mobile client into the cloud [17].

Although computation offloading of satellites is an emerging technique, the mobile edge and cloud computation offloading technique can be leveraged to solve the problem.

3 Design of the Framework

We propose a complete framework for dealing with space-ground missions quickly. As shown in Fig. 1, besides three libraries of demand planning library *(DP Lib)*, task planning algorithm library *(TP Algorithm Lib)* and dynamic task adjustment strategy library *(DTA Strategy Lib)*, the framework is composed of six parts: External Inputs *(EI)*, Demand Planning *(DP)*, Joint Task Planning *(JTP)*, Space-Ground Task and Resources Adjustment *(SGTRA)* which includes Space-Ground Resources Adjustment *(SGRA)* and Space-Ground Task Adjustment *(SGTA)*, Virtualized Resource Pool *(VRP)* and Dynamic Resource Monitoring and Management *(DRMM)*.

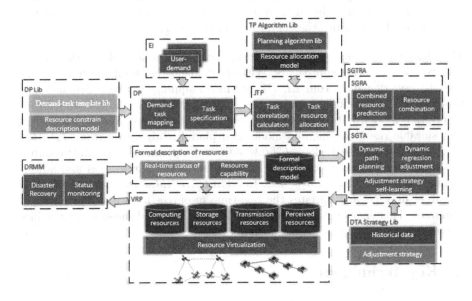

Fig. 1. Framework

EI: It accepts plenty of demands as external inputs of this framework and submits them to *DP* for analysis.

DP: With the demand-task template in *DP Lib* and the real-time virtualized resource status and capability, *DP* changes the input demands into task sets and merges the task sets with task constraints. Then it generates merged sets and description of resource demands.

JTP: It plans the generated task sets. It looks for matched task type and planning algorithm in *TP Algorithm Lib*, calculates task order with task relationship and use the matched model to allocate resources for each task. Then tasks will be delivered to the corresponding computing resources.

SGTRA: It predicts the state of resources with the combined resource forecasting approaches and monitored real-time status of resources. It can dynamically adjust the resources allocated for the tasks by combining resources. It can also plan the execution communication path of the space-ground task and change the way of using resources by adjusting tasks.

VRP: Space-ground resource is heterogeneous. It consists of remote sensing satellites, communications satellites, navigation satellites, receiving resources and many other computing resources. *VRP* uses virtualization form to shield the effect of heterogeneity and provides tasks with unified access interface. It uses software-defined approach to map virtual resources and physical resources, so that its dynamic adjustment is invisible to tasks that use virtual resources.

DRMM: By monitoring virtual resources and physical resources, *DRMM* adjusts the mapping relations between them to balance workload. Also, *DRMM* can realize the disaster recovery of the assigned virtual resources on demand to improve the completion of the tasks.

The above subsystems are integrated together based on formal description and resource virtualization approaches. With the demand-task template from *DP Lib* and the user demands from *EI*, *DP* produce mappings between demands and tasks; with the resource constrain description model from *DP lib* and formal description model, it produces task specification. *JTP* acquires task sets from *DP*, suitable resource planning model and planning algorithm from *TP Algorithm Lib* to plan the tasks. *SGTRM* adjust the planning path and resources according to real-time resources in formal description of resources and adjustment strategy in *DTA Strategy Lib*. In addition, *DRMM* monitor the status of resources in *VRP* and updates the real-time resources in formal description of resources. This enables rapidly planning for space-ground missions and unified management of the space-ground resources.

4 Key Techniques

This paper mainly focuses on five parts: demands planning, joint task planning, on-demand resource adjustment, dynamic task adjustment and edge plus cloud computation offloading.

4.1 Rapid Planning for Large-Scale User Demands

The goal of this technique is to achieve unified management and planning for large-scale user demands, including demand-task mapping mechanism in *DP* based on *DP Lib*, task specification approach in *DP* and formal description

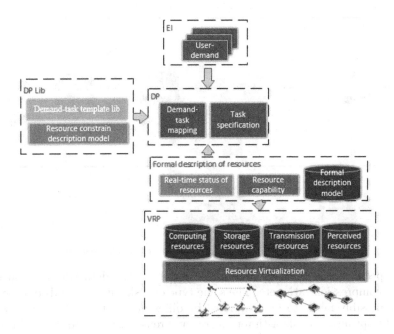

Fig. 2. Demand planning sub-framework

model for resource and task resource demands connecting *DP* with *VRP*. The framework of this part is shown in Fig. 2, which is a part of the integrated framework in Fig. 1. The aspects involved are as follows:

A Demand-Task Mapping Based on Self-learning Task Template

The task set mapped to user demand is determined according to the real-time status of the cloud resource. Thus, the specific user demands should be mapped to a communication path with multiple tasks in a workflow template which contains multiple possible communication paths. That is, there will be a large number of demand-task mapping templates in the *DP Lib*, and each specific user demand will be mapped to a certain communication path in the template according to the real-time state of the resources to generate a specific workflow instance. An example of demand-task template can be shown in Fig. 3 which will be used in Sect. 5. After the demands are mapped into the task set, the feedback execution effect will be used to improve the demand-task mapping template through self-learning to provide a more scientific and rational task mapping template for the planning of subsequent demands.

B Task Specification for Large-Scale User Demand Planning Based on Efficient Reuse

In planning for large-scale user demands, it is necessary to optimize the constraints of the demands and to constrain the resulting task set in order to produce a compact and efficient task set. In addition to the description of the functional semantics, the user demands also contain the demands for the quality attributes

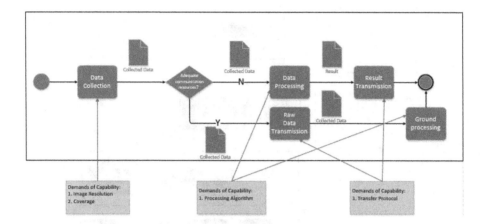

Fig. 3. Demand-task template of investigative missions

of the specific tasks, such as the image resolution, the data transmission rate and the compression ratio, etc. The same type of task with demands of different quality possibly needs to be completed by different resources. Therefore, when using the optimization algorithm to merge and reuse tasks in order to reduce the intensity of task execution and improve resource utilization, the system should make sure that the quality of demands are satisfied.

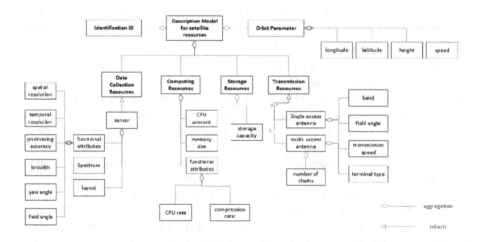

Fig. 4. Description model for satellite resources

C Scalable Formal Description Model for Resource Capability and Task Resource Demands

The premise of realizing automatic task planning is that the task set generated in the *DP* must have a formal description of the resource demands. The satellite resources can be described by UML graph, as shown in Fig. 4. The execution of any task demands requires appropriate resources and the description of the resource demands will be used as a basis for resource scheduling and allocation. Only if a formal description is given, task resource demands can be automatically matched to a formal description of the resource capabilities. This is the basic guarantee for automatically task planning. As the types and capabilities of space-ground resources may continue to expand in the future, the formal description of resource capacity and task resource demands must have good scalability to ensure that the system can adapt to the description of the types and capabilities of new resources automatically.

4.2 Intelligent Planning for Space-Ground Joint Tasks Based on Deep Learning

This technique focuses on planning of generated task set, including task correlation computation and resource allocation as shown in Fig. 5. The details are shown as follow.

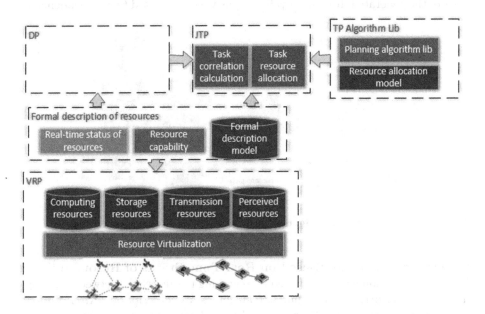

Fig. 5. Task planning sub-framework

A Task Type Classification Management in TP Algorithm Lib Based on Deep Learning

The algorithms for *JTP* of different types of tasks are not the same, because they require resources of different types and capability. Therefore, in this system, *TP Algorithm Lib* will classify the algorithms by its corresponding task type. Specifically, it is to manage the parameter of dynamic programming, autoregressive average movement, taboo search and simulated annealing algorithm separately in each task type and also the algorithm selection strategy. This system also re-aggregates and classifies the tasks with the historical data according to deep learning, extending the task types and algorithm to meet the new demands in the future.

B Task Correlation Computation Based on Graph Calculation

There are data dependencies or control dependencies between tasks in a task set. However, the result of large scale *DP* is several task sets defined by the task set specification instead of one task set. Based on the data dependencies and control dependencies, the system can determine the order of task execution reasonably and generate the *JTP* solution by compute the task correlation in these task sets. Through the task correlation computation, the system can avoid the redundant computation and reuse the generated data sets to reduce the resource consumption of task. This can also balance the utilization of cloud resources to achieve the optimal use of resources. Task correlation computation is achieved through graph computing techniques. The system executes task planning on the basis of the generated directed acyclic graphs with associated task dependencies.

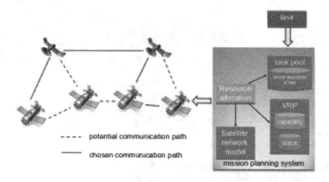

Fig. 6. Resource allocation

C Resource Allocation Based on Real-Time Status of Resource

Resource allocation will be achieved by searching the matching between resource demands description and resource real-time state description. After finding matched resources, task will be assigned to matched resource in a chosen communication path as shown in Fig. 6. Complex solutions including resource combinations can also be searched without affecting the performance. The objects of resource allocation are virtualized resources that can be placed on any physical machine which meets the resource demands. But different placement strategies can have different effects on the reliability, performance, and utilization of physical resources. Therefore, the system place and manage the virtual resources by combining the global optimization of the data center with the local optimization of the single data center. To balance the load of physical resources and minimize the interference between virtual resources is the goal of resource allocation.

4.3   Rapid On-demand Adjustment for Space-Ground Resources

This technique aims to implement on dynamic resource adjustment, as shown in Fig. 7. The aspects involved are as follows:

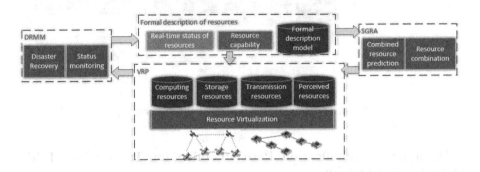

Fig. 7. Dynamic resource adjustment sub-framework

A Rapid Adjustment of Cloud Resources Based on Combination of Reaction and Prediction

Adjustment based on reaction relies on real-time monitoring of resource status in *DRMM*. It is easy to implement, but it may result in lag in resource adjustment solution. The fixed model of space-ground joint missions makes it possible for adjustment based on prediction. The forecast adjustment approach will make use of historical data to predict future resource load and reliability, achieving timely resource adjustment. The combination of reaction and prediction is used to achieve the dynamic reallocation of resources for different types of tasks by using multiple knapsack and other greedy algorithms, aiming to balance resource utilization and ensure task performance. It is the key of on-demand cloud resources rapid adjustment.

B Resource Allocation Based on Resource Combination

Facing with emergency or unable to find matched resources, combination of resources should be tried to meet demands. For example, if the data translation resource needed by a mission is using by a high-priority mission and there is no more data translation resource meets the demands, the system can try to combine several resources to meet the demands. Because the algorithms chosen here may have low convergence efficiency(such as greedy algorithm), a timeout should be set to avoid spending too much time. After timeout, a feasible option is chosen instead of the best option.

4.4   Rapid Adjustment for Space-Ground Tasks Based on Dynamic Communication Path Planning

This technique aims to implement on dynamic task adjustment, as shown in Fig. 8. The details are shown as follow:

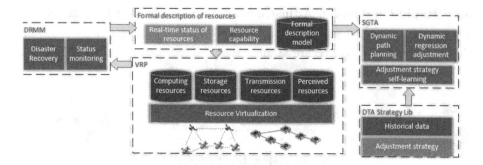

Fig. 8. Dynamic task adjustment sub-framework

A Dynamic Communication Path Planning for Tasks with Multi-objective Optimization

Excessive task size may bring difficulties to task adjustment. At this time, task decomposition should be executed so that the system can generate a multi-objective optimized resource configuration solution for each subtask. By controlling the flow of sub tasks and gathering the execution results, the dynamic communication path planning of tasks can be achieve. Task decomposition and sub-task dynamic combination is achieved based on the task real-time state. For this kind of NP problem, we can use the heuristic pruning algorithm to make the solution space converge rapidly. So that we can find the desired solution, or find out that there is no solution.

B Dynamic Regression Adjustment Algorithm for Multi Task Set

Since the task set is a compact set obtained after combination, there is a large degree of correlation between them. After dynamic communication path planning is performed on a task, it is necessary to execute dynamic regression adjustment on the set of all the tasks associated with it. The system needs to adjust the data and control the dependencies in time, and re-calculate the execution relationship between the tasks through the graph calculation technique to ensure that the results of the task adjustment do not result in serious problems that do not meet the task demands. Because of the high degree of association, this regression adjustment may cause ripple effects and recursive effects, resulting in higher cost of adjustment. Therefore, the system is only required to generate acceptable regression results, not demanding that all tasks be completed in accordance with the original quality standards.

C DTA Strategy Lib Based on Large Data Analysis

Through the analysis of the historical data of *SGTA*, we can summarize the strategy of dynamic task reassignment and resource reorganization. These strategies have a clear applicable scenario of task adjustment, so that they can be adopted by subsequent task adjustments. At the beginning of the system, since the amount of historical data is not big enough, the sparse data set interpolation analysis approach is used to determine the initial strategy for task dynamic adjustment. With the increase in the amount of data, these strategies will be revised and improved, and ultimately meet the actual needs, improving the completion rate of tasks and utilization rate of space-ground resources.

4.5   Edge Plus Cloud Computation Offloading

This technique is used to determine whether a task should be executed on a satellite or on the ground. By using the techniques above, a space-ground joint mission can be divided into a task set. Taking into account the computation capability of satellite resources, the system should offload some of the computation tasks to the ground cloud resources. In this way, we can mitigate the computational pressure of satellite and reduce the execution time as well. This is helpful especially when facing large amount of demands. For those tasks which must be done by satellite, a satellite with too much pressure can also offload some of the tasks to the edge side composed with many other satellites. The system can use the strategies similar to those of mobile edge computation offloading and cloud computation offloading to achieve the edge plus cloud computation offloading in space information network.

5   Case Study

5.1   Scenario

Consider a situation:
There are three investigative missions (M1, M2 and M3) of area $N = \{n_1, n_2 \ldots n_t\}$.

> M1: Search for a signal ("♡") left by the spy in area $ni \in N$. The maximum acceptable delay is 5 min.
> M2: Determine the impact area of Typhoon in area $n_j \in N$. The maximum acceptable delay is 50 s.
> M3: Look for the position of a sunken ship in area N. The maximum acceptable delay is 5 min.

For simplicity, we assume that there are 2 high-orbit satellites ($A1\,and\,A2$), 3 low-orbit satellites ($B1, B2\,and\,B3$) and 2 mid-orbit satellites ($C1\,and\,C2$) and all the satellites have the same computing resources and storage resources. In addition, all the satellites have the same data collection resource, except B2, whose sensor does not have the ability to collect high resolution images. Only high-orbit and mid-orbit satellites have transmission resources. We assume that at this time, A1 and B1 are full loaded while others are idle.

5.2   Process

At the beginning, with the demand-task template in *DP Lib*, the mission planning system changes the three demands into task sets T and description of constrains C. The matched demand-task template of this example is shown in Fig. 3 in Sect. 4.

T:
T1 $\{collection1; processing1; transmission1\}$,
T2 $\{collection2; processing2; transmission2\}$,
T3 $\{collection3; processing3; transmission2\}$,

C:
C1$\{high\,resolution, area\,n_i; approach1; STP\}$,
C2$\{low\,resolution, area\,n_j; approach2; STP\}$,
C3$\{high\,resolution, area\,N; approach3; STP\}$,
where STP stands for Satellite Transport Protocol.

Because the investigative area of collection1 and collection3 are repetitive and their image constrains are the same, the system can merge collection1 and collection3.

Then the task sets are planned following the process in Fig. 9 which shows the detail of Fig. 3.

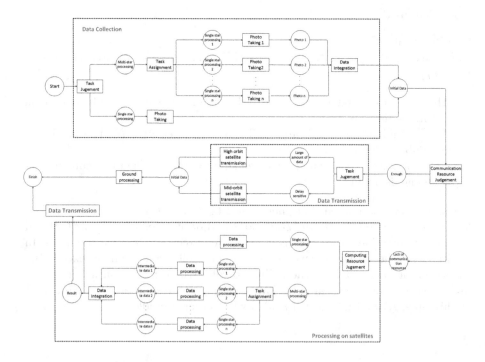

Fig. 9. Process flow chart based on swim lane

T1+T3:

Because the size of area N is out of the range of a single satellite, this joint task should be assigned to several satellites. B3 is chosen as one of the resources. However, there is no other resource which can meet the demands. So C1 is adjusted to be used for data collection (C'). "$Collection1 + 3$" is assigned to B3 and $C1'$. Then, as there are enough high-orbit and mid-orbit satellites, the collected pictures can be transmitted without processing. Because the data size of T3 is large, the collected pictures of T3 are transmitted to high-orbit satellite A2 and A2 transmits them to the ground. Similarly, the collected pictures of T1 are transmitted to mid-orbit satellite C2. Then the two missions can be processed by ground cloud resources.

T2:

Because the size of n_j is not large, collection2 is assigned to a single satellite B2. However, the communication resource is not enough, so the collected pictures should be processed on satellites. Processing2 is assigned to B2, and after processing, the result is transmitted to A2. A2 transmits them to the ground and finally M2 is finished.

The process flow described above is shown in Fig. 10, in which each swim lane stands for a resource and red ones represent full-loaded resources.

Compared to other systems, this framework is integrated. Some optimization is considered to reduce the response time and ensure the performance. This is reflected in three parts:

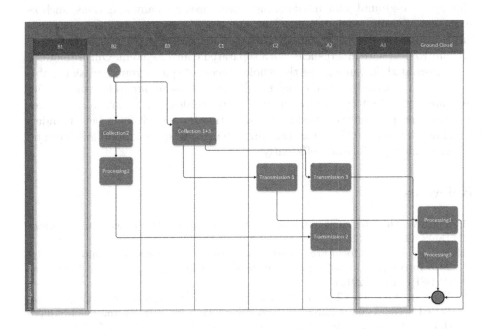

Fig. 10. Process flow chart based on swim lane (Color figure online)

(1) This framework provides task reuse for large scale demand according to task correlation computation. In the case above, we can see that collection1 and collection3 are merged. This optimization helps the system avoid the redundant computation and reuse the generated data sets to reduce the resource consumption of task.
(2) The system adjusts the path dynamically to ensure the generated path is the optimal solution of the current state and the planning algorithms are designed to be constantly optimized by deep learning. In the example, we can find that the path of a task is not decided at the beginning. At every sub-process (data collection, data transmission and processing on satellites), the system will look for an optimal solution according to its current state for the task.
(3) This framework supports on-demand dynamic resource adjustment for demands over capacity, which especially benefits emergent demands. In this case, T1+T3 is assigned to several satellites instead of only one and $C1'$ is changed from C1 to meet the requirements.

6   Conclusion

In this paper, we purpose an integrated framework for mission planning in space information network. We provide the design of the framework, the details and a case study for a better understanding. With the development of space techniques, space-ground joint missions have been used in many situations, such as sea rescue, disaster relief, anti-terrorism and etc. Planning, assigning and adjusting this kind of missions manually seriously decrease the efficiency. Also, it is difficult to deal with emergencies with separated control system. Our framework is an integrated one, managing the whole process of space-ground missions, able to plan space-ground joint missions rapidly and adjust resources for emergencies dynamically and automatically. In case study, we design a situation with three missions and present their basic process in this framework for a better understanding. We believe this framework can help manage space-ground missions and resources more flexibly and efficiently.

References

1. Song, X.: The integrated course of US army command information system. Foreign Tanks **11**, 11–16 (2012)
2. Shi, L., et al.: OpenFlow based space information network architecture. In: 2015 International Conference on Wireless Communications & Signal Processing (WCSP). IEEE (2015)
3. Yang, Z., Xiao, B., Chen, Y.: Modeling and verification of space-air-ground integrated networks on requirement level using STeC. In: 2015 International Symposium on Theoretical Aspects of Software Engineering (TASE). IEEE (2015)
4. Qi, W., Hou, W., Guo, L., Song, Q., Jamalipour, A.: A unified routing framework for integrated space/air information networks. IEEE Access **4**, 7084–7103 (2016)

5. Zhang, N., et al.: Software Defined Space-Air-Ground Integrated Vehicular Networks: Challenges and Solutions. arXiv preprint arXiv:1703.02664 (2017)
6. Peng, Z., et al.: Improved maximizing deviation decision-making model and its application in multi-mission planning of near space system. Syst. Eng. Theory Pract. **34**(2), 421–427 (2014)
7. Deng, Q.: Cooperative Task Planning Technology for Multi-UAVs. Dissertation, Beijing Institute of Technology (2014)
8. Shen, L., et al.: Theories and Methods of Autonomous Cooperative Control for Multiple UAVs. National Defence Industry Press, Beijing (2013)
9. Coutinho, E.F., Gomes, D.G., de Souza, J.N.: An autonomic computing-based architecture for cloud computing elasticity. In: 2015 Latin American Network Operations and Management Symposium (LANOMS). IEEE (2015)
10. Amazon Auto Scaling[EB/OL]. http://aws.amazon.com/cn/autoscaling/
11. Ali-Eldin, A., Tordsson, J., Elmroth, E.: An adaptive hybrid elasticity controller for cloud infrastructures. In: 2012 IEEE Network Operations and Management Symposium (NOMS). IEEE (2012)
12. Mao, Y., Zhang, J., Letaief, K.B.: Dynamic computation offloading for mobile-edge computing with energy harvesting devices. IEEE J. Sel. Areas Commun. **34**(12), 3590–3605 (2016)
13. Chen, M.-H., Dong, M., Liang, B.: Joint offloading decision and resource allocation for mobile cloud with computing access point. In: 2016 IEEE International Conference on Acoustics, Speech and Signal Processing (ICASSP). IEEE (2016)
14. You, C., Huang, K.: Multiuser Resource Allocation for Mobile-Edge Computation Offloading. arXiv preprint arXiv:1604.02519 (2016)
15. Kosta, S., et al.: Thinkair: dynamic resource allocation and parallel execution in the cloud for mobile code offloading. In: 2012 Proceedings IEEE INFOCOM. IEEE (2012)
16. Kemp, R., Palmer, N., Kielmann, T., Bal, H.: Cuckoo: a computation offloading framework for smartphones. In: Gris, M., Yang, G. (eds.) MobiCASE 2010. LNICST, vol. 76, pp. 59–79. Springer, Heidelberg (2012). https://doi.org/10.1007/978-3-642-29336-8_4
17. Kovachev, D., Yu, T., Klamma, R.: Adaptive computation offloading from mobile devices into the cloud. In: 2012 IEEE 10th International Symposium on Parallel and Distributed Processing with Applications (ISPA). IEEE (2012)

A Space-Circle Architecture Design and Performance Analysis of Spatial Backbone Network Based on Geostationary Satellite Collocation

Yong Jiang[1,2(✉)], Yongjun Li[1], Shanghong Zhao[1], Yitao Zhang[1], and Xiao Jie[3]

[1] Air Force Engineering University, Xi'an 710077, China
v.jiangyong@aliyun.com
[2] 96620 Troops of PLA, Baoding 072653, China
[3] 94860 Troops of PLA, Nanjing 210018, China

Abstract. With the development of satellite technology, and continuous improvement of relay, communication, navigation, remote sensing and meteorological satellite systems in China, massive heterogeneous spatial information needs for convergence, integration, storage, transmission, processing, forwarding and so on had put forward higher requirements to the construction of spatial backbone network. Proceeding from the architecture design of spatial backbone network, using the method of geostationary satellite collocation to build the backbone node was proposed. And then several typical geostationary satellite collocation styles were analyzed and compared. Using Orbital dynamics and spherical geometry theory, a fly around model with space-circle configuration was designed, and its AER performance was analyzed through simulation software and optimization algorithm. The simulation results showed that the configuration completely meet design requirements of spatial backbone network.

Keywords: Space-Circle Architecture · Geostationary satellite collocation
Spatial backbone network · Architecture design · Performance analysis

1 Introduction

The various platforms of spatial information network were distributed at different heights in the space environment, with characteristics of dynamic, complex relationships between nodes and network topology heterogeneous. As national information infrastructure, taking considering of limited in global station construction, space information network had basically taken consensus architecture shape of "backbone network + access network" in China [1–5].

This paper is supported by National Natural Science Foundation of China (No. 61701522).

Q. Yu (Ed.): SINC 2017, CCIS 803, pp. 50–65, 2018.
https://doi.org/10.1007/978-981-10-7877-4_5

Space-based Backbone Networks (SBN) were generally composed by integrated GEO satellite backbone nodes with function of broadband access, data relay, routing and switching, information storage, processing and integration. Although the network topology was simple, but massive heterogeneous business access requirements in the future, made the single platform capacity and scarcity of orbital resources to be challenges. How to overcome these challenges, there were two solutions: one was the lager GEO platform and payload; the second was Geostationary Satellite Collocation [6].

However, lager platforms would face vexed problems such as launching, on-orbit Assembly and invulnerability etc. The structure of Geostationary Satellite Collocation means that multi-satellite shares the same orbital, and working collaboratively to recover the lack-ness of single lager platform. The ideal solution had advantages of (1) allowed space modular growth and (2) could be used in distributed computing (3) was more robust and (4) platform design and launching were simple. But Geostationary Satellite Collocation would also cause internal clusters structure optimization, reasonable designing backbone cluster node with stable structure and little maintaining cost was the first problem to be solved.

2 Research Progress

2.1 Geostationary Satellite Collocation Architecture

In terms of Geostationary Satellite Collocation architecture design, many famous Aerospace experts in the field of service and engineering were gathered by Italian Alcatel Space, Spain GMV company, Switzerland kangtelafusi company, Luxembourg SESAstra and the Canadian Telesat company. And then the SkyLAN system concept was proposed [7]. The system was actually a space network composed by multiple GEO satellites based on the standard inter-satellite communication interface. This concept was making functions of single satellite separated to multiple different, smaller satellites in the same orbit. Therefore, SkyLAN was a satellite cluster which exchange information via ISL, and execute comprehensive and integrated functions. The conceptual diagram was shown in Fig. 1.

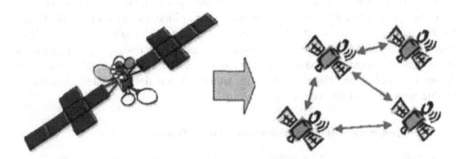

Fig. 1. SkyLAN conceptual diagram

In order to replenish and maintain military failure satellites timely in the war of future, the United States launched the operational responsive space (ORS) program, through the rapid Assembly, Integration and Test (AIT) and the deployment of small, low-cost satellites, complete development of response, enhance or supplement the space forces, enhancing the use of space and space control capabilities. In order to verify the above ideas, US DARPA proposed and invested the F6 development plan as an important part of the ORS program. The F6 program was shown in Fig. 2 [8]. F6 system put a full-function lager satellite into a few special platform groups. These small platforms exchange data wirelessly. This "plug and play" network could make updating and changing task simply by add a new satellite.

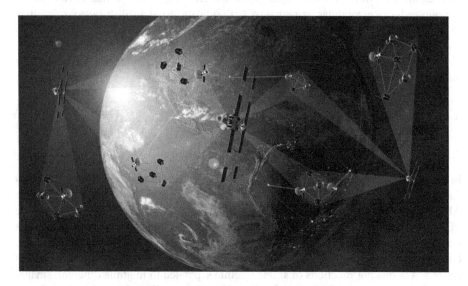

Fig. 2. The constellation diagram of F6 plan [9]

DARPA planned to implement F6 in four stages. First stage was concept design of satellite system, designing project framework using orbit dynamics. And also, contract team would develop a test-bed based on hardware in loop for software simulation on task of spacecraft module separation. Second stage was accomplishing system detail design, hardware and software development of satellite function module. Third stage was completing function module development for system integrated and ground simulation test validation. Fourth stage was launching function module, compositing satellite network, and on-orbit demonstration.

2.2   Geostationary Satellite Collocation Orbital Design

Because of the great potential technical advantages of Geostationary Satellite Collocation, it had very broad applications in military and civilian field, and was wildly researched by many experts and scholars. The fixed circular orbit model was assumed by Ross [10], and the linear mathematical expressions were given under the J2 perturbation. However, intersection node perturbation and apsides rotating under J2 perturbation making the model available only in a short time. Analytical expression for the relative motion of the satellite was given using method of unit spheres by Vadali [11]. And a linear approximate solution of near-circular orbit was given by constructing transfer matrix using the spherical geometry method by Schweighar and Sedwick [12]. A higher order moving model based on the Gauss equation was given, and a method for solution of nonlinear relative motion was proposed in [13]. A trajectory design method of distributed constellations was given and applied in Earth observation satellite systems in [14]. A least squares estimation method for satellite formation flying orbit design was given in [15], using least squares estimation method to design the orbital elements of rest concomitant satellites under reference satellite orbital elements and relative motion. A orbital phase control method to achieve orbit approach and fly-around orbit parameters design in [16]. These methods above were only suitable for distributing low-orbit remote sensing satellite orbit design, and orbit resources does not need to be considered. Taking into account the particularity of the GEO satellite with the scarcity of orbital resources, not only to ensure the stability of group structure, but also ensure flying-around satellite cannot interfere with other satellites in orbit, Existing methods cannot meet the configuration requirements for Geostationary Satellite Collocation.

3   Backbone Network Architecture Analysis of Geostationary Satellite Collocation

3.1   Analyze Requirements

According to spatial development strategy of information network in China, as an important part of the future global information infrastructure, space-based backbone network would be the center of information gathering, management and control for space information system, and could accomplish three core functions of user, control and operation management. As the core node of space information system, the backbone network was designed to work with existing satellite system cluster together to complete the mission requirements, and accomplish interconnection of heterogeneous satellite systems, user's random access and information sharing, and could apply to modern military activities as well as Government and industry sectors. Space-based backbone network design must take into account the following factors:

- The SBN will be an information network that has regional expanding to global coverage. When designing satellite constellation, the ability of global coverage should be considered. And the GEO satellites to construct the constellation should be best choice.
- The SBN will provide various services including information gathering, integration, forward and management for various heterogeneous space platforms of spatial information network, and must have the link transmission capability of large capacity. Since lager GEO platform design, launching, assembly is facing a bottleneck, Geostationary Satellite Collocation will eliminate the disadvantages of

platform, allows modular growth of space segment, at the same time reduce the initial investment cost of the system;

- The SBN is a global coverage constellation, constricted by setting the abroad ground and TT&C stations. It requires the network running autonomously to solve the TT&C problem out of our country and to improve network survivability.

Therefore, under the analysis of space environment characteristics and the space-based platform ability, facing the different application requirements of national defense and military, a service oriented uninterrupted SDN architecture was designed. In Fig. 3, the schematic of SBN structure was given follow. It was divided to six core nodes, and each core node cluster includes 4–5 GEO satellites, those satellites work cooperatively to meet service needs for SBN.

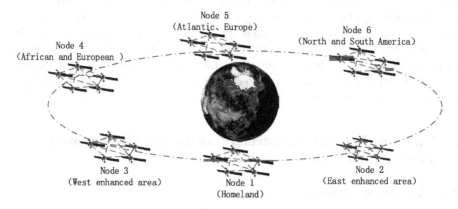

Fig. 3. Schematic of space-based backbone network structure

3.2 Configuration Analysis of Backbone Node Cluster

According to SBN design, its core node uses the configuration of distributed Geostationary Satellite Collocation cluster, this configuration can greatly improve system survivability, self-organization capability, and so on. At present, the typical cluster configuration includes fly-with, sway, fly-around, each configuration has their own advantages and disadvantages. After research and analysis, the applicable space-based trajectory design method for core node will be determined.

- Fly-by cluster configuration

The Fly-with distributed cluster configuration is shown in Fig. 4. All nodes construct a queue to form a distributed cluster, the advantage of this configuration is the constellation design simple, relatively simple position change the relationship between adjacent satellites. But for GEO constellation, this configuration occupies multiple adjacent orbital positions. Considering of GEO orbit resource scarcity currently, engineering implementation is almost impossible.

- Sway cluster configuration

The sway cluster configuration is shown in Fig. 5. All nodes are swing in one orbit position to form distributed cluster, this configuration has advantage of simply constellation design, and only occupy one GEO orbit position. But the azimuth, elevation and range between adjacent node change dramatically, taking inter-satellite high speed directional antenna for example, it is great challenge for antenna Acquisition Tracking Pointing (ATP).

- Fly-around cluster configuration

The fly-around distributed cluster is designed in Fig. 6. Setting a main fix GEO satellite node, the others fly around the fix node in circle to form a distributed cluster. The advantage of this configuration is making the relative position fixed by orbital optimization designed. And because of adding eccentricity, it can effectively avoid crash with other GEO orbital satellite. While its design is much more complex, need to optimize the orbital elements, and belong to multi-objective optimization problem.

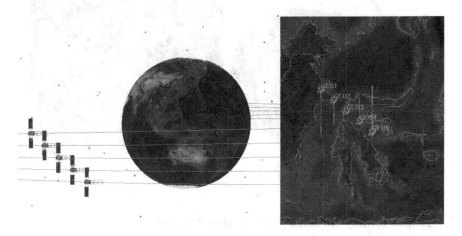

Fig. 4. Fly-with cluster configuration

From the three kinds of distributed cluster configuration analysis above, coplanar fly-around of GEO distributed cluster configuration scheme is more suitable for SBN node design. By working cooperatively between flying around node and master node, it can effectively meet the needs for space information network service, and the configuration can be lunch satellites according to the need of service to improve the scalability of the system.

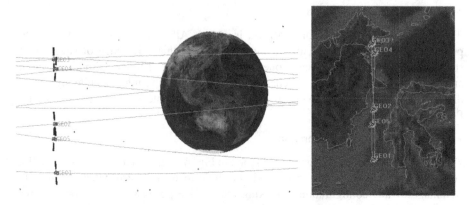

Fig. 5. Sway cluster configuration

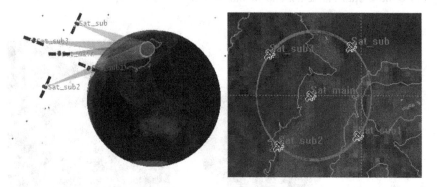

Fig. 6. Fly-around cluster configuration

4 Geostationary Satellite Collocation Design and Performance Simulation

4.1 Mathematic Model

Orbital element is a set of parameters used to describe the satellite running state, including semi-major axis a, eccentricity e, inclination i, RAAN Ω, perigee ω and mean anomaly M, represented in vector form as:

$$\vec{e} = [a, e, i, \Omega, \omega, M]^{T} \qquad (1)$$

In formula (1), semi-major axis a and eccentricity e determine the size and shape of the orbit, inclination i, RAAN Ω and perigee ω determine the orbit space pointing, and the mean anomaly M show the instantaneous position of the satellite in orbit.

In Geostationary Satellite Collocation, each satellite node distribute into a small region, so the orbital elements except perigee ω and mean anomaly M are almost equal. In the relative motion model described by orbital elements, the relative orbital elements are used to analyze the position relationship between satellite nodes. The relative orbital elements are defined as the difference between orbital elements of each node, represented as follow:

$$\Delta \vec{e} = \vec{e}_{cir} - \vec{e}_{ref}$$
$$= [\Delta a, \Delta e, \Delta i, \Delta \Omega, \Delta \omega, \Delta M]^{T}$$

(2)

The subscripts $[\cdot]_{ref}$ and $[\cdot]_{cir}$ respectively represent the relative motion of reference satellite flying-around satellite.

The relative motion relationship of reference satellite flying-around satellite is shown in Fig. 7, the O, S_{ref} and S_{cir} represent earth center, reference satellite and fly-around satellite respectively. In order to describe the trajectory of fly-around satellite relative to reference, the relative coordinate system is defined as follow: the coordinate origin is reference, x axis along the line from the earth to coordinate origin, and y axis is the direction of satellite operation, and z axis is perpendicular to the orbital plane, and x, y axis meet the right hand role.

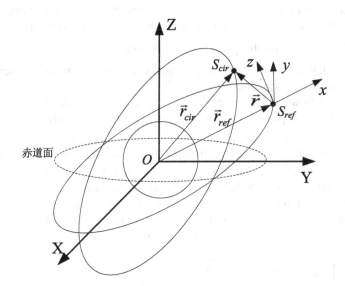

Fig. 7. The relative motion relationship of reference satellite flying-around satellite

According to Fig. 7, transferring fly-around coordinate to reference coordinate, the vector $\vec{r} = M_{ref-cir}\,\vec{r}_{cir} - \vec{r}_{ref}$ is gotten as the fly-around trajectory. The transfer matrix is represented as follow:

$$
\begin{aligned}
M_{ref-cir} &= M_z\big[u_{ref}\big]M_x[-\Delta i]M_z[-u_{cir}] \\
&= \begin{bmatrix}
\cos \Delta u & -\sin \Delta u & -\Delta i \,\sin u_{ref} \\
\sin \Delta u & \cos \Delta u & \Delta i \,\cos u_{ref} \\
\Delta i \,\sin u_{cir} & \Delta i \,\cos u_{cir} & 1
\end{bmatrix}
\end{aligned}
\tag{3}
$$

In formula above, the $M_x[\cdot]$ and $M_z[\cdot]$ represent the rotation matrix of circled over x axis and z axis, the u_{ref} and u_{cir} represent the geocentric angle from relative ascending node to present position of reference satellite and fly-around satellite.

Applying formula (3) on $\vec{r} = M_{ref-cir}\,\vec{r}_{cir} - \vec{r}_{ref}$, by triangular transformation and further consolidation, we can get equation following:

$$
\begin{cases}
x = -ae_A \cos(nt + \theta) \\
y = 2ae_A \sin(nt + \theta) + a\Delta\lambda \\
z = a\Delta i \,\sin(nt + \psi)
\end{cases}
\tag{4}
$$

In formula (4), n represents orbital angular velocity of reference satellite, and e_A, θ, $\Delta\lambda$ and Ψ are meddle variables in formula deduction progress. Form formula (4), we can conclude that: ① the component in x and y axis meet equation $\left(\frac{x}{ae_A}\right)^2 + \left(\frac{y-a\Delta\lambda}{2ae_A}\right)^2 = 1$, so the projection of fly-around trajectory in $x - y$ plane is ellipse with 2:1 long-short axle ratio. ② z axis component is an independent simple harmonic vibration, and its amplitude is $a\Delta\lambda$.

Assume the fly-around satellite as space circle configuration, its radius is r, the short axle of $x - y$ plane meets $p = ae_A = r/2$, the amplitude in z axis meet $s = a\Delta i = r\sqrt{3}/2$, the Initial phase meets $\alpha = \theta - \psi = \pi/2$ or $3\pi/2$. In actual satellite orbit design, the orbital parameters of reference satellite are usually known. Only if $\Delta\vec{e} = [\Delta a, \Delta e, \Delta i, \Delta\Omega, \Delta\omega, \Delta M]^T$ is calculated, the orbital parameters of fly-around satellite are gotten. In order to grantee the cluster could keep the original configuration after running one period, each satellite of cluster must have the same orbital semi-major axis a, as well $\Delta a = 0$. The relationship of relative motion parameters and orbital elements is given in follow equations:

$$
\begin{cases}
e_{cir} = \sqrt{\left(\frac{p}{a}\right)^2 + e_{ref}^2 + 2\frac{p}{a}e_{ref}\cos\theta} \\
i_{cir} = arc\,\cos\left(-\dfrac{\sin\Delta\Omega\,\cos(w_{ref}-\theta+\alpha)-\sin(w_{ref}-\theta+\alpha)\cos\Delta\Omega\,\cos i_{ref}}{\sin k}\right) \\
\Omega_{cir} = \Omega_{ref} + \Delta\Omega \\
w_{cir} = k + \theta - \alpha - \phi + \frac{l}{a} \\
M_{cir} = M_{ref} + \phi
\end{cases}
\tag{5}
$$

$\Delta\Omega$ is the difference of RAAN, k and φ are middle various, and shown in follow formulas.

$$\Delta\Omega = \arctan\left(\frac{\sin(w_{ref} - \theta + \alpha)}{\cos(w_{ref} - \theta + \alpha)\cos i_{ref} + \sin i_{ref}\cot\left(\frac{s}{a}\right)}\right) \tag{6}$$

$$k = \arctan\left(\frac{\sin(w_{ref} - \theta + \alpha)}{\cos(w_{ref} - \theta + \alpha)\cos\left(\frac{s}{a}\right) + \sin\left(\frac{s}{a}\right)\cot i_{ref}}\right) \tag{7}$$

$$\phi = \arctan\left(\frac{2ape_{ref}\sin\theta}{a^2\left(e_{cir}^2 + e_{ref}^2\right) - p^2}\right) \tag{8}$$

Assume the fly-around satellite number is N, the semi-major axis a, eccentricity e, inclination i and perigee ω are fixed, the relationship of RAAN Ω and mean anomaly M is shown as follow.

$$\begin{cases} M_n = \frac{n-1}{N}\pi + M_0 \\ \Omega_n = \Omega_0 + M_0 - M_n \end{cases} \tag{9}$$

Thus, the entire fly-around orbit parameters are calculated, which could provide theoretical references for data relay satellite constellation designed based on Geostationary Satellite Collocation. According to the orbital elements of the satellite constellation, we construct the constellation in the STK software, calculate the AER characteristics, and analyze its performance in detail.

4.2 Constellation Construction

Taking the GEO satellite above China for example, the initial ephemeris time set as "2016/12/02 04:00:00.000 UTCG", the fly-around satellite number is four, distributed evenly, the fly-around radius is 100 km. Using the method and formula above, the orbital parameters are given in Table 1. And its constellation configuration is shown in Fig. 8.

4.3 AER Performance Analysis

Through analyzing the inter-satellite link performance of main-sub and adjacent sub satellite, the constellation performance parameters and configuration realization will be given mathematically. The change relationship of Azimuth, Elevation and Range (AER) along with latitude between main and sub satellites is shown in Fig. 9. And its

Table 1. Orbital parameters of main and sub satellites

Satellite name	Perturbation	Semi-major axis (km)	Eccentricity	Inclination (°)	Perigee (°)	RAAN/longitude(°)	Mean anomaly (°)
Sat_main	J2	42166.3	0	0	0	249.431/118E	0
Sat_sub	J2	42166.3	0.0012	0.12	90	159.431/117.869E	0
Sat_sub1	J2	42166.3	0.0012	0.12	90	69.431/117.876E	90
Sat_sub2	J2	42166.3	0.0012	0.12	90	−20.569/117.883E	180
Sat_sub3	J2	42166.3	0.0012	0.12	90	−110.569/117.889E	270

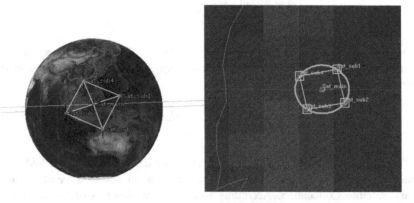

Fig. 8. Constellation configuration with four fly-around satellites

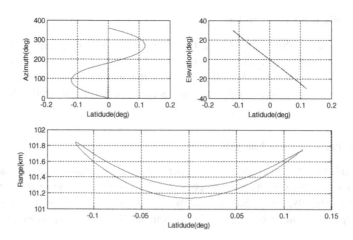

Fig. 9. AER change relationship along with latitude of main-sub satellite

relationship along with time is given in Fig. 10. From these two figures, we can find that, change region of the azimuth, elevation and range are 0 deg–360 deg, ±30 deg and 101.1 km–101.85 km respectively, can meet the configuration requirement.

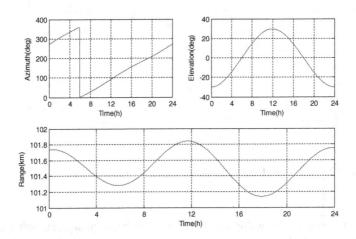

Fig. 10. AER change relationship along with time of main-sub satellite

The AER rate change relationship along with latitude between main and sub satellites is shown in Fig. 11. And its relationship along with time is given in Fig. 12. From these two figures, we can find that, change region of the azimuth rate, elevation rate and range rate are 6.1×10^{-5}deg/s–8×10^{-5}deg/s, $\pm 3.5 \times 10^{-5}$deg/s and $\pm 0.75 \times 10^{-6}$ km/s respectively. AER rate is in 10^{-5} magnitude, and the links are stable to meet the ATP requirement.

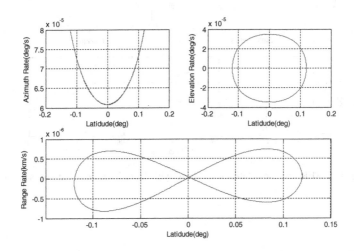

Fig. 11. AER rate change relationship along with latitude of main-sub satellite

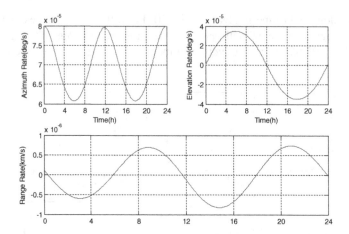

Fig. 12. AER rate change relationship along with time of main-sub satellite

The AER change relationship along with latitude between adjacent sub satellites is shown in Fig. 13. And its relationship along with time is given in Fig. 14. From these two figures, we can find that, change region of the azimuth, elevation and range are 0 deg–360 deg, ±30 deg and 143.1 km–143.9 km respectively, can meet the configuration requirement.

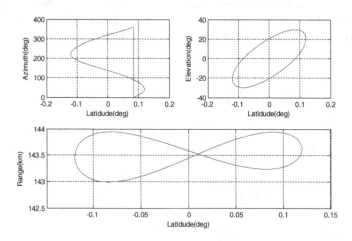

Fig. 13. AER change relationship along with latitude of adjacent sub satellite

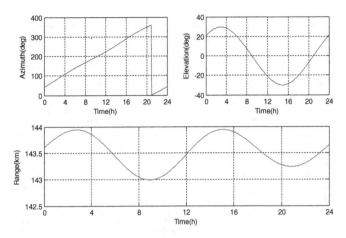

Fig. 14. AER change relationship along with time of adjacent sub satellite

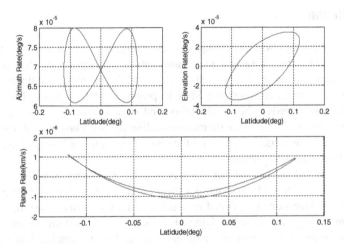

Fig. 15. AER rate change relationship along with latitude of adjacent sub satellite

The AER rate change relationship along with latitude between main and sub satellites is shown in Fig. 15. And its relationship along with time is given in Fig. 16. From these two figures, we can find that, change region of the azimuth rate, elevation rate and range rate are 6.1×10^{-5}deg/s–8×10^{-5}deg/s, $\pm 3.5 \times 10^{-5}$deg/s and $\pm 1.2 \times 10^{-6}$ km/s respectively. AER rate is in 10^{-5} magnitude, and the links are stable to meet the ATP requirement.

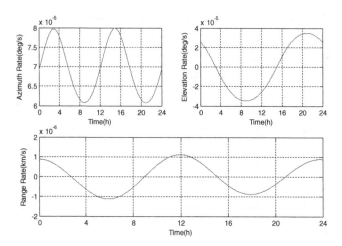

Fig. 16. AER rate change relationship along with time of adjacent sub satellite

5   Conclusion

Based on the actual application, facing on present urgent needs of spatial information networks efficient networking and mass information transformation, drawing on the latest technology and latest achievements, the method that using Geostationary Satellite Collocation mechanism to construct SBN is proposed in this paper. Multi-satellite coordination may improve the survivability and organizational ability of backbone nodes, meanwhile could significantly reduce satellite platform launch and design costs, and could provide theoretical support for the current problems of less capacity of single satellite and orbit resource scarce.

Therefore, based on analysis of three typical Geostationary Satellite Collocation configurations, using the orbital dynamics theory and spherical Geometry methods, the space-circle configuration is analyzed in detail. Then a fly-around constellation orbital design example is given, which is lying above China with 100 km radius. Then the AER performance of main-sub and adjacent sub satellite is simulated in detail. The simulation result shows that this configuration is best with little AER change character, and total meeting the antenna ATP requirement.

References

1. Yu, Q., Wang, J.C.: System architecture and key technology of space information network. Chin. Comput. Commun. **12**(3), 21–25 (2016)
2. Shen, R.J.: Some thoughts of Chinese integrated space-ground network system. Eng. Sci. **8** (10), 19–30 (2006)
3. Zhang, N.T., Zhao, K., Liu, G.L.: Thought on constructing the integrated space-terrestrial information network. J. China Acad. Electron. Inf. Technol. **10**, 223–230 (2015)
4. Min, S.Q.: An idea of China's space-based integrated information network. Spacecr. Eng. **22** (5), 1–14 (2013)

5. Huang, H.M., Chang, C.W.: Architecture research on space-based backbone network of space-ground integrated networks. J. China Acad. Electron. Inf. Technol. **10**(5), 460–491 (2015)
6. Wang, J.C., Yu, Q.: System architecture and key technology of space information network based on distributed satellite clusters. ZTE Technol. J. **22**(4), 9–13 (2016)
7. Gou, L., Xie, Z.D., et al.: SkyLAN: a cluster of geostationary satellites for broadband communications. Dig. Commun. World **1**, 37–40 (2013)
8. Liu, H., Liang, W.: Development of DARPA's F6 program. Spacecr. Eng. **19**(2), 92–98 (2010)
9. Brown, O., Eremenko, P.: Value-centric design methodologies for fractionated spacecraft: progress summary from phase 1 of the DARPA system F6 program. In: AAIA Reinventing Space Conference, 6540, pp. 1–15 (2009)
10. Ross, I.M.: Linearized dynamic equations for spacecraft subject to J2 Perturbations. J. Guid. Control Dyn. **26**(4), 657–659 (2003)
11. Vadali, S.R.: An analytical solution for relative motion of satellites. In: 5th Dynamics and Control of Systems and Structures in Space Conference, Cranfield University, Cranfield, U.K., July 2002
12. Schweighart, S.A., Sedwick, R.J.: High-fidelity linearized J2 model for satellite formation flight. J. Guid. Control Dyn. **25**(6), 1073–1080 (2002)
13. Sengupta, P., Vadali, S.R., Alfriend, K.T.: Second-order state transition for relative motion near perturbed, elliptic orbits. Celest. Mech. Dyn. Astron. **97**, 101–129 (2007)
14. Zhao, J., Xiao, Y.L.: Orbit configuration design of formation flying satellites to be used for earth observing and positioning. J. Astronaut. **24**(6), 563–568 (2003)
15. Dong, Z., Zhang, X.M., You, Z.: Satellite formation flying orbit design based on least-squares estimates. J. Tsinghua Univ. **46**(2), 210–213 (2006)
16. Li, G.F., Zhu, M.C., Han, C.: An orbit transfer method for concomitant satellite approaching and flying-around. J. Astronaut. 30(6), 2182–2187 (2009)

Adaptive Interference Mitigation from IMT-2020 BS to Mobile-Satellite Service

Shuaijun Liu[1,2(✉)], Bo Li[1,2], Gaofeng Cui[1,2], Xin Hu[1,2],
and Weidong Wang[1,2]

[1] Key Laboratory of Universal Wireless Communications,
Ministry of Education, Beijing University of Posts and Telecommunications,
Beijing 100876, China
lsj_bupt@163.com
[2] Information and Electronics Technology Lab,
Beijing University of Posts and Telecommunications, Beijing 100876, China

Abstract. This paper investigates an adaptive interference mitigation (AIM) technique at International Mobile Telecommunications for 2020 (IMT-2020) base station (BS) transmitters to improve the frequency sharing of terrestrial and satellite systems. In contrast to the conventional schemes, we take into account the mobile earth station (MES) and planar array antenna (PAA) rather than the fixed earth station (FES) nor linear array antenna (LAA), respectively. MES motion has an effect on the interference mitigation (IM) performance mainly due to the uncertain MES location resulting in exceeded interference. This paper firstly modeled the MES mobility and then derived the relation between MES velocity and MES location updating period. An adaptive interference mitigation (AIM) scheme is proposed next. Furthermore, simulation results are presented to illustrate the performance of the proposed scheme.

Keywords: Interference Mitigation (IM) · Frequency sharing
International Mobile Telecommunications (IMT)
Mobile Satellite Service (MSS) · Updating period

1 Introduction

The development of IMT-2020 (5G) and beyond is expected to enable new use cases and address rapid traffic growth, for which contiguous and broader spectrum bandwidths than currently available for IMT systems would be desirable. Frequency bands below 3 GHz can be viewed as the most favorable for IMT services for its good propagation characteristics, but it seems hardly to find an available contiguous large bandwidth to support the extremely high throughput use case. This suggests the need to consider spectrum resources in higher frequency ranges [1]. The recent past WRC-15 has adopted the study item 1.13 on frequency-related matters for IMT identification including possible additional allocations to the mobile services on a primary basis for the future development of IMT for 2020 and beyond [2]. However, some bands have already been allocated on a co-primary basis to mobile-satellite service (MSS) [3], thus making it necessary and meaningful to study the sharing and compatibility of IMT-2020 and MSS.

© Springer Nature Singapore Pte Ltd. 2018
Q. Yu (Ed.): SINC 2017, CCIS 803, pp. 66–78, 2018.
https://doi.org/10.1007/978-981-10-7877-4_6

Lots of work has done on sharing studies of IMT and satellite services, most of which are limited to IMT-2000/IMT-Advanced systems. International Telecommunication Union (ITU) has published the relating reports on sharing of IMT-2000 terrestrial and satellite components in [4], and that of IMT-Advanced and geostationary satellite networks (GSO) in the fixed-satellite service (FSS) system in [5, 6]. However, frequency higher than 6 GHz sharing of IMT-2020 and satellite system is in its infancy due to the propagation model not been reached yet, etc. Study of coexistence between 5G small cells and Fixed Service (FS) at 39 GHz is done in [7], where required frequency rejection is given for tolerable interference on FS resulting from IMT-2020. [8] focuses on the spectrum sharing between IMT-2020 and Fixed Satellite Service (FSS) at 28 GHz, where the achievable performance of 5G under the FSS interference is simulated.

We consider the IMT-2020 as secondary systems and MSS as primary (or incumbent) system for that some bands have been allocated to MSS before. A series of cognitive techniques can be used for satellite terrestrial coexistence including interweave, underlay and overlay schemes. Among these, underlay technique exploits the interference tolerance capability of the primary systems that allows the secondary users to transmit even in the presence of the primary users. In this context, the interference mitigation (IM) [10–12] on interfering transmitter or interference reduction (IR) [12–16] on victim receiver both based on multi-input and multi-output (MIMO) are proposed. [11, 12, 14, 16] adopted transmitting or receiving beamforming (BF) techniques, while [13, 15] introduced additional antennas on ES for interference signal process (ISP). [10] proposed an efficient and robust IM technique based on null-steering multi-user multi-input and multi-output (MU-MIMO) spatial division multiple access (SDMA) scheme.

It should be noted here that IM or IR algorithms state of the art mainly limited to linear array antenna (LAA) in IMT BSs and FESs in FSS system, which is quite different for our concerned coexistence scenario of IMT-2020 and MSS. Compared with LAA, planar array antenna (PAA) can realize bigger beamforming gain or higher order MU-MIMO especially suitable for millimeter wave due to its smaller footprint. Predictably, PAA and millimeter wave will be used in IMT-2020 downlink providing extremely high throughput service. What's more, the effect of mobility is rarely considered.

Assuming the knowledge of direction of concerning nodes (DoCN), for example, the concerning node is the earth station (ES) of victim satellite downlink in [10]. DoCN is updated through accessing the ES location database periodically or other spatial spectrum estimation techniques. Motion of ES is ignored in FSS systems [10–16], while things changed when we consider MSS systems characterized by mobile earth station (MES). Then a series of problems should be clarified, including to what extent the mobility of victim ES affect existing IM or IR performance, and how to modify the existing techniques, etc.

In fact, the motion of MES mainly affects the estimation accuracy of DoCN, thus degrading the IM or IR performance. Updating DoCN more frequently can improve the DoCN accuracy, while it can increase the system overhead and be wasteful for the low velocity or static MESs. On the other side, low updating frequency increases the uncertain interference probably exceeding the victim MES interference threshold (IT) due to DoCN error. This paper aims at following two aspects:

- Derived the relation between DoCN updating period and MES mobility;
- Proposed adaptive IM based on the MES mobility prior information.

The rest of this paper is organized as follows: Sect. 2 is the system model. Then the relation of MES mobility and DoCN updating period is derived and AIM scheme is proposed in Sect. 3. Simulations are conducted in Sect. 4. At last Sect. 5 concluded the paper.

2   System Model

2.1   Coexistence Scenario

We consider the frequency sharing of IMT-2020 system and MSS system with both networks operating in downlink mode co-frequency. The MSS space station is supposed geostationary satellite (GEO Sat) and IMT-2020 is deployed here to provide hot-spot service. Coexistence scenario of these two systems is illustrated as Fig. 1.

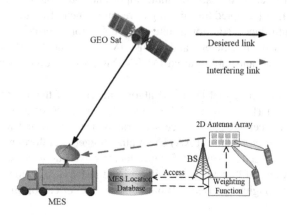

Fig. 1. Coexistence scenario of IMT and MSS

In this context, the desired signal is the GEO Sat downlink signal while the interfering signal is the BS transmitting signal. Interference from IMT BS on the MES should not exceed the IT to keep the underlay cognitive coexistence. Supposing the 2D array antenna with $N_V \times N_H$ elements is deployed at the IMT-2020 BS transmitter. IMT system can access the MES location database periodically to acquire the MES geographic location[1].

---

[1] In case the database does not exist or unavailable, other techniques such as spatial spectrum estimation should be adopted to acquire the MES direction.

2.2 Planar Array Antenna Radiation Pattern

Planar array antenna consisting of identical radiating elements located in yz-plane with a fix inter-element distance $\lambda/2$ is supposed for IMT-2020 BS antenna pattern, thus realizing high order MU-MIMO transmission in downlink. 2D array antenna geometry is illustrated as Fig. 2. Where, θ is the elevation angle ranging from –90 to 90°, φ is the azimuth angle ranging from –180 to 180°.

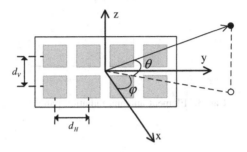

Fig. 2. Planar array antenna model geometry

As we know, array antenna radiation pattern is depended on both antenna element pattern and array factor. Antenna element radiation pattern in horizon and vertical is represented as Eqs. (1) and (2) respectively:

$$A_{E,H}(\varphi) = -\min\left[12\left(\frac{\varphi}{\varphi_{3\,\text{dB}}}\right)^2, A_m\right] \tag{1}$$

$$A_{E,V}(\theta) = -\min\left[12\left(\frac{\theta}{\theta_{3\,\text{dB}}}\right)^2, SLA_v\right] \tag{2}$$

where, A_m is the front-to-back ratio and SLA_v is side-lobe level limit both in dB scale, $\varphi_{3\,\text{dB}}$ and $\theta_{3\,\text{dB}}$ is horizontal and vertical 3 dB bandwidth, respectively. Vertical and horizon radiation pattern of element antenna is illustrated as Fig. 3. And the element antenna pattern gain at (φ, θ) is as Eq. (3).

$$A_E(\varphi, \theta) = G_{E,\max} - \min\{-\left[A_{E,H}(\varphi) + A_{E,V}(\theta)\right], A_m\} \tag{3}$$

where $G_{E,\max}$ is the maximum element antenna gain. Element antenna radiation pattern is shown in Fig. 4, with $G_{E,\max} = 6\,\text{dBi}$, $\varphi_{3\,\text{dB}} = \theta_{3\,\text{dB}} = 65°$, $A_m = 30\,\text{dB}$, $SLA_V = 30\,\text{dB}$.

2.3 MES Mobility Model

Different from FSS system ES-static characteristic, mobility characteristic of MES should be considered. MES mobility can be described by moving velocity and moving direction etc. Here for simple, we take MES with linear motion specifically into

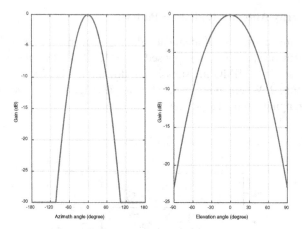

Fig. 3. Element antenna radiation pattern

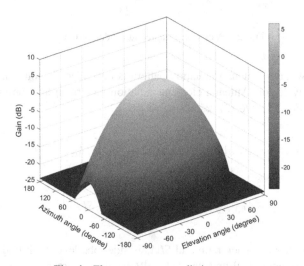

Fig. 4. Element antenna radiation pattern

consideration. As BS can acquire the MES location periodically with updating period T_{ud}, DoCN can be calculated based on the relative position of BS and MES as illustrated in Fig. 5.

At given time $t = t_1$, the DoCN is calculated based on the latest acquired MES location at time t_0, where $t_0 = t_1 - \Delta t$ $(0 \leq \Delta t < T_{ud})$. While the real DoCN is the θ_1 with a difference of $\Delta\theta = \theta_1 - \theta_0$ depending on the MES moving direction θ_v, moving velocity v, time interval Δt and the distance d_0 between MES and BS. Thus, MES all possible locations form an uncertain area (UA) with radius $r_{ua} = v \times T_{ud}$.

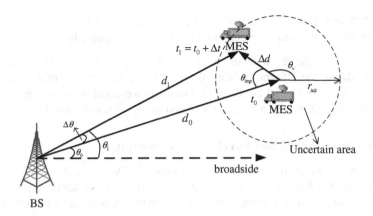

Fig. 5. MES mobility scenario

Based on the cosine theorem, d_1 and $\Delta\theta$ can be calculated as Eq. (6).

$$d_1 = \sqrt{d_0^2 + \Delta d^2 - 2 \times d_0 \times \Delta d \times \cos\theta_{tmp}} \tag{4}$$

$$\theta_1 = \theta_0 + \Delta\theta \tag{5}$$

$$\Delta\theta = \cos^{-1}\left(\frac{d_0^2 + d_1^2 - \Delta d^2}{2 \times d_0 \times d_1}\right) \tag{6}$$

where $\theta_{tmp} = \theta_0 + (\pi - \theta_v)$, $\Delta d = v \times \Delta t$, $0 \le \Delta t < T_{ud}$.

3 Proposed IM Technique

3.1 IM Based on Null-Steering Algorithm

For IMT-2020 2D array antenna with $N_V \times N_H$ elements, the array antenna radiation pattern $A_A(\theta, \varphi)$ in dB scale is illustrated as Eq. (7).

$$A_{A,Beami}(\theta, \varphi) = A_E(\theta, \varphi) + 10\log_{10}\left(\left|\sum_{m=1}^{N_H}\sum_{n=1}^{N_V} w_{i,n,m} \cdot v_{n,m}\right|^2\right) \tag{7}$$

where $w_{i,n,m}$ and $v_{n,m}$ are the super position vector and the weighting vector.

Basic concept of the IM-NS is to form nulls in the spatial spectrum that correspond to the DoCN. Here, it's necessary to give a brief review on IM-NS algorithm.

- Step 1: Compute the null points θ_{null} generated by n_T precoding vectors $e_{g,m}$ ($m = 0, 1, \cdots, n_T - 1$).
- Step 2: Calculate the n_T precoding vectors $w_{g,m}$ depending on DoCN θ_0 and the null points θ_{null} computed in Step 1.

- Step 3: Select the $n_T - 1$ precoding vectors, $w_{g,n}$ $(n = 0, 1, \cdots, n_T - 2)$, forming nulls at DoCN θ_0 from n_T precoding vectors $w_{g,m}$ computed in Step 2.

Figure 6 shows the BS transmit antenna radiation pattern with IM-NS algorithm applied. It shows the BS transmitting power on direction θ_{NS} is mitigated largely improving satellite terrestrial coexistence. Detailed theoretical derivation and analysis can refer to [10]. BS radiation pattern illustrated as Fig. 6 is considered in this paper[2].

3.2   Protection Criteria and Interference Assessment

According to the ITU report, an interference criteria of $I/N = -12.2\,\text{dB}$ $(\Delta T/T = 6\%)$ is chosen as the MES protection criteria, where N is the clear-sky satellite system noise. Let I_1 denote the possible receiving interference changing with the MES location and can be denoted by Eq. (8).

$$I_1 = P_{BS} + G_{T,wi}(\theta_1) + G_R(\varphi_0) - L_1 \tag{8}$$

where the P_{BS} is the BS transmitting power, $G_{T,wi}(\theta_1)$ is the BS antenna transmitting gain towards the direction θ_1 with IM-NS shown in Fig. 6, $G_R(\varphi_1)$ is the MES antenna receiving gain at the off-axis angle of φ_1. L_1 is the propagation loss between BS and MES including path-loss, 3 dB polarization difference loss and bandwidth loss which accounts for the fraction of interfering signal power that appears in the band of the victim MES. It should be noted here all parameters in Eq. (8) is in decibel (dB) scale.

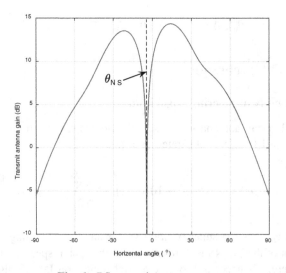

Fig. 6. BS transmit antenna pattern

---

[2] This IM algorithm would require the use of other frequencies to cover the area where the BS transmit antenna gain is reduced, here specified as θ_{NS}.

Here, we model the path-loss as the free space path-loss model as Eq. (9). However, in practice more accurate attenuation models can be considered, e.g., diffraction loss, etc. This leads to extra attenuation, and thus the free space path-loss model is the worst case scenario. Due to variation of propagation characteristics in bands above 6 GHz, it is appropriate to investigate the propagation characteristics of these frequency bands independently. Some preliminary investigations were conducted by both industry and academy, and a more precise path loss model used for analysis will be our further study.

$$L_{PL} = 92.44 + 20 \lg(fc/GHz) + 20 \lg(d/km) \tag{9}$$

As MES's uncertain location in UA illustrated in Fig. 5, the maximum receiving interference should not exceed the IT. From Fig. 6, we can know $G_{T,wi}(\theta_1)$ rises sharp when real DoCN θ_1 away from the null-steering direction θ_0 with a difference of $\Delta\theta$. Compared to $G_{T,wi}(\theta_1)$, the other three factors remain static or slowly varied. It is clear that maximum interference is received in the condition when $\Delta\theta$ obtained the max-value $\Delta\theta_{max}$. From the Eq. (6), we can get the $\Delta\theta_{max}$ as Eq. (10).

$$\Delta\theta_{max} = \sin^{-1}\left(\frac{v \times T_{ud}}{d_1}\right) \tag{10}$$

From this Eq. (10), we know updating period T_{ud} is nearly inverse proportional to MES velocity. For a given MES, reducing the updating period T_{ud} can mitigate the interference.

3.3 Adaptive IM-NS Algorithm

As there is a great correlation between the MES location for the current moment and next, we modify null-steering point from θ_0 to θ_m. Clearly the more close for θ_m to θ_1, bigger interference mitigation gain can be acquired. In particular, we take into account the case in which the BS performs a spatial linear prediction for the possible MES location. Thus proposed adaptive IM-NS forms null at DoCN of θ_m, where θ_m is calculated by

$$\theta_m = \max_{p(\theta_v)}\left(\theta_0 + \cos^{-1}\left(\frac{d_0^2 + d_1^2 - v^2 \times \Delta t^2}{2 \times d_0 \times d_1}\right)\right) \tag{11}$$

Here, a preliminary concept of adaptive IM-NS algorithm is proposed. More precise prediction on MES location and its performance is our further study.

4   Simulation Results

4.1   Simulation Parameters

We focus primarily on the interference modes where the interfering signal emitted from one IMT BS impacts one MSS MES. Operating center frequency of 25.5 GHz is supposed. The characteristics of typical GEO MSS systems as described in the ITU-R Report M.2360-0 are used in simulation. Detailed simulation and link budget parameters for both the IMT and MSS systems are provided in Table 1.

Table 1. System parameters

Parameter	Value
IMT-2020 BS characteristics	
Carrier frequency	25.5 GHz
Bandwidth	20 MHz
BS transmit power	46 dBm
Antenna pattern	3-sector with $\theta_{3\,\mathrm{dB}} = 70°$
Transmit antenna peak gain	15 dBi
BS feeder loss	1 dB
MES characteristics	
Receive antenna diameter	0.33 m
Receive antenna peak gain, G_R	36.4 dBi
Receive antenna polarization	linear
System noise temperature, T_{sys}	246.2 K
IF Receive Bandwidth at -3 dB	16.2 MHz
Receive noise power	−102.6 dBm
Interference criteria, I/N	−12.2 dB
Moving velocity	[20 60 120] km

4.2   Relation Between I/N and Separation Distance

The required separation distance for different MES velocity and updating period are plotted in Fig. 7. From the simulation results, required separation distance for static MES is about 2.8 km. While for MES velocity $v_{MES} = 120$ km/h with updating period $T_{ud} = 10$ s, required separation distance increased to about 37 km.

By reducing the updating period to $T_{ud} = 1$ s, separation distance reduced to a half about 17 km. From the Fig. 7, other conclusions can be proved: (1) the bigger MES velocity is, required separation distance is larger; (2) the updating period is shorter, separation distance is smaller.

4.3   Relation Between MES Velocity and Updating Period

Figure 8 shows the relation between MES velocity and updating period under the interference criteria $I/N = −12.2$ dB. From the results, needed updating period T_{ud}

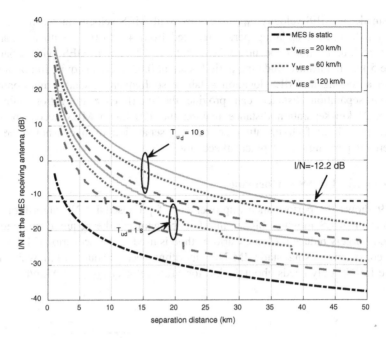

Fig. 7. Relation between I/N and separation distance

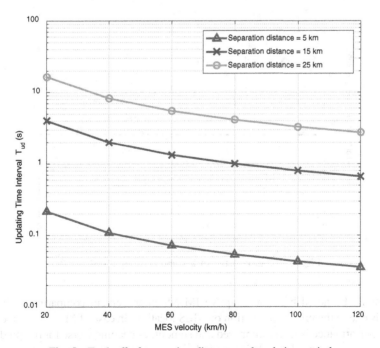

Fig. 8. Tradeoff of separation distance and updating period

grows smaller as MES velocity v_{MES} increases. With MES velocity increasing from 20 to 120 km/h, needed updating period reduced from 4 s to 0.6 s with a separation distance 15 km. It should be noted here that for 120 km/h MES with separation distance 5 km, the needed updating period is about 0.03 s. This is quite impossible for IMT BS accessing the MES location database so frequently. Under this condition, additional separation distance can provide the interference mitigation gain. For example, 25 km separation distance making the 120 km/h MES needs about 3 s updating period. In fact, updating period and separation distance should be both considered depending on the practical scenarios.

4.4   Adaptive IM-NS Performance

Figure 9 shows the performance improvement of proposed IM-NS algorithm. With prediction on MES moving, bigger interference gain can be acquired and required distance is largely reduced. Monte Carlo method is used in this scenario [17]. From the figure, coexistence using static IM-NS algorithm needs about 28 km while using adaptive IM-NS only needs about 11 km for MES velocity $v_{MES} = 60$ km/h.

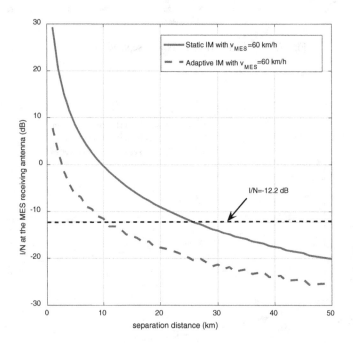

Fig. 9. Relation between I/N and separation distance

It should be noted here the adaptive IM-NS improvement comparing with static IM-NS is due to the precise prediction on MES location. In case of MES with stochastic motion, performance is rarely improved and sometimes become worse for big prediction error. In fact, reducing the updating period can compensate the performance loss.

5 Conclusion

Frequency sharing of IMT-2020 and MSS was investigated in this paper. We studied the required separation distance for different MES velocities. It was shown that the MES with high velocity suffered more interference from IMT BS. The relation between MES velocity and updating period is given. Further, we have shown that AIM algorithm can reduce the separation distance.

Acknowledgement. This work is supported by the National Natural Science Foundation of China (No. 91438114 and No. 61372111).

References

1. ITU-R Reports M.2376: Technical feasibility of IMT in bands above 6 GHz, July 2015
2. ITU-R: Final Acts WRC-15, World Radiocommunication Conference. Geneva (2015)
3. ITU-R: Radio Regulations (2012)
4. ITU-R Report M.2041: Sharing and adjacent band compatibility in the 2.5 GHz band between the terrestrial and satellite components of IMT-2000 (2003)
5. ITU-R Report M.2109: Sharing studies between IMT-Advanced systems and geostationary satellite networks in the fixed-satellite service in the 3400–4200 and 4500–4800 MHz frequency bands (2007)
6. ITU-R Report M.2292-0: Characteristics of terrestrial IMT-Advanced systems for frequency sharing/interference analyses, December 2013
7. Kim, J., Xian, L., Maltsev, A., Arefi, R., Sadri, A.S.: Study of coexistence between 5G small-cell systems and systems of the fixed service at 39 GHz band. In: 2015 IEEE MTT-S International Microwave Symposium, Phoenix, AZ, pp. 1–3 (2015)
8. Guidolin, F., Nekovee, M.: Investigating spectrum sharing between 5G millimeter wave networks and fixed satellite systems. In: 2015 IEEE Globecom Workshops (GC Wkshps), San Diego, CA, pp. 1–7 (2015)
9. Park, J.M., Oh, D.S., Park, D.C.: Coexistence of mobile-satellite service system with mobile service system in shared frequency bands. IEEE Trans. Consum. Electron. **55**(3), 1051–1055 (2009)
10. Jo, H.S., Yoon, H.G., Lim, J., Park, Y.H., Yook, J.G.: Coexistence method to mitigate interference from IMT-advanced to fixed satellite service. In: 2007 European Conference on Wireless Technologies, Munich, pp. 158–161 (2007)
11. Sharma, S.K., Chatzinotas, S., Ottersten, B.: Transmit beamforming for spectral coexistence of satellite and terrestrial networks. In: 8th International Conference on Cognitive Radio Oriented Wireless Networks, Washington, DC, pp. 275–281 (2013)
12. Lagunas, E., Sharma, S.K., Maleki, S., Chatzinotas, S., Ottersten, B.: Resource allocation for cognitive satellite communications with incumbent terrestrial networks. IEEE Trans. Cogn. Commun. Network. **1**(3), 305–317 (2015)
13. ITU-R Report S.2150: An interference reduction technique by adaptive-array earth station antennas for sharing between the fixed-satellite service and fixed/mobile services, September 2009
14. Sharma, S.K., Chatzinotas, S., Ottersten, B.: Spatial filtering for underlay cognitive SatComs. In: International Conference on Personal Satellite Services, pp. 186–198. Springer International Publishing, Cham (2013)

15. Sharma, S.K., Maleki, S., Chatzinotas, S., Grotz, J., Ottersten, B.: Implementation issues of cognitive radio techniques for Ka-band (17.7–19.7 GHz) SatComs. In: 2014 7th Advanced Satellite Multimedia Systems Conference and the 13th Signal Processing for Space Communications Workshop (ASMS/SPSC), Livorno, pp. 241–248 (2014)
16. Sharma, S.K., Chatzinotas, S., Grotz, J., Ottersten, B.: 3D beamforming for spectral coexistence of satellite and terrestrial networks. In: 2015 IEEE 82nd Vehicular Technology Conference (VTC Fall), Boston, MA, pp. 1–5 (2015)
17. ITU-R Recommendation M.1634: Interference protection of terrestrial mobile service systems using Monte Carlo simulation with application to frequency sharing (2003)

An Optimization Deployment Methodology of HAP-VMIMO Broadband Communication Network with Matching the Demand Distribution

Shuzhu Tang, Dawei Yan, Peng You$^{(\boxtimes)}$, and Shaowei Yong

National University of Defense Technology, Changsha, China
Tangshuzhu612@163.com, ysw_nudt@vip.126.com

Abstract. Aiming at the optimal design of the space information network with the usage of high altitude platform (HAP) as base station, this paper proposed a multi-objective optimal deployment methodology for HAP broadband communication network base on network capacity resource matching the demand distribution. Firstly, a virtual multi-input and multi-output (VMIMO) broadband communication network model is consisted by multi HAP. Secondly, the network ergodic capacity and the matching degree which is characterized as Hash fingerprint difference between demand distribution and capacity distribution that are taken as the optimal objectives. In order to solve this model, the non-domination sorting genetic algorithm-2(NSGA-2) with restriction judgment strategy was used. The simulation result shows the effectiveness of the proposed optimization methods.

Keywords: High altitude platform · Virtual multi-input multi-output
Optimization deployment

1 Introduction

Owing to the usage of high altitude platform (HAP) as base station, the space information network can be compatible with the terrestrial network, and has unique advantages in region coverage enhancement and emergency communication [1]. While the communication capacity and coverage range are very limited provided by single HAP, due to its power, bandwidth and height restrictions, generally through interjecting multi-HAP to form a collaborative communication network [2]. Multi-input multi-output (MIMO) technology is an effective means to improve the capacity of HAP network. It help achieve high-speed transmission and enhance link reliability by increasing spatial freedom degree, which require configure multiple antennas at transmitter and receiver. The current relate research mainly focus on HAP-MIMO network with plurality of antennas configure on single HAP [3, 4]. Since the short distance between transmitter antennas and the high altitude that HAP deployed, this making the links which established between HAP and same ground that experience basically same wireless environment. This leads to the construction's poor ability to overcome large-scale fading. Therefore, each HAP configure a single antenna, and

© Springer Nature Singapore Pte Ltd. 2018
Q. Yu (Ed.): SINC 2017, CCIS 803, pp. 79–92, 2018.
https://doi.org/10.1007/978-981-10-7877-4_7

multiple HAP collaboration constitute a virtual multiple-input multiple-output (VMIMO) network, which can make the communication links more robust [5, 6].

Celcer et al. studied the possibility and effectiveness of providing wireless broadband access services for high-speed rail users through space-time coding mechanism in HAP-VMIMO network [5]. Aiming at the problem of overlapping coverage and diversity reception in HAP-VMIMO systems, Dong et al. studied quantitatively the effects of different antenna configurations and channel parameters on the system performance [6]. The above studies are performed on the link performance when multiple HAP positions are pre-fixed, and not consider furthering enhancing network performance by optimizing the deployment of HAP. To optimize the deployment of HAP network with the goal of satisfied more user demand, Zong et al. applied the game learning algorithm which embed the Restricted Spatial Adaptive Play strategy, and obtained Nash equilibrium solution [7]. And it's resulting in a low coverage rate amount area because only user distributions are taken into account. Zhu et al. optimized HAP's position by maximizing joint communication coverage of the cyberspace based on Linearly Decreasing Weighted Particle Swarm algorithm, without matching user demand [8]. Dong et al. proposed a HAP network optimal model which aims to maximum network capacity per cost and guarantees the QoS index and user demand, also integrate multiple indicates into one to optimal [9]. The existing literature mainly focuses on how to deploy HAP to cover more users, instead of improving system performance from the perspective of entire network, and without considering optimization of multiple indicators simultaneously. Based on above, this paper proposed a multi-objective optimal deployment method for HAP broadband communication network which capacity resource is matching demand distribution. In this method, to construct VMIMO system based on multi HAP, and making the Hash fingerprint difference between capacity map and demand map to indicate the matching degree, then the non-dominated sorting genetic algorithm-2 (NSGA-2) which applied the constraint judgment strategy is used to solve the optimization models.

The remainder of this paper is organized as follows: Sect. 2 describes the HAP-VMIMO network model; Sect. 3 presents the multi-objective optimal deployment model, and introduces the Percept Hash and NSGA-2 algorithm; Sect. 4 conducts a numerical simulation and analyzes the results. Section 5 concludes the paper.

2 Network Model

2.1 HAP-MIMO Model

Multiple HAPs configured cooperative communication network through network interconnection, which can enhance the user rate, improve the capacity and reduce the outage probability in the target area. The following describes the HAP-VMIMO network model, as shown in Fig. 1.

In HAP-VMIMO, this with the same coverage area's HAP can be interoperable through inter-platform-link interconnection. At the same time, HAP establish backhaul link with terrestrial fixed base station or satellite backbone network, this help the network to obtain strict time synchronization. The model simply considers that HAP is

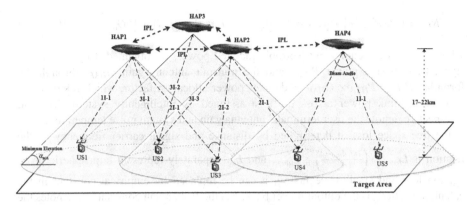

Fig. 1. HAP-VMIMO model

configured with single antenna and enable provide single beam. A plurality of antennas is equipped on the user receiver to establish communication links with the overhead HAP. The carrier and phase synchronization of the received signal is realized at the same time slot by signal processing technique. Whether the ground receiver can establish a link with the HAP is determined by whether the receiver is within the coverage of the HAP, which equivalent to compare the degree between the elevation angle formed by the link and the minimum constraint one. In a multi-covered area, all the overhead HAP base stations with unique antenna can be equivalent to a distributed multi-antenna system, which combine with the ground receivers constitute a virtual multi-input multi-output network (VMIMO). Under this circumstance, the distance between the antennas is very far, the probability of all links being blocked at the same time is very low, and the channel correlation is very small, so it can approximately reach the advantage of MIMO technology. To be noted, it's assumed that the user receiver possessed software radio function which permit user can freely adjust the communication mode to avoid the interrupted affection when its' moving in different coverage areas.

2.2 Downlink Carrier to Noise Ratio

In the broadband communication network, the downlink transmission rate is generally much higher than uplink. For the sake of simplicity, this paper assumes that the uplinks are ideal and only analyzes the downlink carrier to noise ratio (CNR). Under the HAP-VMIMO model, signals received by user in the same coverage area are all useful, so the interference caused by multi HAP is not considered here. In this circumstance, the attenuation of signal propagation mainly comes from transmitter and receiver's circuit system, free space loss, atmospheric propagation loss and small-scale fading, etc. As a digital communication system, in combination with the above analysis, the user's downlink CNR can be solved by the following equation ('[]' represents the dB value).

$$[CNR] = [EIRP] + [Y] + [G_{US}/T] - [L_{free}] - [L_{atmos}] - [L_{ssf}] - [BO_o] - [k] - [B_n] \quad (1)$$

where EIRP is the equivalent isotropic radiated power, we obtained it by the HAP's signal transmission power P_{HAP}, and the transmit antenna gain G_{HAP}, through the formula $EIRP = P_{HAP} \times G_{HAP}$; Y denotes power allocation factor, which refers to the ratio of the link power across the area assigned by intelligently system; G_{US} and T respective denote the user terminals' antenna gain and system noise temperature; L_{free} is the free space loss, it determined by distance and signal carrier frequency f_c, the relation is $L_{free} = \left(\frac{4\pi f_c d_{HAP,us}}{c}\right)^2$; L_{atmos} and L_{ssf} separately represent atmospheric propagation loss and small scale fading, it can be replaced by empirical constant in the calculation; $[BO]_o$ is the output power back; k is the Boltzmann constant; B_n denotes the noise bandwidth of receiver. Then, the transmit signal's signal-to-noise ratio (SNR) is directly determined by this:

$$CNR = \frac{P_C}{kB_nT} = \frac{E_b}{n_0}\frac{R_b}{B_n} = SNR\frac{R_b}{B_n} \quad (2)$$

where P_C denotes signal power after propagation loss; R_b is the bit rate of transmission link; n_0 is single sideband noise power spectral density.

2.3 Capacity Model

Analyze the capacity in HAP-VMIMO network, since the random characteristics of fading channel, this paper mainly considering the ideal expected capacity that user can obtain under coverage multiplicity and antenna configuration. The way that enhance the network performance through multiple coverage and multi-antenna configuration, it's essentially using two or more statistical independent sub-paths to achieve path classification, and finally improves the reliability of data transmission. Then the capacity model is analyzed in detail.

Here supposed the cooperative communication HAP's number is N_T, then the beam forming vector forming the virtual antenna array is $\mathbf{w}(N_T \times 1)$; the number of receiver's antenna is, then the received beam vector is $\mathbf{v}(N_R \times 1)$. When the transmit power is expected to be 1, the receivers SNR_R can be obtained by transmitting's SNR_T combine with fading channel matrix:

$$SNR_R = \left|\mathbf{v}^H\mathbf{H}\mathbf{w}\right|^2 SNR_T \quad (3)$$

where H denotes the complex conjugate transpose operation and the fading channel matrix $\mathbf{H}(t) = [h_{ij}(t)]_{N_R \times N_T}$ is obscured Rician fading. Only the relationship between transmitting and receiver's SNR is considered, we don't specifically analyzing the link's fading channel matrix. In order for the receiver to obtain the maximum SNR, the way that transmitted beam and received beam formed is usually in maximum ratio transmit and in maximum ratio merging. After the eigenvalue decomposition of the signals cross correlation matrix, the optimal beam vector can be obtained, as follows:

$$\begin{cases} \mathbf{H}^H\mathbf{H} = [\mathbf{u}_1, \mathbf{u}_2, \dots, \mathbf{u}_{N_T}]diag(\lambda_1, \lambda_2, \dots, \lambda_{N_H})[\mathbf{u}_1, \mathbf{u}_2, \dots, \mathbf{u}_{N_T}]^H \\ \mathbf{w} = \mathbf{u}_1, \mathbf{v} = \mathbf{Hu}_1/\|\mathbf{Hu}_1\|_F \end{cases} \tag{4}$$

where the diagonal matrix in the formula is a descending diagonal matrix, and λ_1, $\mathbf{u}_1$ represent the largest eigenvalues and the corresponding eigenvectors, respectively; $\|\cdot\|_F$ demotes the Frobenius norm.

The synthetically transmitter's SNR can be expressed in the sum of multi-antenna's SNR. Link obtained the ideal capacity through the Shannon formula. For simplicity, the channel matrix in HAP-VMIMO model is transformed into independent uncorrelated subchannels, and the subchannels' number is determined by the rank of channel matrix, $r = \min(N_T, N_R)$. Consider the maximum ergodic capacity that the network can obtained, it is assumed that the subchannel can reach the ideal channel state information (CSI) according to the "water injecting" theorem, and the rational power allocation is carried out to obtain the optimal data rate. Then the resulting channel capacity is:

$$C = \max_{\sum \gamma_i = N_H} W \sum_{i=1}^{r} \log_2(1 + SNR_T \gamma_i \lambda_i) \tag{5}$$

where W is the work bandwidth, γ_i is the power allocation factor, λ_i is subchannel channel gain (equivalent to $\mathbf{H}(t)$'s non-zero eigenvalue).

Since the ideal CSI is generally not available, this paper adopts the equal power allocation method to carry out the signal transmission, as this $\gamma_i = 1/N_T$. Then under the VMIMO operating mode, the ergodic capacity of the user with multiple antennas is deduced by the sum of expected values of all subchannel capacities. Express as follow:

$$C = E\left(W \sum_{i=1}^{r} \log_2\left(1 + \frac{\lambda_i R_b}{B_n N_T} \sum_{j}^{N_T} CNR_j\right) \right) \tag{6}$$

The establishment of the network capacity model is to study the HAP-VMIMO network's ergodic capacity under different coverage circumstances and receiver configuration; therefore, the propagation channel matrix should be treated specially in the simulation calculation.

3 Deployment Optimization Method

Since HAP's deployment neither be constrained by landform condition like terrain base station, nor be constrained by dynamic of orbits like satellite, it's prone to optimizing resource distribution by matching user demands which could be targeted to allocate high capacity to strong demand's area. In this we propose a deployment optimization methodology of HAP-VMIMO network with matching the demand distribution based on p-Hash and NSGA-2 algorithm.

3.1   Core Idea

Considering the strategy that matching image through "fingerprint" in the image retrieval process, applied it to deployment design method. Take the demand distribution as the test chart, and let the capacity map library formed by design vector library become the image library. Constantly optimize the design victory through the guidance of matching degree's comparison between the test chart and the image library's fingerprint. Finally, the optimum design variable library with the largest matching degree can be obtained. The flowchart is shown in Fig. 2.

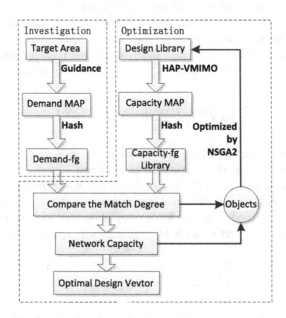

Fig. 2. The flowchart of optimized deployment method

The whole optimization process is divided into two phase. The first-investigation phase: the main task is obtaining the "demand fingerprint" which possesses the function of demand guidance. According to the analysis of target area's demand, generate the user demand map. Then using the p-Hash algorithm to extract and quantify the map's feather to get the "demand fingerprint". The second-optimization phase: the phase is the core process of the method. On commence, random spanning a set of design vector satisfied constraints to construct the design vector library. Each of them is leaded into HAP-VMIMO model to calculate its capacity performance and generate the capacity map, and get the ones "capacity fingerprint" in the same way. Then comparing the match degree with the demand map between the individuals in the capacity map library, we can get the priority of the individual rank in library. Based on this, the design library could be optimized by using modern optimization method NSGA-2 after certain iterative process. And finally we could obtain the best design vector through the performance and cost analysis. The definitions of some concepts are described below.

(1) *User demand map:* is a grid diagram which representing the size and distribution of the user demand for communication services in target area. The area is gridded at a certain resolution, and each grid is assigned a numerical value after analysis, these consist of a numerical matrix become the demand map.

$$\mathbf{D} = [demand(grid)], \; grid \in Area \tag{7}$$

(2) *Capacity map:* similar to above, is a grid diagram which representing the size and distribution of the capacity that the network could offer in the target area. The grid value is determined by the calculation according to design vector and network model.

$$\mathbf{C} = [capacity(grid)], \; grid \in Coverage \tag{8}$$

(3) *Hash:* refers to an algorithm that can extract and quantify the contents of a document and form a unique brief summary, as well as possess the character of unidirectional and anti-collision. Hear using the p-hash algorithm to achieve the function.

$$fg(Map) = Hash(Map), \; Map = \mathbf{D} \, or \, \mathbf{C} \tag{9}$$

3.2 Optimization Model

The HAP-VMIMO broadband communication network studied in this paper doesn't involve the specific communication system and antenna technology. The method target is to obtain a network deployment plan that network recourse is well matched with the user demand distribution. Design variables, optimization objectives and design constraints are given below.

3.2.1 Network Design Vector

The set of all variables is the system design vector. This method is at the standpoint of deploying network, so the design variable should be directly and significantly affected at the system level. The main effects could be divided into three aspects: coverage characteristic, complexity and cost. Table 1 shows the selected variables.

Table 1. Table captions should be placed above the tables.

Label	Design variable	Symbol	Directly related character
$\Gamma(1)$	HAP number	N_{HAP}	Coverage, complexity, cost
$\Gamma(2)$	Location (longitude, latitude)	$\left\{ Long_i^{HAP}, Lat_j^{HAP} \right\}$	Coverage
$\Gamma(3)$	Minimum elevation	$\left\{ \alpha_i^{min} \right\}$	Coverage
$\Gamma(4)$	Receiver antenna number	N_R	Complexity and cost
$\Gamma(5)$	Transmit power cost	$\left\{ P_i^{HAP} \right\}$	Cost
$\Gamma(6)$	HAP antenna gain	$\left\{ G_i^{HAP} \right\}$	Cost

The design vector is $\mathbf{\Gamma} = [N_{HAP}; \{Long_i^{HAP}, Lat_i^{HAP}\}; \{\alpha_i^{min}\}; N_R; \{P_i^{HAP}\}; \{G_i^{HAP}\}]$. If all variables in vector are optimized would result in the consequent that impossible to obtain the optimal solution because of excessive amount of computation (if $N_{HAP} = 5$, the variables' number is $(2 + 5N_{HAP})$, even if the search space of each is only 10, then the solution space size is 10^{27}). For simplify, we choice the HAP number, location and minimum elevation which directly related the coverage character as optimized variable, and the rests are in predetermined.

3.2.2   Optimization Object

The matching optimization is to obtain the optimal design vector corresponding to the largest match degree between capacity map and demand map. Because the fingerprint generated by hash algorithm is a fixed-length sequence, the difference between fingerprints could be represented by Hamming distance. Then the optimal object-match degree could be expressed as the reciprocal of fingerprint difference. Meanwhile, the designed network should provide as large capacity as possible, it's equally important with the match degree. So the other object is set to network capacity. After the above, the mathematical model of optimal object is shown below:

$$\begin{cases} \max \Phi_1(\mathbf{\Gamma}) = \|fg(\mathbf{D}) \text{ xor } fg(\mathbf{C_\Gamma})\|^{-1} \\ \max \Phi_2(\mathbf{\Gamma}) = \|\mathbf{C_\Gamma}\| \end{cases} \quad (10)$$

where xor denotes an exclusive-OR operation.

3.2.3   Deployment Constraints

In order for the deployed HAP-VMIMO network to be closer to reality, it's necessary to analyze the major constraints in the deployment implementation.

(1) *The overlap upper limit:* Considering the complexity in realizing and the problem of signal interference, the number of the links accepted by any grid should be less than one upper limit. Even if the visible HAP's number is greater than limit at one grid, it should select appropriate HAP to satisfy the constraint, as the follows.

$$\forall grid \in Area, \; N_T(grid) \leq N_T^{max} \quad (11)$$

(2) *Minimum HAP spacing:* Although HAP can long time endurance, it's not completely static in the air and its position would change slightly over time. To avoid HAP collision need to limited the spacing between HAPs, as shown below.

$$\forall i \neq j, \; d_{HAP_i, HAP_j} \geq d_{min} \quad (12)$$

where d_{min} denotes the minimum HAP spacing, d_{HAP_i, HAP_j} is the virtual distance between two HAP.

(3) *Minimum transmission power:* To ensure the normal communication between the HAP and any grid under its coverage, sufficient transmission power is required. For simplicity, the unit power per unit area of HAP in its coverage is required to be greater than a certain minimum value, as shown below.

$$\forall i \leq N_H, \frac{P_i^{HAP} G_i^{HAP}}{S_i^{Cover}} \geq P_{min}^{grid} \tag{13}$$

where P_{min}^{grid} denotes the certain minimum transmission power, S_i^{Cover} is the HAP's coverage size which can be calculated according to its minimum elevation: $S_i^{Cover} = \pi(\frac{H}{\tan(\alpha_i^{min})})^2$.

3.3 Optimization Algorithm

In the flow chart, the two main algorithms are the p-Hash that generates the fingerprint and the NSGA-2 which can optimize multiple objects simultaneously. The following is a detail introduction.

3.3.1 p-Hash for Generating Fingerprints

The perception Hash algorithm is widely used in the field of digital image recognition. There are three basic algorithms in image retrieval technology, include the mean hash algorithm based on low frequency, enhanced hash algorithm based on discrete cosine transform, and differential hash algorithms, etc. In this paper, the matching demand map and capacity map are both two-dimensional matrices, which belong to simple images, so using the simplest algorithm-mean hash. The main steps are as follows:

Step 1: Scale the MAP in standard size m × m by using bilinear interpolation method;

Step 2: Calculate the MAP matrix's pixel mean value in target area (or in coverage);

Step 3: Compare the matrix's pixel: if the value is greater than the mean, then record 1, else record 0;

Step 4: Generating fingerprint: encode the comparative results in a fixed order to form a numeric fingerprint.

3.3.2 Non-dominated Sorting Genetic Algorithm-2

The optimization model presented in this paper is a multi-objective and multi-constraint model. And it's obvious that the model is a non-linear, non-convex and non-continuous optimization problem. Because of the large search space and complex solution of objective function, it's a typical NP-Hard problem, and the traditional optimization methods are no longer applicable. Similarly complex global constellation design problems, multi-objective evolutionary algorithms are widely used as an effective tool [10]. Therefore, this paper applied the non-dominated sorting genetic algorithm-2 in multi-objective evolutionary algorithm to solve the problem.

NSGA-2 is an unconstrained multi-objective optimization algorithm, but the model contains several. To induce the population's evolutionary direction within the constraints, it's essential to disposed of infeasible solutions. In this paper, we add a constraint judgment process during the execution of the algorithm: If one individual does not satisfy the constraint, setting its object to the "worst" level directly and without any calculate continued. The NSGA-2 pseudocode is given in Table 2.

Table 2. The pseudocode of NSGA-2.

Initialize: population size- M , generation- N_G , mutation and crossover, fingerprint $fg(\mathbf{D})$

1: Generate initial population: based on constraints, random generate $P_0 = [\boldsymbol{\Gamma}_1, \boldsymbol{\Gamma}_2, ..., \boldsymbol{\Gamma}_M]$;

2: Individual constraint judge and objects calculate:
    for m = 1 to M
        Based on HAP-VMIMO, calculate *Design-Constraint*($\boldsymbol{\Gamma}_i$) ;
        if Design-Constraint($\boldsymbol{\Gamma}_i$) *satisfied*
            Generate capacity map fingerprint $fg(\mathbf{C}(\boldsymbol{\Gamma}_i))$;
            Combine with demand map fingerprint $fg(\mathbf{D})$, calculate [$\Phi_1(\boldsymbol{\Gamma}_i)$, $\Phi_2(\boldsymbol{\Gamma}_i)$];
        else directly set individual $\boldsymbol{\Gamma}_i$ *'s objects:* [$\min(\Phi_1)$, $\min(\Phi_2)$];
        end
    end

3: for $g = 1$ to N_G **do**

4: Genetic variation forms offspring: $Q_{i-1} = GeneticOperator(P_{i-1}, p, q)$;

5: Offspring fitness value calculation: the same as *step2*;

6: Elitist retention strategy: $F_i = Q_{i-1} \cup P_{i-1}$;

7: Fast non-dominated hierarchical ordering: $[T_1, T_2, ...] = NonDominatedSort(F_i)$;

8: Same layer's crowding distance: $\{T_1, T_2, ...\} = CrowdingDistanceAssignment([T_1, T_2, ...])$;

9: Tournament strategy select parent: $P_i = TournamentSelect(\{T_1, T_2, ...\}, M)$;

10: end

---

4   Simulation and Analysis

In this section, the Yangtze River Delta urban region is used as the target area for simulation, which to verified the effectiveness of the proposed optimization deployment method. The simulation software is MATLAB R2014a.

4.1   Target Area and Parameters

It's complicated to directly investigate the demand distribution of the broadband communication network in the city. And it's manifest that the size of demand is positively correlated with the population. Therefore, here replace the user demand map with the Night Lights Map that can reflect the population distribution which published by NSGA2106. The region of the Yangtze River Delta (118.5°E–122.5°E, 29.6°N–32.4°N) is selected as the target area, and rasterized with 0.005° × 0.005° to constitute the demand map, as shown in Fig. 3.

In order to make the simulation of experiments close to actual and more comparative, in Table 3 gives the preset fixed parameters in the model. These parameters remain unchanged during the simulation.

Fig. 3. The Yangtze River Delta's night lights map

Table 3. Simulation parameters.

Parameter	Symbol	Value
HAP high altitude	H_{HAP}	17 km
Carrier frequency	f_c	48 GHz
Noise temperature	T	135 K
Antenna gain	G_{US}	41 dB
Noise bandwidth	B_n	1.544 Mbps
Output power back	$[BO]_o$	3 dB
Atoms-propagation loss	Δ_{atmos}	16 dB
Minimum HAP spacing	d_{min}	400 m
Overlap upper limit	N_T^{max}	5
Minimum trans power	P_{min}^{grid}	60 dB

4.2 Algorithm and Experimental Setup

We used the adaptive constraint NSGA2 which with real coding and analog binary cross strategy to evolution constant generates to obtain the Pareto solution. The algorithm's parameters are identical in each experimental, which the population size is 50, the evolutionary generation is 100, the mutation and the crossover probability are 10% and 90% respectively.

By setting up different deployment parameters, multiple experiments are carried out. After repeated iterations, the Pareto optimal solutions are obtained and compared. Pre-set EIRP to 2000 W. Set a total of 8 different parameters of the experiment: the deployment of HAP number is 12 or 18, the minimum elevation is variable value of 10°–20° or fixed value of 15°, the receiver antenna number is 2 or 4 and so on.

4.3   Comparison and Analysis of Results

After optimized, we obtained the Pareto solution of the eight experiments object values of the match degree and the network capacity as shown in Fig. 4. (Note: the left and right sides are the solution of the receiver antenna number is 2 and 4 respectively, and all have been normalized.)

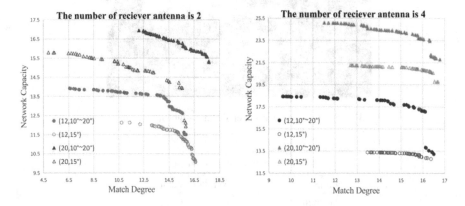

Fig. 4.   The optimal solution.

From the commonalities of the experiments can be found: The greater the individual's matching degree, the smaller the network capacity. It is proved that the two objects are mutually limited in the individual level, and it is difficult to get the HAP deployment scheme to achieve the best of both high capacity and matching user demand. Moreover, the variation range of the matching degree in each experiment is much larger than that of the network capacity. This shows that as long as the deployment parameters contain the number of HAP, the minimum elevation limit and receiver antenna number have been identified, the obtained total capacity are in tiny discrepancy between different deployment schemes in VMIMO mode. However, different deployment schemes result in significant difference in the matching degree of capacity resources and user demand. This explains the indeed need for optimal deployment of the HAP-VMIMO network to matching demand.

From the comparison of each experiment can be found: When the number of receiver antennas remains constant, the greater the number of HAP is deployed, the greater the network capacity is, and this is obviously, while the optimal match obtained in the individual is also greater. As the number of HAP increases, in addition to the increase in power source, it also increases the number of overlapping covers in the target area, which can gain a larger capacity gain. When the number of receiver antennas is from 2 to 4, the network capacity of each group is greatly increased, and the difference of network capacity between the same groups is reduced. Because of the increase in the number of receiver antennas, the VMIMO network formed is more efficient, and the receiver can more fully obtain the capacity gain through the HAP multi-repetition cap. When a fixed number of HAP, compare the minimum elevation angle constraint is a variable values of 10°–20° or a fixed value of 15°, its show that in the same experiment, the individuals with the same amount of network capacity have better matching degree when the minimum elevation is variable, and which converse is also the same. Because the deployment scheme can be more flexible when configured an adjustable minimum elevation, but the actual variable minimum elevation is more difficult to implement.

Figure 5 gives the typical HAP distribution of simulation when the receiver antenna number is 4. It can be found that the typical solutions are well matched with the demand distribution in the Yangtze River Delta urban agglomeration. Comprehensive the above results and analysis, the optimization deployment method is reasonable and effective, and it is shown that the HAP position distribution with high matching degree and network capacity can be optimized under different parameter configurations, which is able to give some reference to the actual deployment of HAP network.

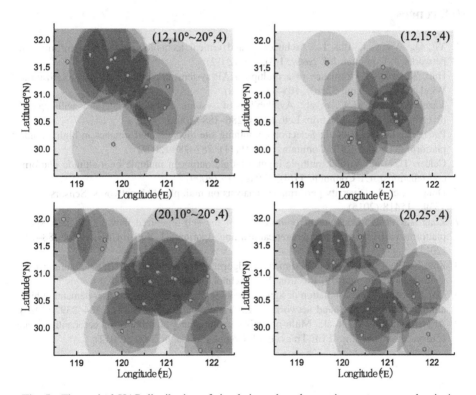

Fig. 5. The typical HAP distribution of simulation when the receiver antenna number is 4.

5 Conclusion

In the circumstance of using multiple HAP's interconnection to construct the space information network, this paper present a multi-objective optimal deployment method for HAP broadband communication network base on capacity matching demand.

Firstly, the HAP-VMIMO network model is established. After analyzed the single HAP's CNR, the network capacity model is given when covered area's overlap and receiver antennas' number are different. Secondly, according to the principle of image retrieval, the paper proposes an optimized deployment idea that minimizes the Hash fingerprint difference between the capacity map and the user demand diagram. And considering the entire network's performance that let the match degree and the network capacity both as optimal objectives, then the NSGA-2 which applied the constraint judgment strategy is used to solve the nonlinear, discontinuous and non-convex optimization model. Finally, set The Yangtze River Delta as the target area for simulation. After several experiments, the optimization results of different parameters such as the HAP quantity, the minimum elevation angle and the receiver antenna number are obtained, which verified the method's effective.

References

1. Yu, Q., Wang, J., Bai, L.: Architecture and critical technologies of space information networks. J. Commun. Inf. Netw. 1(3), 1–9 (2012)
2. Hult, T., et al.: Performance of a multiple HAP system employing multiple polarization. Wirel. Pers. Commun. 52(10), 105–117 (2010)
3. Vázquez-Castro, M.A., et al.: Availability of systems based on satellites with spatial diversity and HAPS. Electron. Lett. 6(38), 286–288 (2002)
4. Panagopoulos, A.D., et al.: Selection combining site diversity performance in high altitude platform networks. IEEE Commun. Lett. 10(11), 787–789 (2007)
5. Celcer, T., et al.: Virtual multiple input multiple output in multiple high-altitude platform constellations. IET Commun. 11(3), 1704–1715 (2009)
6. Dong, F., et al.: Diversity performance analysis on multiple HAP networks. Sensors 7(15), 15398–15418 (2015)
7. Zong, R., et al.: Deployment optimization of the self-organized network on near space platforms based on the game theoretical learning algorithm. J. Xidian Univ. 40(5), 188–193 (2013)
8. Zhu, Z., et al.: Deployment optimization algorithm for regional MANET containing near space vehicles as a part. J. Electron. Inf. Technol. 33(4), 915–921 (2013)
9. Dong, F., et al.: A constellation design methodology based on QoS and user demand in high altitude platform broadband networks. IEEE Trans. Multimedia 18(12), 2384–2397 (2015)
10. Arias-Montano, A., et al.: Multi-objective evolutionary algorithms in aeronautical and aerospace engineering. IEEE Trans. Evol. Comput. 16(5), 662–694 (2012)

Distributed Cooperative Storage Management Framework for Big Data in Satellite Network Operation and Maintenance

Fu Yinjin[1], Hou Rui[2(✉)], and Xie Jun[1]

[1] College of Command and Information System,
Army Engineering University, Nanjing 210007, China
[2] Institute of China Electronic System Engineering Corporation,
Beijing 100039, China
1808072450@qq.com

Abstract. In recent years, China's rapid growth on the demand for satellite communication application, not only impels the continuous expanding on the management scale of network operation and maintenance (O&M) system, but also puts forward higher demand for intelligent network management and control. Under this circumstance, the data management function, which services as the core of the satellite network O&M system, is faced with the serious management challenges brought by the huge amount and complex datasets. In this paper, we study the distributed cooperative storage management technologies for big data management issue in satellite network O&M. We propose a distributed cooperative big data storage model for the satellite network O&M, and further study the intra-site hybrid database management strategy and inter-site fast data synchronization technology, to improve the scalability and disaster tolerance of data service in the O&M application. Finally, we evaluate the hybrid database architecture based on Oracle and HBase using the benchmark, and compare the theoretical network traffic with the actual flow measured by GoldenGate, then perform the quantitative analysis on the system disaster tolerance of data services.

Keywords: Satellite network · Operation and maintenance · Big data
Distributed storage · Hybrid database · Data synchronization
Disaster tolerance

1 Introduction

The operation and maintenance (O&M) management of satellite communication network is the critical service for the whole system running in reliability, safety, high efficiency and cost-efficiency [1]. It includes station control, network control and operating control services. The station control service is responsible for the terminal device control and operational management in the earth station. The network control service is responsible for the communication networking between earth stations and the dynamic resource management in the network. The traffic control service is responsible for the coordinated allocation of the unified managed satellite transponder resources

© Springer Nature Singapore Pte Ltd. 2018
Q. Yu (Ed.): SINC 2017, CCIS 803, pp. 93–104, 2018.
https://doi.org/10.1007/978-981-10-7877-4_8

among various networks. Through the monitoring and management of network equipment, server, database and all kinds of application services, network O&M management can improve the efficiency and service level agreement of application in satellite communication network, to meet the needs of various users. Data service, as the core service of the satellite communication network O&M system, is responsible for managing the massive system operation log information, as well as the configuration and status information of all kinds of equipment and services. With the developing of satellite communication applications in China, not only the management scale of the operation and maintenance system will soon reach more than a hundred satellites, hundreds of ground stations, millions of mobile users, but also it put forward higher requirements in the intelligent network control, the professional application services and the fine-grained resources usage. The scale expansion of satellite network and the increasing of data category cause the satellite communication network O&M system to be faced with the big data challenge of massive complex operation and maintenance dataset [2].

Different from the application demand of traditional distributed storage system, the satellite communication network O&M data management application, not only faces the traditional big data storage management challenges, but also brings the complexity problems from the space-ground integrated network due to the combination of terrestrial networks and satellite networks [3]. At present, the branches of satellite network O&M site collect and manage data independently, and the information in each site cannot be shared because of the management authority and the security responsibility reasons. But in the event of earthquake, flood, large area blackout and even war, data service of one or more sites in the whole system will fail or even be destroyed. This traditional information isolated management model cannot make full use of the limited storage resources in the site to manage the massive operation and maintenance data, and cannot further meet the disaster recovery needs of the core data services in O&M applications [4, 5]. We study distributed cooperative storage technology by combining the big data storage management challenges of satellite network O&M and the complexity characteristics of space-ground integrated network, to enhance the system scalability and disaster recovery capabilities of O&M data service in the satellite network.

In this paper, we will study the key technologies of distributed cooperative storage for satellite communication network O&M, including big data storage architecture, hybrid database management strategy and fast data synchronization technology.

In traditional network O&M systems, data management is relatively independent, and without distributed collaborative design, which makes the insufficient capability in data disaster recovery and low utilization rate of IT resources in the site [6]. We design an integrated distributed collaborative big data storage framework to support data sharing, disaster recovery and heterogeneous architecture for big data management requirements of satellite communication network O&M system.

Due to the diverse variety and complex structure of operation and maintenance data, a single relational data management model has been unable to effectively manage the big data in satellite network O&M. The application demands of the massive, complex and highly distributed O&M data storage force the data management system to scale out, and drive us to adopt the hybrid database management technology to support the network O&M data service.

The distributed cooperative big data management for network O&M application has greatly increased the demand for inter-site data replication, and it seriously affects the quality of service in data management [7], since the O&M sites are connected by a wide area network and the network bandwidth is very limited. By mining the potentiality to optimize data migration in remote disaster tolerance, we study the fast data synchronization mechanism to improve the recovery capability of the O&M data service when part of the system fails.

The rest of the paper is structured as follows. Section 2 presents the necessary background and related work. Section 3 describes the architecture of our distributed cooperative data storage system, hybrid database management strategy and database synchronization technique. Section 4 evaluates the system prototype in system fault tolerance, hybrid database performance, data synchronization throughput, and Sect. 5 draws conclusions.

2 Related Work

According to the research content of distributed cooperating storage management technology for big data in satellite network O&M application, we introduce the related work in the three aspects: distributed storage system, hybrid database management and database synchronization technology.

2.1 Distributed Storage System

The research in distributed storage system for massive data management began in 1980s, and then had drawn great interests from both the industrial and academic communities. The core technology of the distributed storage system is distributed file system, it includes: network file system, SAN cluster file system and object based file system to support the distributed storage management for massive dataset.

Network file system: it focuses on file sharing in network environment, and mainly solves the interaction between client and file server. The server architecture is basically symmetrical structure, and each server stores a directory subtree to support the storage management of large dataset. It provides a unified namespace, but the storage server does not share the storage space between the servers, and there is no load balancing and fault tolerance mechanism among the servers. The representative products include: AFS [8] developed by Carnegie Mellon University and Sun's product NFS [9].

- SAN cluster file system: it replaces the SCSI bus with network, and a file can be written into several storage nodes in parallel by data striping, which can significantly improve the I/O throughput. All computing nodes share storage space to maintain a unified namespace and file data. But because of the tight coupling characteristics of shared critical resources, distributed locks are required to perform complex cooperation and exclusive operations among nodes, which makes it difficult to scale out in large-scale server nodes. The typical SAN cluster file systems include IBM's GPFS [10] and VMFS [11] developed by VMware.

- Object based file system: it utilizes object-based storage devices with intelligent ability, and divides the file into a plurality of objects, which are stored separately into different object-based storage devices. This can significantly reduce the file metadata. The object-based storage devices are completely independent, so that the object based file system can be expanded to large scale, and effectively solved the capacity expansion problem of the storage system. The current widely used object-based parallel file system: Panasas [12] developed by Carnegie Mellon University, Oracle's Lustre file system [13], Ceph [14] developed by University of California, Santa Cruz, Google file system (GFS) [15] and the open source project HDFS [16] launched by Yahoo.

With the function expansion of distributed storage system software, compared with the traditional storage system with dedicated hardware, the standard open hardware platform can achieve all their storage function by using software, which makes the Software Defined Storage (SDS) as an emerging concept. Compared with the traditional distributed file system, besides the storage function, SDS has obvious advantages in scalability, availability, flexibility, management and cost efficiency. The typically representative products include: VMware VSAN [17], EMC ScaleIO [18], Nutanix NDFS [19], and Huawei Fusion Storage [20]. In recent years, SDS had extended to Hyper Converged Infrastructure (HCI) to support virtualization in computing, storage and network source. HCI makes the equipment units can be aggregated through the network to form a unified resource pool with seamless modularize scalability. Comparing with the traditional distributed architecture, the HCI architecture have some merits in system reliability, performance, availability, scalability, cost-efficiency, deployment and maintenance, and we build a HCI based software defined storage to implement the upper level hybrid database system, and provides dynamically scalable system resources in computing and storage, in order to support the fast, safe and reliable big data management in satellite network O&M application.

2.2 Hybrid Database Management

In the era of big data, we need to use a variety of architectures to support different applications in order to cope with the needs of big data management. The existing database management systems can be broadly divided into three categories: SQL database for transaction processing, NoSQL database for Internet applications and NewSQL database for data analysis. But in some complex scenarios, single database architecture cannot completely meet the application requirements of storage management, association analysis, complex query, real-time processing and control of construction costs and other aspects for massive structured and unstructured data. Therefore, hybrid database architecture has become the inevitable choice to meet the complex application.

Nowadays, the design and development of hybrid database has become a research focus in big data management. HyPer [21] is a main-memory-based relational DBMS for mixed OLTP and OLAP workloads, which is developed by Technical University of

Munich. Its OLTP throughput is comparable or superior to dedicated transaction processing systems and its OLAP performance matches the best query processing engines. Google has launched a new cross data center hybrid database called F1 [22] to support the AdWords business. It combines high availability, the scalability of NoSQL systems like Bigtable [23], and the consistency and usability of traditional SQL databases. It also provides synchronous cross-datacenter replication, strong consistency and hidden commit latency. Alibaba's HybridDB [24] is an online massively parallel processing data warehousing service based on the open source Greenplum database. It enables mixed use of row and column stores, and supports real-time analytics on JSON, XML and fuzzy strings data in SQL syntax. Xeround [25] is an in-memory distributed database to provide database as a cloud service for applications based on MySQL database. It offers MySQL as a front-end, on the back-end it is a NoSQL system distributed on a large number of physical nodes.

The existing hybrid data management techniques are designed and optimized for the specific application scenarios. According to the needs of massive complex O&M data management in satellite network, we carry out data classification according to different data acquisition source and application management, choose SQL and NoSQL hybrid model to efficiently manage different types of data in the suitable databases.

2.3 Database Synchronization

Database synchronization refers to the exchange of data between two independent databases so that any change in a database will occur in the same way in another database. With the development of SQL and NoSQL database applications, the typical SQL database (such as Oracle [26]) and the mainstream NoSQL database (such as HBase [27]) support data synchronization technology for disaster backup management.

Oracle database mainly provides four kinds of data synchronization technology: Advanced Replication, Streams, DataGuard and GoldenGate. Advanced Replication uses "internal trigger" to capture updates when data operating, and these operations are encapsulated in remote procedure calls (RPCs), then pushed RPCs to the target database with transaction queue, the target database executes these RPCs using "internal trigger" to finish data replication. Streams capture process extracts the changes from the redo log files in the source database and formats each change into a logical change record (LCR), which is stored in a queue, then propagates LCRs to another queue and can then apply the LCRs to the destination database. The principle of DataGuard has to transfer redo, and then apply redo, redo consists all the changes made in the database in the form of the log files that are required by oracle database to recover a database transaction. GoldenGate is implemented by extracting the source database Redo Log or Archive Log, and then delivered to the target database through TCP/IP, and finally analyze and decode the log to the target database for synchronization; it also supports Oracle, DB2, SQL Server, Sybase, MySQL, Teradata and other database platform for heterogeneous data synchronization. According to the application characteristic difference among these database synchronization methods, the comparative analysis is shown in Table 1, GoldenGate is the preferred way for Oracle data synchronization due to its prominent advantages in every aspect.

Table 1. The comparative analysis of Oracle data synchronization methods

Characteristics	Advanced Replication	Streams	DataGuard	GoldenGate
Replication Topology	Bi-directional	Bi-directional	Uni-directional	Bi-directional
Replication Granularity	Database, Schema, Table	Database, Schema, Table	Database	Database, Schema, Table
Data Timeliness	Medium	Medium	Good	Good
Data Conversion	Unsupported	Supported	Unsupported	Supported
Transmission Compression	Unsupported	Unsupported	Unsupported	Supported
Bilateral Version	Can be different	Can be different	Must same	Can be different
Maintenance	Hard	Hard	Medium	Medium

HBase database can use Distcp, CopyTable, Export/Import, Snapshot and Replication commands for data backup or disaster recovery. The basic idea of data synchronization between HBase clusters is: At first, the target cluster establishes the same tables as the source cluster, and then copies the data to the destination by Snapshot, moreover, start real-time synchronization by Replication between the two clusters, finally the target cluster copy data generated between Snapshot starting and Replication starting using the MR tasks.

To meet the business continuity of the satellite network O&M application, according to the hybrid data management architecture based on NoSQL and SQL, we study the data synchronization technology based on Oracle and HBase to provide reliable data services when man-made and natural disasters appear, and it can also be used for load balancing, data transfer and database merger without interruption or loss, when the database access pressure is too large.

3 Distributed Cooperating Data Management Framework

To meet the demand of big data management for satellite network O&M application, we propose a distributed cooperative data storage management framework. Firstly, we design a scalable distributed cooperative big data storage architecture. Then, a hybrid database management strategy over this architecture is described. Finally, a fast data synchronization technique with network topology awareness is designed.

3.1 Distributed Cooperative Big Data Storage Architecture

As shown in Fig. 1, we propose the scalable network storage system architecture for the distributed cooperative management of massive complex data in satellite communication network O&M. This architecture consists of in-site database server clusters

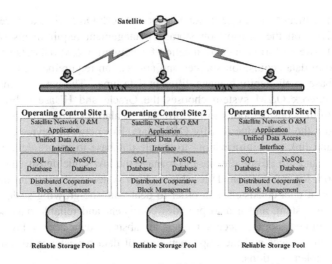

Fig. 1. Distributed cooperative big data storage architecture

with the back-end reliable storage pool and inter-site interconnection with wide area networks (WAN) or the alternative satellite communication network. It can be divided into five logical layers: storage device layer, block management layer, database layer, satellite network O&M application layer and network interconnection layer. In operating control site, the storage device layer is a highly reliable storage pool based on HDD and SSD hybrid storage; it can manage the local storage resource independently. The distributed cooperative block management layer supports the in-site fault tolerance management for the massive O&M data by building the scalable database cluster system based on HCI, so as to improve storage sharing and I/O performance. The database layer supports hybrid data management model with traditional SQL database and novel NoSQL database, and provides unified data access interfaces for the upper application by leveraging the abstraction over various database interfaces. Satellite network O&M application layer includes service monitoring, configuration management, performance management, fault management, accounting management and security management to support the normal operation of satellite communication network. The network interconnection layer is to build interconnection between operating control sites by the conventional ground network and emergency satellite communications network, and provide an inter-site distributed cooperative data management services using database synchronization technology, and enhance the disaster recovery capability of satellite communication network O&M application.

3.2 Hybrid Database Management

Traditional relational databases are inadequate in dealing with data intensive applications due to their disadvantages in flexibility, scalability and performance. The application demands of the massive, complex and highly distributed network O&M data storage force the data management system to scale out, and drive us to adopt the hybrid database management technology to support the network O&M data service. Through in-depth analysis on the distribution storage management requirements of network O&M big data, we perform data classification for network O&M datasets according to the difference in data acquisition sources and application requirements, and select the suitable database to efficiently manage different data types. The database management of satellite network O&M system chooses the Oracle and HBase hybrid database scheme due to the considerations in performance, scalability, compatibility and reliability. We store the high value density O&M data, like network device configuration information and link state information, to Oracle database to ensure data consistency and efficiency, and use HBase database to manage the low value density data network, such as network log information. This achieves high system scalability for data storage at the expense of data consistency in order to deal with the growing scale of satellite communication system, and it also provides consistent and reliable data service. To create an integrated storage access model, an abstract data access layer is added between system services and the implementation of data persistence to hide different data storage implementations.

3.3 Fast Data Synchronization

Because of the complexity of data synchronization requirements in the satellite network O&M management, a large number of nodes adapt network topology with two-way business center or multiple-service center, and the long physical distance between nodes, low the network speed and poor system reliability, result in a large number of backlogged data. To support big data management, we not only perform data synchronization in both relational database and non-relational database to achieve conjoint analysis for structured and unstructured data. According to the application scenarios of satellite network O&M requirements, we select GoldenGate for synchronous replication between Oracle databases, and multiple copy commands for data synchronization among multiple HBase databases, and we can choose single table independent processing or multi-table batch processing for data synchronization. According to the difference in sharing permissions and disaster recovery requirements of in-site database table, we can firstly build the shared logic network topology for sites with the same sharing permission, then establish one-to-one, broadcast (one-to- many), polymerization (many-to-one) and bi-directional synchronous transmission among the directly adjacent sites in its logical network topology, in order to improve the I/O performance of data sharing, disaster recovery capability of data service in network O&M application.

4 Evaluation

We carry out the demonstration experiments on disaster tolerance ability of our proposed distributed cooperative big data storage architecture, the query performance of our hybrid database management system and the network throughput of data synchronization mechanism.

4.1   Disaster Tolerance

As shown in Fig. 2, we built a highly fault-tolerant HCI platform based on VMware VSAN virtualization software consists of four Dawning I620 servers connected by two Huawei Gigabit S6700 switch, on total 512 GB memory capacity, 6.4 TB SSD capacity, 48 TB enterprise HDD capacity, to verify the feasibility and disaster tolerance of our proposed distributed storage system architecture for satellite network O&M data. We create eight virtual server nodes on the HCI platform, including two nodes for Oracle RAC database server cluster and six nodes for HBase highly available server cluster. In operating control site, the two database cluster can support server level fault tolerance, due to the double replica configure of HDFS based HBase and the nature of Oracle RAC system, and both of them can tolerate half of the nodes fail.

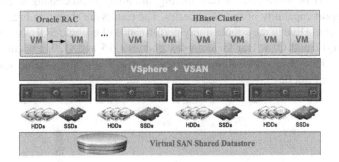

Fig. 2. Hybrid database cluster system based on HCI.

For the inter-site data disaster tolerance, we currently only implement the remote data synchronization between two operating control sites, and the average network latency of two Oracle databases is 5.2 s, and 6.5 s for that of two HBase databases replicate data update operations. The reason for high network latency is that the wide area network interconnection between two sites is not a private network, and there is great potentiality for optimization on the synchronization delay of the databases. But it can still meet the needs of disaster recovery for the critical data in satellite network O&M application. According to the data replication mechanism in Sect. 3.3, each of shared logical network topology in the distributed storage architecture can tolerate at least one site data service failure.

4.2   Hybrid Database Performance

To support unified data access interface under the hybrid database management framework, we install the Phoenix [28] on the HBase to provide the SQL like access interface to hide the difference of various database access interfaces. We mainly focus on the performance impact of HBase and Phoenix integration since there are many existing works related to the Oracle database performance research. We employ 6 virtual server nodes with Ubuntu12.04 LTS version in the HBase database system, to verify the efficiency of the conversion between HBase platform and Phoenix interface, and our experimental platform deploys the following software: Hadoop-1.2.1,

HBase-0.98.6.1, Zookeeper-3.4.5, Hive-0.13.1, Pig-0.13.0, Phoenix-4.0.0. We test each test value more than 5 times to calculate the average value.

Phoenix is a high-performance relational database layer for low latency applications in HBase, enabling the use of SQL statements on HBase database, which is open-sourced in 2014. The founder of Phoenix project James Taylor believes that the existing SQL solutions for NoSQL data storage cannot achieve horizontal compression, and cannot adapt to the large amount of data changes. As a result, Phoenix has been developed for better scalability and faster response time. Adding Phoenix's SQL interface layer between data access and operation execution of HBase can simplify the use of HBase, reduce the amount of code, and optimize the query operation.

We selected the decision support benchmark TPC-H running on the data warehouse Hive [29] over Hadoop platform with the Phoenix over HBase for the comparative analysis. TPC-H is developed for data mining and analysis processing to evaluate the decision support capability of specific queries. The results are shown in Fig. 3. Phoenix differs little from Hive in the simple query performance of a single SQL statement, such as Q1, Q6, Q12 and Q14. But for complex queries Q15 and Q20, Phoenix performs much better than Hive, since these queries contain both single table queries and multi-table joint queries.

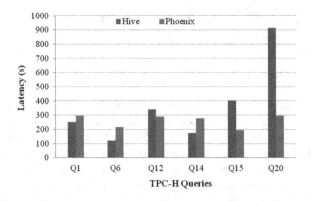

Fig. 3. The comparison test on Hive and Phoenix over HBase.

4.3 Data Synchronization Throughput

We select two Oracle RAC clusters in two remote operating control sites, which are configured as bidirectional data replication with Goldengate middleware. We feed the platform with the simulation dataset of the operation and maintenance application in satellite network, that the metadata and access characteristics are the same as the real operation and maintenance application, but fill the data content with random data. We deploy two cluster as the Active-Active mode, different from uni-directional Active-Passive mode, we create a Extract and Data Pump process on the target side pointing to the source terminal based on the original uni-directional replication, and create a Replicat process at the source to execute the Trail file pass over by the target side. We generate 61.5 MB Trail files at two sides, and perform data synchronization in about

10 min. Through simple calculation, the theoretical value of network traffic throughput is 102.5 KB/s for uni-directional replication, and 205 KB/s for bidirectional replication. The traffic firewall monitoring data analysis for database bi-directional replication with GoldenGate is shown in Fig. 4. The theoretical network traffic throughputs in two directions are basically consistent with the actual traffic flow monitored by the traffic firewall. The maximum range of data fluctuation is about 1100 KB, the average value is about 230 KB, and the replication processing is stable, the average value does not greatly fluctuate with time.

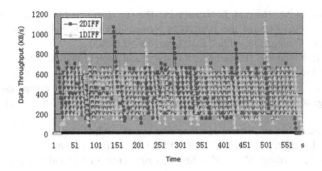

Fig. 4. The difference analysis of database replication.

5 Conclusion

In this paper, we integrate distributed cooperative big data storage technology into the satellite network operation and maintenance application, and provide the technical support for the planning, scheduling and adjustment of the data storage resources of the satellite network O&M. We study the distributed cooperative storage management for the massive complex network O&M data management, and break through the thinking mode of information isolation management among the satellite network operating control sites. We not only design a distributed data storage management framework to support the reliable and scalable data services among multiple sites, but also create an integrated storage access model on Oracle and HBase hybrid database, and an efficient network-topology aware data synchronization mechanism, to enhance the scalability and disaster tolerance in the massive complex O&M data management system.

Acknowledgements. This research was supported by the National Natural Science Foundation of China under Grant No. 61402518.

References

1. Maral, G., Bousquet, M., Sun, Z.: Satellite Communications Systems: Systems, Techniques and Technology. Wiley, Chichester (2009)
2. Yang, W.: Theory and progress of active operation and maintenance of mobile internet based on big data. Big Data Res. **2**(6), 97–109 (2016)
3. Suto, K., Avakul, P., Nishiyama, H., Kato, N.: An efficient data transfer method for distributed storage system over satellite networks. In: 77th IEEE Vehicular Technology Conference, vol. 14(6), pp. 1–5 (2013)

4. Frey, J., Corbo, T.: Managing networks in the age of cloud, SDN, and big data: network management megatrends. Enterprise Management Associates, April 2014

5. Das, A., Lumezanu, C., Zhang, Y., Singh, V., Jiang, G., Yu, C.: Transparent and flexible network management for big data processing in the cloud. In: Proceedings of the 5th USENIX Workshop on Hot Topics in Cloud Computing (HotCloud 2013), June 2013

6. Ford, D., Labelle, F., Popovici, F., et al.: Availability in globally distributed file systems. In: Operating Systems Design and Implementation (2010)

7. Muthitacharoen, A., Chen, B., Mazierres, D.: A low-bandwidth network file system. In: Proceedings of the 18th ACM Symposium on Operating Systems Principles, pp. 174–187, October 2001

8. Satyanarayanan, M., Howard, J., Nichols, D.: The ITC distributed file system: principles and design. In: Proceedings of the 10th ACM Symposium on Operating Systems Principles, Orcas Island, Washington, United States, pp. 35–50 (1985)

9. Sandberg, R., Golgberg, D., Kleiman, S.: Design and implementation of the sun network file system. In: Proceedings of the Summer 1985 USENIX Conference, pp. 119–130, June 1985

10. Schmuck, F., Haskin, R.: GPFS: a shared-disk file system for large computing clusters. In: Proceedings of the Conference on File and Storage Technologies (FAST 2002), pp. 231–244 (2002)

11. VMware, Inc. VMware Virtual Machine File System. White Paper (2007)

12. Welch, B., Unangst, M., Abbasi, Z., et al.: Scalable performance of the panasas parallel file system. In: Proceedings of the 6th USENIX Conference on File and Storage Technologies, San Jose, California (2008)

13. Lustre File System [EB/OL]. http://wiki.lustre.org/

14. Weil, S., Brandt, S., Miller, E., et al.: Ceph: a scalable, high-performance distributed file system. In: Proceedings of the 7th Symposium on Operating Systems Design and Implementation (OSDI 2006) (2006)

15. Ghemawat, S., Gobioff, H., Leung, S.: The google file system. In: Proceedings of SOSP 2003, Bolton Landing, New York, USA, October 2003

16. Hadoop [EB/OL]. http://hadoop.apache.org/

17. VSAN [EB/OL]. http://www.vmware.com/cn/products/virtualsan.html

18. ScaleIO [EB/OL]. https://www.emc.com/storage/scaleio/index.htm

19. Nutanix Distributed File System [EB/OL]. https://www.nutanix.com/products/software-editions/

20. Fusion Storage [EB/OL]. http://www.huawei.com/cn/

21. Kemper, A., Neumann, T.: HyPer: a hybrid OLTP& OLAP main memory database system based on virtual memory snapshots. In: Proceedings of the ICDE 2011, pp. 195–206 (2011)

22. Shute, J., Vingralek, R., Samwel, B., et al.: F1: a distributed SQL database that scales. In: Proceedings of the 39th International Conference on Very Large Data Bases, 26–30 August 2013, Trento, Italy (2013)

23. Chang, F., Dean, J., Ghemawat, S., et al.: Bigtable: a distributed storage system for structured data. In: Proceedings of OSDI 2006, pp. 205–218 (2006)

24. Alibaba HybridDB [EB/OL]. https://help.aliyun.com/product/35364.html

25. Xeround Cloud Database [EB/OL]. http://xeround.com/

26. Oracle [EB/OL]. https://www.oracle.com/index.html

27. HBase [EB/OL]. http://hbase.apache.org/

28. Phoenix [EB/OL]. http://phoenix.apache.org/

29. Thusoo, A., Sarma, J., Jain, N., et al.: Hive - a petabyte scale data warehouse using Hadoop. In: IEEE 26th International Conference on Data Engineering (ICDE), Long Beach, USA, pp. 996–1005. IEEE (2010)

A Design of Multi-band and Multi-mode Real-Time Information Collection System Based on a Global Space Information Network

Liu Xianfeng, Yan Lei$^{(\boxtimes)}$, Fan Chenguang, Wu Shuai,
and Guo Jianming

College of Aerospace Science and Engineering,
National University of Defense Technology, Changsha, China
501722228@qq.com

Abstract. With the rapid development of navigation and aviation, more and more countries are being urged to quickly collect the state information of marine and aerial targets. The satellite network has been applied information collection. At present, the two systems of AIS and ADS-B are mature marine and aerial targets monitoring systems. Considering the information collection and returning, this paper proposed a design of multi-band and multi-mode information collection based on global space information network. A design of multi-band and multi-mode information collection payload based on software radio is proposed. The method of covering band is used to design the constellation. Inter-satellite links are also applied to the satellite network. Finally, based on hardware-in-the-loop simulation, this paper provides a ground testing experiment which contains testing performance of payload and the satellite network.

Keywords: Space information
Multi-band and multi-mode information collection payload · Ground testing

1 Introduction

Globalization causes the indicators of aviation and navigation, such as traffic volume, the business of lane, become an important representation of the world economy. Collecting static and dynamic information (identity, location, velocity, etc.) of marine and aerial targets can achieve real-time tracking and even management of the targets [1]. Recently, the global information collection with the satellite constellation has been the prevailing trend [2]. Moreover, the type and amount of information gradually increases, leading to an imperious demands that information collection platform needs to have the characteristics of lower cost, rich function and easy configurability [3]. For instance, the Orbcomm company plans to carry AIS (Automatic Identification System) payload on its second system [4]. And the operation of the Argos has been changed from single-tasking mode to multi-tasking mode [5]. At present, there are two relatively mature monitoring systems for marine and aerial targets. They are AIS and ADS-B (Automatic Dependent Surveillance – Broadcast) system [6, 7] respectively. But they have unique communication standard. Usually, satellite platform needs to carry

© Springer Nature Singapore Pte Ltd. 2018
Q. Yu (Ed.): SINC 2017, CCIS 803, pp. 105–116, 2018.
https://doi.org/10.1007/978-981-10-7877-4_9

different payloads. Actually, for the payload, the satellite has strict limitation on their size and weight. To save cost and space, this paper proposes a method of multi-band and multi-mode real-time information collection system based on SDR (software-defined radio). In addition, for the globally distributed marine and aerial targets, a constellation scheme that can cover global region is proposed in real-time. And inter-satellite links are also designed for guaranteeing collecting and returning information timely.

The rest of the paper is organized as follows. In Sect. 2, we will describe the principle of the payload of multi-band and multi-mode real-time information collection. In Sect. 3, we will develop a constellation scheme. And we will analyze the communication performance based on the time delay. Moreover, a method based on hardware-in-the-loop simulation shall be proposed for testing constellation scheme on the ground. We summarized our findings in Sect. 4.

2   Multi-band and Multi-mode Real-Time Information Collection Payload

AIS and ADS-B use VHF (Very High Frequency) and L band as their carrier frequency respectively. And their signals have different requirement on the antenna gain, leading to the result that they cannot share the same antenna. The way based on SDR can receive different signals from different targets at the same time. The diagram about two types of signals collection is shown in Fig. 1.

For improving efficiency of information collection, AIS and ADS-B needs to have two antennae respectively. One of two antennae is at an angle of 45° to the movement of the satellite while the other is at an angle of −45° to the movement of the satellite.

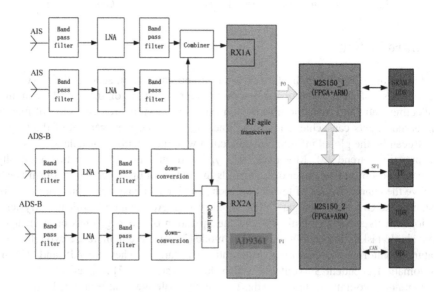

Fig. 1. Signals collection and processing

Due to electromagnetic wave in VHF having longer wavelength, the VHF antenna needs the big size antenna. Regarding the antenna gain, the L band antenna adopts to single helix antenna. From Fig. 1, we can know that firstly, signals will enter the band-pass filter, which can filter some noise out of band. And then the low noise amplifier improves gain of signals. Secondly, the important part is RF (radio frequency) agile transceiver which can process signals containing quick AD/DA, frequency conversion, etc. Lastly, the FPGA processing unit achieves baseband conversion, demodulation and grouping. For reducing complexity, it is noticeable that ADS-B signals needs to switch into VHF band before the RF agile transceiver. AIS and ADS-B signals have different characteristics as shown in Table 1.

Table 1. Signals parameters

	Modulation frequency (MHz)	Modulation	Checkout
AIS	156.775/156.825/161.975/162.025	GMSK/BT = 0.5	CRC-16
ADS-B	1090	PPM	CRC-16

And then we will describe the design of the payload containing frequency dividing and signals processing.

2.1 Frequency Dividing

The hardware of the payload includes a variety of the nonlinear thyristors. It is inevitable that signals carried by different frequency will produce inter modulation distortion [8]. Usually, the third intermodulation severely affects signals processing. The distortion item of the third intermodulation can be expressed by (1)

$$2f_1 - f_2 \quad \text{and} \quad 2f_2 - f_1 \tag{1}$$

Where f_1 and f_2 are different carrier frequencies. AIS signals contain four types of frequencies. The frequency spectrum and the third intermodulation are shown in Fig. 2.

In the first frequency conversion, ADS-B signals should approach the AIS frequency. Besides, ADS-B signals need 3 MHz bandwidth as transitive band. Regarding 1 MHz as the allowance, ADS-B signals can be converted into 148 MHz–152 MHz.

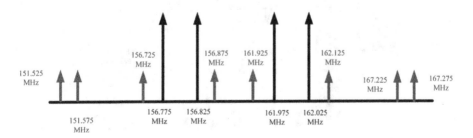

Fig. 2. Frequency spectrum

2.2 Multiple Sub-channels Modulation

AIS signals are modulated by GMSK (Gaussian Filtered Minimum Shift Keying). Generally, they can be demodulated by coherent demodulation or non-coherent demodulation. For the microsatellite which has the weak ability of computing on orbit, the signals processing scheme should not be complex. And considering the high velocity of the satellite and limitation on preambles, this payload employs non-coherent differential demodulation [9]. Moreover, high-speed motion of satellite leads Doppler frequency offset of received signals, which deteriorate the performance of demodulation scheme. However, the method that signals are directly extracted and then used to estimate frequencies by the FFT (Fast Fourier Transformation) will cost much time and resources. Therefore, according to different frequency, we set several sub-channels to deal with signals consistently. For instance, AIS signals contain four frequencies. At present, the number of ships using 161.975 MHz and 162.025 MHz is more than these with 156.775 MHz and 156.825 MHz [4]. For reducing packets loss due to many signals arriving simultaneously, the signals transmitted by the former two frequencies are modulated by the method of multiple sub-channels modulation. The Doppler frequency offset ranges from −4 kHz to 4 kHz. From the Sect. 2, the single antenna can receive signals with either positive or negative frequency. For instance, one of the antenna can receive signals with the positive frequency offset. These signals can be put into eight sub-channels to process. The frequency offsets of eight sub-channels are 3.5 kHz, 3.0 kHz, 2.5 kHz, 2.0 kHz, 1.5 kHz, 1 kHz, 0.5 kHz, 0 kHz. However, signals with 156.775 MHz and 156.825 MHz can be processed by directly extracting present signals and estimating frequency offset. The procedure of signals processing is shown in Fig. 3.

ADS-B uses the PPM (Pulse Phase Modulation) which is similar to amplitude modulation. The code mode is bidirectional level code. The procedure of demodulation is that: firstly, we reshape the baseband wave of the impulse signals. Secondly, we ensure the location of message head and identify type of message. Finally, the correct

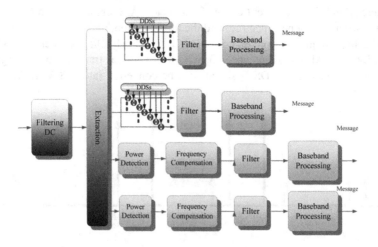

Fig. 3. Processing of signals

ADS-B messages can be obtained after they pass the CRC (Cyclic Redundancy Code). The whole procedure is shown in Fig. 4.

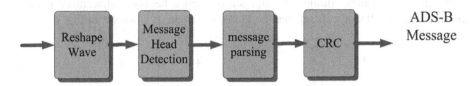

Fig. 4. Processing of ADS-B signals

3   Design of Constellation and Communication Performance

3.1   Performance of Coverage

The building of architecture is the precondition of designing space information network. For obtaining the good performance of receiving signals globally, this paper designs a polar orbit constellation which can almost cover the earth based on covering band method. The covering band method makes use of overlapping coverage with several satellites in the same orbit to form a consequent area. It is shown in Fig. 5.

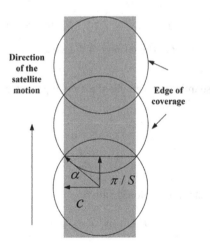

Fig. 5. The covering band

From the Fig. 5, we know that the semi-geocentric angle α and the width of covering band satisfy the following geometric relation.

$$c = \arccos\left[\frac{\cos \alpha}{\cos(\pi/S)}\right] \tag{1}$$

The adjacent satellites in different orbit can display the two relative movements. They are the direct orbit and contrary orbit respectively. The satellites in direct orbit need to keep fixing phase relation while the phase of satellites in contrary is varying. Through the reasonable design of longitude difference between adjacent orbits, the polar orbit constellation can achieve the global coverage. It is shown in Fig. 6.

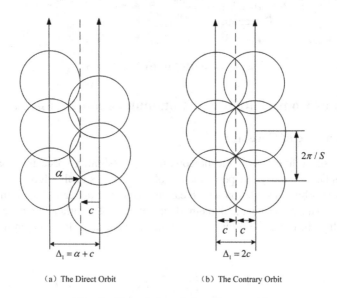

(a) The Direct Orbit   (b) The Contrary Orbit

Fig. 6. The relation of the adjacent orbit

For ensuring the seamless coverage, the two types of orbits need to satisfy the following relation respectively.

$$\Delta_1 = \alpha + c \tag{2}$$

$$\Delta_2 = 2c \tag{3}$$

The polar orbit constellation should satisfy

$$(P - 1)\Delta_1 + \Delta_2 = \pi \tag{4}$$

We put (2), (3) and (4) into (5). And then we can obtain

$$(P - 1)\alpha + (P + 1)\arccos[\frac{\cos \alpha}{\cos(\pi/S)}] = \pi \tag{5}$$

Where P is the number of the orbits. S counts the satellites. α as the semi-geocentric angle depends on the height of the orbit h and the minimum elevation angle θ. Their relation is shown in Fig. 7.

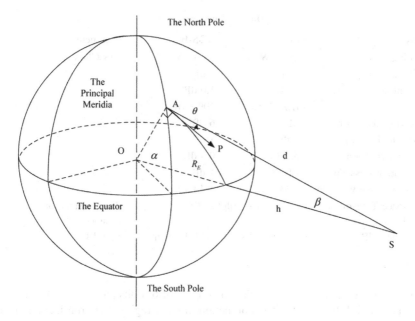

Fig. 7. The coverage of the satellite

From the Fig. 7, we can know that

$$\alpha = 90° - \beta - \theta \tag{6}$$

In the triangle

$$\frac{R_E}{\sin \beta} = \frac{R_E + h}{\sin(\theta + 90°)} \tag{7}$$

By the law of cosines, the distance from the satellite to edge of its coverage can be obtained

$$d^2 = R_E^2 + (h + R_E)^2 - 2 * R_E * (h + R_E) * \cos \beta \tag{8}$$

According to above, α is determined with the value of h and θ. The whole constellation is based on the LEO microsatellite. In the simulation, we set $h = 600$ km and $E = 5°$. Moreover, there are some requirements to receive signals in orbit. The half beam angle of the antenna need to satisfy $\beta' < \beta$. According to criterion of AIS and ADS-B, the needed parameters about computing the value of communication link are shown in Table 2.

From the Table 2, if the allowances of AIS and ADS-B outperform 10 dB, the furthest of communication distances are 718 km and 722 km respectively. Since the AIS antenna has almost the same coverage as the ADS-B antenna, we set $d = 718$ km. Moreover, according to (7) and (8). we set $\beta = 65.5°$ and $\alpha = 19.4°$. The outcome of

Table 2. Link parameters

Items	AIS	ADS-B	Comment
Emitting Power P	10.9 dBW	25 dBW	AIS Class A
Emitting Gain Gpt	2 dBi	0 dBi	
Transmission Loss Lt	1.0 dB	1.0 dB	
Frequency f	161.xx MHz	1090 MHz	
Receiving Gain Grp	0 dBi	6 dBi	
Feed Line Loss Lr	0.5 dB	1 dB	
Atmospheric Loss Lg	0.5 dB	0.5 dB	
Polarization Loss Lp	1 dB	1 dB	
Receiver Sensitivity Sen	<-133dBW	<-134dBW	
Free space Transmission Loss Ls (dB)	Ls = 32.44 + 20lgf + 20lgd		d is transmission distance
Allowance (dB)	P + Gpt-Lt-Ls-Lg + Grp-Lp-Sen		>10 dB

simulation indicates that the constellation consists of 6 orbits and 13 satellites in every orbit. To avoid different satellites' confliction in polar region, the orbit inclination and the difference of longitude of the direct orbit are designed as 85° and 31° respectively. The simulation time is from 5 Apr 2017 04:00:00 to 6 Apr 2017 04:00:00. And the architecture and coverage of the constellation are shown in Figs. 8 and 9.

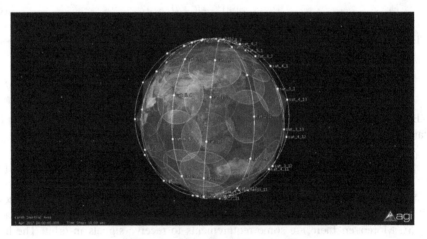

Fig. 8. The architecture of constellation

From the Fig. 9, we can know that the ratio of single-time global coverage reaches 99.83%, which almost guarantees global information collection. Besides, the inter satellite link needs to be designed to ensure information returning to the ground station in time.

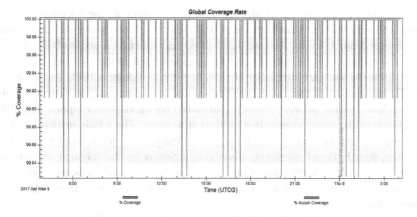

Fig. 9. Performance of constellation coverage

3.2   Performance of Communication

Based on the characteristic of multi-band and multi-mode real-time information, this section proposes a testing scheme based on hardware-in-the-loop simulation to test performance of space information network. The principle is shown in Fig. 10.

The whole testing scheme contains the hardware performance and the software simulation. The hardware performance' testing mainly includes transmitting and receiving simulated signals correctly. It is highlighted in non-dashed parts in Fig. 10.

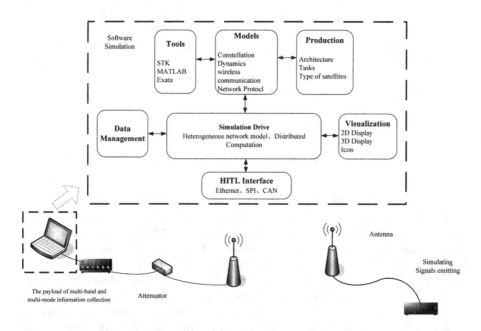

Fig. 10. The makeup of hardware-in-the-loop simulation

The main equipment consists of signals simulators, antennae, the attenuator and the payload of multi-band and multi-mode information collection. Moreover, the emitting power ranges from 3–15 W. And the value of power reduction is about 40–70 dB. The signals are received by the antenna and then demodulated in the payload. The rest of the Fig. 10 is the software simulation. In this part, the computer collects and sends data by HITL interface. And these data are used to produce heterogeneous network modes. And then based on the network protocol and some constraints, the computer establishes the architect of the space information collection network. The whole procedure of this testing scheme can be divided into three parts. Firstly, the signals simulator produces simulating signals based on targets distribution. Secondly, the payload receives and demodulates signals. Finally, the computer counts the received messages and adjusts the architect of the constellation based on the performance of receiving signals and the network protocol.

And then we need to estimate the number of data possibly received by this information collection system. We regard AIS as an example and utilize AIS data collected by the 'Tiantuo III' satellite during some time to plot a ships distribution map which is shown in Fig. 11.

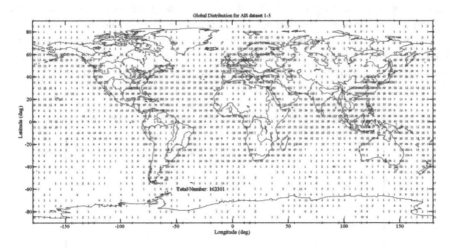

Fig. 11. Ships distribution map

The map is divided into many regions in a difference of longitude and latitude. The number of every region is marked by the red figure. There are about 130 thousand of ships installing the AIS on the global maritime space [11]. Moreover, the probability of ships detection is one of the significant indicators of the space AIS. And the probability is mainly influenced on distribution of ships. According to the above, we have had simulation. The outcome indicates that the probability of ships detection is about 41.3%, which is corresponding to that proposed in recent papers [12]. Assuming every ship emits message with per 10 s, we can compute that the space information collection network can receive 463881600 AIS messages during the 24 h. Moreover, in the coverage of the single satellite, a large number of ships result in collision of uplink signals. However, it can narrow the antenna width or use method of signals separation to alleviate the collision.

Moreover, the design of inter satellite link is significant for data returning. Since the communication distance cannot be too far, the inter satellite link is deserved to be established within adjacent satellites. The total time delay is shown as follow

$$t_{delay} = t_{delay}^c + t_{delay}^h + t_{delay}^p \tag{9}$$

Where t_{delay}^c is the time of signals transmission. t_{delay}^h is the time during which information passes several hops and t_{delay}^p is sum of time of processing in every satellite node. The simulating outcome based on STK indicates that the average communication distance of adjacent satellite is 3339.9 km in the same orbit while that is 3172.4 km in the adjacent orbit. The information passes maximum hops is 6. The total time delay is kept in level of millisecond, which can satisfy the requirement of signals emission cycle of AIS (10 s) and ADS-B (about 4 s) [13, 14].

4 Conclusion

Considering the data collection based on space multi-band and multi-mode information collection network, this paper proposes the design of payload and constellation networking. In the design of payload, this paper proposes the scheme of frequency band dividing and multi-band and multi-mode signals demodulation. Moreover the constellation has been designed based on covering band method. It can cover 99.83% of the global region in real-time. At the end of this paper, we design the hardware-in-the-loop simulation to test performance of space information network based on time delay and ships distribution. In a word, the scheme of multi-band and multi-mode information collection can provide design of future space information network as a reference.

References

1. Perez, C.A., Jimenez, M., Soto, F., et al.: A system for monitoring marine environments based on wireless sensor networks. In: OCEANS 2011. IEEE, Spain (2011)
2. Wang, S., Hou, Y.: Requirement analysis on air space information transmitted systems. Ordnance Ind. Autom. **28**(12) (2009)
3. Zhang, Z., Jiang, C., Ren, Y.: Design of space based information transmission network. In: Proceedings of the 1st Space Information Network Academic Forum, August 2016
4. Yaping, Z., Xuming, H.: ORBCOMM-commercial LEO system for short data communication. Electron. Technol. **28**(2) (2001)
5. Jie, B.: Application and study on arctic sea ice buoy of argos satellite communication system. Thesis, Northeastern University (2012)

6. te Hennepe, F., Rinaldo, R., Ginesi, A., Tobehn, C., Wieser, M., Helleren, Ø.: Feasibility of an European constellation for space detection of AIS signals. In: European Symposium on Satellite-AIS, December 2010

7. Department of Transportation, Federal Aviation Administration: Automatic Dependent Surveillance-Broadcast (ADS-B) Out Performance Requirements to Support Air Traffic Control (ATC) Service; Final Rule, 14 CFR Part 91, Washington, DC, 28 May 2010

8. Gongliang, L., Hui, L.: Satellite Communication Network Technology. Posts and Telecom Press, Beijing (2015)

9. Mingshan, Z.: Suppression of 3rd—Order Intermodulation Distortion in RoF Based on Feed Foward Method. Thesis, Dalian University of Technology (2013)

10. Benvenuto, N., Salloum, A., Tomba, L.: Further results on differential detection of GMSK signals. IEEE Trans. Commun. (7), 32–49 (2012)

11. Cheng, Y., Chen, L.H., Chen, X.Q.: Beam scanning method based on the helical antenna for space-based AIS. J. Navig. **68**, 52–70 (2015)

12. Yun, C.: Research on the key technology of micro/small satellite-based AIS. Thesis, National University of Defense Technology (2015)

13. International Telecommunication Union: Technical characteristics for an automatic identification system using time division multiple access in the VHF maritime mobile frequency band. ITU-R.M.1371-2 (2007)

14. Delovski, T., Werner, K., Rawlik, T., Behrens, J., Bredemeyer, J., Wendel, R.: ADS-B over satellite the world's first ADS-B receiver in space (2014)

Multi-detection Based CSMA Protocol for Micro-satellite Ad Hoc Network

Feng Tian[1(✉)], Lin Gui[2], Xinglong Jiang[1], Siyue Sun[1], Guang Liang[1], and Yining Cao[3]

[1] Shanghai Engineering Center for Micro-satellite, Shanghai 201203, China
tianfeng_microsat@163.com
[2] Department of Electronic Engineering,
Shanghai Jiao Tong University, Shanghai 200230, China
[3] Institute of China Electronic System Engineering Company,
Beijing 100141, China

Abstract. Micro-satellite ad hoc network has attracted a lot of interest from both the academia and industry, due to its better performance of earth coverage, data access delay and so on. MAC protocol design is one of the key and important problems in the micro-satellite ad hoc network. In this paper, we propose the Multi-Detection based CSMA protocol for the micro-satellite ad hoc network named as MD-CSMA, in which each satellite senses the channel by multiple detections. Compared with the traditional CSMA, the MD-CSMA protocol provides better performance of channel utilization ratio and guarantees the space mission with high-level priority. First, the related works about MAC protocols and micro-satellite ad hoc network are reviewed, and we show that the CSMA protocol better suits the micro-satellite ad hoc network than the TDMA protocol. Then, we propose the MD-CSMA protocol and its analysis. Finally, we construct various simulations to verify that the MD-CSMA protocol has better performance in terms of channel utilization ratio, mission satisfied ratio, and average latency of data access than the CSMA/CA protocol and the TDMA protocol.

Keywords: Micro-satellite · Ad Hoc network · CSMA protocol
Multi-detection

1 Introduction

Compared with one single big satellite, the micro-satellite ad hoc network can not only implement the full function of the single big satellite, but also provide higher efficiency gain by promoting adaptability, scalability, reconfigurability, and affordability [1]. Therefore, micro-satellite network has become an efficient and economical approach to resolve many new space missions, such as navigation,

This work is supported by the National Natural Science Foundation of China, under Grants 61401278, and CAS Innovation Fund, under Grants CXJJ-15S086.

© Springer Nature Singapore Pte Ltd. 2018
Q. Yu (Ed.): SINC 2017, CCIS 803, pp. 117–126, 2018.
https://doi.org/10.1007/978-981-10-7877-4_10

communications, remote sensing, and scientific research [2]. The MAC protocol is an important and key role in the micro-satellite network. In this paper, we design a multi-detection based CSMA protocol, named MD-CSMA, to improve the performance of channel utilization, mission satisfied ratio, and data access latency.

In order to make the best use of micro-satellite ad hoc network and complete various kinds of space missions. The Medium Access Control (MAC) protocol should be designed by considering the network and mission features, such as network topology, micro-satellite number, mission priority [3], and so on.

There has been many MAC protocols proposed for satellite network [4–7]. In [7], the authors proposed the Time Division Multiple Address (TDMA) protocol for a cluster of micro-satellite, in which time is divided into time slots and each micro-satellite is allowed to transmit or receive in one time slot. The Frequency Division Multiple Access (FDMA) protocol for micro-satellite network is analyzed in [8], in which multiple satellites can communicate at the same time by using different frequencies. However, when the number of micro-satellites is huge, TDMA will cost a high data access delay, and FDMA will waste channel resources. The Carrier Sense Multiple Access with Collision Avoidance (CSMA/CA) protocol is proposed in [9,10], in which transmitting node detects the channel state by using Request-to-Send (RTS) and Clear-to-Send (CTS) signals. With the increase of the micro-satellite number, the performance of CSMA/CA will deteriorate caused by too many collisions. In this paper, we propose a multi-detection based CSMA protocol to improve the performance of channel utilization ratio and mission satisfied ratio by multiple collision detections.

In MD-CSMA protocol, we divide a time slot into multiple mini-time slots, containing multiple mini-time slots for contention (denoted as contention mini-time slot) and one mini-time slot for data transmission (denoted as data mini-time slot). The length of contention mini-time slot is much shorter than the length of data mini-time slot. In the contention mini-time slot, transmitting micro-satellites contend for the data mini-time slot. If there is a collision happened in this contention mini-time slot, each micro-satellite will stop contending with a retreat probability in order to avoid contention. The retreat probability relates to the mission priority. The MD-CSMA protocol can increase the channel utilization by multiple contentions, and guarantee the high-level priority mission by retreat probability.

The main contributions of the paper are as follows.

- We are the first to propose the MD-CSMA protocol for micro-satellite network. In this protocol, the micro-satellite contends channel in the multiple contention mini-time slots when it has transmission mission, which increases the channel utilization ratio by multiple detections.
- We propose the retreat probability, which guarantees the high-level priority mission. The retreat probability relates to the mission priority, i.e., the lower-level space mission owns the higher retreat probability. Therefore, the higher-level space missions are satisfied with higher probability.

- We construct various simulations to evaluate the efficiency of the MD-CSMA protocol. Evaluation results show the proposed MD-CSMA protocol outperforms the traditional CSMA protocol and the TDMA protocol in terms of channel utilization ratio, mission satisfied ratio, and data access latency.

The remainder of our paper is organized as follows. In Sect. 2, we briefly review the related work. Then we propose the MD-CSMA protocol in Sect. 3. In Sect. 4, we propose the theoretical analysis about the MD-CSMA protocol. We present the evaluation results in Sect. 5. Section 6 concludes our work and propose our future work.

2   Related Work

With the development of Chinese economy and the advancement of One Belt And One Road policy, the number of space missions experiences a huge explosion. Because of the adaptability, reconfigurability, and affordability, the micro-satellite ad hoc network has become a promising and economical approach to resolve the explosion space mission. In [11], the authors reviewed the Project "F6" of Defense Advanced Research Project Agency (DARPA), which propose the Distributed Satellite System (DSS).

The MAC protocol plays an important role in the inter-satellite communication [4]. There has been lots of research on the MAC protocol design for micro-satellite ad hoc network, which can be generally divided into two categories: conflict-free protocols and contention based protocols. Some basic protocols of the conflict-free protocols are TDMA (Time Division Multiple Access), FDMA (Frequency Division Multiple Access), and CDMA (Code Division Multiple Access). Their common idea is that each satellite use different time slot, or frequency, or code to transmit, which ensures that collision of data transmission never occurs. In [6], the authors analyzed multiple contention based protocols, such as ALOHA, CSMA, BTMA (Busy Tone Multiple Access), ISMA (Idle Signal Multiple Access), and so on. Their common idea is that satellites contend for the channel. Due to the scalability of network and the difficulty of synchronization, the conflict-free protocol might not be the best option for inter-satellite ad hoc network. Therefore, we propose a contention based protocol, which adapts the changes in the network size and network topology.

3   The MD-CSMA Protocol

In this paper, G is used to denote the micro-satellite network. We take micro-satellite i as an example to illustrate the MD-CSMA protocol. We assume that micro-satellite i has N neighboring micro-satellites. And some of the micro-satellite i's neighboring micro-satellites request to communicate with the micro-satellite i, denoted as the requesting micro-satellites.

In the MD-CSMA protocol, a time slot is divided into multiple mini-time slots, containing multiple contention mini-time slots and one data mini-time slot, as shown in Fig. 1. The requesting micro-satellites contend in the contention mini-time slots, and complete the communication mission in the data mini-time slot. Figure 2 illustrates the framework of the contention mini-time slot. The contention mini-time slot contains two sub-mini-time slots. In the first sub-mini-time slot, the transmitting micro-satellites transmit the Request To Send (RTS) to the micro-satellite i. In the second sub-mini-time slot, micro-satellite i feedbacks the Clear To Send (CTS) if it receive a RTS successfully.

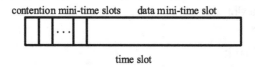

Fig. 1. A motivation example for movement.

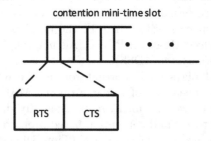

Fig. 2. The framework of contention mini-time slot.

Figure 3 illustrates the successful reservation and collision. Figure 3(a) illustrates the successful reservation between micro-satellite i and one of its neighboring micro-satellites. More specially, there is only one micro-satellite transmitting RTS to micro-satellite i. Once micro-satellite i receives the RTS, it will feedback the CTS to the transmitting micro-satellite. If the transmitting micro-satellite receives the CTS, they reserve the data transmission successfully and the other micro-satellite i's neighboring micro-satellites know this reservation by receiving this CTS (since this CTS contains the id of micro-satellite i and the id of the transmitting micro-satellite.). Figure 3(b) illustrates the collision, in which there are more than one micro-satellite i's neighboring micro-satellites transmitting RTS to micro-satellite i. That causes a collision in micro-satellite i, and none of these neighboring micro-satellites can reserve data transmission.

If a requesting micro-satellite wins in the contention mini-time slot, it will transmit data to micro-satellite i in the data mini-time slot. If there is a collision, in the next contention mini-time slot some transmitting micro-satellites will stop contending with a retreat probability in order to decrease the probability of collision.

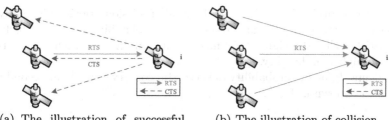

(a) The illustration of successful reservation.

(b) The illustration of collision.

Fig. 3. The illustration of contention.

Generally, there are many kinds of space missions with different priority in the micro-satellite ad hoc network. In order to satisfy the high-level-priority mission, the high-level priority mission has a lower retreat probability. In our paper, we assume that there are M levels. The lower-level space mission owns the higher retreat probability. We define the retreat probability of the m-th level space mission as

$$P_m = 1 - \frac{1}{m}. \tag{1}$$

The length of the contention mini-time slot is much shorter than the length of data mini-time slot, which increase the channel utilization ratio.

4   Analysis of the Protocol

In this section, we propose the theoretical analysis of the MD-CSMA protocol. To clarify the presentation, we list the notations used in the analysis here.

- i: the micro-satellite i,
- N: the number of micro-satellite i's neighbors,
- N_0: the number of micro-satellite i's neighbors requesting to communicate with micro-satellite i at t_0-th time slot,
- M: the number of mission kinds,
- m: the level of mission priority, $m = 1, 2, \ldots, M$,
- p_m: the retreat probability of the m-th mission,
- K: the number of contention mini-time slots.

There are N_0 micro-satellites requesting to communicate with micro-satellite i at t_0-th time slot, and these N_0 will transmit RTS at the first contention mini-time slot of the t_0-th time slot. If there are more than one micro-satellites transmitting RTS to micro-satellite i, there is a collision in micro-satellite i. We define $(1 - P_1)$ as this probability. In order to avoid the collision, these N_0 micro-satellites will stop contending in the second contention mini-time slot with the corresponding retreat probabilities.

The retreat probability relates to the level of mission priority. Generally, the mission with higher priority has lower retreat probability (as shown in Eq. 1), which satisfies that the higher-level mission can win in the contention mini-time slots with higher probability.

We define P_2 as the probability of successful conservation at the second mini-time slot, as shown in Eq. 2.

$$P_2 = (1 - P_1) \cdot \sum_{n=1}^{N} ((1 - p_n) \cdot \prod_{n_0 \neq n} p_{n_0}). \tag{2}$$

$(1 - P_1)$ is the probability that these $N_0 > 1$ requesting microsatellites lost in the first contention mini-time slot. $(1 - p_n) \cdot \prod_{n_0 \neq n} p_{n_0}$ is the probability that the micro-satellite n wins in the second contention mini-time slot, where $(1 - p_n)$ is the probability that micro-satellite n transmitting RTS at the second contention mini-time slot, $(1 - p_n)$ is the probability that the other micro-satellites stop transmitting RTS at the second contention mini-time slot. Therefore, there is one micro-satellite winning in the second contention mini-time slot is P_2. Similarly, we define P_k as the probability that there is a micro-satellite winning at the k-th contention mini-time slot, as shown in Eq. 3.

$$P_k = \prod_{1,\cdots,k-1} (1 - P_{k-1}) \cdot \sum_{n=1}^{N} ((1 - p_n) \cdot \prod_{n_0 \neq n} p_{n_0}). \tag{3}$$

$\prod_{1,\cdots,k-1}(1 - P_{k-1})$ is the probability that there is no micro-satellite winning before the k-th contention mini-time slot. N_{k-1} is the number of micro-satellites transmitting RTS at the $(k-1)$-th contention mini-time slot, and the micro-satellite n is one of these N_{k-1} micro-satellites. $((1 - p_n) \cdot \prod_{n_0 \neq n} p_{n_0})$ is the probability that the micro-satellite n wins at the k-th contention mini-time slot.

We define P as the probability that there is a micro-satellite winning in K contention mini-time slots, as shown in Eq. 4.

$$P = P_1 + \sum_{k=2}^{K} P_k. \tag{4}$$

P_1 is the probability that there is a micro-satellite winning in the first contention mini-time slot. P_k is the probability that there is a micro-satellite winning at the k-th contention mini-time slot.

The number of contention mini-time slots has an influence on the performance of the MD-CSMA protocol. On one hand, too many contention mini-time slots will cause waste. On the other hand, if there is not enough contention mini-time slots, there may be no micro-satellite winning in the K contention mini-time slots. In Eq. 5, we analyze how to get the minimum number of contention mini-time slots that guarantees $P > P_0$ (P_0 is a given probability.).

$$minK \tag{5}$$

$$st. \quad P \geq P_0 \tag{6}$$

In Eq. 5, P is an increasing function of K. Therefore, we can easily get the result of Eq. 5.

5   Experimental Evaluation

In this section, we construct various simulations to evaluate our proposed MAC protocol. In order to illustrate the outperformance of the MD-CSMA protocol, we compare our proposed MAC protocol with the TDMA protocol and the CSMA/CA protocol. In the TDMA protocol, a time slot is divided into N mini-time slots for the N neighboring nodes. In the CSMA/CA protocol, each satellite contend at a random time slot. When there is a collision, they stop contending for a random period.

The following three metrics are used for evaluating our proposed protocol.

- Channel utilization ratio: the ratio of channel reserved successfully. It refers to the effective bandwidth utilization
- Mission satisfied ratio: the ratio of space missions being satisfied. It refers to the efficiency of the MD-CSMA protocol.
- Average latency of data access: the average delay over all the generated queries, where data access delay is defined as the time elapsed between generation of query and the reservation.

We construct various simulations in two different scenarios. In the first simulation scenario, the number of micro-satellites varies from 48 to 288. There are 12 Low Earth Orbits (LEO), each containing 4/5//24 micro-satellites. Micro-satellite uses directional antenna, and its beam width is 5°. The number of each micro-satellite's neighboring micro-satellites varies from 2 to 10. Due to the mobility of micro-satellites, each micro-satellite cannot meet all of its neighboring nodes at the same time. In the traditional TDMA, we divide a time slot into 10 mini-time slots. There are 10 levels of mission priority. And the distribution of mission priority obeys to the Zipf-distribution, i.e., $p_m^{mission} = \frac{1}{m^s}/(\sum_{m=1}^{M} \frac{1}{m^s})$, where m is the mission priority level, M is the number of mission priority levels, $s = 1$. Each micro-satellite transmits RTS with probability P_m.

Figure 4 shows the performance comparison of channel utilization. With the increase of micro-satellite number, each micro-satellite has more neighboring micro-satellites. The X-axle denotes the number of neighboring nodes. The Y-axle denotes the channel utilization ratio. Figure 4 shows that the proposed MD-CSMA protocol outperforms the CSMA/CA protocol in terms of channel utilization ratio. When P_m is large, the MD-CSMA protocol outperforms the TDMA protocol. The reason is as follows. The MD-CSMA protocol provides a better channel utilization ratio than the CSMA/CA protocol by using multiple contention. Since the time slot structure of the TDMA protocol is fixed, the MD-CSMA protocol can provide a better performance of channel utilization ratio.

Figure 5 shows the performance comparison of mission satisfied ratio. Generally, the MD-CSMA protocol outperforms the CSMA/CA protocol in term of

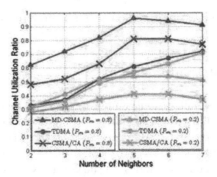

Fig. 4. Channel utilization.

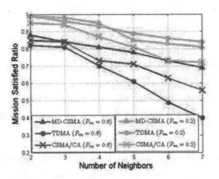

Fig. 5. Mission satisfied ratio.

mission satisfied ratio by multiple contentions. When $P_m = 0.8$, the MD-CSMA protocol outperforms the TDMA protocol in terms of mission satisfied ratio. The reason is as follows. The MD-CSMA protocol provides a better mission satisfied ratio than the CSMA/CA protocol by using multiple contention mini-time slots. Since the time slot structure of the TDMA protocol is fixed, when P_m is large, the MD-CSMA protocol can provide a better performance of mission satisfied ratio.

Figure 6 shows the performance comparison of data access delay. Generally, the MD-CSMA protocol outperforms the CSMA/CA protocol in term of data access delay by using multiple contention mini-time slots. When $P_m = 0.2$, the MD-CSMA protocol outperforms the TDMA protocol in terms of data access delay. The reason is as follows. The time slot structure of the TDMA protocol is fixed, when P_m is small the MD-CSMA protocol can satisfied the space mission with less delay than the TDMA protocol.

In the second simulation scenario, there are 12 Low Earth Orbits (LEO), each containing 24 micro-satellites. And each micro-satellite has 10 neighboring micro-satellites. P_m ($m = 1, 2, \ldots, 288$) is the probability that the micro-satellite m is a requesting micro-satellite. We various P_m from 0.2 to 0.8.

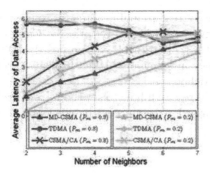

Fig. 6. Average latency of data access.

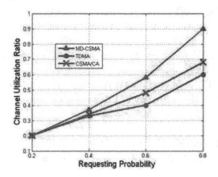

Fig. 7. Channel Utilization ratio comparison.

Figure 7 shows the performance comparison of channel utilization ratio. The MD-CSMA protocol outperforms the CSMA/CA protocol and the TDMA protocol in term of channel utilization. And the performance improvement is more significant with a larger requesting probability. The reason is as follows. The time slot structure of the TDMA protocol is fixed, the requesting micro-satellite cannot use the time slot of the other micro-satellites (even these micro-satellites are not requesting micro-satellites). The MD-CSMA protocol makes the best use of the channel resource by using the multiple contention mini-time slots. Therefore, the MD-CSMA protocol achieves a better performance of mission satisfied ratio. We have got the similar comparison results in terms of mission satisfied ratio and average data access latency.

6   Conclusion and Future Work

In this paper, we propose a new MAC protocol for the micro-satellite ad hoc network, named Multi-Detection Carrier Sense Multiple Access (MD-CSMA), where the micro-satellites reserve the mission mini-time slot by multiple contention. When there is a collision, the transmitting micro-satellite stop contending by a retreat probability. The retreat probability relates to the mission priority, which guarantees the space mission of high-level priority. Compared with the TDMA protocol and the CSMA/CA protocol, our proposed MD-CSMA protocol provides better performance in terms of channel utilization ratio, mission satisfied ratio, and data access delay.

In the future, we will research how to set the retreat probability by considering the game theory, in order to improve the efficiency of contention mini-time slot.

References

1. Zhan, Y., Ma, Z., Cao, Z.: Technology of modern micro satellite and its development direction. Chin. J. Electron. **7**, 102–106 (2000)
2. Dai, Y., Seng, Y.: Development and Inspiration of Space Technology, vol. 3, pp. 7–14 (2014)
3. Wertz, J.R., Larson, W.J.: Space Mission Analysis and Design. Space Technology Library, New York (2008)
4. Radhakrishnan, R.R., Edmonson, W.W., Afghah, F., Rodriguez-Osorio, R.M., Pinto Jr., F., Burleigh, S.C.: Survey of inter-satellite communication for small satellite systems: physical layer to network layer view. IEEE Commun. Surv. Tutor., 1 (2016)
5. Tang, Z.: Research on MAC Protocols of Self-Organizing Networks in Small Satellite Constellation. A thesis of Master from National University of Defense Technology
6. Goldsmith, A.: Wireless Communications. Cambridge University Press, New York (2005)
7. Kang, H., Jiang, X., Xiong, W.: STDMA for inter-satellite communication in low earth orbit. In: Liang, Q., Mu, J., Wang, W., Zhang, B. (eds.) Proceedings of the 2015 International Conference on Communications, Signal Processing, and Systems. LNEE, vol. 386, pp. 391–398. Springer, Heidelberg (2016). https://doi.org/10.1007/978-3-662-49831-6_39
8. Heidari, G., Truong, H.: Efficient, flexible, scalable inter-satellite networking. In: IEEE Wireless for Space and Extreme Environments (WiSEE) 11, pp. 1–6 (2013)
9. Sidibeh, K., Vladimirova, T.: Communication in LEO satellite formations, adaptive hardware and systems. In: NASA/ESA Conference (2008)
10. Radhakishnan, R., Zeng, Q.A., Edmonson, W.W.: Inter-satellite communications for small satellite systems. Int. J. Interdiscip. Telecommun. Netw. **5**, 11–24 (2013)
11. Liu, H., Liang, W.: Development of DARPAs F6 program. Chin. J. Spacecr. Eng. **2**, 92–98 (2013)

Frequency Sharing of IMT-2020 and Mobile Satellite Service in 45.5–47 GHz

Shuaijun Liu[1,2(✉)], Xin Hu[1,2], and Weidong Wang[1,2]

[1] Key Laboratory of Universal Wireless Communications,
Ministry of Education, Beijing University of Posts and Telecommunications,
Beijing 100876, China
lsj_bupt@163.com
[2] Information and Electronics Technology Lab,
Beijing University of Posts and Telecommunications, Beijing 100876, China

Abstract. In this paper, the possibility on frequency sharing of IMT-2020 and mobile satellite systems (MSS) in the 45.5–47 GHz band is investigated. This study is of great importance to related research community, industry and regulators which are currently investigating spectrum requirements and technology options for IMT-2020 and beyond. Focusing on the scenario of MSS GSO uplink as victim, we analyzed the interference from IMT-2020 to the MSS receiving GSO satellites (Sat) and compared that with the predefined threshold to assess whether the frequency sharing is possible. Different density of IMT-2020 stations and elevation areas are considered in sharing analysis. In addition, separation distance needed is simulated in terms of separation longitudes.

Keywords: International Mobile Telecommunication (IMT)
Mobile Satellite Service (MSS) · Frequency sharing · Interference assessment

1   Introduction

The development of IMT for 2020 and beyond is expected to enable new use cases and applications and addresses rapid traffic growth, for which contiguous and broader channel bandwidths than currently available for IMT systems would be desirable. This suggests the need to consider spectrum resources in higher frequency ranges [1]. The recent past WRC-15 has adopted the resolution of studies on frequency-related matters for IMT identification including possible additional allocations to the mobile services on a primary basis including 45.5–47 GHz bands for the future development of IMT for 2020 and beyond [2]. However, this band has been allocated on a co-primary basis to MSS [3], thus making it necessary and meaningful to study the sharing and compatibility of IMT-2020 and MSS.

Lots of work has done on sharing of IMT and other services, most of which are limited to IMT-2000 and IMT-Advanced systems. International Telecommunication Union (ITU) has published the relating reports on sharing of IMT-2000 and other services in [4], and that of IMT-Advanced and other services in [5, 6]. However, sharing of IMT-2020 and other services is in its infancy. Study of coexistence between

Q. Yu (Ed.): SINC 2017, CCIS 803, pp. 127–135, 2018.
https://doi.org/10.1007/978-981-10-7877-4_11

5G small cells and Fixed Service (FS) at 39 GHz is done in [7], where required frequency rejection is given for tolerable interference on FS resulting from IMT-2020. [8] focuses on the spectrum sharing between IMT-2020 and Fixed Satellite Service (FSS) at 28 GHz, where the achievable performance of 5G under the FSS interference is simulated. [9] analyzed the coexistence of MSS and MS in 2.1/1.9 GHz band, and interference from MS on MSS is done assuming the MS CDMA scheme.

However, existing research mainly focused on the interference to earth stations (ES) and few concerned that to receiving Sat. Besides, aggregate interference from IMT on MSS is analyzed without consideration of IMT stations numbers. To the authors' best knowledge, few studies has assessed on frequency sharing of IMT-2020 and MSS at 45.5–47 GHz band. We focus on the interference from IMT systems to MSS receiving GSO Sat in 45.5–47 GHz with co-channel interference specified.

Existing work can be guide on our study, but still many challenges are undergo. Propagation model, power control schemes and antenna radiation patterns can all do effect on the frequency sharing of IMT-2020 and MSS. In particular, we consider the parameters provided by ITU, 3GPP and other newly publications. We first verify the interference scenarios and classify the interference cases in detail. Then we analyze the interference of IMT-2020 on MSS satellites in terms of different operating elevations and various densities of IMT nodes. In addition, the separation between IMT systems and MSS is simulated in terms of separation longitude with different operating latitudes. The contributions of this paper are twofold as follows:

- We evaluate and analyze the interference from IMT-2020 to MSS receiving GSO Sat in the band of 45.5–47 GHz with co-channel interference specified.
- We test different IMT station densities on simulation. Effective area percentage and equivalent UEs density are defined to describe aggregate interference from IMT to MSS.

The paper is organized as follows: Sect. 2 is the system model and interference assessment. Section 3 describes the simulation methods and the results analysis. Section 4 concludes the paper.

2   System Model and Interference Assessment

2.1   Sharing Scenario

We consider the coexistence scenario of MSS and IMT networks as illustrated in Fig. 1 where the MSS spot beam GSO satellite (Sat) and IMT-2020 is specified. In addition, no cooperation of these two networks is assumed.

2.2   Interference Assessment

The interference scenario from IMT to MSS uplink can be illustrated as Fig. 1. Detailed interfering model can be classified into 2 cases and separately denoted by C1–C2 in Fig. 1.

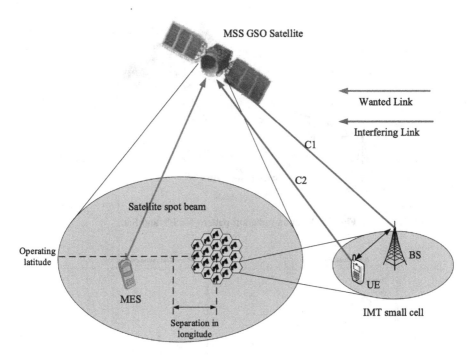

Fig. 1. Frequency sharing scenario of IMT and MSS

- **Case 1:** IMT downlink interfere MSS uplink, denoted by C1.
- **Case 2:** IMT uplink interfere MSS uplink, denoted by C2.

For C1–C2 each case, the interfering link contains two nodes, that is IMT transmitting nodes and MSS received nodes, denoted by Tx and Rx separately, where Tx limits to the IMT BS or UE while Rx limits to the MSS Sat. Transmit powers of i_{th} Tx is denoted by $P_i(Tx)$. Interference j_{th} Rx received from i_{th} Tx is $I_{j,i}$ and can be expressed as Eq. (1):

$$I_{j,i} = P_i(Tx) + G_i(Tx,\ \theta_d) + Gj(Rx,\ \theta_a) - PL_{j,i} \tag{1}$$

where the θ_d is the angle of departure for transmitting signals and the θ_a is the angle of arrive for the receiving signals, as illustrated in Fig. 2.

Omnidirectional radiation pattern is supposed as IMT-2020 BS antenna, with the vertical radiation pattern is referenced in [10]. For MSS Sat antenna pattern, we assumed a tapered circular apertures antenna with uniform distribution, described in Eq. (2) with $n = 0$ [11].

$$G(\phi) = G_{\max} \left| 2^{n+1}(n+1)! \frac{J_{n+1}(\phi)}{(\phi)^{n+1}} \right|^2 \tag{2}$$

Antenna patterns for MSS Sat and IMT-2020 BS are shown in Fig. 3.

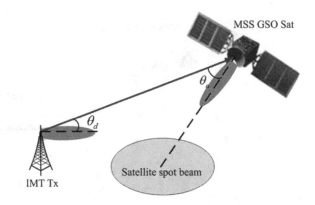

Fig. 2. Antenna radiation pattern for BS and Sat

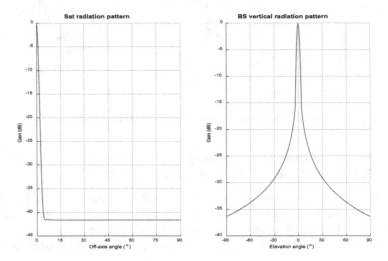

Fig. 3. Antenna radiation patterns for IMT BS and MSS Sat

Note that Tx power is assumed to be controlled with an LTE-like power control mechanism [12]. The uplink power control parameter PL_{x-ile} value is modified to 105.9 dB, with shadowing effect considered.

The path-loss $PL_{j,i}$ is calculated based on line-of-sight (LOS) in Recommendation ITU-R P.2001-2 [13] expressed as follows:

$$PL = 92.44 + 20\lg(fc/GHz) + 20\lg(d/km) + L_o \tag{3}$$

where L_o means other losses, characterized by operating frequency, MES elevation and local climate etc. L_o is mainly determined by rain attenuation with other inevitable factors like atmospheric attenuation and cross-polarization discrimination. Rain attenuation for p% percent of the time where p ranges from 0.001 to 1.0 is calculated about 13 dB for a typical city with specific p = 0.01, 58 mm/h rain drops is supposed [14].

Then the interference on j_{th} Rx considering number of N_{Tx} Tx should be summed as described in Eq. (4):

$$I_j = \sum_{i=1}^{N_{Tx}} I_{j,i} \tag{4}$$

The whole interference of IMT on MSS will be averaged as Eq. (5):

$$I = \frac{1}{N_{Rx}} \sum_{j=1}^{N_{Rx}} I_j \tag{5}$$

Interference from IMT systems on existing MSS systems should be compared with the pre-defined interference threshold. We select an equivalent satellite link noise temperature rise, $\Delta T / T = 6\%$, as the maximum interference threshold [15], where $\Delta T / T$ is defined as follow:

$$\frac{\Delta T}{T} = \frac{I}{N_0 B_{ref}} \tag{6}$$

where I is the receiving interference in the bandwidth of B_{ref}, N_0 is the thermal noise density corresponding to the equivalent noise temperature of the satellite link, B_{ref} is the MSS link reference bandwidth.

3 Performance Evaluation

3.1 Simulation Environment

Deterministic calculations, while being simple, do not always provide a complete picture of the interference scenarios that arise. For this reason, we use the recommended Monte Carlo method in simulation analysis [16]. Table 1 lists the system parameters in simulation.

3.2 Results and Analysis

3.2.1 Different IMT-2020 Stations Density

For area of satellite spot beam and IMT small cell are greatly different in size, and number of IMT BSs or UEs can do make difference on aggregate interference assessment. We define the effective area percentage (EAP) to describe the deployed IMT area in a spot beam.

Table 1. System parameters

Parameter	Value
IMT-2020 system	
Carrier frequency	46 GHz
Inter-site distance	200 m
BS transmit PSD	36 dBm/MHz
BS antenna pattern	Equation (1d) Ref [10]
BS feeder loss	1 dB
UE transmit PSD	7.5 dBm/MHz
UE feeder loss	1 dB
MSS system	
Sat transmit power	50 W
Sat antenna main lobe gain	41.6 dBi
Sat antenna radiation pattern	Equation (2)
Link noise temperature	501 K

$$EAP = \frac{Area\ of\ IMT}{Area\ of\ spot\ beam} \qquad (7)$$

Figure 4 shows the interference of IMT BSs to MSS receiving GSO Sat on different EAP and MES elevations. The results show that $\Delta T/T$ always exceeds the threshold of $\Delta T/T = 6\%$, making it scarcely possible to deploy IMT-2020 downlink co-frequency with MSS uplink in the same geographical region.

We define the Equivalent UEs Density (EUD) as the ratio of total UEs and area of spot beam, described as Eq. (8).

$$EUD = \frac{Number\ of\ UEs}{Area\ of\ spot\ beam} \qquad (8)$$

Figure 5 shows the interference from IMT UEs to MSS receiving GSO Sat on different EUD. The results show that $\Delta T/T$ exceeds the threshold of $\Delta T/T = 6\%$ when EUD exceeds about $600/km^2$. Typical IMT-Advanced active UE density is $18/km^2$ for dense urban macro, $115/km^2$ for dense urban micro [5]. Considering the IMT-2020 new arising Machine-to-Machine (M2M) services, M2M device subscribers will occupy an increasingly large proportion in UEs. For example, subscriptions in China in 2030 are predicted to be 22.7 billion, about 450 times of 50 million in 2013 [17]. Likelihood or not of sharing between IMT-2020 interfering UEs and MSS receiving GSO Sat will be possible only once whether used for M2M services in this band, the accurate EUD of IMT-2020 and that of specific RF technical characteristics in a satellite spot beam will be made available.

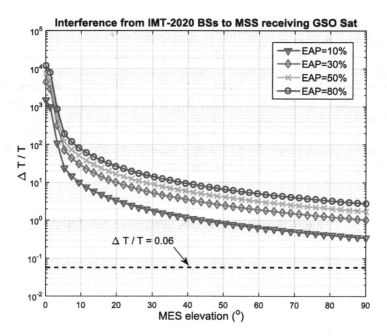

Fig. 4. Interference from IMT-2020 BSs to MSS receiving Satellite

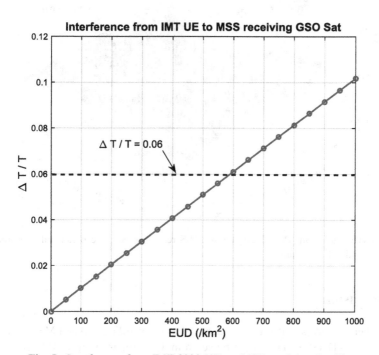

Fig. 5. Interference from IMT-2020 UEs to MSS receiving Satellite

3.2.2   Separation Needed in Longitude

To keep the interference of IMT BSs to victim MSS GSO Sat under the threshold, additional loss should be provided by alternative geographic separation, here particular refer to separation in longitude (SiL) as illustrated in Fig. 1. Same latitude of satellite spot beam and IMT deployment, IMT BSs density of *EAP* = 30% are supposed.

Figure 6 shows the interference of IMT BSs to MSS receiving GSO Sat in terms of different of MES elevations and SiLs. It shows that the needed SiL differentiate with the operating MES elevation. The SiL increases as MES elevation is smaller for IMT BSs has bigger antenna gain towards MSS receiving GSO Sat. From Fig. 6, the SiL should be more than about 7° when MES elevation is 90° to guarantee the MSS GSO Sat.

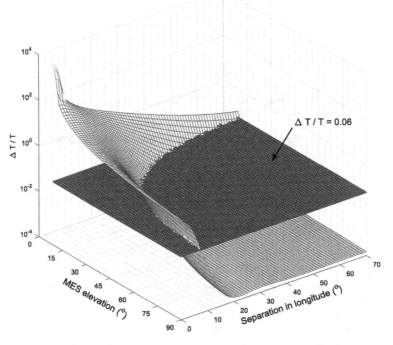

Fig. 6. Interference from IMT-2020 BSs to MSS receiving Satellite under different longitude separations and MES elevations

4   Conclusion

In this paper, we investigated the frequency sharing of IMT-2020 and MSS in the band between 45.5–47 GHz. The interference from IMT on receiving MSS GSO Sat is simulated and compared with the predefined threshold. Particularly, we analyzed the interference in terms of different IMT deployment densities and MES elevations. In addition, the separation needed to protect the MSS GSO Sat from IMT BSs excessive interference is given in terms of longitude separation. Simulation can be reference guide for spectrum relating issues for IMT-2020 and beyond.

Acknowledgement. This work is supported by the National Natural Science Foundation of China (No. 91438114 and No. 61372111).

References

1. ITU-R Rep. M.2376: Technical feasibility of IMT in bands above 6 GHz, July 2015
2. ITU-R: Final Acts WRC-15, World Radiocommunication Conference, Geneva (2015)
3. ITU-R: Radio Regulations (2012)
4. ITU-R Rep. M.2041: Sharing and adjacent band compatibility in the 2.5 GHz band between the terrestrial and satellite components of IMT-2000 (2003)
5. ITU-R Rep. M.2109: Sharing studies between IMT-Advanced systems and geostationary satellite networks in the fixed-satellite service in the 3400–4200 and 4500–4800 MHz frequency bands (2007)
6. ITU-R Rep. M.2292-0: Characteristics of terrestrial IMT-Advanced systems for frequency sharing/interference analyses, December 2013
7. Kim, J., Xian, L., Maltsev, A., Arefi, R., Sadri, A.S.: Study of coexistence between 5G small-cell systems and systems of the fixed service at 39 GHz band. In: 2015 IEEE MTT-S International Microwave Symposium, Phoenix, AZ, pp. 1–3 (2015)
8. Guidolin, F., Nekovee, M.: Investigating spectrum sharing between 5G millimeter wave networks and fixed satellite systems. In: 2015 IEEE Globecom Workshops (GC Wkshps), San Diego, CA, pp. 1–7 (2015)
9. Park, J.M., Oh, D.S., Park, D.C.: Coexistence of mobile-satellite service system with mobile service system in shared frequency bands. IEEE Trans. Consum. Electron. **55**(3), 1051–1055 (2009)
10. ITU-R Rec. F.1336-4: Reference radiation patterns of omnidirectional, sectoral and other antennas for the fixed and mobile services for use in sharing studies in the frequency range from 400 MHz to about 70 GHz, February 2014
11. Stutzman, W.L., Thiele, G.A.: Antenna Theory and Design, 3rd edn, p. 389. Wiley, New York (2012)
12. 3GPP TS 36.942 V12.0.0: Evolved Universal Terrestrial Radio Access (E-UTRA); Radio Frequency (RF) system scenarios, September 2014
13. ITU-R Rec. P.2001-2: A general purpose wide-range terrestrial propagation model in the frequency range 30 MHz to 50 GHz, July 2015
14. ITU-R Rec. P.618: Propagation data and prediction methods required for the design of Earth-space telecommunication systems, July 2015
15. ITU-R Rec. S.739: Additional methods for determining if detailed coordination is necessary between geostationary-satellite networks in the fixed-satellite service sharing the same frequency bands (1992)
16. ITU-R Rec. M.1634: Interference protection of terrestrial mobile service systems using Monte Carlo simulation with application to frequency sharing (2003)
17. ITU-R Rep. M.2370-0: IMT traffic estimates for the years 2020 to 2030, July 2015

Research on Task-Oriented Dynamic Reconstruction of Space Information Networks

Qi Zhang[✉], Lin Gui, Hui Yu, Feng Tian, and Shichao Zhu

Department of Electronic Engineering, Shanghai Jiao Tong University,
Shanghai 200240, China
{qizhang_sjtu,guilin,yuhui,ronaldo1,zhushichao}@sjtu.edu.cn

Abstract. Due to its high coverage and communication capacity in bat-
tlefield and disaster area, space information networks have become an
important apart in the next generation communication system. As the
surging demand of burst business in hotspot regions, existing architectures of space information networks lack scalability and cannot meet the
demand for high quality of service. This paper first proposes a flexible network architecture with dynamic reconstruction capability. Next,
space task sensing and traffic prediction technology are introduced to
forecast space task types and acquire the optimization objective of
dynamic reconstruction problem. Finally, we formulate the utility and
cost functions about different dynamic reconstruction strategies and then
select the optimal dynamic reconstruction scheme to satisfy the surging
demand of sudden business around the world.

Keywords: Space information networks · Network architecture
Task-oriented · Dynamic reconstruction

1 Introduction

Space information networks are carried by space platforms (including geostationary orbit satellites, nonsynchronous medium earth orbit satellites, nonsynchronous low earth orbit satellites, stratospheric airship, near-space UAVs
(Unmanned Aerial Vehicles) and so on). They can support space information
acquisition, transmission and processing in real time [1]. As a national strategic
infrastructure, space information networks have more prominent advantages in
various significant applications such as earth observation, aerospace measurement
and control, emergency communications, air transport and ocean voyage [2]. With
the rapid development of Chinese military and economy as well as the promotion
of the "the Belt and Road" initiative, the interests and influence of China in the

---

Q. Zhang—This work was supported in part by the National Natural Science Foundation of China (61471236, 61420106008, 61671295), the 111 Project (B07022), and
the Shanghai Key Laboratory of Digital Media Processing; it is also partly sponsored
by Shanghai Pujiang Program (16PJD029).

Q. Yu (Ed.): SINC 2017, CCIS 803, pp. 136–144, 2018.
https://doi.org/10.1007/978-981-10-7877-4_12

world are expanding. At the same time, the number of various space missions has risen rapidly, especially in hotspots, where sudden space missions occur with high possibility. These large and unexpected missions put forward higher requirements for the dynamic scalability of space information networks.

The GEO orbit resources and global ground stations are all limited in China [3]. Existing space information networks cannot serve for the increasing number of space users, especially in regional hotspots with the proliferation of resource requirement. It becomes a great challenge to build a space information network to meet the increasing and sudden space tasks. In this paper, we propose a methodology about task-oriented dynamic reconstruction of space information networks.

In view of the large scale, time-varying, space-varying and high dynamic characteristics of space information networks, many scholars and research institutions have explored the dynamic reconstruction technology of space information networks. The high-throughput distributed spacecraft network (Hi-DSN) proposed in [4] could provide a vertically integrated network infrastructure and maintain high-throughput multi-hop communications among mobile spacecraft operating in diverse orbits, Hi-DSN also supported the dynamic extension when adding new nodes. The authors in [5] introduced a cluster network model and proposed an efficient scheme for satellites communication and self-healing when suffering damage. The routing protocol under the star cluster structure was proposed to support the dynamic reconstruction of nodes and links. Liang et al. in [6] proposed an in-orbit reconfigurable software/hardware architecture for LEO satellite communication system so that the satellites could be developed according to the latest technology and updated on orbit by means of load reconstruction. These existing researches on dynamic reconstruction of space information networks mainly focused on physical layer, MAC layer and network layer and provided some theoretical basis for dynamic reconstruction separately. However, to the best of our knowledge, there is lack of task modeling and systematic analysis, which cannot specifically guide the dynamic reconstruction of space information networks.

2   Architecture of Space Information Networks

The architecture design of Space information networks is the prerequisite of dynamic network reconstruction, so we combine the current research status and the space information network characteristics and propose a task-oriented reconfigurable network architecture. Recently, most researches have assumed the architecture of space information networks is hierarchical, i.e., "backbone network + access network" [7–9]. We analyze the TSAT system of the U.S. as an example. Its backbone network consists of 5 GEO satellites which complete the interconnection by laser link, while other space nodes and sub networks get access to the backbone network. It's a typical kind of "backbone + access" network [7]. In order to deal with the burst regional traffic, we introduce the supplement of the backbone network as "region enhancement layer" based on the existing "backbone + access" network architecture. Region enhancement layer is temporarily constructed to increase service capacity for hotspot regions by various satellites and aerial platforms interconnecting with each other. Since satellites and aerial platforms constantly enter and leave, region enhancement layer changes dynamically and should be constructed through the least costly way. The two-layer backbone network architecture, "backbone + regional enhancement", can improve the data transmission ability for regional emergency business due to its dynamic reconstruction capacity. We abstract the space information network into a backbone network characterized by resource supply and an access network characterized by resource requirements, as shown in Fig. 1. The resources in this paper mainly refer to the communication resources carried by network nodes (including bandwidth, antenna, power, frequency, etc.), computing resources, cache resources and so on. Taking the communication resources as an example, in the hotspots (red dotted circle in Fig. 1 represents a large number of new users in this region), the backbone network needs to use MEO/LEO satellites and aerial communication platforms to get more communication resources for data transmission. We construct the "region enhancement layer" pertinently as a supplement of the "GEO backbone layer" to ensure that the backbone network can provide enough resources for surging business in hot spot regions, which improve the space information backbone network service capacity and ensure the whole network's quality of service. Because of the MEO/LEO satellite' time-varying orbit characteristics, a part of satellites will leave the "region enhancement layer", while another part of satellites will come to the hot spot region and be incorporated into the "region enhancement layer". In this scenario, we formulate the network dynamic reconstruction problems as minimizing the reconstruction cost to satisfy the traffic carrying capacity of space information networks. In terms of space information networks with two-layer backbone architecture, the following challenges will be considered:

Network heterogeneity: Two-layer backbone network architecture in space information network has obvious heterogeneity. One the one hand, High orbit backbone nodes, such as relay satellites, have a relatively fixed position due to the characteristics of their orbits. According to the evolution trend, high orbit nodes will accomplish laser interconnection and form an available efficient high orbit backbone network with fixed topology. On the other hand, the satellite nodes located in the MEO/LEO have periodic dynamic topology because of their periodic motion characteristics. Due to the different periods of satellite motion in different orbits, the region enhancement layer shows the characteristic of dynamic connections. Thus, the backbone of a space information network shows an obvious heterogeneity feature that high orbit satellites have static topology and MEO/LEO satellites have dynamic topology.

Dynamic reconstruction: In order to enhance the backbone network's capacity, MEO/LEO satellites or aerial communication platforms are scheduled to construct temporary regional enhanced network based on various mission demand. We regard all kinds of satellites with communication function as "resources satellites", which carry different resources. Thus, we can not only use orbiting satellite nodes, but also temporarily expropriate MEO/LEO satellite nodes or aerial

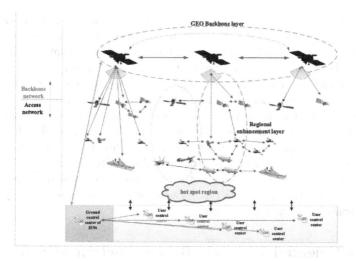

Fig. 1. An example of dynamic reconstruction of the space information networks. (Color figure online)

communication platforms to build the temporary region enhancement layer. At the same time, due to the motion characteristics of MEO/LEO satellites, some satellites will shift out of the region enhancement layer, while other MEO/LEO satellites will move into the hot spots area, so the network needs to be reconfigured in order to maintain the adequate service capacity. After space tasks are completed, the network connection of region enhancement layer should be canceled to release the communication resources of MEO/LEO satellites and aerial communication platforms. Thus, the backbone layer of the space information network has an open network structure, which can accept new satellite nodes to enter the backbone layer and support dynamic reconstruction.

Heterogeneous space resources: Satellite resources under the two-layer architecture differ from each other greatly due to intergenerational update and distinct missions of satellites. As far as the relay satellites are concerned, different generations will coexist for some time. The satellite resources, including the communication frequency, bandwidth, antenna type, cache, computing and power are all dissimilar. Satellites in the region enhancement layer will also show the difference about their communication, storage and computing capability. For example, the earth observation satellites have broadband communication capability, while the communication bandwidth of navigation satellites is relatively narrow. We can also regard the air communication platforms as a special "resources satellites". Thus, the space information networks have various and heterogeneous space resources.

Space missions with large quantity, massive types, and regional burst: According to the task type, network services can be classified as high-speed service (such as remote sensing service), low-speed service (such as measurement and control services); from the users' motion characteristics, services can be classified as those with predictable motion track (such as spacecraft users) and others with random motion track (such as ground mobile users); from delay characteristics, services can be classified as real-time service (such as real-time voice, video communication) and non-real-time service (such as the playback of remote sensing data); from the access mode, services can be classified as pre planned service and burst service. The resource requirements of these services have some consistency, but also have differences in many aspects, especially for the regional burst traffic which has obvious region characteristics. From the view of whole network, demands for resources are unevenly distributed.

The heterogeneity of backbone network, heterogeneous node resources and diversity of space task demands put forward some challenges to maximize the utility of space information networks.

3 Task-Oriented Dynamic Reconstruction of Space Information Networks

In this paper, we aim at improving the service carrying capacity of space information networks by dynamically reconstructing the backbone network. First of all, the modeling and analysis of three classical space tasks are presented, which are image transmission, measurement and control and voice service. We present a cognitive scheme for fast and accurate space task prediction and grasp the resource demand from the task level. Then, the network reconstruction goal of service carrying capacity is introduced. Next, this paper will study the service carrying capacity gain and implementation cost under different network dynamic reconstruction methods and propose a reasonable reconstruction strategy so that the space information networks can finally meet the regional task needs.

3.1 Space Task Perception and Prediction

Space information networks mainly serve three classical tasks. One is image transmission task (such as earth observation), which is characterized by high return speed and severe asymmetry between forward and backward links. By 2020, the data transmission rate of most earth observation satellites will reach 2Gbit/s, the highest requirement is about 8Gbit/s. The second category is the measurement and control task, which has a high reliability, low rate characteristics. The in-orbit measurement and control of satellite requires that the forward control and the backward telemetry constitute a closed loop alignment mechanism. The forward control and backward telemetry data rates of satellites are generally only a few Kbit/s, and the small part of spacecraft can reach dozens of Kbit/s. The third type of task is voice service. Because of the harsh conditions of space environment, the space modem's switching processing capability is generally not high.

In order to perceive distinct tasks in space information networks, we sense the traffic types through data transmission rate and the correlation between data frames. Firstly, the decision threshold TH_1 is set according to past network data transmission rate, this parameter should be constantly modified according to the decision feedback result. Then, the data transmission rate c to be analyzed in the space information networks is measured. If $c < TH_1$, it is considered that the measured task is the measurement and control task; otherwise it is image transmission task or voice service. Next, in order to further sense the image transmission task, we intercept a part of data stream, and extract the adjacent M frames. Let $X(i)$ denote the frame i, and $X(i)_j$ denotes column of j. We define ρ as the correlation coefficients of frame i,

$$\rho_i = \max_{1 \le j \le M, 1 \le k \le M, j \ne k} \frac{< X(i)_j, X(i)_k >}{\|X(i)_{j_2}\| \|X(i)_{k_2}\|}. \tag{1}$$

And further define as the mean correlation coefficient, denoted as

$$\rho = \frac{1}{M} \sum_{i=1}^{M} \rho_i, \ i \in [1, M]. \tag{2}$$

The threshold TH_2 is first set according to the experience value of network data transmission, this parameter also needs to be constantly modified according to the feedback of the decision result. Taking into account the high correlation of image data frames, if $\rho \ge TH_2$, it is considered that the measured task is image transmission task; otherwise it is voice service.

The classical tasks carried on the space information networks are different from that on the terrestrial mobile communication network or the traditional service on the Internet. In general, the space tasks have typical arrival laws and task attributes, which are more conducive to the task prediction of space information networks. However, due to the complexity of space information network topology and the uncertainty of space transmission link, it brings challenges to space mission prediction and service support. This paper focuses on breaking the traditional coarse-grained traffic measurement and analysis model, and studies the effective traffic analysis, modeling and resource demand forecasting for space tasks, so as to realize the precise perception of network traffic status, reveal the law of space task and optimize network resources configuration.

In this paper, a fast and accurate space task prediction and service decision result are obtained by establishing a cognitive method for space users' quality of experience. The details of forecasting process are as follow:

(1) Get the type, and requirements of different tasks for different space users.
(2) Build a dynamic database of classical tasks for space information networks and maintain multidimensional information (constraints, priority, task model and QoE) of classical space tasks and network states.
(3) By means of data mining, statistical analysis and evolutionary prediction, the model of distinct types of task is established, the task characteristics are extracted, and the clustering decision is implemented.
(4) To match the knowledge database and then formulate the traffic analysis and resource requirements analysis of space tasks.

(5) Based on the current state of the network, user demand status and network optimization scheme, we can predict the task type and resource requirements of current space information network, and then the demand of burst service for network access capability and data transmission capability can be obtained.
(6) Release relevant forecast information and service strategy.

3.2   Reconstruction Strategies of Space Information Networks

After obtaining the demand of network access capability and data transmission capability in hotspot region, we then reconstruct region enhancement layer to satisfy the burst demand accordingly. The region enhancement layer in backbone network of space information networks has a variety of dynamic reconstruction methods, including upgrading satellite nodes in orbit, expropriating temporary satellites, launching new air communication platforms. These dynamic reconstruction methods bring different carrying capacity gain and implementation cost. Our objective is to compare distinct reconstruction strategies and select one to satisfy the actual demand with least cost.

We take the expropriation of in-orbit satellites as an example. First, we calculate the gain of the backbone network access capacity by expropriating a satellite v_i, denoted as $\Delta\lambda_{v_i}$. Next, we analyze in detail the gain of the data transmission capability the backbone network. When the space information network expropriate a new satellite, the link of the original network needs to be reconstructed to achieve maximum data transmission capability. Using the graph theory and dynamic programming theory, the gain of the data transmission capability of the backbone network caused by dynamic reconstruction can be calculated. The detailed solution is as follows:

Let T be the satellite node set of current backbone network, and $v_i \in T$ denotes the new satellite node which is going to be added to T. We further define U_{v_i} as the set of nodes in T that can connect with v_i. The discussion is divided into two cases: backbone network without isolated nodes and that with isolated nodes:

(1) Backbone network without isolated nodes
Find the node v_i in U_{v_i} with the largest weight of edge (v_i, v_j). Assume that v_j has connected with v_m, then compare the weight of edge (v_i, v_j) and that of edge (v_j, v_m).

(a) if $E_{v_i,v_j} > E_{v_j,v_m}$, then disconnect the original link (v_j, v_m) and establish a new link (v_i, v_j). For the node v_m whose link is disconnected, find the optimal solution again.
(b) if $E_{v_i,v_j} \le E_{v_j,v_m}$, keep the original link (v_j, v_m) of v_j and find the edge with second largest weight in U_{v_i}, then find the optimal solution again.

(2) Backbone network with isolated nodes
Assuming that the isolated node $v_g \in T$, if we have $v_g \notin U_{v_i}$, then the reconstruction scheme of v_i is the same as that of without an isolating node.

If $v_g \in U_{v_i}$, find the node v_j in U_{v_i} with the largest weight of edge (v_i, v_j) and assume that has connected with v_m.

(a) If $E_{v_i,v_g} + E_{v_j,v_m} \geq E_{v_i,v_j} + \max(\Delta E_{v_m})$, then keep the original link (v_j, v_m) of v_j, find the edge with second largest weight in U_{v_i}, then find the optimal solution again. If the above equation still holds after the traversal, then we connect the new node and the isolated node.

(b) If $E_{v_i,v_g} + E_{v_j,v_m} \leq E_{v_i,v_j} + \max(\Delta E_{v_m})$, then disconnect the original link (v_j, v_m) and establish a new link (v_i, v_j). For the node v_m whose link is disconnected, find the optimal solution again.

In the above formula, $\max(\Delta E_{v_m})$ is defined as the increased maximum data throughput after removing node v_i, v_j, v_m and merging v_m into T. Through the above algorithm, the data transmission capacity gain ΔC_{v_i} of the backbone network is calculated.

When reconstructing the network, we should strike a better tradeoff between the gain of the network carrying capacity and the implementation cost. We define $f(v_i)$ as the implementation cost function of expropriating the new satellite v_j. Moreover, we can calculate the access demand $\Delta\lambda_0$ of new emergency service and the transmission capacity requirements ΔC_0 for backbone network by space task perception and prediction method introduced in the Sect. 3.1. In order to satisfy the new unexpected tasks in the hot spot regions via dynamic reconstruction with the minimum implementation cost, we formulate the optimization problem as (3).

$$\min \sum_{v_i} f(v_i)$$

$$s.t. \sum_{v_i} \Delta C_{v_i} \geq \Delta C_0 \qquad (3)$$

$$\sum_{v_i} \Delta\lambda_{v_i} \geq \Delta\lambda_0$$

The optimal reconstruction strategy of space information networks can be given by resolving the above optimization problem.

4 Conclusion

In this paper, the "backbone + regional enhancement" two-layer backbone architecture of space information networks was proposed. We have studied the task-oriented dynamic reconstruction of space information networks and proposed novel reconstruction schemes, which can provide support for improving the dynamic scalability of space information networks. Specifically, in view of the surging business in hotspot area, this paper firstly established a cognitive traffic prediction model and then obtained the burst service requirements for network access capacity and data transmission capacity which were regarded as the dynamic reconstruction target. By formulating an optimization model, the optimal dynamic reconstruction strategy can be selected to satisfy the demand for task carrying capacity under the condition of minimal reconstruction cost.

References

1. Li, D.R., Sheng, X., Gong, J.Y., Zhang, J., Lu, J.H.: On construction of China's space information network. Geomat. Inf. Sci. Wuhan Univ. **06**, 711–715+766 (2015)
2. Yu, Q., Wang, J., Bai, L.: Architecture and critical technologies of space information networks. J. Commun. Inform. Netw. **1**(3), 1–9 (2016)
3. Li, Y.H., Huang, H.M., Zheng, J.: Efficiency improvement technologies for tracking and data relay satellite system. Chin. Space Sci. Technol. **01**, 71–77 (2014)
4. Bergamo, M.A.: High-throughput distributed spacecraft network: architecture and multiple access technologies. Comput. Netw. **47**(05), 725–749 (2005)
5. Jiang, Y.Q., Wu, Q.: A dynamic reconstruction strategy applied to star cluster. Digit. Technol. Appl. **09**, 115 (2012)
6. Liang, G., Gong, W.B., Liu, H.J.: The design of reconfigurable LEO satellite communication system. J. Astronaut. **01**, 185–191 (2010)
7. Pan, Q., Hu, X.J., Zhang, X.Q.: Network Centric Warfare Equipment System. National Defense Industry Press, Beijing (2010)
8. Fei, L.G., Fan, D.D., Kou, B.H., et al.: Research on the demonstration of space information network based on TDRSS. J. China Acad. Electron. Inform. Technol. **10**(05), 479–484 (2015)
9. Medium and long term development plan of national satellite navigation industry. Satellite Application 06, pp. 38–43 (2013)

Topology Analysis of Inter-Layer Links for LEO/MEO Double-Layered Satellite Networks

Hongcheng Yan[✉], Jian Guo, Xianghui Wang, Yahang Zhang,
and Yong Sun

Institute of Spacecraft System Engineering,
China Academy of Space Technology, Beijing 100094, China
hongcheng.yan@gmail.com

Abstract. Due to the relative orbiting of Low Earth Orbit (LEO) satellite and Medium Earth Orbit (MEO) satellite, the inter-layer links (IIL) of LEO/MEO Double-Layered Satellite Networks (DLSN) have to switch dynamically, resulting in dynamic changes of satellite network topology, which has an impact on the data transmission performance of DLSN. In this paper, the IIL topology of LEO/MEO DLSN is analyzed and simulated. Firstly, the visibility calculation method and establishment strategy of IIL between LEO and MEO satellite as well as the calculation and optimization of system snapshots is analyzed. Then, simulation analysis regarding the number and duration of system snapshots, IIL switching time for LEO, the number of switching IIL in each system snapshot, the number of IILs that each MEO needs to establish are presented. Finally, the future research trends of DLSN IIL topology are discussed, such as how to reduce the maximum IIL number for MEO and so on.

Keywords: Double-Layered Satellite Networks · Inter-layer link
Snapshot optimization · Simulation analysis

1 Introduction

In non-geostationary orbit satellites, Low Earth Orbit (LEO) satellites have a lower transmission latency, lower link loss and thus low requirements to user terminals due to its low altitude. However, the coverage of a single LEO satellite is limited and usually need a larger constellation to achieve global coverage thus having a big system investment. Meanwhile, Medium Earth Orbit (MEO) satellites have a higher altitude, higher transmission latency and higher link loss, thus have higher requirements to user terminals. However, due to the higher altitude and wide coverage of MEO satellites, global coverage only needs a dozen MEO satellites and thus having a low system investment. Moreover, the long distance transmission latency of MEO constellation is better than LEO constellation. Therefore, LEO/MEO Double-Layered Satellite Networks (DLSN), which can combine the advantages of both LEO and MEO satellites, has become a research focus in satellite communication network field [1].

© Springer Nature Singapore Pte Ltd. 2018
Q. Yu (Ed.): SINC 2017, CCIS 803, pp. 145–158, 2018.
https://doi.org/10.1007/978-981-10-7877-4_13

In LEO/MEO DLSN, LEO satellites have to establish Inter-Layer Link (IIL) with MEO satellite in addition to establishing Inter-Satellite Links (ISL) with intra-orbit LEO satellites and inter-orbit LEO satellites. MEO satellites also have to establish IILs with LEO satellites in addition to establishing ISLs with intra-orbit and inter-orbit MEO satellites [2]. Because MEO satellites cannot always be visible to LEO satellites, the IILs have the characteristics of dynamic switching. Meanwhile, the ISLs in LEO constellation and MEO constellation can generally be fixed by choosing a reasonable constellation configuration [3]. Therefore, it can be concluded that the topological dynamics of LEO/MEO DLSN are mainly due to the dynamic change of the IIL.

At present, the academia mainly focuses on the satellite network routing algorithm [4, 5], and the research on the dynamic of satellite network topology is relatively little [3, 6–11]. Markus et al. [3] proposed that choosing an inclined walker constellation can achieve fixed laser ISLs for broadband LEO satellite networks. Wang et al. [6] presented an analysis on how to reduce the dynamics of LEO satellite network topology by choosing a reasonable constellation configuration. Wang et al. [7] proposed an equal-duration snapshot optimization method for LEO satellite networks. The above researches are mainly focus on topology analysis and optimization for single layer satellite networks. Wang et al. [8] argued that the LEO constellation selection has an impact on the topology dynamics of multilayered satellite network. Wu and Wu [9] proposed a centralized IIL establishment strategy for LEO/MEO DLSN and made a performance evaluation. Zhou et al. [10] and Long et al. [11] proposed a snapshot optimization method based on snapshot merging and achieved a remarkable improvement.

The establishment strategy of IIL in LEO/MEO DLSN is generally based on satellite grouping and routing protocol [1], that is, LEO satellite will choose MEO satellite with the longest predicted coverage time to establish IIL. Each time the IIL changes, one new snapshot will be generated. Since the strategy did not initially take into account the snapshot optimization problem, the number of snapshots generated was high and the duration of the snapshot was short. Large number of snapshots makes the satellite network topology more dynamic and requires more storage space of the satellite; short duration of snapshots makes a higher demand for the convergence speed of the satellite routing algorithm. The snapshot optimization method based on snapshot merging proposed by Zhou-Long can greatly reduce the number of snapshots while increasing the duration of snapshots.

Since the IIL topology of LEO/MEO DLSN has not been thoroughly analyzed and simulated in the literature, therefore this paper will try to fill the gap and point out the future research direction. Firstly, the visibility calculation method and establishment strategy of IIL are presented. Secondly, the calculation and optimization of system snapshots proposed by Zhou-Long is analyzed. Thirdly, simulation analysis regarding the number and duration of system snapshots, IIL switching time for LEO, the number of switching IIL in each system snapshot, the number of IILs that each MEO needs to establish are presented. Finally, the future research trends are discussed.

2   The Establishment Strategy of IIL

The architecture of LEO/MEO DLSN is shown in Fig. 1. LEO constellation generally needs a larger number of satellites to achieve global coverage due to its low orbit altitude while MEO constellation only need a dozen or more satellites to achieve global coverage due to its high altitude. Each LEO satellite generally establishes ISLs with two intra-orbit satellites and two inter-orbit satellites while each MEO establishes ISLs with MEO satellites according to the same strategy. Meanwhile, each LEO satellite will also choose an MEO satellite to establish IIL. Since the ISLs in LEO layer and in MEO layer can be fixed by choosing reasonable constellation configuration, the topology of LEO constellation and MEO constellation can be regarded as static. However, due to the relative orbiting of LEO and MEO satellites, the IILs are characterized by dynamic switching. Then, it can be concluded that the topological dynamics of LEO/MEO DLSN are mainly due to the dynamic change of the IIL.

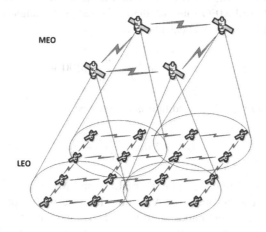

Fig. 1. Architecture of LEO/MEO DLSN

At present, the establishment strategy of IIL is generally based the longest coverage time strategy proposed in satellite grouping and routing protocol [1], that is, the LEO satellite will choose the MEO satellite with the longest predictable coverage time in all visible MEO satellites to establish IIL until the MEO satellite can no longer cover itself. Then, the LEO satellite will use the same longest coverage time strategy to select the next MEO satellite to establish IIL. Each time the IIL changes, one new snapshot will be generated.

Since LEO satellite and MEO satellite must be visible to each other to establish IIL between them, we first formulate the LEO-MEO visibility condition which is shown in Fig. 2 [1]. O is the earth center and A is an MEO satellite while B is the LEO satellite. A' is the crossing point of line OA and the sphere with the radius $(R + h_L)$ where R is the radius of the earth and h_L is the radius of LEO constellation.

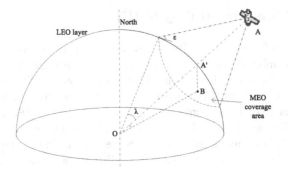

Fig. 2. Visibility condition between LEO and MEO satellite

Assume the radius of the MEO constellation is h_M and ε is the minimum elevation angle between LEO and MEO satellite, the half-sided center angle of the MEO coverage area on the LEO layer λ is calculated as:

$$\lambda = 90 - \varepsilon - \arcsin\left(\frac{R + h_L}{R + h_M} \sin(90 + \varepsilon)\right)$$

Then, LEO-MEO visibility condition is as follows:

$$\angle A'OB = 2\arcsin\frac{|A'B|/2}{R + h_L} \leq \lambda$$

According to the visibility conditions of LEO and MEO, the visible period of a LEO for all MEOs can be obtained. According to these visible periods, we can get MEO satellites that LEO will choose to establish IILs and the switching time of IILs. For all LEO satellites to perform the above operations, we will be able to get all IIL switching time of all LEO. All IIL switching time of all LEOs together constitute the division time of the system snapshot.

Since the satellite grouping and routing protocol does not take into account the optimization of the snapshot at first, the number of snapshots generated by the above method is large which makes the topology of DLSN highly dynamic. At the same time, the resulting snapshots have a short duration which makes a higher demand for the convergence speed of the satellite routing algorithm. In order to solve the above problems, Zhou-Long proposed a snapshot optimization method which can greatly reduce the number of snapshots while increasing the duration of the snapshots. The snapshot optimization method will be introduced in the following section.

3 Snapshot Optimization Method

Assume t_i is one division time of the system snapshots. At t_i one LEO satellite will switch ILL from one MEO satellite to another MEO satellite with longest predictable coverage time. Assume tip1 is another division time of the system snapshots. At t_{i+1} one LEO satellite L_i will no longer be visible to one MEO satellite M_i. Therefore, the ILL between L_i and M_i will be disconnected and L_i will select another MEO satellite M_{i+1} according to longest coverage time strategy. This situation is shown in Fig. 3 [11].

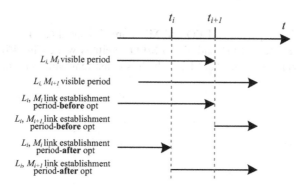

Fig. 3. Snapshot optimization method

Since L_i disconnects ILL with M_i and establishes a new ILL with M_{i+1} at t_{i+1}, a new division time t_{i+1} of the system snapshots is generated, resulting in a new snapshot. Because L_i is visible to both M_i and M_{i+1} at time t_i, Zhou-Long tried to advance the ILL switching time of L_i with M_i and M_{i+1} from t_{i+1} to t_i, thereby reducing a system snapshot.

As regarding to implementation of the snapshot optimization method, it is possible to traverse the division time of the system snapshots which are sorted by time, and for each division time t_i, search for division time t_{i+1} that can be merged with t_i. Whether t_i and t_{i+1} can be merged is based on two conditions: the first one is that the start time of the visible period of L_i and M_{i+1} is earlier than t_i; the second one is that the end time of the visible period of L_i and M_i is later than t_i (Since t_{i+1} is greater than t_i, therefore the second condition must be satisfied).

4 Simulation Analysis of IIL Topology

In this section, the IIL topology is analyzed by simulation. The simulation time is one solar day and the simulation step is 1 s. In the simulated LEO/MEO DLSN, LEO layer uses a Celestri constellation and MEO layer uses an ICO constellation [12]. The constellation parameters of LEO and MEO are shown in Table 1. Celestri constellation is an inclined walker constellation, so ISLs within LEO layer can be fixed.

Table 1. Constellation parameters of LEO/MEO DLSN

Constellation parameter	LEO	MEO
Inclination (°)	48	45
Altitude (km)	1400	10390
Number of planes	7	2
Number of satellites per plane	9	5
Inter-spacing of planes (°)	51.43	180
Inter-spacing of satellites in one planes (°)	40	72
Phase factor	5	0

Firstly, the visible period of LEO and MEO are simulated and Fig. 4(a) shows the visible periods between LEO1 and all 10 MEO satellites while Fig. 4(b) is the simulation result of STK (Systems Tool Kit) which is consistent with our simulation result.

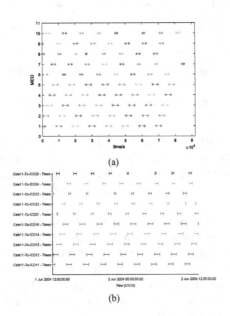

Fig. 4. Visible periods between LEO1 and all 10 MEO satellites. (a) Our simulation results; (b) STK simulation results.

For each LEO satellite, based on the longest predictable coverage time strategy to select an MEO satellite to establish ILL, we can obtain the ILL switching time of each LEO as shown in Fig. 5. Figure 5(a) is the ILL switching time of each LEO before snapshot optimization while Fig. 5(b) is the ILL switching time of each LEO after snapshot optimization. In Fig. 5 the horizontal coordinate is time while the vertical coordinate is LEO satellite.

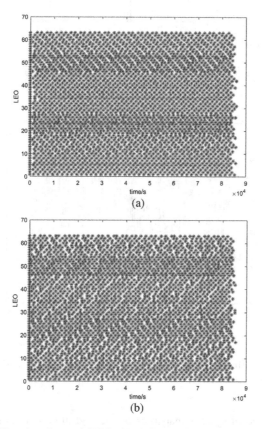

Fig. 5. ILL switching time for each LEO. (a) Before optimization; (b) After optimization.

Since the ILL switching time is plotted densely (one LEO has to switch ILLs 42 times at least while 52 times at most), it is difficult to find the ILL switching time improvement after snapshot optimization from Fig. 5. So the number of ILL switching

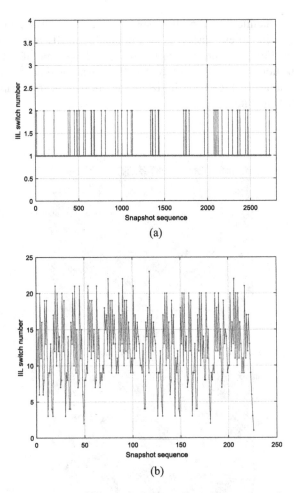

Fig. 6. The number of IIL switching at each division time of system snapshots before and after snapshot optimization. (a) Before optimization; (b) After optimization.

at each division time of system snapshots before and after snapshot optimization are collected and shown in Fig. 6. As we mentioned earlier, all IIL switching time of all LEOs together constitute the division time of the system snapshot. Therefore, Fig. 6 is the combination of IIL switching time of all LEO in Fig. 5. Before snapshot optimization, the number of IIL switching at each division time of system snapshots is only 1 or 2 or 3 at most. While after snapshot optimization, the number of IIL switching at each division time of system snapshots is 12 in average and 23 at most. In another word, the snapshot optimization makes many IILs that have been switched in difference times to switch at the same time, thereby reducing the number of system snapshots.

Figure 7 shows the distribution of the number of ILL switching at each division time before and after optimization. From Fig. 7(a) we can see that before snapshot optimization, the number of ILL switching at each division time is mostly 1. While after snapshot optimization, the number of ILL switching at each division time increases dramatically.

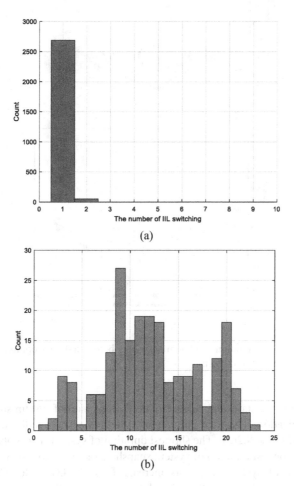

(a)

(b)

Fig. 7. The distribution of the number of ILL switching at each division time before and after optimization. (a) Before optimization; (b) After optimization.

The number and duration of system snapshots before and after optimization is shown in Fig. 8.

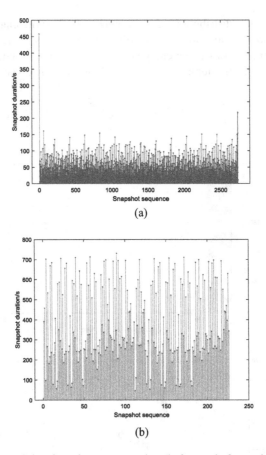

Fig. 8. The number and duration of system snapshots before and after optimization. (a) Before optimization; (b) After optimization.

Table 2 shows the statistical characteristics comparison of system snapshots before and after optimization. The total number of system snapshots reduced from 2737 to 226, i.e. reduced to the 8.26%. The shortest duration of system snapshots increase from 1 s to 46 s. The longest duration of system snapshots increase from 458 s to 731 s. The average duration of system snapshots increase from 31.4370 s to 378.6593 s. The reduction of the number of system snapshots can reduce the topology dynamics of DLSN while the increase of snapshot duration can make the routing algorithm have enough time in each snapshot to converge, which is of great importance to improve the data transmission performance of DLSN.

Table 2. Statistical characteristics comparison of system snapshots

Statistical characteristics	Before optimization	After optimization	Improvement
Total number	2737	226	Reduced to 8.26%
Shortest duration/s	1	46	46 times
Longest duration/s	458	731	1.6 times
Average duration/s	31.4370	378.6593	12 times

Figure 9 shows the distribution of system snapshot duration before and after optimization and it can be seen more clearly that the snapshot optimization has reduced the number of snapshots and increased the duration of snapshots.

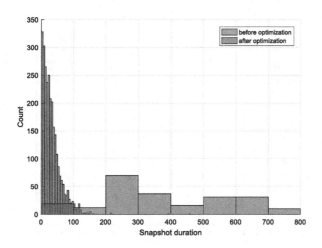

Fig. 9. The distribution of system snapshot duration before and after optimization.

For the optimized system snapshots, the number of ILL that MEO needs to establish is analyzed. Figure 10(a) shows the statistical properties of the number of ILL for all MEOs in each system snapshot while Fig. 10(b) shows the statistical properties of the number of ILL in all snapshots for each MEO. It can be seen that MEO needs to establish 10 ILLs at most and 2 ILLs at least. The average ILL that MEO has to establish is 7 (The statistical result is 6.3).

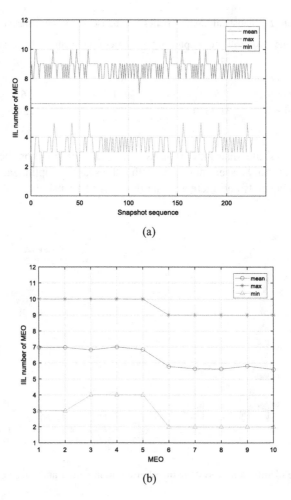

Fig. 10. The statistical properties of the number of IIL MEO need to establish. (a) The number of IIL for all MEOs in each snapshot; (b) The number of IIL in all snapshots for each MEO.

5   Discussion and Future Research Trends

When constructing a DLSN, each LEO satellite will generally be equipped with one IIL while the number of IILs that MEO satellites needs to be equipped should be the maximum number of IIL established by all MEO satellites. Therefore, the simulated DLSN should equip 10 IIL for MEO satellites. However, due to the reason that some MEO satellites only needs to establish 2 IILs at some time, so 8 IILs will be idle. From the point of view of efficient use of resources, this will result in wasted IIL resources. Ideally, all MEO satellites equipped with 7 IILs should be the optimum configuration. Therefore, future research emphasis should be put on how to reduce the maximum number of IILs that MEO satellites needs to establish or to conduct multi-beam antenna research to achieve multiple IILs with one antenna.

In addition, since MEO satellites should be equipped with 6–10 IILs to connect with LEO satellites as well as 4 ISLs to connect with other MEO satellites, how to equip so many antennas on one MEO satellite platform is also a problem that needs further study.

If an MEO satellite platform can only be equipped with limited IILs (e.g., less than the average 7), then there will be some LEO satellites that cannot establish IIL with MEO satellites. Therefore, how to assign IILs among all LEO satellites to achieve optimum network topology is also a research problem.

6 Conclusions

In this paper, the IIL topology of LEO/MEO DLSN is analyzed and simulated. Firstly, the visibility calculation method and establishment strategy of IIL between LEO and MEO satellite as well as the calculation and optimization of system snapshots is analyzed. Then, simulation analysis regarding the number and duration of system snapshots, IIL switching time for LEO, the number of switching IIL in each system snapshot, the number of IILs that each MEO needs to establish are presented. Finally, future research trends are discussed.

It should be pointed out that although this paper is for LEO/MEO DLSN, but the analyzed method is also applicable to GEO/MEO, GEO/LEO and other DLSN. At the same time, multi-layer satellite networks such as GEO/MEO/LEO also is applicable. Unlike double-layer satellite networks, multi-layer satellite networks needs to perform snapshot optimization in each DLSN (GEO/MEO and MEO/LEO), and combines the two DLSN optimized snapshots into whole system snapshots.

Acknowledgements. This work is supported by the National Science Foundation of China (No. 91438102).

References

1. Chen, C., Eylem, E., Ian, F.A.: Satellite grouping and routing protocol for LEO/MEO satellite IP networks. In: Proceedings of the 5th ACM International Workshop on Wireless Mobile Multimedia, pp. 109–116. ACM (2002)
2. Wang, L., Zhang, N., Wang, Y., et al.: Geometric characters of inter satellite links between MEO layer and LEO layer in MEO/LEO networks. Chin. Space Sci. Technol. **24**(1), 26–30 (2004)
3. Markus, W., Jochen, F., Frederic, W., et al.: Topological design, routing and capacity dimensioning for ISL networks in broadband LEO satellite systems. Int. J. Satell. Commun. Netw. **19**(6), 499–527 (2001)
4. Lu, Y., Zhao, Y., Sun, F., et al.: Routing techniques on satellite networks. J. Softw. **25**(5), 1085–1100 (2014)
5. Qi, X., Ma, J., Wu, D., et al.: A survey of routing techniques for satellite networks. J. Commun. Inf. Netw. **1**(4), 66–85 (2016)
6. Wang, J., Li, L., Zhou, M.: Topological dynamics characterization for LEO satellite networks. Comput. Netw. **51**(1), 43–53 (2007)

7. Wang, J., Yan, J., Cao, Z.: Optimization of sequent snapshots routing algorithm in LEO satellite networks. J. Astronaut. **30**(5), 2003–2007 (2009)
8. Wang, J., Xu, F., Sun, F.: Benchmarking of routing protocols for layered satellite networks. In: IMACS Multiconference on Computational Engineering in Systems Applications, pp. 1087–1094. IEEE (2006)
9. Wu, T., Wu, S.: Performance analysis of the inter-layer inter-satellite link establishment strategies in two-tier LEO/MEO satellite networks. J. Electron. Inf. Technol. **30**(1), 67–71 (2008)
10. Zhou, Y., Sun, F., Zhang, B.: A novel QoS routing protocol for LEO and MEO satellite networks. Int. J. Satell. Commun. Netw. **25**(6), 603–617 (2007)
11. Long, F., Xiong, N.X., Vasilakos, A.V., et al.: A sustainable heuristic QoS routing algorithm for pervasive multi-layered satellite wireless networks. Wireless Netw. **16**(6), 1657–1673 (2010)
12. Evans, J.V.: Satellite systems for personal communications. Proc. IEEE **86**(7), 1325–1341 (1998)

Optimal Strategy Routing in LEO Satellite Network Based on Cooperative Game Theory

Songjie Wei[1], Hao Cheng[1(⌧)], Meilin Liu[2], and Milin Ren[3]

[1] School of Computer Science and Engineering,
Nanjing University of Science and Technology,
200 Xiaolingwei, Nanjing 210094, China
{swei,115106000709}@njust.edu.cn
[2] Shanghai Institute of Satellite Engineering,
Shanghai Academy of Spaceflight Technology,
3666 Yuanjiang Rd, Shanghai 201109, China
meilinliu5l@outlook.com
[3] Beijing Engineering Research Center of NGI & Its Major Application
Technologies Co. Ltd., 1 East Zhongguancun Rd,
Beijing 100084, China
rmilin@163.com

Abstract. To overcome the network difficulty such as long propagation delay and traffic load imbalance when forwarding data packets through multiple hops in LEO satellite network, we propose an optimal strategy based routing algorithm for LEO satellite network using the cooperative game theory. With the idea of cooperation for mutual benefit, a LEO satellite node has the motivation of improving its own network performance gain by cooperation with neighbors to accomplish the multi-hop forwarding task of data packets. A satellite node compares the benefits of joining various routing coalitions, and tends to choose a more powerful next-hop coalition member node for data packet forwarding, which effectively distributes and balances the traffic load of the popular nodes. Such preference also improves the utilization of the satellite network resources, and reduces the average network delay of data packets. Our simulation results show that compared with the traditional satellite routing algorithms based on the shortest path, the average packet routing delay using the proposed algorithm is reduced by 18.5% and the traffic load balance of the network is increased by 65.6%. By replacing the shortest routing path with a path of satellite nodes with the expected optimal routing performance benefit, the proposed routing algorithm outperforms the existing algorithm on both the temporal and spatial network performance.

Keywords: Satellite network · Cooperative game theory
Optimal strategy routing

1 Introduction

With the rapid advance in satellite industry, satellite mobile communication is becoming more indispensable to humans' daily life. Compared with the traditional terrestrial mobile communication systems, a satellite mobile communication system is

© Springer Nature Singapore Pte Ltd. 2018
Q. Yu (Ed.): SINC 2017, CCIS 803, pp. 159–172, 2018.
https://doi.org/10.1007/978-981-10-7877-4_14

characterized by the fast deployment to cover a large area without a lot of ground-based supporting infrastructures. For communications in wild mountainous areas, offshore islands, disaster-stricken areas, cruising vessels and voyage aircraft, Satellite-based communication network has unique irreplaceable advantage [1]. Communication satellites can be classified into low-orbit LEO satellites, medium-orbit MEO satellites and geostationary orbit GEO satellites. GEO satellite is more suitable for broadcasting services and stationary users for high-rate data service. Although GEO satellites have been widely used in radio and television services, they are not suitable for real-time communication services due to the long propagation delay of hundred milliseconds. The distance between LEO satellites and ground users is comparably shorter, and the propagation delay of satellite-ground links is thus reduced to the order of milliseconds. A terrestrial mobile terminal only needs a smaller than dish antenna to setup a space-terrestrial link. LEO satellites is time and cost efficient in manufacturing, launching, and operating, which makes it a natural choice in many communication scenarios of service-oriented systems. In 1998, the first truly LEO-based satellite communication network Iridium is deployed with on-board switching and on-board processing capabilities. After that, the heat of academic study and industrial capital investment in LEO satellite networking grows for two decades.

Users of the LEO satellite network have desires real-time data communication with low packet delay, low packet loss ratio and optimal bandwidth utilization. The LEO satellites forms a multi-hop routing, self-organizing network with dynamic topology change by a series of inter-satellite links within the same orbit or between different orbits. However, compared with the random motion of nodes in the ground mobile ad hoc network, the motion of a LEO satellite node has a significantly periodic regularity. The dynamics of a satellite network topology predictable and schedulable. Such regularity can greatly improve the satellite network routing efficiency and resource utilization [2].

In the study of routing algorithms for LEO satellite networks, Werner et al. proposed a routing algorithm for satellite networks based on virtual topology for the first time. They carried out a great deal of in-depth research and discussion on this routing algorithm [3]. The main characteristic of this algorithm is to make full use of the periodic motion regularity of satellite nodes, converting the dynamic topology of LEO satellite network into a series of static topology on time, and conducting the calculation operation of all time slices routing tables in advance. The algorithm does not require too much computing capability onboard in satellite nodes. Ekici et al. designed a satellite network routing algorithm based on virtual nodes [4]. The basic idea is to divide the earth surface into regions and allocate a logical address for each region. The address of the LEO satellite node over each region area uses the same logical address. On this basis, each satellite node calculates its routing table according to the current logical address. Because a satellite node can infer the position of any satellite node in the whole network according to the logical address, it can avoid the link state information interaction among the nodes in the network. This idea shields the impact of satellite motion in the network. There are also a class of satellite network routing algorithms called satellite network dynamic routing algorithm. Its essence is based on the similarity between the satellite network and the ground mobile network. This kind of algorithm migrates the dynamic routing algorithm in the terrestrial network to the satellite network, which is an improvement and extension to the traditional terrestrial network routing algorithm. For example, the LAOR (Location-Assisted On-demand Routing Algorithm) proposed by Karapantazis is to apply the AODV routing algorithm in the mobile ad hoc network to the LEO satellite network [5].

On the basis of the above three categories of satellite routing strategies, other researchers put forward several novel satellite network improved routing protocols [6]. Aiming at the problem that the static route in the virtual topology routing algorithm cannot adapt to the dynamic network traffic, Song et al. proposed a traffic-light-based intelligent routing strategy (TLR) based on traffic signal mechanism [7]. The routing strategy firstly combines the predictability and periodic motion characteristics of the satellite network topology, and calculates multiple routing paths from the source satellite node to the destination satellite node in advance with the propagation delay as the routing cost. Then each satellite node periodically broadcasts its status information such as the queue occupancy rate to the neighbors, which is the traffic light information of the node. In the data packet relay forwarding process, the first routing path is adjusted locally according to the traffic signal information of the neighbor nodes, so as to bypass the congested satellite nodes and inter-satellite links as much as possible. This strategy uses the multi-path routing mechanism combined with static and dynamic planning to avoid and reduce network congestion, so as to balance the network traffic load. However, the application of the routing strategy has a prerequisite that the author believes in which the satellite node congestion can only happen in one or two inter-satellite links. With the progress of satellite network technology and the increasing degree of social informatization, the trend of the rapid increase of satellite network traffic makes this assumption not practical. Local optimization of routing path cannot achieve satisfactory results in the real satellite network. In the following simulation experiments, we compare this routing strategy with the optimal strategy routing algorithm based on cooperative game proposed in this paper, and the result analysis and discussion of these two strategies illustrates this limitation in local optimization.

In recent years, many researchers begin to apply the game theory in economics, especially the non-cooperative game theory to the network resource allocation problems such as bandwidth, power and channel. For example, Baig et al. applied the non-cooperative game theory to mobile ad hoc networks to establish a selfish node incentive mechanism, which makes the selfish nodes tend to participate in the relaying of data packets to get higher returns [8]. Paramasivan and Zheng et al. tried to solve the network security problem in mobile ad hoc networks by dynamic Bayesian signal game [9, 10]. Jiang et al. introduced the Stackelberg game into a hybrid multi-layer satellite network composed of GEO and LEO satellites to implement data packet routing, relay forwarding and network traffic load balancing [11].

In this paper, routing in a LEO satellite constellation network is taken as the problem study scenario, and an optimal strategy routing algorithm based on cooperative game is proposed. Cooperative game can make LEO satellite nodes have better cooperation initiative. According to the predictable topology of the LEO satellite constellation network, a number of routing paths between the source satellite node and the destination satellite node are constructed. The coalitional game is introduced into the data packet forwarding process of the LEO satellite node. The ground of LEO satellite relay nodes on the routing path are treated as an alliance, and the cooperative benefits of the routing alliance are defined by using the nodes' real-time status information and the performance of network routing path. The Shapley value of the coalitional game is used as the solution of the cooperative game and determines the individual benefits of LEO satellite relay node. In the process of forwarding data packets, the LEO satellite nodes independently calculate, compare the gains that can be obtained from each routing game alliance, and then determine the next hop of the data packet. In order to improve its own revenue, LEO satellite nodes tend to join more profitable routing alliances, and select the next hop member node of the alliance to forward the data packets. Therefore, it can bring better node traffic load balancing effect, shorten the network delay of data packets, and significantly improve the utilization rate of satellite resources.

The rest of this paper is organized as follows. Section 2 discusses the proposed coalition routing game. Section 3 presents NS-2 simulation results for the proposed approach and compares the results with those of TLR. Section 4 provides the conclusion and some discussion on future works.

2 Cooperative Gaming Routing Model

The periodic motion of LEO satellite nodes makes the LEO satellite network natural with multipath routing attributes. How to use the multipath routing in LEO satellite network to realize the efficient utilization of satellite resources, and the effective improvement of network performance has become an important subject of current research on satellite networking.

Game theory is a mathematical tool used to solve the cooperation and conflict between individuals. In this paper, we introduce the cooperative game theory to analyze the routing and forwarding of data packets in LEO satellite network, and to solve the typical problems such as unbalanced traffic load, network congestion and low resource utilization rate in LEO satellite network due to the uneven distribution of population on earth.

According to the three elements of game theory: player, strategy space and utility function, this paper defines the relay forwarding behavior of data packets in LEO satellite network as a cooperative game, and achieves the game revenue maximization, a reasonable allocation of resources, network performance optimization through the cooperation between nodes.

2.1 Coalitional Gaming Routing Model

In this paper, a coalitional game [12] is introduced in the data packet forwarding process of the LEO satellite node. A plurality of LEO satellite relay nodes from the source node to the destination node are treated as an alliance. As mentioned earlier, due to the natural multipath routing attributes of the LEO satellite network, a LEO satellite node usually has multiple associations as choices to join. In order to maximize its own benefit, a node tends to join the game alliance that can achieve the highest revenue. A satellite node chooses to join the optimal routing alliance based on the revenue that the node can achieve when joining the alliance, which is the revenue that the routing alliance allocates to the node based on the contribution of the node to the alliance, and the contribution of the satellite node to the routing alliance can be quantified by the Shapley value [13]. This paper uses the Shapley formula as the solution of the coalitional game, that is, the allocation scheme of the coalitional game utility, which can effectively guarantee the rationality and fairness of the cooperative revenue allocation.

In the above cooperative game model, the players of the game are defined as LEO satellite nodes, and the strategy space includes the next hop of the data packet forwarding, or the neighbor node of the current LEO satellite node. Next, we define the revenue of the alliance and the revenue of the node in detail. The alliance's revenue describes the gains that can be obtained by all nodes on a routing path. The revenue of a single node is closely related to the revenue of the alliance, and the higher the revenue of the alliance, the higher the revenue that the node receives from the alliance. In this paper, we use the data packet routing performance and the overall performance of the network to measure the revenue of the routing alliance, because our ultimate goal is to improve the forwarding efficiency of data packets and the overall performance of the network through the cooperative game between satellite nodes. Therefore, the revenue of the alliance is positively correlated with routing performance and network performance, and it is feasible and reasonable to measure the effect of cooperative game with observable routing performance and network performance parameters.

2.2 Routing Coalition Revenue Function Definition

The performance parameters of the LEO satellite node n described in this paper mainly include the current remaining available bandwidth of the node, namely the throughput attribute $throughput(n)$, the node queue delay attribute $queuedelay(n)$, the network packet loss rate attribute $packetloss(n)$, and the node buffer capacity attribute $bufferlength(n)$. These attributes are critical to network routing performance. For a routing path $P = (s, n_1, n_2, \ldots, d)$ from the source satellite node to the destination, its routing performance parameters are computed as follows:

$$throughput(P) = \min_{n \in p}\{throughput(n)\} \qquad (1)$$

$$delay(P) = \sum_{n \in P} queuedelay(n) \qquad (2)$$

$$packetloss(P) = 1 - \prod_{n \in P}(1 - packetloss(n)) \qquad (3)$$

$$bufferlength(P) = \min_{n \in P}\{bufferlength(n)\} \qquad (4)$$

Consider the grouping problem for satellite networks as a coalitional game. Every route from the source to the destination is treated as a coalition. The satellite nodes are the players and the game is concerned with whether a node should join a group or not. How the node may select the best group to join, we need a utility function which reflects the benefit for the node's joining a coalition. Here we use the quality of routing to measure the payoff for a participation node, because quality of routing is shared among every participation node. The payoff function of a path P can be expressed as follows:

$$f(P) = \alpha(throughput(P) - T_{min}) + \beta(D_{max} - delay(P))$$
$$+ \gamma(1 - packetloss(P)) + \lambda(bufferlength(P) - B_{min}) \tag{5}$$

where $throughput(P)$, $delay(P)$, $packetloss(P)$, and $bufferlength(P)$, respectively, denote throughout, delay, packet loss ratio, and buffer capacity for the path as defined in (1), (2), (3), and (4). T_{min}, D_{max} and B_{min} indicate the path's minimal tolerable throughput, maximal tolerable delays and minimal buffer size available, respectively. α, β, γ and λ are the weighting factors for normalizing these requirements. That is to say, the value of α, β, γ, λ itself is of no significance, and the ratio between them is meaningful. By adjusting the ratio between α, β, γ and λ, different routing QoS requirements can be achieved, and different network performance requirements can be improved to meet the needs of different data traffic for different service quality.

2.3   Routing Coalition Revenue Allocation Mechanism

The most important thing in the cooperative game is the allocation of the cooperative revenue, as it relates to whether the cooperative coalition can be maintained steadily. A reasonable, fair and equitable coalition revenue allocation scheme ensures that any one of the participants in the coalition is reluctant to leave the current coalition and join another coalition. Because even if the participant leaves the current coalition to join another coalition, it cannot get higher returns. Based on individual rationality, it has no incentive to leave the current coalition.

As a widely applicable concept, the Shapley value is a solution that assigns a single benefit allocation to benefit sharing games. We choose this solution to a cooperative game since the computational complexity is small and the Shapley value provides relatively anonymous solution by a random ordering of the nodes. It had been proved that the Shapley value is the unique value on the set of games satisfying anonymity, dummy, and additivity. The benefits of the nodes in the coalition are calculated as follows:

$$\varphi_i(f) = \sum_{S \subseteq A \setminus \{i\}} \frac{|S|!(n - 1 - |S|)!}{n!} (f(S \cup \{i\}) - f(S)) \tag{6}$$

In (6), $S \subseteq A \setminus \{i\}$ denotes all coalitions S of A not containing node , where A is a finite set of nodes. $\frac{|S|!(n-1-|S|)!}{n!}$ represents the probability that the participant joins the coalition S, and $|S|$ represents the number of participants in the coalition S. Therefore, $\varphi_i(f)$ indicates the benefit allocation in the benefit sharing game for node i in the coalition $S \cup \{i\}$. There are two coalitions in (6): one is S and the other is $S \cup \{i\}$, and they are all routing coalition. In coalition S, the routing probe cannot arrive at destination node, so the payoff of S is 0. Then the benefit allocation in the cooperative game for node i in the coalition $S \cup \{i\}$ can be written into:

$$\varphi_i(f) = \sum_{S \subseteq A \setminus \{i\}} \frac{|S|!(n - 1 - |S|)!}{n!} (f(S \cup \{i\})) \tag{7}$$

In (7), the benefit allocation in the benefit sharing game for node i decreases with the number of participation being increased and with coalition benefits being decreased. So as a rational node, in order to maximize the benefits, the node tends to join the coalition which has less participation number and more benefits.

2.4 Cooperative Gaming Routing Cost Problem

Although the topology of a satellite network is dynamic, its change is not random, but can be determined in advance according to the laws of the constellation movement. In order to make full use of the periodic motion law of LEO satellite constellation and to reduce the routing control overhead of cooperative game routing algorithm, this paper transforms the dynamic topology of LEO satellite network into static topologies in several time slices by referring to the virtual topology routing mechanism in satellite network. In a certain time slice, we firstly calculate multiple node-disjoint routing paths as the alternative routing coalitions in the cooperative game routing algorithm based on the Dijkstra shortest path algorithm, so as to avoid spending too much unnecessary control overhead to collect network topology information.

The above-mentioned satellite network topology is predictable, but the traffic distribution in the network is unpredictable. We want to construct an adaptive optimal revenue routing algorithm based on cooperative gaming to deal with the dynamic network traffic distribution. In order to collect this dynamic traffic change information and avoid the large additional routing overhead, this paper uses the data piggyback mechanism to collect the state information of satellite nodes and inter-satellite links. These network state information is encapsulated into the data packet traffic, which gradually spreads over the entire LEO satellite network with the relay forwarding of the data packets. Finally, a satellite node uses the collected network state information to calculate the revenue of each routing coalition, and forwards the data packets according to the routing path determined by the routing coalition with the best revenue.

In the network state awareness scheme used in this paper, each satellite node needs to be aware of the state of all its inter-satellite links, which are connected to the neighbor nodes of the satellite. By adding additional piggyback information such as throughput, queue delay, and packet loss ratio to the data packets, LEO satellite nodes can obtain these information in real time during the forwarding of data packets and estimate the traffic load status of other network nodes based on these information [14]. This paper focuses on the cooperative game routing modeling process rather than the network state awareness and its cost analysis. The detailed description of the network state awareness scheme and the analysis of the routing cost can be found in the above referred literature.

3 Experimental Evaluation

To evaluate the performance of the proposed cooperative gaming routing protocol for LEO satellites, we benchmark the new protocol with the two mostly referred and studied ones, the Dijkstra shortest path routing algorithm based on propagation delay and the intelligent multi-path routing strategy TLR based on the traffic light signal mechanism. The corresponding LEO satellite network routing protocols simulation program is implemented on the ns-2 (Network Simulation Version 2) platform. The LEO satellite constellation model uses a polar orbital constellation model of Iridium-like systems.

3.1 Constellation Model Construction

Figure 1 shows the structure of the Iridium-like constellation model experimented in this paper. The LEO satellite constellation model is designed with 6 orbital planes, each with 11 LEO satellites for a total of 66 LEO satellites with an orbital inclination of 86.4° and an orbit height of 780 km. Each LEO satellite has four inter-satellite links connected to the neighbor nodes. An ISL between neighbor satellites in the same plane (orbit) is an intra-plane link, while one connecting cross-plane (cross-orbit) satellites is an inter-plane link. The relative inter-satellite distance and angle is constant inside the same orbit, so that intra-plane ISLs can be built and maintained continuously. The relative distance, speed and angle of satellites are time varying between different orbits. In general, the relative angular velocity between satellites at both ends of the inter-satellite link is significantly increased in the bipolar region, and the satellite antenna cannot maintain satellite communications on different orbits at an ever-changing angular velocity. Therefore, in order to reflect the characteristics of LEO satellite network operation with high fidelity, when a LEO satellite runs to a high latitude area above 60°, it closes its inter-plane links. The cost of building and maintaining cross-seam links is very expensive. Previous research indicates that cross-seam links only have trivial impact on network performance when doing satellite networking and communication, so our experiments do not consider the cross-seam links as others [15].

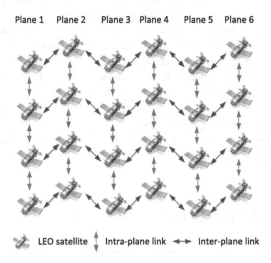

Fig. 1. Network topology with nodes and links in satellite constellation

3.2   Simulation Parameter Configuration

In the above LEO satellite constellation network model, the optimal revenue routing algorithm of cooperative game is simulated. With theoretical analysis and empirical evidence, we determine the ratio of weighting factors α, β, γ and λ as 4:3:2:1, for network traffic load balancing. Therefore, in the simulation experiment, the values of α, β, γ and λ are normalized and then set to 0.4, 0.3, 0.2 and 0.1 respectively. The simulation time for each experiment is 7200 s, which is about one satellite network running period. The data results are the mean of 100 simulation experiments. In order to more directly reflect the performance of the routing algorithm under different network load conditions, 200 data flows are established at the network application layer. The transmission time of each data flow is 15–25 s, and the distribution of data flows is in accordance with the Pareto distribution characteristics. That is, only a small number of satellite nodes transmit and receive data packets, and most of others are only responsible for relaying and forwarding data packets.

Note that this paper only considers inter-satellite routing, assuming that the terrestrial user node has sent the data packet to the source satellite node, and then the data packet is routed by the LEO satellite relay node to the destination satellite node. The main parameters of the LEO satellite network simulation are shown in Table 1.

Table 1. Network simulation parameter setting

Simulation parameters	Value
Packet type	CBR (Constant Bit Rate)
Packet size	512 Byte
Packet rate	1000, 2000, 3000, …, 10000
Link bandwidth	25 M
Queue length	50

3.3   Results and Discussion

In order to fully verify the performance of the cooperative game routing algorithm in the LEO satellite constellation network, especially its ability to balance the traffic load, respectively to measure the network performance of Dijkstra shortest path algorithm, TLR routing algorithm and the optimal revenue routing algorithm under different network loads. The network performance index measured in the experiment mainly includes the packet delivery ratio and the average end-to-end delay. The former reflects the reliability of the routing strategy, while the latter reflects the efficiency of the routing strategy. Finally, we compare the real-time node load variance of the three algorithms in the simulation process. This result is more intuitive to show the traffic load balancing ability of the optimal revenue routing algorithm. In this paper, the network load is divided into three states, including mild network load, moderate network load and heavy network load. The data packet sending rate of mild network load is less than 4000 per second, and the data packet sending rate of heavy network load is higher than that of 7000 per second. The data packet sending rate of moderate network load is between the two.

The packet delivery ratio of the three routing algorithms under different network loads is shown in Fig. 2. When the traffic load is light, the performance of the shortest path routing algorithm, the traffic light intelligent routing algorithm and cooperative game routing algorithm is quite similar with no significant gap. This is because at this point, whether the routing coalition with the best revenue in the cooperative game or the first routing path chosen by the traffic light routing policy is the routing path determined by the shortest path routing algorithm. When the network load is further aggravated, the packet delivery ratio of the three routing algorithms begins to decline. At this point, the input and output buffers of the LEO satellite nodes are gradually filled, and the excess data packets cannot get enough buffer space, or the waiting time in the queue is too long to be discarded.

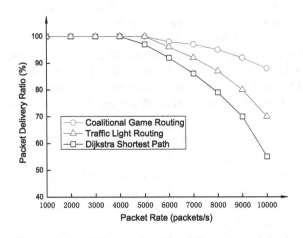

Fig. 2. Packet delivery ratio under different network loads

The shortest path routing algorithm simply uses the minimum hop counts as the routing basis, ignoring the real-time status information of the satellite nodes and the inter-satellite links, such as whether the satellite node is already in the congestion. Traffic light intelligent routing algorithm considers the real-time status of the neighbor nodes when selecting the next hop, and bypasses some congestion nodes by dynamically adjusting the local route, thus improving the packet delivery ratio to a certain extent. The cooperative game routing algorithm implements the maintenance of multiple routing alliances in real time. It evaluates the quality of the routing path by real-time calculation of the cooperative benefit of the coalition. It takes full advantage of the existing network resources to achieve load balancing of traffic, which greatly improves the packet forwarding rate and packet delivery ratio, and reduces the possibility of network congestion. Even if network congestion occurs, the cooperative game routing algorithm can also alleviate network congestion to some extent, especially to improve the performance of the network under heavy load conditions. Therefore, the average packet delivery ratio of cooperative game routing algorithm proposed in this paper is obviously higher than that of shortest path routing algorithm and traffic light intelligent routing algorithm.

Figure 3 shows the average end-to-end delay of the three routing algorithms under different network loads. The end-to-end delay in the LEO satellite network is the sum of the propagation delay of the data packet in the inter-satellite links and the queue processing delay of the data packet in the nodes. The shortest path routing algorithm is based on the number of hops in the routing, only considering the propagation delay of the data packets regardless of its queue processing delay. The traffic light intelligent routing algorithm dynamically selects the next hop relay node according to the real-time queue occupancy rate of each neighbor node, and avoids the over-congestion neighbor node as the next hop. When the network load is heavy, the algorithm can achieve the goal of reducing the overall end-to-end delay by reducing the queue processing delay of data traffic. The cooperative game routing algorithm takes into account the status information of each LEO satellite node and inter-satellite link in the routing coalition in the process of selecting the route. In particular, the algorithm not only considers the number of hops in the choice of routing path, but also takes into account the real-time data packet processing capability such as throughput, queue delay and packet loss ratio of LEO satellite nodes. Therefore, the routing established by cooperative game routing algorithm is more stable, and the algorithm can effectively reduce the end-to-end delay. Especially in the case of heavy network load, the satellite node compares the gains obtained from different cooperative game coalitions, and then selects the routing path determined by the coalition with the highest revenue to forward the data packets, which greatly reduces the waiting latency of the data packets in the queue.

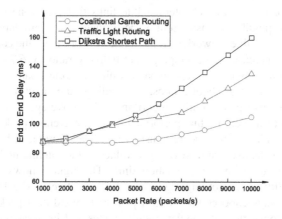

Fig. 3. End to end delay under different network loads

Figure 4 shows the average routing path length of data packets forwarded from a source satellite node to a destination satellite node under different network loads, which is consistent with the results shown in Figs. 2 and 3. With the increasing network load, the number of popular satellite nodes and inter-satellite links increases, and the performance of each routing path is damaged to varying degrees. The traffic light intelligent routing algorithm needs to dynamically adjust the local routing path in most LEO

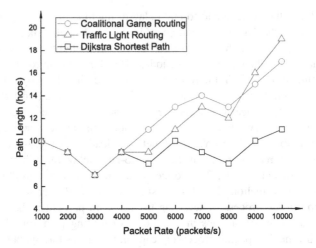

Fig. 4. Path length under different network loads

satellite relay nodes, which results in a significant increase in the average number of hops. The cooperative game routing algorithm proposed in this paper can select the current optimal routing path according to the real-time status of LEO satellite nodes and inter-satellite links in multiple routing alliances, thus improving the satellite network resource utilization and network throughput performance. The cost is also an increase in the number of inter-satellite routing hops, since the selected routing path must bypass some hot nodes and inter-satellite links that are prone to network congestion as much as possible to ensure routing performance. The simulation results show that when the LEO satellite network is in moderate network load, the cooperative game routing algorithm increases the average packet delivery ratio by 6.7% and decreases packet transmission delay by 21.2%, compared with the shortest path routing algorithm with an average increase of about 3 hops. Especially in the heavy network load conditions, the cooperative game routing algorithm with an average increase of about 5 hops to achieve an excellent routing performance that the average packet delivery ratio is increased by 23.7% and the packet transmission delay is reduced by 31.8%.

Figure 5 shows the average load variance values of the satellite nodes under heavy network load varying with the simulation time. The figure shows the traffic load balancing capability of the routing algorithm more intuitively. The Dijkstra shortest path algorithm always chooses the shortest path to forward data packets, which can easily cause the congestion of popular satellite nodes and inter-satellite links. Therefore, the load variance of satellite nodes is not only large but also dramatic. The traffic light intelligent routing algorithm can dynamically adjust the local routing path through the relay nodes to avoid aggravating the congestion of the hot nodes and inter-satellite links. The traffic light intelligent routing algorithm can dynamically adjust the local routing path through the relay nodes to avoid aggravating the congestion of the hot nodes and inter-satellite links. The load variance of satellite nodes is smaller and gentler than the shortest path routing algorithm by locally balancing the network traffic load. The cooperative game routing algorithm proposed in this paper dynamically adjusts the optimal routing path according to the cooperative revenue and balances the network traffic load from the global point of view. Therefore, the traffic load can be distributed evenly across the whole satellite network and the load variance of satellite nodes is the smallest and the most gentle in the three routing algorithms.

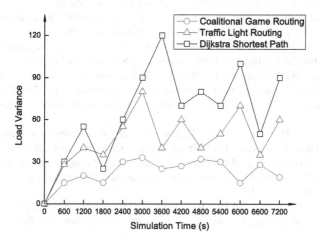

Fig. 5. Traffic distribution under heavy network load

4 Conclusion and Future Work

This paper presents an optimal revenue strategy routing algorithm for LEO satellite network based on cooperative game theory. The motivation of this algorithm design is to reduce the data transmission delay of LEO satellite network and to balance the traffic load of network nodes effectively. The algorithm is based on cooperative game theory to study the collaboration between LEO satellite nodes for data packet forwarding. LEO satellite nodes are more likely to cooperate with their best neighbor nodes to form an alliance, thereby increasing their own benefits. By comparing the benefits of joining the various coalitions, the node tends to select the lighter neighbor node as the next hop for data packet forwarding, which can effectively balance the nodes' traffic load. It can be seen from the experimental results that the cooperative game routing algorithm has significant effectiveness on reducing the transmission delay and balancing the network traffic load.

Acknowledgments. This material is based upon work supported by the CASC Innovation Fund (F2016020013), the CERNET Next-Generation Internet Innovation Project (NGII20160601), and Innovation Projects of Beijing Engineering Research Center of Next Generation Internet and Applications. Opinions and conclusions expressed in this material are those of the authors and do not necessarily reflect the views of the sponsors.

References

1. Wu, W.W., Miller, E.F., Pritchard, W.L., et al.: Mobile satellite communications. Proc. IEEE **82**(9), 1431–1448 (1994)
2. Li, C., Liu, C., Jiang, Z., et al.: A novel routing strategy based on fuzzy theory for NGEO satellite networks. In: IEEE Vehicular Technology Conference, pp. 1–5 (2015)
3. Werner, M.: A dynamic routing concept for ATM-based satellite personal communication networks. IEEE J. Sel. Areas Commun. **15**(8), 1636–1648 (1997)
4. Ekici, E., Akyildiz, I., et al.: A distributed routing algorithm for datagram traffic in LEO satellite networks. IEEE/ACM Trans. Networking **9**(2), 137–147 (2001)
5. Karapantazis, S., Papapetrou, E., Pavlidou, F.N.: On-demand routing in LEO satellite systems. In: IEEE International Conference on Communications, pp. 26–31 (2007)
6. Lu, Y., Zhao, Y., Sun, F., et al.: Satellite network routing technology. J. Software **5**, 1085–1100 (2014)
7. Song, G., Chao, M., Yang, B., et al.: TLR: a traffic-light-based intelligent routing strategy for NGEO satellite IP networks. IEEE Trans. Wireless Commun. **13**(6), 3380–3393 (2014)
8. Baig, O., Ai-Harthi, Y.S., Al-Tubaishi, E.: Game-theoretic algorithm stimulating cooperation in multi-hop wireless networks. In: International Conference on Game Theory for Networks, pp. 1–5. IEEE (2015)
9. Paramasivan, B., Prakash, M.J.V., Kaliappan, M.: Development of a secure routing protocol using game theory model in mobile ad hoc networks. J. Commun. Netw. **17**(1), 75–83 (2015)
10. Zheng, D., Tang, H., Yu, F.R.: A game theoretic approach for security and quality of service (QoS) co-design in MANETs with cooperative communications. In: IEEE Military Communications Conference, pp. 1–6 (2013)
11. Jiang, L., Cui, G., Liu, S., et al.: Cooperative relay assisted load balancing scheme based on Stackelberg game for hybrid GEO-LEO satellite network. In: IEEE International Conference on Wireless Communications & Signal Processing, pp. 1–5 (2015)
12. Saad, W., Han, Z., Debbah, M., et al.: Coalitional game theory for communication networks. IEEE Signal Process. Mag. **26**(5), 77–97 (2009)
13. Shapley, L.S.: A value for N-person games. In: Roth, A.E. (ed.) The Shapley Value, pp. 31–40. University of Cambridge Press, Cambridge (1988)
14. Cheng, H., Liu, M., Wei, S., Zhou, B.: A distributed algorithm for self-adaptive routing in LEO satellite network. In: Yu, Q. (ed.) SINC 2016. CCIS, vol. 688, pp. 274–286. Springer, Singapore (2017). https://doi.org/10.1007/978-981-10-4403-8_24
15. Gavish, B., Kalvenes, J.: The impact of intersatellite communication links on LEOS performance. Telecommun. Syst. **8**(2), 159–190 (1997)

NSOPNet: Dynamic Mode of Near Space Pseudolite Network

Weiyi Chen[✉], Pingke Deng, Xiaoguang Zhang, Yi Qu,
Yinkui Gong, and Hongxia Wang

Academy of Opto-Electronics, Chinese Academy of Sciences, Beijing, China
1242520290@qq.com

Abstract. Near space aerostat has the advantages of all-weather, high maneuverability, easy arrangement, In extreme cases where unexpected events and satellites are unavailable, aerostat platform has become a fast and effective means to provide various communication services. A plurality of aerostat components into a network. Constructing a wide coverage near space network is a key link in the integration of space and ground. Due to the impact of high-altitude air and other environmental factors. The aerostat platform strong mobility and track control difficult. That aerostat is facing network topology changes quickly, routing design complex Based on this, this paper creatively puts forward non connection oriented dynamic opportunity routing in aerostat network-NSOPNet. With the moving of aerostat, In the light of sight, communication is realized by means of store and forward. At the same time, this paper designed routing algorithm- OP-NSR. It requires each aerostat platform maintains a message queue. When the two aerostat can communicate in the light of sight, exchanging messages that are not stored by the other aerostats, Iterate until the source messages are delivered to the destination. The simulation experiment with multi nodes of aerostat. Through the simulation of OP-NSR routing algorithm show that the method can effectively solve the aerostat networking and routing problem in near space.

Keywords: Aerostat · NSOPNet · OP-NSR

1 Introduction

At present, the ground network has been developed for nearly twenty years. Although the coverage of the network is comprehensive, communication services are faced with many challenges. [1] Some remote areas not fully cover the network, Communication services are not provided. Subject to the national territory limits, the ground network cannot be extended to land overseas, ships on the high seas cannot use the ground network for information services. In the event of natural disasters such as earthquakes and typhoons, ground communications facilities have been damaged; in the case of satellite unavailability, the breakdown of communications and navigation services will result in significant economic losses; [2] The near space vehicle because has the characteristics all-weather, long-time, high mobility, easy arrangement [3], Not only can provide long-term service information in remote mountainous areas, but also to

© Springer Nature Singapore Pte Ltd. 2018
Q. Yu (Ed.): SINC 2017, CCIS 803, pp. 173–183, 2018.
https://doi.org/10.1007/978-981-10-7877-4_15

provide information service for the public emergency. as an alternate mode, it can be fully deployed in a short time and take on most of the emergency tasks when in the satellite unavailable state. It costs low and easy to implement. [4] Aerostat is the tethered balloons and the airships as a platform for a lighter than air aircraft equipment. Including the capsule (used for filling gas lift), fairing, tail, nose, equipment rack, power supply system, pressure regulation system etc. The basic structure is shown in Fig. 1, Aerostat has the following advantages. (1) can all-weather work, long, strong endurance, suitable for the provision of emergency communication guarantee for public emergency. (2) High mobility, easy to control, can be arranged in remote areas and mountainous areas. (3) carrying capacity is big, survival ability is strong, can flexibly carry all kinds of communication resources, payload, providing diversified information services [5–7].

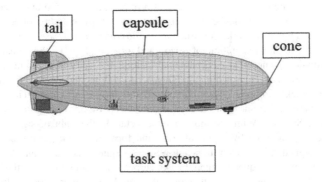

Fig. 1. Basic structure of airship

2   Related Work

2.1   Aerostat Communication

As In 2001, SKY Site company of the United States launched the space data platform, using wireless communication equipment installation of stratospheric aerostats on expanding the coverage of cellular network [9]. In 2009, scholars in Japan put forward the idea of using the ball borne wireless mesh network system for emergency network communication after disasters. The balloon floats at the height of 40–100 m and connects to the ground mobile nodes through the IEEE802.11b/g protocol to access the Internet [10]. At present, the more successful the aerostat application case is Google Project Loon. It is a network operating in the stratosphere. Designed to connect rural and remote areas to fill gaps in network coverage. Google also cited the use of balloons to provide communications services after natural disasters. After a natural disaster like Hurricane Sandy, communications infrastructure in the affected areas will be damaged and will take a long time to recover, while the Loon balloon will become a very useful alternate communication facility. Google balloons can be provided to wireless networks in corresponding areas, with speeds of about 10 Mbps. There are two communication links in the network: (1) the communication network between balloons;

(2) the balloon to the ground station network. ISM band 2.4G/5.8 GHZ [11] is currently in use. Users send signals to their nearest balloon at ISM band via a special antenna, final signal is transmitted to a balloon which connected to the ground network. As the balloon moves, the wireless mesh network will continue to adjust. The signal jumps between the balloons, thereby forming a network of at least 5 balloon nodes. Each balloon can be connected to a balloon within 48 km by radio receivers. Another radio transceiver guarantees that balloons can communicate with hundreds of antennas within 40 km in diameter on the ground. Theoretically, thousands of balloons can cover the whole world, [12–14].

2.2 Aerostat Network

In 2009, a research team at Iwate University in Prefectural, Japan, made a further attempt to form an air balloon network of Mesh mesh to provide a temporary emergency network for earthquake disaster [15]. The network structure of this vision is composed of balloons with wireless devices in the air, which form a network of autonomous networks. These balloons configure themselves by detecting the power density of electromagnetic fields, and they always choose the closest power density balloon to build connections. Once a balloon is blown or damaged by the wind, it is automatically connected with the new adjacent balloon, which ensures the stability of the Mesh network.

Google balloon is really using the air Mesh networking, divided into two parts: the balloon between the Mesh network, balloon and ground stations constitute user network [16], as shown in Fig. 2. Project Loon uses a frequency range of ISM unlicensed bands. The network structure is divided into two parts: horizontal Mesh network and vertical network. The Mesh network adopts IEEE 802.11j protocol, and the vertical network adopts IEEE 802.11b and G protocol. The specific parameters are shown in Table 1.

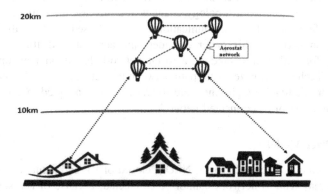

Fig. 2. Google aerostat mesh network

Wireless Mesh network is a good idea, but it is inconvenient to set up and maintain in some remote mountainous areas. In 2012, Simon Morgenthaler, of the University of

Table 1. Google balloon parameter configuration

	Mesh network	Vertical network
Standard	IEEE802.11j	IEEE802.11b,g
Frequency	2.4 GHz	4.9 GHz
Signal power	250 mW	10 mW
Trans speed	54 Mps	54 Mps
Max distance	600 m	100 m
Antenna	Octagonal plains	Co-linear

Bern in Switzerland, proposed a more advanced concept of using UAVs to build Mesh networks, which they call UAVNet. The principle is that the UAV uses the IEEE 802.11s standard to form an air Mesh network [17, 18]. The main contribution of the UAVNet concept is that they propose a networking algorithm for air Mesh networks. Probably the principle is that a drone from a first ground node starting off, and detection from another ground node, then their nearest, the drone to fly to the middle point of the two ground node, node to ground the starting point as the reference point to the direction of moving slowly, until it receives a signal from the starting point of the intensity of the ground node reaches a predefined threshold. Then, another UAV began to lift off, similar to the principle of movement, but the former UAV as a new reference point.

3 Networking System Model

Construction of near space vehicle network is facing many challenges. People cannot accurately control the aerostat move and stay. In many cases, the aerostat between light of sight, unable to realize data exchange, cannot realize the communication each other. The whole state of aerostat intermittent network. With aerostat drift, real-time change of network topology, network topology changes and increase the difficulty of routing, which will affect the entire communication process. Based on this, different from Google's Mesh network, this paper considers the aerostat is drifting continuously moving, put forward a new kind of aerostat network based on new opportunities routing [19]. Technical features is no path between the aerostat. With the movement of the aerostat. In the light of sight, the store-forward mode is adopted to communication under the condition of disconnected network.

3.1 NSOPNet Model

Aerostat movement, layout of sparse, NLOS, closed of RF and signal attenuation etc. Many times may lead to network cannot be connected. because of aerostats moving, that leads to routing problem, In this paper we use the opportunity routing to architecture a aerostat network, The essence of the network is a multi-hop temporary autonomous system. No fixed routers, Nodes in a network can move freely and communicate with each other in any way. Each node in the network does not need to be connected directly. Instead, it is possible to communicate between two NLOS nodes in a relay manner. Traditional wireless networks need to pre-establish routing between communication endpoints before transmitting user data. This work model implies an important assumption that most of the time the network is connected, and that there is at least one complete end-to-end communication path between any node pair. NSOPNet is constructed based on the move characteristics of aerostat. When the two aerostat into mutual communication range, data exchange. The topology of NSOPNet defined as $G(V,E)$, $G(V,E) \propto G(V, E'_{random})$. If the aerostat Vi to Vj in the in LOS, then $(V_i, V_j) \in E'_{random}, V_i \in \{V | 1 \leq i \leq m\}$. m said the number of aerostat.

communicate_field

When part of aerostat is within the scope of communication, The definition of aerostat to form a communication domain field. The topology of the communicate_field is represented as $G'(V', E')$, then $V' \subset V$, is established randomly. The communication field must be able to communication between the two aerostat, Every time the data exchange is realized in Aerostat communication field.

The communication process of the NSOPNet is described as shown in Fig. 3. NSOPNet routing mode is "store-carry-forward", it realizes the communication between the aerostat. When a link to the target domain is present, the message is forwarded, otherwise, the message is stored in the local persistent memory and then waiting for the available link.

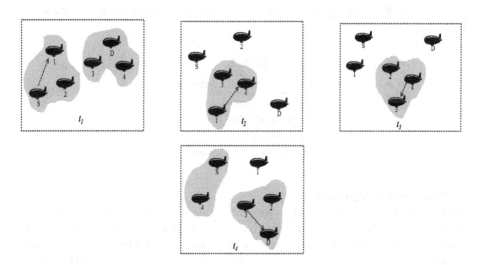

Fig. 3. Communication process of the NSOPNet

3.2   The Design of Aerostat Device Communication

Aerostat network mainly uses shortwave radio communications, The radio communication distance is limited by radio sight distance and link circuit. In the case of smooth link circuit, the radio distance becomes the key factor of communication. The function distance of wireless communication is closely related to the distance of sight. The radio sight distance refers to the maximum distance between the objects to keep barrier free communication monitoring. Relating to many factors such as atmospheric reflection, climate and topography [20].

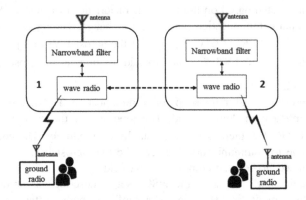

Fig. 4. Composition of aerostat shortwave communication link

As shown in Fig. 4, the composition of aerostat shortwave radio communication link, we must guarantee the surface shortwave radio and aerostat on shortwave radio parameters in the working process are equal. The list of basic devices is shown in Table 2.

Table 2.

Device	Number
Shortwave antenna	2
Narrowband filter	1
Shortwave radio	1
Ground station	Many

OP-NSR routing algorithm

OP-NSR works as a "store - carry - forward" mode. When a destination node is not present in the routing table, the message is cached at the current node. And wait for the appropriate forwarding opportunity as the current node moves. For each message, it is the key to design the efficient routing protocol to determine the best next hop forwarding node and select the appropriate forwarding time. The NLOS_Table format is shown in Table 3.

Table 3. Format of NLOS_Table

Vax	Count1	Count2	...	Countn
Times	2	3	...	1

(1) For each aerostat to maintain a record the times that non line of sight in NLO-S_Table. Definition: County is a variable in NLOS_Table, County said the time that the disconnected between this aerostat and aerostat (i). Let n be the number of aerostat in the network, n-1 is the number of variables for NLOS_Table. Definition: once the aerostat disconnect that is not in the distance of a radio line of sight.

(2) OP-NSR algorithm is divided into two stages, (1) message replication, transmission, (2) find the destination node, direct transmission

In the message replication phase:
The algorithm is described as follows:

(1) aerostat forwarding node selection: (1) according to the description, in each copy of the aerostat distribution, according to the aerostat alternative in the visible range, check the NLOS_Table, select the smallest value represents the least number of disconnected from the candidate County, send a copy of the half forward to corresponding aerostat the.

(2) replication method forwarding information: the sender will have a copy of the message to m, distributed to m aerostat. Select the appropriate aerostat will distribute a copy of m/2 to it, then all have a copy of the aerostat will distribute copies of own amount of 1/2 to the aerostat new proper, before the aerostat and no message copies of the same. This cycle of operation, until all the aerostats are only one copy, said out. The distribution process can be seen as a construction of a two fork tree, as shown in the following Fig. 5, using two trees to represent the process of copying messages. In this process, there is a certain probability of passing the source information to the destination node. If successful, the algorithm is finished, otherwise, the second step is performed.

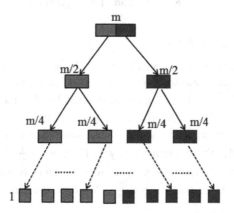

Fig. 5. Data replication distribution process

Find the destination node direct transmission stage:

In the same information m floating device active node, according to the random strategy, an arbitrary source information carrying aerostat can send signals to the target node. If the destination node is not found, communication fails and retransmission is requested.

The flow chart of the algorithm as shown in Fig. 6.

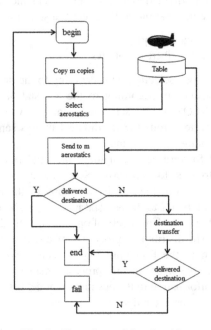

Fig. 6. Flow chart of the algorithm

3.3 Algorithm Delay Analysis

The process as a structure of two binary tree, aerostat to send a message is the root node, a copy of the final m message aerostats is a leaf node, the total number of nodes on this tree is $2^{(\log m + 1)} - 1$. The tree constructed by this method has the fewest number of layers. In a $\sqrt{N} \times \sqrt{N}$ grid, The number of the aerostat is X, the range of move was K, the average delay of the direct transmission is $ED_{dt} = 0.5(0.34 \log N - \frac{2^{k+1} - K - 2}{2^k - 1})$, Ideally, the minimum delay is $ED_{opt} = \frac{H_x - 1}{(X-1)} ED_{dt}$, Where H_x is the harmonic series of the N term of X, The average delay of OP-NSR algorithm is $ED_{op-NSR} \le (H_{x-1} - H_{x-m})ED_{dt} + \frac{X-m}{X-1}\frac{ED_{dt}}{m}$, At $m < x$, the equal sign is established.

Simulation experiment results

Performance evaluation criteria

The transmission delay and transmission success rate are chosen to evaluate the performance of the system.

(1) transmission delay

The data packet is transmitted from the aerostat node to the target node time required for aerostat. The average transmission delay is usually used to measure the transmission delay, which proves that the network performance is better, the routing algorithm has strong transmission capacity, high efficiency and less network resources.

(2) transmission success rate

The ratio of the number of packets sent from the sender to the destination and the total number of transmissions in a given time range. It is an important index to evaluate the packet loss rate of routing algorithms.

The experimental configuration design parameters are shown in Tables 4, 5 and 6 for the operating parameters of the aerostat set in Table 5 for the data set. The random motion mode of aerostat freedom movement (RWP).

Table 4. Operating parameters of the aerostat

	Parameter	Value
Aerostat operation set	Flight area/km	200*200
	Running time/h	12
	Mobility model	RWP
	Aerostat speed/(m/s)	[5, 10]

Table 5. Data set

	Parameter	Value
Communication parameter set	Packet size/KB	[1000,1500]
	Cache size/MB	10
	Transmission rate/(kbit/s)	500
	Transmission range/km	48
	Transmission mode	Broadcast

In accordance with the aerostat network scale is divided into 10, 20, 40, 80 simulation experiments, the corresponding forwarding copy number of 4, 16, 32, 64, as shown in Table 6.

Table 6. Experimental grouping

Aerostst size	10	20	40	80
Copy number	4	16	32	64

The results shown in Fig. 7, that by 6, by 10, in the transmission of aerostat network experiment success rate is about 80%, with the expansion of the scale of aerostat, transmission success rate increase, when the aerostat reaches 80, the success rate is about 90%.

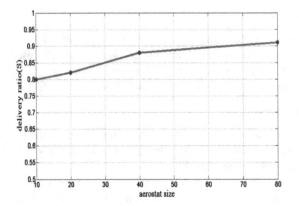

Fig. 7. Transmission success rate

The Fig. 8 shows that when the number of aerostat is 10, the average transmission delay of network maximum is about 0.3 s, when the number of aerostat is 80, the network delay is about 0.05 s.

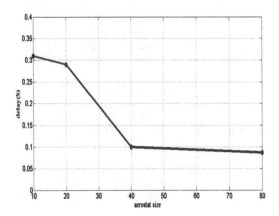

Fig. 8. Average delay of network transmission

It is necessary to point out that the experiment is based on the random motion of the aerostat model, the actual situation is the aerostat in track movement control words, the experiment would be better, because it is a random experiment, the experimental results did not achieve the optimal effect.

4 Conclusion

This paper presents a opportunistic routing method based on near space vehicle network, presents a NSOPNet opportunity network architecture, this architecture is designed on OP-NSR routing algorithm, and analyzed the performance of the algorithm from two aspects of transmission success rate and the average delay, verify the availability and efficiency the higher the method, provides a new research method for aerostat network communication. At the same time in the operation mode of aerostats, considering the flight status is not deep enough, great impact on all kinds of complicated weather conditions, network communication, research in the following work should focus on.

References

1. Song, Q., Jamalipour, A.: A network selection mechanism for next generation networks. In: IEEE International Conference on Communications, vol. 2, pp. 1418–1422. IEEE (2005)
2. Lee, C.S., Knight, D.: Realization of the next-generation network. IEEE Commun. Mag. **43** (10), 34–41 (2005)
3. Yao, W.U., Yao, W., Wang, C., et al.: Thermal characteristics analysis of a near-space aerostat driven by the natural energy. J. Astronaut. **36**, 784–790 (2015)
4. He, L., Wei, P.: Using aerostat to increase ability of detecting and warning in near space. Aerosp. Electron. Warf. **2**, 010 (2009)
5. Lambert, C., Nahon, M.: Stability analysis of a tethered aerostat. J. Aircr. **40**(4), 705–715 (2012)
6. Delaurier, J.D.: A stability analysis for tethered aerodynamically shaped balloons. J. Aircr. **9** (9), 646–651 (1972)
7. SoPTAS: Solar powered tethered aerostat system (2014)
8. Longo, M.R., Lourenco, S.F.: On the nature of near space: effects of tool use and the transition to far space. Neuropsychologia **44**(6), 977–981 (2006)
9. eWeek: Google's Balloon-Powered Internet Ready for Carrier Testing. Eweek (2016)
10. Google's balloon-powered internet for all' is almost ready: multibriefs.com
11. Google to bring balloon-powered Internet to Indonesia's 17,000 islands: uscpublicdi plomacy.org
12. Google's internet balloons can stay aloft for 100 days: multibriefs.com
13. Project Loon: Google's Internet Balloons to Fly over Sri Lanka: questia.com
14. Google Courts the Stratosphere with "Loon" Technology: directionsmag.com
15. Engel, M.: Google's project loon hovers over the satellite industry. Via Satell. (2013)
16. Alleven, M.: Carnival eyes Google's project loon, other emerging technologies for hybrid system at sea, port. Fierce Wirel. Tech. (2014)
17. Morgenthaler, S., Braun, T., Zhao, Z., et al.: UAVNet: a mobile wireless mesh network using unmanned aerial vehicles. In: GLOBECOM Workshops, pp. 1603–1608. IEEE (2012)
18. Javaid, A., Sun, W., Alam, M.: UAVNet simulation in UAVsim: a performance evaluation and enhancement. In: International Conference on Testbeds and Research Infrastructures, pp. 107–115. Springer International Publishing, Cham (2014)
19. Biswas, S., Morris, R.: Opportunistic routing in multi-hop wireless networks. ACM (2005)
20. AIAA: Design and Fabrication of an Aerostat for Wireless Communication in Remote Areas, pp. 654–655 (2007)

Interference-and-Voyage Based Cell Zooming for Maritime Wideband Network

Chuan'ao Jiang[1], Ailing Xiao[1,2], and Liuguo Yin[1(✉)]

[1] Tsinghua National Laboratory for Information Science and Technology,
Beijing 100084, China
yinlg@mail.tsinghua.edu.cn
[2] Department of Electronic Engineering, Tsinghua University,
Beijing 100084, China

Abstract. The remarkable growth of the marine economy has made the maritime wideband communication a research focus. This article presents a multiple backhauls based maritime wideband communication (MBC) architecture to provide the wideband access to the ocean vessels. In MBC architecture, the ships equipped with shipborne LTE base stations (BSs) could autonomously choose the maritime satellites or the onshore high-tower BSs as the backhaul nodes. The other ships carrying the shipborne customer premise equipment (CPE) can access the Internet through the shipborne BSs. Furthermore, an interference-and-voyage based cell zooming strategy is proposed to coordinate the inter-cell interference in the MBC architecture. The proposed strategy adjusts the BS cell size based on the BS inter-ference level and ship voyage. Simulation results using the real ship data show that under the MBC architecture, the proposed cell zooming strategy can effectively coordinate the inter-cell interference and increase the throughput of the maritime wideband network.

Keywords: Maritime wideband communication · Shipborne base station
Cell zooming · Inter-cell interference coordination

1 Introduction

With the remarkable growth of the maritime industry and global shipment, the marine economy has become the new growth point of the world economics and generates extensive marine activities, which results in an increasing demand for the low-cost and wideband maritime communication. Nevertheless, the current maritime communication methods, such as the conventional HF/VHF/UHF [1] and maritime satellite systems significantly lag behind the terrestrial wireless communication methods. To mitigate this gap, many wideband maritime communication systems are developing.

Recently, some novel maritime communication systems is proposed to fulfill the communication need of the marine activities, such as WIreless-broadband-access for SEaPORT (WISEPORT) network and TRITON [2]. WISEPORT is based on the cellular network and provides the wideband access within 15 km from ports, which is too short for the ocean vessels. TRITON system is an application of the mesh

© Springer Nature Singapore Pte Ltd. 2018
Q. Yu (Ed.): SINC 2017, CCIS 803, pp. 184–196, 2018.
https://doi.org/10.1007/978-981-10-7877-4_16

technique. However, it provides a broad wideband coverage at the expense of complicated routing protocols and low service reliability.

In this paper, we provide a novel multiple backhauls based maritime wideband communication (MBC) architecture to enable a low-cost and wideband network at sea. In the MBC architecture, the shipborne BSs with omnidirectional antennas are deployed on specific kinds of ships, and the user ships can get wideband access through these shipborne BSs. We assume that high-tower BSs equipped with phased array antennas regularly deployed onshore, which perform as the backhaul nodes of the shipborne BSs. Besides, maritime satellites provide the shipborne BSs with another backhaul choice. The shipborne BSs can autonomously choose the maritime satellites or the high-tower BSs as the backhaul nodes.

However, in the MBC architecture, due to the mobility of the shipborne BSs, the static radio network planning (RNP) is disabled compared to the terrestrial communication network [3]. The coverage area of the adjacent shipborne BSs may be widely overlapped when two BS ships navigate closely, which means that the ships in the overlapped area are faced with a serious inter-cell interference problem. Therefore, shrinking the overlapped area is an effective way to coordinate the inter-cell interference. The cell zooming technique can dynamically adjust the cell size, which is a method to shrink the overlapped interference area. The author in [4] presents the cell zooming technique to improve the performance of wireless network and proves that the cell zooming can reduce the power consumption when working with the cell sleeping strategy. In the literature [5], a quality of service (QoS) aware cell zooming strategy is proposed to improve the QoS in the regular cellular network, which can improve the energy efficiency without deteriorating the QoS of the users.

However, these cell zooming strategies do not consider the interference coordination as the first target, and they are essentially implemented in the static and regular net-work, where the interference may be mitigated in the RNP stage. They can hardly solve the interference problem if applied in the highly dynamic MBC environment, which motivates us to study the nexus between the cell zooming strategy and the inter-cell interference. In this paper, we propose an interference-and-voyage based cell zooming (IVB-CZ) strategy to coordinate the inter-cell interference in the MBC architecture. The proposed strategy adjusts the size of each cell in terms of the interference level and ship voyage. The simulation results using the real ship data show that the proposed IVB-CZ algorithm can effectively coordinate the inter-cell interference, increase the throughput and reduce the times of user ship handover as well.

Our contributions are as follows: (1) a novel maritime wideband communication architecture is presented to enable the low-cost wideband access at sea; (2) an inter-ference-and-voyage based cell zooming strategy is proposed to coordinate the inter-cell interference. The rest of this paper is organized as follows. Section 2 describes the MBC architecture and the system model. Section 3 describes the IVB-CZ strategy. Performance analyses are discussed in Sect. 4. In Sect. 5, we give the conclusion of this paper.

2   System Model

2.1   The MBC Architecture

The MBC architecture provides a highly dynamic maritime communication network, where both the shipborne BSs and the user ships are mobile. In MBC architecture, we classify the ships into two types: the BS ships and the user ships. The ships deployed with the LTE base stations are the BS ships, and the other ships, which are equipped with shipborne CPE, are the user ships. The BS ships can access the Evolved Packet Core (EPC) through multiple backhauls. As Fig. 1 shows, we assume that there are high-tower BSs regularly deployed along the shoreline. The high-tower BSs are a special kind of BSs equipped with the phased array antennas to dynamically provide backhaul signals for the BS ships in hot spots of the sea. Due to the energy concentration effect of the phased array antennas, the high-tower BSs can provide the coverage up to 150 km offshore. However, the high-tower BSs only enable certain area with the wireless backhaul and the other area without the backhaul signals becomes the coverage holes. For the BS ships within the coverage holes, they can choose the maritime satellites as backhaul nodes to connect with the EPC, which can achieve a link rate ranging from 4 Mbps to 135 Mbps [6]. For the user ships, if covered by the shipborne BS, they can access the wideband network through the surrounding shipborne BSs, otherwise they fall back to the narrowband satellites.

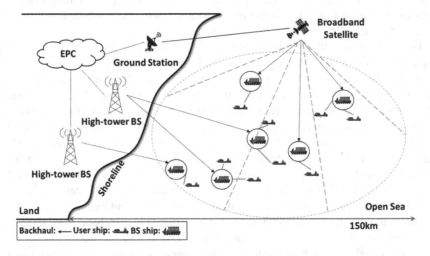

Fig. 1. Illustration of the MBC architecture for wideband maritime communication

Table 1 shows a rough calculation of the MBC architecture based on the real ship data in the China's Yellow Sea, including the user coverage and the average number of BS ships around a user ship within different coverage size of shipborne BSs. It can be seen that if all the shipborne BSs adopt the same fixed cell size, when the cell radius is set to 15 km, the total coverage rate of the user ships is 91.39%. If shrinking or expanding the cell size, a low coverage rate problem or an energy wasting problem will

Table 1. A rough calculation of MBC

Radius (km)	Coverage rate	Avg BS ship
5	57.31%	0.91
10	80.02%	1.31
15	91.39%	2.78
20	92.89%	4.14
25	94.10%	6.53

emerge, respectively. Besides, if setting the cell radius to 15 km, a user can be covered by an average number of 2.78 shipborne BSs, which means that a serious multiple overlapped problem exists in the MBC architecture. As Fig. 2 shows, the coverage area of shipborne BS C is overlapped with A and B and the user ships in the overlapped area will encounter a serious co-channel interference problem. To shrink the overlapped area and coordinate the inter-cell interference, we need a cell zooming strategy to dynamically adjust the cell size.

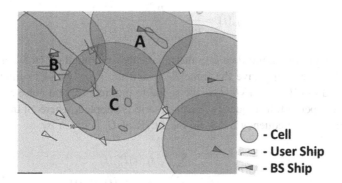

Fig. 2. The schematic map of BS ship distribution under MBC architecture.

2.2   Network and Channel Model

We consider a maritime communication network involving $N(t)$ BS ships and $M(t)$ user ships at time t. The set of shipborne BSs is denoted by $B(t) = \{B_i|i = 1, \ldots, N(t)\}$, and the set of user ships is $U(t) = \{U_j|j = 1, \ldots, M(t)\}$. Each ship has a geographic coordinate $[x_1(t), y_1(t)]$, $1 \in B(t) \cup U(t)$, which can be gathered from the AIS system. Each shipborne BS has a cell coverage radius $R_i(t)$. For a user ship U_j, it can access the shipborne BS B_i if the distance between U_j and B_i is less than $R_i(t)$. For a shipborne BS B_i, the set of assigned user ships is $S_i(t)$. A user ship can be served by only one shipborne BS which means $S_m(t) \cap S_n(t) = \Phi$, $m \neq n$, $\forall m,n \in B(t)$. Besides, we define two variables to describe the relation between B_i and U_j:

$$c_{j,i}(t) = \begin{cases} 1, & \text{if } U_j \text{ is covered by } B_i \text{ at time } t \\ 0, & \text{otherwise} \end{cases} \qquad (1)$$

$$s_{j,i}(t) = \begin{cases} 1, & \text{if } U_j \in S_i(t) \\ 0, & \text{otherwise} \end{cases} \qquad (2)$$

The downlink transmitting power of shipborne BS B_i. is denoted as $P_i^t(t)$, and the received signal power of U_j from B_i is expressed as $P_{j,i}^r(t)$. The $P_{j,i}^r(t)$ is calculated based on the maritime two-ray model [7]:

$$P_{j,i}^r(t) = 10 log_{10}\left[P_i^t(t)\right] + 10 log_{10}\left\{ \left(\frac{\lambda}{4\pi d_{j,i}(t)}\right)^2 \left[2\sin\left(\frac{2\pi.h_i.h_j}{\lambda d_{j,i}(t)}\right)\right]^2\right\} \qquad (3)$$

where λ is the carrier wavelength, h_i and h_j denote the antenna heights of U_j and B_i, and $d_{j,i}(t)$ is the distance between U_j and B_i. We model the channel based on the Shannon theorem, the allocated bandwidth $b_{j,i}$ of U_j from the serving B_i is calculated as:

$$b_{j,i}(t) = \frac{R_{QOS}}{log_2\left(1 + SINR_j(t)\right)} \qquad (4)$$

where R_{QOS} is the minimum data rate that guarantees the required QoS demand. We assume all the user ships have the same R_{QOS} and the R_{QOS} varies as time goes by, which is stated in [9]. The $SINR_j(t)$ is the signal to interference and noise ratio (SINR) of U_j. In this paper, a full frequency reuse scenario is adopted, where all the shipborne BSs share the same frequency band. So the SINR of U_j is given by:

$$SINR_j(t) = \frac{\sum_{i=1}^{N(t)} s_{j,i}(t)P_{j,i}^r(t)}{\sigma^2 + \sum_{i=1,}^{N(t)}\left[1 - s_{j,i}(t)\right]P_{j,i}^r(t)} \qquad (5)$$

where σ^2 is the noise power. Based on the allocated bandwidth, U_j can access the shipborne BS which satisfies the QoS demand:

$$b_{j,i}(t) < b_i^{idle}(t) \qquad (6)$$

where the $b_i^{idle}(t)$ is the unoccupied bandwidth of B_i. If no shipborne BS satisfies (6) for U_j at time t, U_j is blocked. The proportion of the blocked user ships in the network is the blocking rate.

In LTE-A, the number of the user ships which a BS is able to serve is determined by the available bandwidth of BS. From this perspective, when the entire BSs share the B^{total} allocable bandwidth, the normalized load of B_i at time t is given by:

$$L_i(t) = \frac{\sum_{j=1}^{M(t)} s_{j,i}(t) b_{j,i}(t)}{B^{total}} \tag{7}$$

2.3   The Cell Zooming Scheme

For all shipborne BSs, the maximum transmitting power is P_{max} and the maximum coverage radius is r_{max}. According to the cell zooming strategy, the BSs can autonomously change the coverage radiuses by adjusting the transmitting power. In the MBC architecture, a discrete cell zooming method is adopted, which is proved to be suitable for highly dynamic scenario for its robustness in mobility [8].

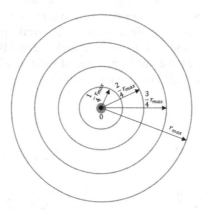

Fig. 3. The schematic map of cell partitioning with K = 4.

Under the discrete cell zooming method, each cell can be partitioned to $K + 1$ concentric circles. The number K is the partitioning factor. Figure 3 shows an example of K = 4 cell partitioning case. In this paper, we partition the cell in an equal distance way [10], so the radius set is:

$$R_{can} = \left\{ 0, \frac{r_{max}}{K}, \frac{2r_{max}}{K}, \ldots, \frac{(K-1)r_{max}}{K}, r_{max} \right\} \tag{8}$$

where BS keeps the maximum radius r_{max} using maximum transmitting power P_{max}. The corresponding transmitting power of other radiuses can be calculated by (3). We define the scaling factor of B_i as γ_i, which represents the degrees that the BS scales down the cell size:

$$\gamma_i = \frac{x}{K}, x = 0, 1, 2, 3 \ldots K \tag{9}$$

3   The Proposed IVB-CZ Strategy

The aim of the cell zooming strategy is to coordinate the inter-cell interference by shrinking the overlapped area between the adjacent shipborne BSs. This section describes the interference-and-voyage based cell zooming strategy.

For shrinking the overlapped area, every shipborne BS is required to adjust the cell size cooperatively. It's a key challenge to decide which shipborne BSs are adjustable to ensure the user experience can still be maintained after the adjustment. What's more, the shipborne BSs with high cell load cannot adjust the cell sizes because shrinking the cell with high load will bring about the blocked users. So we define the load threshold as L_{th} and a cell can adjust the size if the cell load is less than L_{th}. The shipborne BSs with low cell load can reduce the cell sizes and the transmitting power to improve the SINR of the other cell. After decreasing the cell size, the extra users will offload to other ships. Figure 4 illustrates an example of cell zooming strategy. The shipborne BS A and D scale down their cell sizes to shrink the overlapped area. To take in the extra users offloaded by A and D, C expands its cell size and B maintains its cell size. After adjusting the cell sizes, the overlapped area of the example scenario significantly shrinks and hence the inter-cell interference is mitigated.

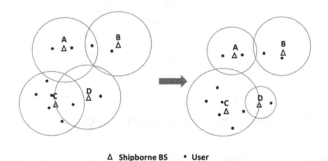

△ Shipborne BS   • User

Fig. 4. An example of cell zooming.

3.1   Voyage-Based User Association Algorithm

In order to be applied for the dynamical MBC architecture, the cell zooming strategy introduces the sailing status to make the decision. We assume that the voyage data of every ship are available in the AIS system. The management entity in the EPC can use the latest updating AIS data to predict the voyage of each ship. These predicted voyage data can be downloaded by shipborne BSs through S1 interfaces. Therefore, the user ships can get all the predicted information from the serving shipborne BSs.

In the MBC architecture, for the user ships, the shipborne BS with a similar direction is the best association choices because they can provide a continuous wide-band access, which can avoid the frequent handover of users and hence relieves the cell load fluctuations. Considering the voyage information, we define the voyage-based received signal power $P_{j,i}^{v}(t)$ as:

$$P_{j,i}^v(t) = \alpha P_{j,i}^r(t) + (1 - \alpha)P_{j,i}^r(t + \tau) \tag{10}$$

where $\alpha \in (0, 1]$, τ is the prediction period, $\forall B_i \in B(t)$, $U_j \in U(t)$. In (10), $P_{j,i}^r(t + \tau)$ is the received signal power in the predicted moment, which is calculated in (3).

Based on this parameter, the voyage-based (VB) user association algorithm is showed in Algorithm 1. The association procedure is operated autonomously in every user ship. The user ship is associated to the shipborne BS with the best voyage-based received signal power as long as the QoS requirement can be guaranteed. Any user unable to hand over to a shipborne BS is blocked.

Algorithm 1.   VB User Association Algorithm

---

1. For U_j in U(t)
2.   **While** B(t) $\neq \emptyset$ **then**
3.   Calculate $P_{j,i}^v(t)$, $i \in B(t)$.
4.   Set $B_m = argmax_{i \in B(t)} P_{j,i}^v(t)$.
5.   **If** $b_{j,m}(t) > b_m^{idle}(t)$ or $c_{j,m}(t) = 0$ **then**
6.   B(t) = B(t) − $\{B_m\}$.
7.   **else**
8. U_j is associated to B_m.
9.   **End if**
10.   **If** B(t) = $\emptyset$ **then**
11. U_j is blocked.
12.   **End if**
13.   **End while**
14. **End for**

3.2   IVB-CZ Algorithm

In the IVB-CZ algorithm, all the channel related information and voyage related information are gathered by EPC, and the cell zooming strategy is operated in a centralized way. When the blocking rate falls below a threshold Pr_{blr}, the cell zooming strategy is triggered. After the optimization results are configured by the BSs, the shipborne BSs keep their status until the next trigger.

To measure the load and interference status of shipborne BS, a utility function $UF(B_i)$ is introduced which considers both the load and interference:

$$UF(B_i, t) = \frac{I_i(t)}{L_i(t)} \tag{11}$$

where $L_i(t)$ is the normalized load of B_i and $I_i(t)$ represents the inter-cell interference that B_i brings to other shipborne BSs, which is given by:

$$I_i(t) = \sum_{j=1}^{M(t)} c_{j,i}(t)[1 - s_{j,i}(t)]P_{j,i}^r(t) \tag{12}$$

The procedure of the IVB-CZ algorithm is described as Algorithm 2. All shipborne BS are initialized with the maximum cell size. Then operator switches off the BSs covering no ship. Among the BSs which satisfy $L_i(t) < L_{th}$, the BS with maximal $UF(B_i, t)$ shrinks its cell without blocking the user ships until $L_i(t) \geq L_{th}$ is satisfied. After associating the extra user ships to other BS, we repeat the above steps. If all the BS in B(t) satisfy $L_i(t) < L_{th}$, end the procedure.

Algorithm 2. IVB-CZ Algorithm

---

1. **Initialization**: Set $P_i^t(t) = P_{max}, \gamma_i = 1, \forall B_i \in B(t)$
2. **If** blocking rate exceeds Pr_{blr} **then**
3.   **For** B_i which $\sum_{j=1}^M c_{j,i} = 0$
4.   Configure B_i with $\gamma_i = 0$ and B(t)=B(t)-$\{B_i\}$.
5.   **End for**
6.   **While** there are user ships satisfying $L_i(t) < L_{th}$ **do**
7.   Sort the BS in B(t) by $UF(B_i, t)$
8.   Find $B_m = argmax_{i \in B(t)} UF(B_i, t)$
9.   **While** no user ship is blocked and $L_i(t) < L_{th}$ **do**
10.   Configure B_m with γ_m.
11.   Using **algorithm 1** to re-associate user ships.
12. $\gamma_m = \gamma_m - 1/K$
13.   **End while**
14.   **End while**
15. **End if**

---

4   Performance Evaluation

In this section, we use the software MATLAB to evaluate the performance of the proposed cell zooming strategy under the real ship data. The IVB-CZ algorithm, the QoS-aware cell zooming algorithm [5] and no cell zooming scenarios are evaluated in terms of the average user SINR, average user throughput, and the normalized handover times. The QoS-aware cell zooming is a method to reduce power consumptions and improve the QoS level, which operates with BS sleeping method. The simulation parameters highlighted in Table 2 are set according to 3GPP LTE specifications [11].

Table 2. Simulation parameter

Parameters	Value
Maximum transmitting power (P_{max})	43 dBm
Maximum cell radius (r_{max})	15 km
Partitioning factor (K)	4
Carrier frequency	1.89 GHz
The allowcable bandwidth (B^{total})	17.6 MHz
Height of S-BSs (h_i)	35 m
Height of user ships (h_j)	15 m
Required data rate (R_{QOS})	3.5 Mbps
Predictable interval (τ)	15 min
α in (9)	0.7
Blocking rate threshold (Pr_{blr})	2.5%
Load threshold (L_{th})	0.75

4.1   Simulation Environment

Figure 5 shows the evaluated region of our work, which is the area within the red boundary lines in China's Yellow Sea. We take 7 days of ship voyage data (Oct. 10–16, 2015) [12] as the simulation data basis. The data is processed as follows:

- All the data is divided by 15 min. The resulting 96 data files are interpolated at 96 moments {0:15, 0:30, 0:45 ... 23:45, 24:00}.
- Choose the passenger vessels, cargo vessels and tankers as BS ships and others as user ships. Mark the ship type in the data file.

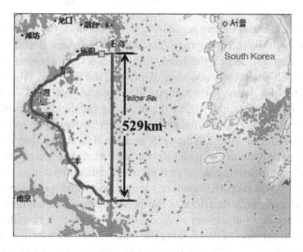

Fig. 5. Evaluated regions in China's Yellow Sea

4.2   Simulation Results

As showed in Fig. 6, the proposed IVB-CZ algorithm can increase the SINR of the user ships compared with the no cell zooming case because the IVB-CZ algorithm can reasonably scales down the cell with low cell load to shrink the signal overlapped area, which can obviously improve the spectral efficiency. However, it's noticeable that the QoS-aware cell zooming algorithm achieves slightly higher SINR than IVB-CZ. It is because the QoS-aware cell zooming algorithm switches off more BSs to reduce energy consumption. So the average distance between the adjacent shipborne BSs is longer and the overlapped area is smaller. Therefore, the spectral efficiency is improved further. Note that the curve of the SNIR fluctuates severely. It's because we use the real ship data as the simulation data basis, the distribution of the ships is nearly random, which makes the SINR performs randomly.

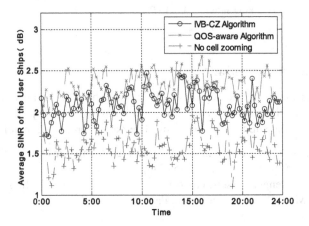

Fig. 6. Average SINR of the user ships

However, since the user experience mostly lies in the throughput of the user ships, a higher SINR cannot directly improve the user experience. Because the network throughputs are also affected by the bandwidth resources. As showed in Fig. 7, compared with the QoS-aware cell zooming algorithm, the IVB-CZ Algorithm can significantly improve the network throughput. It's because that the IVB-CZ algorithm increase the SINR without downsizing the available bandwidth resources. Although QoS-aware cell zooming algorithm achieves a higher performance in terms of SINR, the throughput is reduced. Because the QoS-aware cell zooming algorithm is operated in a distributed way without considering the cell load and interference level. The distributed method downsizing the signaling overheads compared with the proposed IVB-CZ algorithm, however, the operator cannot choose the most appropriate BSs to adjust the cell sizes, which deteriorates the performance in throughput. Besides, the QoS-aware cell zooming algorithm may switch off more BSs to reduce the energy consumption at the expense of downsizing the bandwidth resources and blocking users. In the no cell zooming case, a serious inter-cell interference exists and the throughput is limited by the low spectral efficiency. Therefore, the network throughput is slightly lower than the IVB-CZ algorithm.

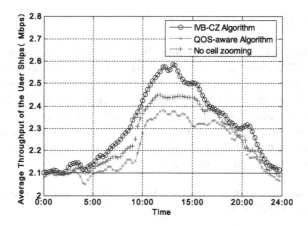

Fig. 7. Average throughput of the user ships

The Fig. 8 demonstrates the normalized handover times which the handover times of the no cell zooming case is normalized to 1. It is noticeable that the handover times of IVB-CZ algorithm are lower than the QoS-aware cell zooming algorithm because compared with QoS-aware cell zooming algorithm, the IVB-CZ algorithm adopts the VB user association algorithm to associate users, which considers the sailing status of both the BS ships and user ships. The user ships will access the BS with the similar sailing direction, which can significantly decrease the handover times of users. Therefore, the user experience can be effectively improved.

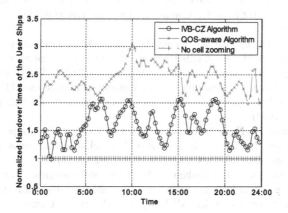

Fig. 8. Normalized handover times of the user ships

5 Conclusions

In this paper, we propose a novel multiple backhaul based maritime wideband communication (MBC) architecture to provide the wideband access for the ocean vessel. To coordinate the inter-cell interference in the MBC architecture, an interference-and-voyage based cell zooming (IVB-CZ) strategy is presented. The IVB-CZ strategy takes the inter-cell interference level and ship voyage into consideration to make the cell zooming decision. Simulation results indicate that the proposed cell zooming strategy is an effective way to improve the performance of maritime communication network in term of the network throughput and the user handover times.

Acknowledgement. This work was supported by the National Natural Science Foundation of China under grant No. 91538203.

References

1. Global Maritime Distress and Safety System (GMDSS). http://www.egmdss.com/gmdss-courses/mod/resource/view.php?id=2349
2. Zhou, M.-T., Hoang, V., Harada, H., et al.: TRITON: high-speed maritime wireless mesh network. IEEE Wirel. Commun. **20**(5), 134–142 (2013)
3. Challita, U., Al-Kanj, L., Dawy, Z.: On LTE cellular network planning under demand uncertainty. In: Proceedings of the IEEE Wireless Communications and Networking Conference (WCNC), pp. 2079–2084, April 2014
4. Niu, Z., Wu, Y., Gong, J., Yang, Z.: Cell zooming for cost-efficient green cellular networks. IEEE Commun. Mag. **48**(11), 74–79 (2010)
5. Le, L.B.: QoS-aware BS switching and cell zooming design for OFDMA green cellular networks. In: 2012 IEEE Global Communications Conference (GLOBECOM), pp. 1544–1549. IEEE (2012)
6. Hecht, Y.: Implementing VoIP support in a VSAT network based on SoftSwitch integration. In: Fan, L., Cruickshank, H., Sun, Z. (eds.) IP Networking over Next-Generation Satellite Systems, pp. 309–316. Springer, New York (2008). https://doi.org/10.1007/978-0-387-75428-4_20
7. Zhao, Y., Ren, J., Chi, X.: Maritime mobile channel transmission model based on ITM. In: 2nd International Symposium on Computer, Communication, Control and Automation. Atlantis Press (2013)
8. Balasubramaniam, R., Nagaraj, S., Sarkar, M., et al.: Cell zooming for power efficient base station operation. In: 2013 9th International Wireless Communications and Mobile Computing Conference (IWCMC), pp. 556–560. IEEE (2013)
9. Alam, S.A., Dooley, S.L., Poulton, S.A.: Traffic-and-interference aware base station switching for green cellular networks. In: Proceedings of the IEEE 18th International Workshop on Computer Aided Modeling and Design of Communication Links and Networks (CAMAD), pp. 63–67, September 2013
10. Khamesi, A.R., Zorzi, M.: Energy and area spectral efficiency of cell zooming in random cellular networks. In: 2016 IEEE Global Communications Conference (GLOBECOM), pp. 1–6. IEEE (2016)
11. GPP TS 36.213, Evolved Universal Terrestrial Radio Access (EUTRA); Physical layer procedures
12. BLM Shipping Software. www.boloomo.com/

Nano/Microsatellite Universal Ground Station Design Based on SDR

Bao-Shan Wang[✉], Li-Hu Chen, and Quan Chen

College of Aerospace Science and Engineering,
National University of Defense Technology, Changsha, China
Wangbaoshan90@163.com, clh2055@163.com,
chenquan9311@163.com

Abstract. With the development of nano/micro-satellite technology, cluster flying and space networking become the trend of development. The contradiction between the numbers of satellites and ground stations have become increasingly prominent. Through the analysis of micro satellite common modulation system, three kinds of modulation system were selected: FM, GMSK, and BPSK. By using GNU Radio & USRP software radio platform, a universal ground station based on amateur radio frequency band was designed to realize the telemetry data receiving and demodulating functions of micro satellites on different communication system.

Keywords: SDR · GNU Radio · Nano/microsatellite
Telemetry demodulation · Ground station

1 Introduction

Satellites weighing from 1–50 kg, commonly known as Nano/Micro-satellite, have advantages of low cost, high flexibility, and short development cycle over bigger satellites. They can perform a variety of tasks, such as earth observation, remote sensing, communication, technical experiment and scientific research. According to "Small Satellite Market Observations" [1], the number of micro-satellites launch is increasing year by year, from 92 in 2013 to 158 in 2014.

The future development of nano/microsatellite has a trend to be based on hadoop and informatization. SpaceX has planned to build satellite constellation consisting of more than 4,000 satellites. The satellite network technology can not only improve service efficiency of satellites, but also reduce duplication of investment [2].

At present, a wide variety of satellites are developed to perform different tasks. However, traditional ground stations customize TT&C tasks for individual satellites. They need certain time of preparation before and after satellite passing. With the development of nano/micro-satellites and satellite constellations, the TT&C system will be challenged by new problems such as several different satellites passing simultaneously and the shorter interval between successive satellites' pass. The contradiction between the numbers of satellites and ground stations have become increasingly prominent. The traditional single-satellite TT&C system has been unable to meet the demands.

© Springer Nature Singapore Pte Ltd. 2018
Q. Yu (Ed.): SINC 2017, CCIS 803, pp. 197–203, 2018.
https://doi.org/10.1007/978-981-10-7877-4_17

After analyzed the commonly used modulation system, we designed a satellite ground station based on Software Defined Radio platform. In theory, it is possible to realize the reception of telemetry data for most of the nano/micro-satellites with amateur radio frequency after knowing the key parameters such as the center frequency of the satellite. And it is successfully used on "NUDTSat", which is a cubesate designed by National University of Defense Technology.

2 Experimental Platform

Radio Software Defined Radio (SDR) [3], is a radio communication system where components that have been typically implemented in hardware (e.g. mixers, filters, amplifiers, modulators/demodulators, detectors, etc.) are instead implemented by means of software program on a personal computer or embedded system. Based on the platform to load the Standardized, modular, universal software, SDR is able to realize a variety of wireless communication functions.

GNU Radio [4] is an open source software that allows to build a radio communication system via a minimum level of hardware. GNU Radio provides a signal processing module library, called blocks, including modulation methods, filters, FFT, convolution, etc. By connecting blocks, GNU Radio form a complete flowgraph to realize an operational application. In addition, GNU Radio provides OOT (out-of-tree) tool to extend the function. GNU Radio is more flexible compared to other software.

Universal Software Radio Peripheral (USRP) [5] is a hardware platform used with the GNU Radio software suite. The basic design concept is to complete all the waveform-related processing such as modulation and demodulation on the host CPU, and other high-speed general operations such as digital conversion, sampling and interpolation are processed on the FPGA (Field Programmable Gate Array).

The experimental platform shown in Fig. 1. The USRP B210 provides a fully integrated, single-board USRP platform with continuous frequency coverage from 70 MHz–6 GHz. Programs in this paper are developed based on Ubuntu 14.04 LTS and GNU Radio Companion 3.7.8.

3 Ground Station Simulation

Most of the nano/micro satellites are developed by universities, amateur radio organizations and groups, and VHF/UHF band signals are widely adopted. Based on the requirements of specific task, modulations include FM, FSK, PSK, MFSK, BPSK, GMSK, OFDM were chosen. In particular, Lilacsat [6], BY70-1 [7] integrated FM function. AISAT [8], GALASSIA [9], GOMX-1 [10] used GMSK modem. Part of the QB50 project satellites and FUNcube [11] choose BPSK modulation.

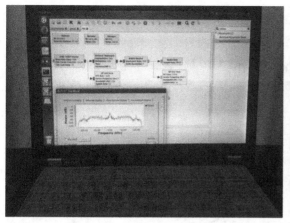

Fig. 1. The experiment platform

3.1 Frequency Demodulation

The frequency modulation (FM) is the carrying of information over an electromagnetic wave by varying its frequency. Its most common application is FM broadcasting. Many satellites on orbit have integrated FM module because of its anti-noise performance.

Figure 2 shows a FM receiver demodulation flowgraph. The signal received by USRP is transmitted to GNU Radio, and the sample rate are changed in Rational Resampler block. The message is then FM-demodulated by WBFM Receive block which can be replaced by NBFM Receive block as well. At last, the demodulated signals are converted into audio signals in Audio Sink block.

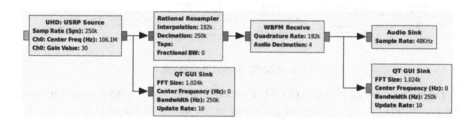

Fig. 2. FM demod flowgraph

Figure 3 shows the FM demodulated waveform and the original signal waveform after signals from of music channel broadcast are received.

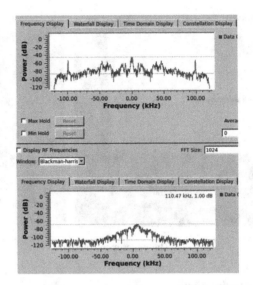

Fig. 3. FM Spectrogram

3.2 Gaussian Minimum Shift Keying Demodulation

Gaussian Minimum Shift Keying or GMSK is a continuous-phase frequency-shift keying modulation scheme which is based on the MSK. MSK modulated baseband signal is a rectangular waveform. GMSK first shapes signal with a Gaussian filter before being applied to a frequency modulator, which has the advantage of reducing sideband power (Fig. 4).

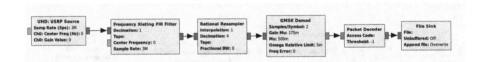

Fig. 4. GMSK demod flowgraph

Figure 5 shows an example of GMSK demodulation flowgraph for common cases. The parameters can be determined according to the actual situation.

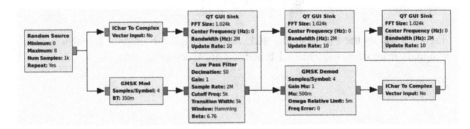

Fig. 5. GMSK mod and demod flowgraph

Since we do not have GMSK source, so we build a modulation and demodulation flowgraph for test showed in Fig. 5.

GMSK frequency spectrogram and the waterfall graphic are shown in Fig. 6. As can be seen from the Frequency Display, GMSK modulation and demodulation module is running correctly. From the Waterfall Display it can be seen that, after filtering demodulation, the signal has been significantly strengthened.

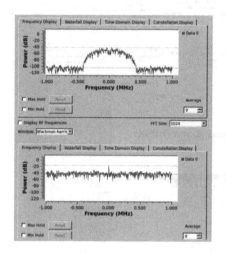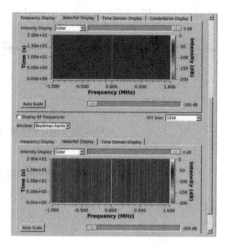

Fig. 6. GMSK spectrogram and the waterfall

3.3   Simulation of Ground Station Based on NUDTSat

NUDTSat [12] is a double unit CubeSat developed by NUDT. The downlink uses Binary Phase Shift Keying (BPSK) modulation.

Figure 7 illustrates the GNU Radio flowgraph for the NUDTSat ground station. To improve the quality of signals, the signal source, which has been stored as a File Source here, was transited to the Low Pass Filter block which helps to discard unwanted portions of the signal and Feed Forward AGC (Automatic Gain Control) block which adjust the input-to-output gain to a suitable value. After FLL (Frequency Locked Loop) Band-Edge block, which is for frequency lock, signals will be display in QT GUI Frequency Sink block to compare with origin signals. Polyphase Clock Sync block is for recovering timing and Costas Loop block compensates for possible phase and frequency offset. LMS DD Equalizer means Least Mean Square Direct Decision Equalizer for reducing inter-symbol interference. Finally, After BPSK demodulation block and HDLC decode, the signal is stored in the File Sink block as a binary file. The Throttle block is designed to prevent CPU from full load. The spectrum and constellation are shown in Fig. 8.

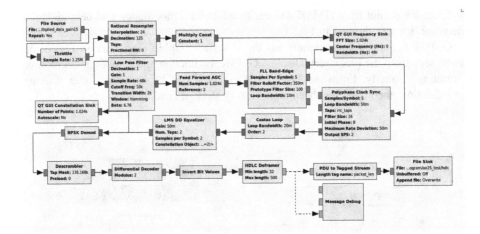

Fig. 7. NUDTSat ground station (BPSK)

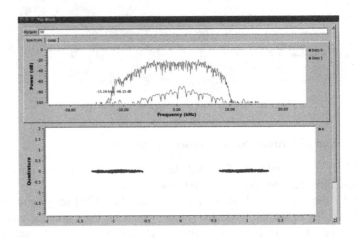

Fig. 8. BPSK spectrogram and constellation

4 Conclusion

A GNU Radio application is summarized as "source - modem - sink" model, as we shows in Sect. 3.1. Moreover, as demonstrated in GMSK simulation, an appropriate block for signal processing is needed to receive high quality signals. However, it is more complex that we design a ground station based on software defined radio for specific satellite, illustrated by NUDTSat.

In fact, the differences between various satellites still exist, and there is no general pattern to manage all satellites temporarily. In theory, when a complete universal ground station is developed, it is able to receipt and sync the signals from a variety of satellites, and demodulate and decode signal to valid data by diversifying blocks.

References

1. Buchen, E.: Small Satellite Market Observations (2015)
2. Zhou, Y.-Q., Luo, C.: Development trend of the commercialized microsatellite industry. Space Int. **5**, 37–43 (2016). (in Chinese)
3. Yang, X.-N., Lou, Y.-C.: Software Radio Technology and Applications. Beijing Institute of Technology Press, China (2010). (in Chinese)
4. GNU Radio Wiki. http://gnuradio.org/redmine/projects/gnuradio/wiki
5. USRP Wiki. https://en.wikipedia.org/wiki/Universal_Software_Radio_Peripheral
6. Lilacsat Information. http://lilacsat.hit.edu.cn/?page_id=257
7. BY70-1 Information. http://space.skyrocket.de/doc_sdat/by70-1
8. AISAT Information. https://directory.eoportal.org/web/eoportal/satellite-missions/a/aisat
9. Galassia-1 Information. https://eoportal.org/web/eoportal/satellite-missions/content/-/article/galass-1
10. Gomx-1 Information. https://directory.eoportal.org/web/eoportal/satellite-missions/g/gomx-1
11. FUNcube Information. https://amsat-uk.org/satellites/communications/ukube-1
12. NUDTSat Information. http://space.skyrocket.de/doc_sdat/nudtsat

Theory and Method of High Speed Transmission

A Novel Relay-Assisted Coded Cooperation Scheme in the Stratospheric Communication System

He Di[1,3(✉)], He Chen[2], and Jiang Lingge[2,3]

[1] Shanghai Key Laboratory of Navigation and Location-Based Services,
School of Electronic Information and Electrical Engineering,
Academy of Information Technology and Electrical Engineering,
Shanghai Jiao Tong University, Shanghai 200240, China
dihe@sjtu.edu.cn

[2] Department of Electronic Engineering, School of Electronic Information
and Electrical Engineering, Shanghai Jiao Tong University,
Shanghai 200240, China
{chenhe,lgjiang}@sjtu.edu.cn

[3] National Mobile Communications Research Laboratory,
Southeast University, Nanjing 210096, China

Abstract. In this study, a novel relay-assisted coded cooperation scheme used in the stratospheric communication system is proposed. The corresponding research and performance analyses especially focus on the relay-assisted coded cooperation device-to-device (D2D) communication under the co-channel interference (CCI) in the stratospheric communication system platform is given. The purpose of the proposed coded cooperation scheme is to reach a better performance of multi-user communications with higher capacity especially under CCI. The relay-assisted D2D communication idea is introduced here to choose the best relay platform in the stratospheric communication system, and a novel approach to select the best relay node (BSR) is also proposed in the study. Both the theoretical analyses and the computer simulation results show that the proposed approach can reduce the outage probability and the average symbol error rate (SER) more efficiently than the conventional methods under the circumstances without BSR selection and without relay-assisted coded cooperation.

Keywords: Stratospheric communication · Co-channel interference (CCI)
Relay-assisted coded cooperation

1 Introduction

In the air-ground communications network and system, the High Altitude Platforms (HAPs) are supposed to be a kind of useful infrastructure which can help to realize the high-efficiency communications between the HAPs and the mobile users at the ground [1].

While in the stratospheric communication system, the mobile users at the ground realize the communications through the connections of HAPs. Although the HAPs possess the good property that each HAP could cover a much more area and lots of users than a mobile base station on the ground, it will also encounter the problems of

© Springer Nature Singapore Pte Ltd. 2018
Q. Yu (Ed.): SINC 2017, CCIS 803, pp. 207–217, 2018.
https://doi.org/10.1007/978-981-10-7877-4_18

signal blocking or shadowing, serious line-of-sight (LOS) signal fading, low elevation angles and so on, which may result in the decreasing of communications quality of service (QoS), such as increasing of outage probability or average symbol error rate (SER). At the same time, the co-channel interference (CCI) will also introduce serious performance deteriorations.

To solve the above mentioned problem, a kind of relay-assisted coded cooperation device-to-device (D2D) communication scheme under CCI in the stratospheric communication system is proposed in this study. In recent years, the D2D communications have arisen a lot of research interests among wireless communication area [2–4]. While in the conventional ground cellular networks, when two mobile users are in close proximity, they can directly communicate with each other using the radio resource allocated by the base station. Based on this idea, we introduce the D2D communication concept between a pair of HAPs, say HAP 1 and HAP 2, in case that when we want to establish the communication between the mobile user and HAP 1, but the LOS signal between the mobile user and HAP 1 is blocked or seriously fading, while the LOS signal between the mobile user and HAP 2 is unblocked. Obviously, this is a better scheme to improve the communications QoS. In addition, D2D communications between HAPs can also have benefits to increase the capacity of the whole system.

In [2], the analysis of the relay-assisted D2D communication shows it can ensure the call quality and the channel capacity. Within the discussions in this research which is mainly related to the interference management, the main idea is to reuse the same spectrum when the power control and the good D2D QoS can meet the threshold under the premise of the position limit. When the quality of D2D channel is not good enough, a D2D pair will communicate which is assisted by some other users within the free space as a relay node.

In [3], the authors propose a relay assisted system based on coded cooperation, despite the decode-and-forward (DF) and coded cooperation is very similar, there are still some differences. Laneman proposed several cooperation agreements, which include DF, amplify-forward (AF), and so on [5]. The purpose of coded cooperation proposed with the relay nodes is to increase the channel capacity. While in this study, the corresponding analysis and conclusion is mainly based on [4]. The main innovations and contributions of our research work are as followed:

(1) The original D2D communication systems are based on the relay strategy of DF mode. In this study, the cooperative relay encoding strategy is introduced, for example, the relay node does not encode the information transmitted from the source node, but only transmits a part of the encoding information through the independent channels.
(2) The proposed cooperative relay D2D transmission mode can improve the validity of the transmission capacity of the system, for example decreasing the outage probability and the average SER even under CCI circumstances.

The remaining of the paper is arranged as follows: In Sect. 2, the system model and the D2D communications best relay node selection scheme are introduced. Based on the proposed idea, the system performance analyses are given in Sect. 3, which include the outage probability analysis and the average SER analysis. Computer simulation results are presented in Sect. 4, which shows the validity of the proposed scheme. And the final conclusions are given in Sect. 5.

2 System Model and Best Relay Selection Scheme

In the stratospheric communication system, it is supposed that there exists a pair of source-destination nodes, which is plotted in Fig. 1. While in Fig. 1, the node s is the source node which is placed on one of the HAPs, and the node d is the destination node which is placed on the ground (or the mobile user). In the communications, when the LOS signal path from s to d is blocked or possesses critical fading, the communication QoS may be influenced seriously.

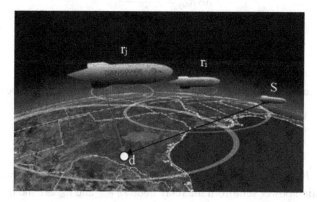

Fig. 1. Basic structure of the relay-assisted coded cooperation stratospheric communication

At the same time, to realize a wide area communication through the stratospheric HAPs, many platforms will be placed in the stratosphere to make the information exchange. Assume that the stratospheric HAPs (except the node s) are defined as an HAP set $\Lambda = \{r_1, r_2, \cdots, r_J\}$, where $r_j \in \Lambda$ $(j = 1, 2, \cdots, J)$ represents the jth HAP and J is the total number of HAPs in the stratospheric communication system (except the node s).

Based on the idea of D2D communication, we introduce the relay-assisted coded cooperation technique to solve the problem mentioned above. Firstly, all the stratospheric HAPs except the node s are regarded as the possible relay nodes to help the information transmission from s to d. When the source-destination pair cannot communicate with each other directly and fluently, one idle HAP in Λ will be chosen as the relay node to assist the direct link. The main idea in this technique is to set up a cooperation system combining the LOS path and the relay path so that the different parts of the information codewords can be transmitted from the source node s to the destination node d directly and through the relay node r_j indirectly.

Figure 1 illustrates the relay-assisted coded cooperation stratospheric communication. The codewords transmitted from the source node s are divided into two successive time segments which are called information frames. In the first frame, the source node s transmits a rate-R_1 codeword (N_1 symbols) to the destination node d, and transmits a rate-R_2 codeword (N_2 symbols) to the selected relay node r_j. If the relay node r_j decode the rate-R_2 codewords successfully (checked by CRC), the relay node r_j

will transmit the N_2 information symbols to the destination node d in the second frame. If the N_2 symbols cannot be decoded by the relay node r_j, the relay node will not transmit any symbols to the destination node d.

If the source node s transmits the information codewords to the relay node r_j and the destination node d at the same time, the instantaneous signal-to-noise ratio (SNR) received by the nodes r_j and d, denoted by SNR_{sr_j} and SNR_{sd} respectively, can be expressed as

$$SNR_{sr_j} = \frac{P_s|h_{sr_j}|^2}{N_{sr_j}}, \tag{1}$$

$$SNR_{sd} = \frac{P_s|h_{sd}|^2}{N_{sd}}, \tag{2}$$

and the instantaneous SNR in the path r_j-d, denoted by SNR_{r_jd}, can also be expressed as

$$SNR_{r_jd} = \frac{P_{r_j}|h_{r_jd}|^2}{N_{r_jd}}, \tag{3}$$

where P_s and P_{r_j} denote the transmitting power sent from the source node s and the relay transmitting power sent from the relay node r_j; h_{sr_j} and h_{sd} are the pathloss fading coefficient of the relay link from the source node s to the relay node r_j and the LOS link from the source node s to the destination node d respectively; h_{r_jd} is the pathloss fading coefficient of the relay link from the relay node r_j to the destination node d; N_{sr_j}, N_{sd} and N_{r_jd} are the CCI plus channel noise powers received by the relay path s-r_j, LOS path s-d and the relay path r_j-d, respectively.

According to [6], when there doesn't exist the relay path, the outage probability of the direct path s-d, denoted by $p_{out(s-d)}$, satisfies

$$P_{out(s-d)} = 1 - \exp(-\frac{SNR_{th}}{SNR_{sd}}), \tag{4}$$

where SNR_{th} denotes a certain SNR threshold to meet the corresponding communication QoS requirement, generally it can be chosen to reach the maximal channel capacity.

If a relay path is also available, the outage probability of the link from the source node s to destination node d, denoted by $p_{out(s-r_j-d)}$, will be changed to

$$P_{out(s-r_j-d)} = \left[1 - \exp(-\frac{SNR_{th}}{SNR_{sd}})\right] \cdot \left[1 - \exp(-\frac{SNR_{th}}{SNR_{sr_j}}) \cdot \exp(-\frac{SNR_{th}}{SNR_{r_jd}})\right]. \tag{5}$$

To simplify the analysis complexity, it is assumed that the SNR thresholds for each communication path are the same.

Based on the above analyses, when there exists the relay path, how to select the best relay node is also a very important and serious problem as shown in Fig. 2. While it can be found in Fig. 1, the source node s transmits the information data into two different segments. In the first frame, the relay node r_j receives a rate $R_1 = R/\beta$ codeword, where β is the coefficient of the cooperation model. The channel will be in outage when the rate R_1 is larger than the capacity. In other words, the relay node r_j cannot decode the codeword sent from transmitter. It may possess two possible cases according to whether the relay node r_j could decode the codeword successfully or not.

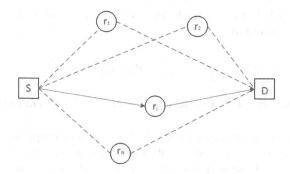

Fig. 2. Best relay node selection

Case 1 ($\theta = 1$): In this case, the relay node r_j successfully decodes the codeword transmitted from the source node s. The corresponding condition is defined as

$$C_{sr_j}(SNR_{sr_j}) = \log_2(1 + SNR_{sr_j}) > R/\beta, \tag{6}$$

where C_{sr_j} and SNR_{sr_j} denote the capacity and instantaneous SNR of the channel between the source node s and relay node r_j.

In the second frame, both the relay node r_j and source node s send codewords to the destination node d. The corresponding condition is

$$C_{sd}(SNR_{sd}, SNR_{r_jd}|_{\theta=1}) = \beta \log_2(1 + SNR_{sd}) \\ + (1 - \beta) \log_2(1 + SNR_{r_jd}) < R \tag{7}$$

where C_{sd} denote the capacity of channel between the source node s and destination node r_j.

Case 2 ($\theta = 2$): In this case, the relay node r_j cannot decode the codeword sent from the source node s in condition that the rate R_1 exceeds the channel capacity, that is

$$C_{sr_j}(SNR_{sr_j}) = \log_2(1 + SNR_{sr_j}) < R/\beta. \tag{8}$$

So in the second frame, the destination node d can only receive the codeword from the source node s. So we have

$$C_{sd}(SNR_{sd}|_{\theta=2}) = \log_2(1 + SNR_{sd}) < R. \tag{9}$$

Here, the capacity of direct link and relay link can be expressed respectively by

$$C_{sr_j}(SNR_{sr_j}) = \log_2(1 + SNR_{sr_j}), \tag{10}$$

$$C_{r_jd}(SNR_{r_jd}) = \log_2(1 + SNR_{r_jd}). \tag{11}$$

where $SNR_{sr_j} = \frac{P_s|h_{sr_j}|^2}{N_{sr_j}}$, $SNR_{r_jd} = \frac{P_s|h_{r_jd}|^2}{N_{r_jd}}$.

Since the relay link is combined by two independent channels, the capacity of the relay link can be expressed as

$$C_{sr_jd} = \frac{1}{2}\min(C_{sr_j}(SNR_{sr_j}), C_{r_jd}(SNR_{r_jd})), \tag{12}$$

where C_{sr_jd} denotes the capacity of the relay channel from node s to node d through the relay node r_j.

The principle to choose the best relay node in the coded cooperation we used here is to find the relay node which can have the maximal relay link capacity. To reduce the relay time delay, we choose only one relay node to decode and forward the information codewords transmitted from the source node s. And the other relay nodes are then set into the idle state. While the best relay selection criterion can be describe as follows

$$r_j^{opt} = \arg\max_{j\in\Lambda}(C_{sr_jd}), \tag{13}$$

where r_j^{opt} is the best selected relay (BSR) node or the optimal selected relay (OSR) node.

3 Performance Analyses

3.1 Outage Probability Analysis

Outage probability is an important parameter to measure the performance of relay-assisted communications.

In the coded cooperation system, define the outage probability into two independent cases. When the channel capacity is less than the expected rate of the codewords, the channel will be interrupted. According to the analysis in last Section, and let SNRth to reach the maximal channel capacity, the outage probability can be expressed by

$$\begin{aligned}
p_{out} = {}&\Pr\{SNR_{sr_j^{opt}} > 2^{R/\beta} - 1\} \cdot \Pr\{(1 + SNR_{sd})^\beta \\
&\cdot (1 + SNR_{r_j^{opt}d})^{1-\beta} < 2^R\} + \Pr\{SNR_{sr_j^{opt}} < 2^{R/\beta} - 1\} \\
&\cdot \Pr\{SNR_{sd} < 2^R - 1\},
\end{aligned} \tag{14}$$

In the stratospheric communication system, to simplify the analysis, assume that both the LOS path and the relay path obey the Rayleigh fading, then it can be derived according to the results in last Section that

$$\Pr\{(1+SNR_{sd})^{\beta}(1+SNR_{r_j^{opt}d})^{1-\beta}<2^R\}$$
$$=\int_0^{+\infty}\Pr\{SNR_{r_j^{opt}d}<H(x)\}e^{-x}dx, \tag{15}$$

where the function $H(x)$ is defined as

$$H(x)\overset{\Delta}{=}\sqrt[1-\beta]{\frac{2^R}{(1+SNR_{sd}\cdot x)^{\beta}}}-1, \tag{16}$$

Due to the fact that $SNR_{r_j^{opt}d}$ is non-negative, so we should have $H(x)>SNR_{r_j^{opt}d}>0$, and the range of x belongs to

$$0<x<\frac{2^{(R/\beta)}-1}{SNR_{sd}}, \tag{17}$$

Hence, Eq. (15) can be simplified to

$$\Pr\{(1+SNR_{sd})^{\beta}(1+SNR_{r_j^{opt}d})^{1-\beta}<2^R\}$$
$$=\int_0^{\frac{2^{(R/\beta)}-1}{\gamma_{sd}}}[1-\exp(-\frac{H(x)}{SNR_{r_j^{opt}d}})]e^{-x}dx, \tag{18}$$

Therefore, the outage probability of the relay system can be expressed as

$$P_{out(s-r_j^{opt}-d)}=\Pr\{SNR_{sr_j^{opt}}>2^{R/\beta}-1\}$$
$$\cdot\Pr\{(1+SNR_{sd})^{\beta}\cdot(1+SNR_{r_j^{opt}d})^{1-\beta}<2^R\}$$
$$+\Pr\{SNR_{sr_j^{opt}}<2^{R/\beta}-1\}\cdot\Pr\{SNR_{sd}<2^R-1\}$$
$$=\exp\left(\frac{2^{R/\beta}-1}{SNR_{sr_j^{opt}}}\right)\cdot\int_0^{\frac{2^{(R/\beta)}-1}{SNR_{sd}}}\left[1-\exp(-\frac{H(x)}{SNR_{r_j^{opt}d}})\right] \tag{19}$$
$$\cdot e^{-x}dx+\left\{1-\exp\left[-\frac{2^{R/\beta}-1}{SNR_{sr_j^{opt}}}\right]\right\}$$
$$\cdot\left\{1-\exp\left[-\frac{2^R-1}{SNR_{sd}}\right]\right\}.$$

3.2   Average SER Analysis

Based on the SNRs defined in Eqs. (1)–(3) and use the moment generating function (MGF) based approach in [7], the MGF of the proposed relay-assisted coded cooperation communication system, denoted by Mr(s), can be expressed by

$$M_r(s) = \beta \cdot E_1\left(P_s \cdot e^{-s \cdot SNR_{sd}}\right) \\ + (1 - \beta) \cdot E_2\left(P_{r_j} \cdot e^{-s \cdot SNR_{r_j d}}\right), \tag{20}$$

where the functions $E_1(.)$ and $E_2(.)$ are defined by

$$E_1\left(P_s \cdot e^{-s \cdot SNR_{sd}}\right) = \int_0^{+\infty} P_s \cdot e^{-s \cdot SNR_{sd}} f_{|h_{sd}|^2}(h_{sd}) dh_{sd} \\ E_2\left(P_{r_j} \cdot e^{-s \cdot SNR_{r_j d}}\right) = \int_0^{+\infty} \int_0^{+\infty} P_{r_j} \cdot e^{-s \cdot SNR_{r_j d}} \\ \cdot f_{|h_{sr_j}|^2}(h_{sr_j}) f_{|h_{r_j d}|^2}(h_{r_j d}) dh_{sr_j} dh_{r_j d}, \tag{21}$$

while $f_{|h_{sd}|^2}(h_{sd}), f_{|h_{sr_j}|^2}(h_{sr_j})$ and $f_{|h_{r_j d}|^2}(h_{r_j d})$ are the probability density functions (PDFs) of variables h_{sd}, h_{sr_j} and $h_{r_j d}$, respectively. And when the BSR node is selected according to (13), Eq. (20) can be changed to

$$M_r^{opt}(s) = \beta \cdot E_1\left(P_s \cdot e^{-s \cdot SNR_{sd}}\right) \\ + (1 - \beta) \cdot E_2\left(P_{r_j^{opt}} \cdot e^{-s \cdot SNR_{r_j^{opt} d}}\right). \tag{22}$$

Then based on the above MGF analysis results and the average SER analysis results in [7, 8], and if the source signal is transmitted as M-PSK modulation, the average SER of the proposed relay-assisted coded cooperation D2D communication with co-channel interference in the stratospheric communication system can be calculated by

$$SER_{M-PSK} = \frac{1}{\pi} \int_0^{\theta_M} M_r\left(\frac{g_{M-PSK}}{\sin^2 \theta}\right) d\theta, \tag{23}$$

where we have $\theta_M = \pi(M - 1)/M$ and $g_{M-PSK} = \sin^2(\pi/M)$.

In the real applications, the following accurate approximation can be used to calculate the average SER in M-PSK as [8]

$$SER_{M-PSK} = \sum_{i=1}^3 a_i M_r(b_i), \tag{24}$$

where $a_1 = \frac{\theta_M}{2\pi} - \frac{1}{6}$, $b_1 = g_{M-PSK}$, $a_2 = \frac{1}{4}$, $b_2 = \frac{4}{3} g_{M-PSK}$, $a_3 = \frac{\theta_M}{2\pi} - \frac{1}{4}$, $b_3 = \frac{g_{M-PSK}}{\sin^2(\theta_M)}$. And for some other modulations such as M-PAM and M-QAM, the approximate average SER calculation results can also be found in [8].

4 Numerical Simulation Results

In this section, we give the computer simulation results of the proposed relay-assisted coded cooperation D2D communication with co-channel interference in the strato-spheric communication system with the selected BSR node, relay-assisted coded cooperation D2D communication with co-channel interference without the selected BSR node (the relay node is selected randomly), and the non-cooperative stratospheric communication system with only LOS path (non-cooperation).

In the computer simulations, we choose the parameters as follows: the co-channel interference power is $N_{sd} = N_{sr_j} = -130\,\mathrm{dBm}$, $\beta = 1/2$, the expected rate of coded cooperation system is $R = 1$ bps/Hz. For comparisons, we also give the simulation results under $R = 2$ bps/Hz. The system parameters for numerical computer simulations are given in Table 1.

Table 1. System parameters for numerical simulations

Source node power	17 dBm
Interference power	−130 dBm
Modulation	8-PSK
Number of Monte Carlo simulation times in each simulation points	10^{10}

Figure 3 shows the comparison of outage probability performance under R = 1 bps/Hz. It can be found that when the rate of coded cooperation is 1 bps/Hz and when the outage probabilities approach 10^{-4}, the proposed approach (BSR) can achieve about 3 dB SNR gain than the randomly selected relay method (no-BSR), and about 12 dB SNR gain than that in the non-cooperation. Figure 4 shows the same simulation results under R = 2 bps/Hz, and the outage probability is increased under the same SNR compared to the results under R = 1 bps/Hz. At the same time, it can be found that when the outage probabilities approach 10^{-4}, BSR can achieve about 5 dB SNR gain than that of the no-BSR case.

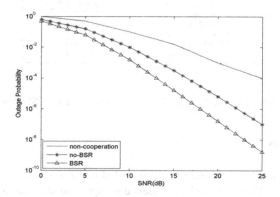

Fig. 3. Comparison of outage probability performance under R = 1 bps/Hz

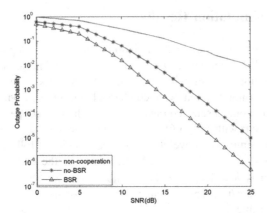

Fig. 4. Comparison of outage probability performance under R = 2 bps/Hz

Figure 5 shows the average SER performance comparison results under 8-PSK modulation. While in plotting the theoretical result of the proposed BSR approach, the approximation equation in (24) is used. It can be found that the SER performance of the randomly selected relay method is better than that of non-cooperation method, and the SER performance of the proposed BSR approach is better than that of the randomly selected relay method. It can also be observed that in all these three methods, the simulation results coincide with the corresponding theoretical results well, which also verify the correctness of the SER theoretical analyses results in last Section.

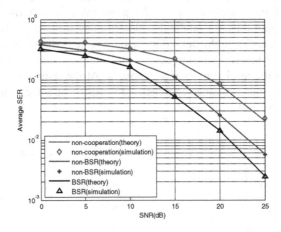

Fig. 5. Comparison of average SER performance under 8-PSK modulation

5   Conclusions

In this study, we proposed a kind of relay-assisted coded cooperation and BSR node selection method with co-channel interference to optimize the stratospheric communication system. The strategy takes advantage of relay-assisted coded cooperation to increase the capacity of system and selects the best relay node to increase the SNR gain. Both the theoretical analyses and numerical simulation results show that the proposed BSR method can effectively reduce the outage probability and decrease the average SER performance compared with those of no-BSR method and non-cooperation method.

Acknowledgements. This research work is supported by the National Natural Science Foundation of China under Grant Nos. 91438113 and 61771308, the Important National Science and Technology Specific Project of China under Grant No. 2016ZX03001022-006, the Shanghai Science and Technology Committee under Grant No. 16DZ1100402, and the open research fund of National Mobile Communications Research Laboratory of Southeast University under Grant No. 2017D11.

References

1. Tozer, T.C., Grace, D.: High-altitude platforms for wireless communications. Electron. Commun. Eng. J. **13**(3), 127–137 (2001)
2. Ni, Y., Jin, S., Wong, K.K., Zhu, H., Shao, S.: Outage analysis for device-to-device communication assisted by two-way decode-and-forward relaying. In: 2013 International Conference on Wireless Communications and Signal Processing, pp. 1–6 (2013)
3. Wen, S., Zhu, X., Lin, Y., Lin, Z., Zhang, X., Yang, D.: Achievable transmission capacity of relay-assisted device-to-device (D2D) communication underlay cellular networks. In: 2013 IEEE 78th Vehicular Technology Conference (VTC Fall), pp. 1–5 (2013)
4. Min, H., Lee, J., Park, S., Hong, D.: Capacity enhancement using an interference limited area for device-to-device uplink underlaying cellular networks. IEEE Trans. Wireless Commun. **10**(12), 3995–4000 (2011)
5. Laneman, J.N., Tse, D.N.C., Wornell, G.W.: Cooperative diversity in wireless networks: efficient protocols and outage behavior. IEEE Trans. Inf. Theory **50**(12), 3062–3080 (2004)
6. Behnad, A., Rabiei, A.M., Beaulieu, N.C.: Generalized analysis of dual-hop DF opportunistic relaying with randomly distributed relays. IEEE Commun. Lett. **17**(6), 1057–1060 (2013)
7. Simon, M.K., Alouini, M.S.: Digital Communication over Fading Channels, 2nd edn. Wiley, Hoboken (2005)
8. McKay, M., Zanella, A., Collings, I., Chiani, M.: Error probability and SINR analysis of optimum combining in Rician fading. IEEE Trans. Commun. **57**(3), 676–687 (2009)

Exploiting DTN Routing Algorithms Under Resource Constraints

Risu Cha, Yutao Chen, Liang Wan, and Jian Wang[✉]

School of Electronic Science and Engineering,
Nanjing University, Nanjing 210023, China
mf1623002@smail.nju.edu.cn, wangjnju@nju.edu.cn

Abstract. Delay/disruption tolerant network (DTN) is originated from the pioneer research into interplanetary internet and later, researchers found that DTN can also be applied to many challenged networks. Several DTN routing protocols have been presented to improve the routing performance, since message delivery is difficult in such networks due to the absence of stable end-to-end paths. However, the protocols ignore the fact that the nodes in DTN like satellites and other wireless devices usually have very limited resources like battery, bandwidth, and storage. In this paper, we introduce four existing routing algorithms and two new routing algorithms we propose, and compare their performances of delivery ratio and latency in the case of limited buffer size under both ground and space environment. We obtain the curves of the network throughput varying with the network load, and find it showing a congestion phenomenon, from which we can compare the congestion control capacities of the routing protocols. Simulation results show that our newly proposed routing protocols can successfully cope with the congestion caused by storage constraints.

Keywords: Social networks · Forwarding algorithms
Delay-tolerant networks

1 Introduction

Delay/disruption Tolerant Networks (DTNs) are characterized by their intermittent connectivity, time evolving topology, long message delays, and lack of stable end-to-end paths. DTNs can be divided into terrestrial DTN and spatial DTN according to the different scenes. The terrestrial DTN is composed of a variety of wireless devices like smart phone, laptop, or even vehicles, while the space DTN is mainly consist of satellites. Millions of devices are connected via the Internet, providing reliable communications over the standard protocol set on the transmission control protocol/Internet Protocol (TCP/IP). However, the Internet relies on some assumption like continuous bidirectional end-to-end paths, short round trips, symmetric data rates, and with the proliferation of wireless devices, the Internet has limitations to provide a satisfactory performance in connecting the millions of wireless devices popping up [1]. At the same time, due to the constraints of satellite platforms and inter-satellite links (ISL), only limited number of ISLs can be equipped on the satellites (e.g., only one ISL can be

© Springer Nature Singapore Pte Ltd. 2018
Q. Yu (Ed.): SINC 2017, CCIS 803, pp. 218–226, 2018.
https://doi.org/10.1007/978-981-10-7877-4_19

equipped on one satellite) and the ISLs in space networks will subject to long delay, intermittent connectivity and asymmetric bandwidth [2]. It is worth mentioning that the nodes of space DTN are not limited to satellites. With the rapid development of China's aerospace industry, the traditional spatial information transmission mode cannot meet the needs of complex space operation, so the establishment of a heterogeneous spatial information network has become the key to promote the process of information [3].

Due to the absence of end-to-end connection, traditional routing protocols for the Internet cannot be applied on DTN directly, so several routing algorithms for DTN have been proposed. The main purpose of many existing routing algorithms is to find a relay node that is more likely to transfer the data to the destination. To determine such a relay node, a variety of approaches are used including estimating node meeting probabilities, packet replication, network coding, and leveraging prior knowledge of mobility pattern [4].

DTN routing protocols can be classified as replication-based and forwarding-based according to their forwarding patterns. For replication-based DTN routing protocols, like Epidemic routing [5], Spray and Wait [6], the message is duplicated from one node to his several neighbors according to certain rules, so there will be several copies of the message transfer in the network. Such protocols can improve the delivery ratio while at the cost of increasing transmission overhead and buffer occupancy. On the other hand, for forwarding-based routing algorithms, like Direct Transmission, FRESH [7], and SimBet Routing [8], each packet has a single copy since it is forwarded to the neighbor and deleted from the current node. With the application of rational forwarding strategy, forwarding-based routing can also gain improved routing performance.

Early proposed routing protocols concentrate on improving the routing performance, and assuming there is no resource constraint. However, DTNs are often subject to severe constraints of resource like transmission bandwidth, buffer size, and energy. Therefore, several recently done works addressed some transmission scheduling and buffer management problems in their proposed DTN routing schemes [9, 10]. Due to the resource constraint, there always exist congestion in DTNs, so some measures should be taken to control congestion. Congestion control mechanism of DTN can be classified as proactive or reactive control [11]. Proactive congestion control (also known as congestion avoidance) schemes take a preventive approach and try to prevent congestion from happening in the first place; in reactive congestion control, end systems typically wait for congestion to manifest itself before any action is taken. Proactive congestion control can ease congestion by controlling the data rate of the source node, however, when congestion is severe, this method cannot effectively alleviate congestion.

In this paper, we study the routing in DTNs where buffer sizes of nodes are constrained, and compare the performance of four existing routing protocols and two newly proposed routing protocols under such situation. We further measure the throughput under different network loads, and find that when the load increases to a certain value, the congestion occurs, from which we can compare the congestion control abilities of different routing protocols.

2   DTN Routing Protocols

In this section, we introduce four existing routing protocols and two proposed routing protocols. Epidemic routing, Direct Transmission, FRESH and Simbet Routing are existing routing protocols proposed in the previous works, while FRESH_BM and SimBet_BM are newly proposed routing protocols in this paper.

2.1   Existing Routing Protocols

Epidemic routing. Epidemic routing is a typical flooding based routing algorithm, which is named for its data transmission process that similar to the spread of infectious diseases. In such routing procedure, two encounter nodes send all of their carrying messages to each other, and finally have identical sending lists. Since a large number of copies of messages transmitted in the network, Epidemic routing can reach the optimal delivery ratio at the expense of huge resource consumption. Therefore, the Epidemic routing is suitable for networks with high bandwidth and large buffer size. However, for the networks of limited storage capacity, it may lead to the decrease of routing efficiency due to frequent packet loss.

Direct Transmission. Direct Transmission is one of the simplest DTN routing algorithms. The idea of the algorithm is that if and only if there is a link between the source node and the destination node, the message is transmitted directly from the source to the destination, otherwise, the message still stay with the source node. Data transmission does not pass any intermittent nodes, so there exist only one copy for each message at any time. The advantage of Direct Transmission is that it has the lowest consumption of network resources. However, the source node needs to wait for a long time or even a permanent wait to transmit data to the destination node, which can result in large delay and low success rate. The Direct Transmission is suitable for scenarios where the network topology is known and the nodes' mobility is a priori, such as the urban public transport network.

FRESH. FRESH is an enhanced version of Direct Transmission. For FRESH, each node store the newest encounter time with the nodes it meet. When two nodes encounter, if the former node has a fresher encounter time with the destination, the message is forwarded to it. Otherwise, the node carries the message and waits for next encounter. Compared to Direct Transmission, FRESH achieve improved success rate, and also increased cost, but the cost of it is still much less than Epidemic routing.

SimBet. SimBet is a kind of social-based DTN routing protocol, which utilizes the similarity and betweenness centrality for making forwarding decision. The similarity is defined as the common neighbors of two nodes, as shown in (1),

$$sim(i,j) = N(i) \cap N(j) \tag{1}$$

where N(i) and N(j) are the sets of neighbors of node i and j. The betweenness centrality measures the extent to which a node lies on the paths linking other nodes and it is calculated as (2),

$$C_B(i) = \sum_{j=1}^{N} \sum_{k=1}^{j-1} \frac{g_{jk}(i)}{g_{jk}} \qquad (2)$$

where g_{jk} is the total number of geodesic paths linking node j and k, and $g_{jk}(i)$ is the number of those geodesic paths that include node i. When two nodes encounter, if the former node has a higher similarity with the destination, or it has a higher betweenness centrality, the message is forwarded to it. Otherwise, the message stays with the nodes. The goal is to find the right community of destination, where nodes in it have higher similarity with each other than other nodes. To let the messages home in there community, central nodes with high betweenness centrality are used to carry them between communities.

2.2 Proposed Routing Protocols

In this subsection, we propose two new routing algorithms that add buffer management to FRESH and SimBet.

FRESH_BM. FRESH_BM is based on FRESH and is designed to address the lack of buffer management in FRESH. At each node, it calculate the Freshness Value (FV) of each message from the latest encounter time between nodes, and sort the messages according to their FVs. The FV of message M_k at node i is calculated as (3),

$$FV(M_k, i) = \frac{1}{CT - ET(d_k, i)} \qquad (3)$$

where CT is the current time, d_k is the destination node of the message M_k, and the ET is the latest encounter time of two nodes. FV indicate the freshness of the contact between two nodes. Therefore, we assume that the messages with higher FV have greater probabilities to be delivered since the current node more likely to meet the destination of them. When two nodes encounter, the sending node traverses the sending queue, which is sorted by the descending order of the FV, and if the buffer size of receive node is full, the node drop the messages from the queue tail, until it can accommodate the message.

SimBet_BM. SimBet_BM is familiar with the FRESH_BM, but it sort the message according to the SimBet Value (SV) instead of FV, and choosing the relay nodes as SimBet do. Definition of SV is of message M_k at node i is shown as (4),

$$SV(M_k, i) = 0.5sim(d_k, i) + 0.5bet(d_k) \qquad (4)$$

where d_k is the destination node of the message M_k, $sim(d_k, i)$ is the similarity of d_k and i, and $bet(d_k)$ is the betweenness centrality of the d_k. SV indicates the social relation between two nodes, and messages with higher SV is more likely to be delivered, so messages are also sorted by the descending order of the SV. Like FRESH_BM, SimBet_BM also transmit the messages from the queue head, and delete the messages from the queue tail.

3   Simulation Settings and Performance Metrics

3.1   Simulation Settings

In this paper, all simulations are based on NetworkX, a complex network analyzing package of Python. We use two data sets MIT and SPACE for simulations. MIT data set [12] is mobility traces collected from real network environment, while SPACE [2] is a synthetic contact simulating the communication between satellites.

MIT. The MIT contacts were collected in the Reality Mining project [12], where 97 students and employees of MIT were equipped with ceil phones scanning every 5 min for Bluetooth devices in proximity during 9 months. For our simulations, we define time slice as day, and classify contacts according to their date. We cut the traces by using contacts reported between February 2005 and March 2005.

SPACE. The SPACE contacts model is composed by a medium earth orbit (MEO) satellite constellation, and it is inspired by the work of Yan et al. [2]. The satellite constellation is walker-δ 24/3/2 which has 24 satellites in 3 orbits and each orbit has 8 satellites, and each satellite is equipped with one half-duplex ISL.

3.2   Performance Metrics

The protocols are evaluated for two performance metrics: delivery ratio and latency. They can be illustrated as:

Delivery ratio. Delivery ratio is the percentage of delivered packets. Increasing message delivery ratio is the main goal of any DTN routing protocol. Message delivery ratio is given by:

$$DeliveryRatio = \frac{1}{M} \sum_{k=1}^{M} R_k \tag{5}$$

where M is the number of messages created and $R_k = 1$ if message m_k is delivered, otherwise $R_k = 0$.

Latency. Latency is the total time spent between message creation and delivery. The latency measure of protocol can be done by calculating the average latencies of messages. The average latency is calculated as:

$$Latency = \frac{1}{N} \sum_{k=1}^{N} ReceiveTime_k - CreationTime_k \tag{6}$$

where N is the total number of messages received, the parameters $ReceiveTime_k$ and $CreationTime_k$ represents the receiving time and creation time of message k.

4 Result and Discussion

Although DTN has a variety of resource constraints, the buffer size is often the most important resource since if it is set unreasonably, it will lead to a large number of packet loss or a serious waste of resources. So we focus on the impact of buffer size on the routing protocols, and compare their optimal delivery ratios and the corresponding minimum buffer sizes. To simulate the buffer-size constraint of network, we set a buffer size (i.e. length of data storage list) and initially create messages for all other nodes for each node. When two nodes exchange messages, only if the former node's buffer has more space, the message can be forwarded to it. We measure the delivery ratio and latency of each protocol under different buffer size, and compare them in Figs. 1 and 2.

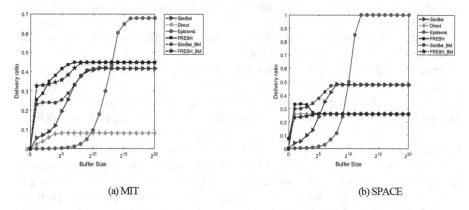

(a) MIT   (b) SPACE

Fig. 1. Effect of increasing buffer size on delivery ratio

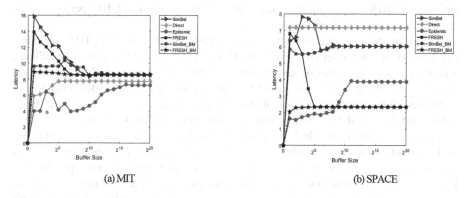

(a) MIT   (b) SPACE

Fig. 2. Effect of increasing buffer size on latency

As Fig. 1 implies, the delivery ratios initially increase and then achieve a nearly constant value as the buffer size is increased. This is because initially there is an increased message drop rate due to low buffers, resulting in the low values of delivery ratio, and as the buffer size is increased, delivery ratio also improves due to decrease in message drops. However, when it increases to a certain value, it can fully satisfy the requirement of buffer size for data transmission, so increasing the buffer size makes no sense anymore.

As is shown in Fig. 2, the latencies of Epidemic routing and Direct Transmission are very slight at the beginning, and gradually increase with the increase of buffer size. This is because when the buffer size is tiny, only a small amount of messages between close nodes are delivered, and with the stabilization of the delivery ratios, the latencies also tent to be stable. At the contrast, the latencies of SimBet and FRESH are high at the beginning, and decrease with the buffer size increase. From Fig. 1, we know that they can achieve high delivery ratios even with small buffer size, but with the limit of buffer size, it can not make the most advisable choice for the relay nodes, which leads to a larger delay at the beginning. However, the Epidemic routing and Direct Transmission will not encounter such problems, since they do not have selection strategy for relay nodes. The latencies of FRESH_BM and SimBet_BM are both very smooth, almost no impact on the size of the cache.

Based on the simulation results, it can be concluded that Epidemic routing has the highest delivery ratio (67.87% for MIT and 100% for SPACE), and lowest latency for MIT (7.24) but the buffer size it needs to achieve optimal performance is much larger than others. On the other hand, FRESH and SimBet are achieving both high delivery ratios and reasonable latencies, since there routing strategy is more intelligent than Epidemic routing and Direct Transmission. We also observe that on the MIT contact, which represents the terrestrial DTN, FRESH outperforms SimBet with greater delivery ratio and lower latency, while SimBet achieves higher delivery ratio but also higher delay on the SPACE contact. The performances of newly presented protocols FRESH_BM and SimBet_BM are also shown in the graph, and we find that when the buffer size is tiny, two new protocols perform better than their older versions with higher delivery ratio and lower latency, and the optimal performances is identical with the older. Therefore, we can infer that FRESH_BM and SimBet_BM performs well even with the limited buffer size.

To further compare the performance of FRESH, SimBet, FRESH_BM, and Sim-Bet_BM, we set the buffer size to 2^7 for MIT and 2^5 for SPACE, and add different network loads to the network and observe the changes in network throughput. The network throughput here is measured by the number of messages delivered to the destination. When network load is k, it means that there has $k \times N \times (N - 1)$ messages to be transmitted in the network, where N is the number of nodes in the network.

From the results shown in Fig. 3, we observe that with the increment of network load, throughput of both Simbet and FRESH initially increases as network load increases, however, when the load reaches a certain value, it begin to sharply decline. The reason for such behaviour is that initially the load (i.e. number of messages) of the network is far less than the buffer size, so the number of packets delivered increase with the increment of load. However, when the load reaches the buffer size, the message transmission became difficult and the throughput decrease.

When the congestion reaches a certain level, the data transmission of the SimBet and FRESH will be almost stagnant, making the network in a state of paralysis. However, for FRESH_BM and SimBet_BM, the throughputs increase at the beginning,

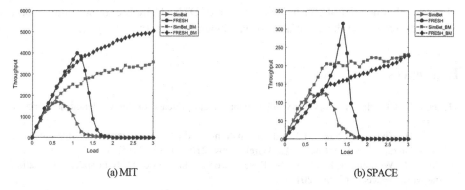

(a) MIT   (b) SPACE

Fig. 3. Effect of increasing network load on throughput on Simbet and FRESH

and maintain a certain value when the network loads reach a certain value, and Sim-Bet_BM even can improve the optimal throughputs of the network. This is because we sort the messages according to their priority, and the messages with higher priorities are preferentially transmitted during the data transmission, at the same time, if the buffer size of receive node is full, we drop some messages that with lower priorities to accept the newly coming messages. With the data dropping policy, there are always data transmitting in the network, and congestion caused by the heavy network load can be eased to a certain extent. But it is also very "dangerous" since it may lead to heavy data lost.

5 Conclusion and Future Work

Many previously proposed DTN routing protocols focus on performance improvement and ignore the resource constraints such as transmission bandwidth, buffer size, and energy. In this paper, we analyze and compare the performance of four DTN routing protocols (i.e. Epidemic routing, Direct Transmission, SimBet and FRESH) under the buffer size constrained situation, and propose two new routing protocols (i.e. FRESH_BM and SimBet_BM). The results show that SimBet and FRESH perform better than the other two, since the Epidemic routing has the highest delivery ratio but also needs highest buffer size, and the delivery ratio of Direct Transmission is too low. We also find that FRESH performs better on the MIT, while SimBet has a better performance on the SPACE than FRESH, and both of FRESH_BM and SimBet_BM achieve better performances than their older versions when the buffer size is small. For further discussion, we observe the network throughput of SimBet, FRESH, Sim-Bet_BM, and FRESH_BM under different network loads. The results show that congestion generated on SimBet and FRESH with the increase of the network load, and SimBet_BM and FRESH_BM can ease the congestion with the dropping policy.

Although the data dropping policy can ease the congestion, but it also leads to heavy data lost, So our future work will concentrate on the combination of the proactive and reactive congestion control mechanisms, to better control the congestion and reduce the data dropping. In this paper, we only discuss the buffer size constraint, which is only one kind of constrained resource of DTN. Therefore, in our future work, we will consider also the constraints of bandwidth and energy.

References

1. Jain, S., Chawla, M.: Survey of buffer management policies for delay tolerant networks, 1 (2014)
2. Yan, H., Zhang, Q., Sun, Y.: Local information-based congestion control scheme for space delay/disruption tolerant networks. Wirel. Netw. **21**(6), 1–13 (2015)
3. Shen, J., Weiming, L.I., Zhang, S.: Research on application of DTN in space information network. Spacecraft Eng. (2015)
4. Balasubramanian, A., Levine, B., Venkataramani, A.: DTN routing as a resource allocation problem. SIGCOMM Comput. Commun. Rev. **37**(4), 373–384 (2007)
5. Vahdat, A., Becker, D.: Epidemic routing for partially-connected Ad Hoc networks (2000)
6. Spyropoulos, T., Psounis, K., Raghavendra, C.S.: Spray and Wait: an efficient routing scheme for intermittently connected mobile networks. In: Proceedings of the 2005 ACM SIGCOMM Workshop on Delay-Tolerant Networking, pp. 252–259 (2005)
7. Dubois-Ferriere, H., Grossglauser, M., Vetterli, M.: Age matters: efficient route discovery in mobile Ad Hoc networks using encounter ages. In: Proceedings of the 4th ACM International Symposium on Mobile Ad Hoc Networking and Computing, pp. 257–266 (2003)
8. Daly, E.M., Haahr, M.: Social network analysis for routing in disconnected delay-tolerant MANETs. In: Proceedings of the 8th ACM International Symposium on Mobile Ad Hoc Networking and Computing, pp. 32–40 (2007)
9. Dimitriou, S., Tsaoussidis, V.: Effective buffer and storage management in DTN nodes. In: 2009 International Conference on Ultra Modern Telecommunications Workshops, pp. 1–3 (2009)
10. Zhang, X., Zhang, H., Gu,. Y.: Impact of source counter on DTN routing control under resource constraints. In: Proceedings of the Second International Workshop on Mobile Opportunistic Networking, pp. 41–50 (2010)
11. Silva, A.P., Burleigh, S., Hirata, C.M., et al.: A survey on congestion control for delay and disruption tolerant networks. Ad Hoc Netw. **25**(PB), 480–494 (2015)
12. Eagle, N., Pentland, A.: Reality mining: sensing complex social systems. Pers. Ubiquit. Comput. **10**(4), 255–268 (2006)

Performance of Fountain Code Based Photon Counting Deep-Space Communication Systems

Chenjia Wei, Yueying Xiang, Xiaolin Zhou[(⊠)], Chongbin Xu,
and Xin Wang

Key Laboratory of EMW Information, Fudan University, Shanghai, China
zhouxiaolin@fudan.edu.cn

Abstract. Deep space communications have characteristics such as long communication distance, heavy channel fading and limited equipment and source, leading to a more stringent requirement than that of ground communication. To this end, this paper proposes a fountain code based deep-space communication system. The fountain code has low decoding complexity and good error performance to meet the requirement of the channel coding for the deep space communication. Building on the proper model of deep space channel, we combine the photon counting scheme and fountain coding to combat the channel fading in deep-space communications. The simulation results show that the error probability of the proposed system can approach 10^{-3} for the transmit distance of 1.5×10^8 km, with a transmit power of 1 W and coding rate of 1/3, thereby meeting the demand of deep space communications.

Keywords: Deep space communication · Fountain code · Poisson shot noise
Photon counting

1 Introduction

Due to the long transmission distance, loss of link and severe bit error, deep space communication is facing the problem of transmission delay and low received SNR that neither satellite communication nor terrestrial wireless communication has [1]. Therefore, traditional forward error correction (FEC) and feedback retransmission technique cannot be applied in deep space communication. In order to realize reliable communication in channels where power is constrained, channel coding technique plays a vital role in improving the performance of the system. What traditional channel coding technique mainly does is to correct error of information in physical layer. Automatic repeat request mechanism has to be adopted to guarantee the reliable communication when the correcting process fails. However, automatic repeat request is hard to meet the demand of deep space communication because of the limit of over long transmission time of the link. At present, fountain code [2] has been utilized to realize the reliable communication in deep space as a rising coding method.

Fountain code is an FEC coding method based on group coding. In the encoding process, the original data is divided into several groups, and each group generates redundant information during the coding to eliminate the influence of channel on data. The transmitter sends the encoding information continuously, and the redundant

© Springer Nature Singapore Pte Ltd. 2018
Q. Yu (Ed.): SINC 2017, CCIS 803, pp. 227–235, 2018.
https://doi.org/10.1007/978-981-10-7877-4_20

information is generated and sent just as a fountain, until the receiver can completely recover the original file [3]. Therefore, this kind of mechanism can recover data efficiently without the feedback channel, complete the reliable transmission of information, and avoid long waiting for feedback confirmation. Fountain codes can meet the requirements of deep space communication for information transmission reliability and communication quality, and have great potential in the field of deep space communications [4].

In deep space communications, wireless optical communication, as a rising high rate wireless communication technology, has been in the spotlight due to its high-speed data transmission rate [5]. The European Space Agency and NASA considered it as the next generation of technology used in satellite communication [6, 7]. Because of the quantum effects in optical communications, Poisson channel model is often adopted in deep space communication based on photon counting channels [8]. Dolinar et al. [9] studied on the limited transmission rate of Poisson channel under the modulation of on-off keying (OOK) and pulse position modulation (PPM); Matuz et al. [10] discussed the performance of LDPC codes in Poisson channel under PPM modulation. In recent years, Poisson channel based on photon counting has gradually become the focus of research on optical communication systems. The performance of the system is analyzed by theoretical deduction and simulation [11].

Based on the analysis and modeling of deep space channels, a deep space communication system based on photon counting technique and fountain code coding is proposed in this essay. After modeling and calculating the link budget for deep space channel, this paper analyzes the attenuation of wireless optical signal caused by deep space channel, designs a deep space communication system based on photon counting Poisson model and fountain codes encoding technology, and deducts the likelihood ratio of received signals as well as iterative decoding algorithm based on the principle of decoding of fountain codes.

2 Channel Model and Link Budget

Deep space channel is composed of ground part and free space part. When signal travels through the atmosphere, absorption and reflection of waves by the ionosphere can lead to signal attenuation, and high frequency waves will be absorbed by the atmosphere as well; for the free space part, transmission signal can be affected by Cosmic noise and solar radiation. We assume that the modulation mode is OOK, so that we have the Average input signal power [12]

$$P = \frac{1}{2} r |\alpha|^2 f_c h, \tag{1}$$

where r is the number of optical pulses transmitted per second, f_c is signal center frequency, and h is Planck constant. If the receiving end adopts Poisson photon counting, the number of photon that is received satisfies the Poisson distribution [13], so for the received codes r_j we have probability mass function

$$P(r_j|\lambda) = \frac{\lambda^{r_j}}{r_j!}e^{-\lambda}, \, j = 1,\ldots,N, \tag{2}$$

where j is the Serial number of the received signal, and λ is the average number of the received photons:

$$\lambda = D_f \cdot n_s \cdot c_j + n_b, \tag{3}$$

where D_f is the Fresnel number in free space transmission [13], n_s is the number of received photons when transmitted code $c_j = 1$, and n_b is the Photon interference introduced by Background light radiation. In Far field free space communication, the transmitting end and the receiving end communicate with each other through two Circular antennas. We assume A_t, A_r respectively represent the area of transmitting antenna and receiving antenna, f_c is Signal center frequency, and L is the Signal transmission distance, then the Fresnel number in free space transmission is [11]

$$D_f = \frac{A_t A_r}{c^2 L^2}f_c^2, \tag{4}$$

where c is the speed of light. In the case of Narrowband transmission, deep space communication can be divided into near field communication $(D_f \gg 1)$ and far field communication $(D_f \ll 1)$ according to the Order of magnitude of the Fresnel number. Thus we can have the Log Likelihood Ratio of the received signal as

$$L_{ch}^j = \log\frac{P(r_j|c_j = 1)}{P(r_j|c_j = 0)} = r_j \cdot \log\left(1 + \frac{D_f \cdot n_s}{n_b}\right) - D_f \cdot n_s, \, j = 1,\ldots,N, \tag{5}$$

where $P(r_j|c_j)$ is the conditional probability density function of the deep space channel.

3   Fountain Code Encoding and Decoding

Fountain code is a sparse graph code which is widely used in erasure channels. The sender keeps encoding and transmitting packets as a fountain, while the receiver decodes the received packets. When the receiver receives enough coding information, it can decode successfully, and then the sending end stops sending the encoded information [14]. Luby Transform (LT) is one of the most common-used fountain codes. We suppose a K-bit sequence as $s = \{s_1, s_2, \ldots s_K\}$, and the encoder generates the Coding vector $g_n = [g_{n1}, g_{n2}, \ldots, g_{nK}]$ according to the set Degree distribution function, noting the nth coded bit as $c_n = \left(\sum_{k=1}^{K} s_k \bullet g_{nk}\right)$ mod 2. The relationship between the coded bit $c = \{c_1, c_2, \ldots c_N\}$ and the information bit can be described as

$$\mathbf{c} = \mathbf{Gs}, \tag{6}$$

where the Generating matrix $\mathbf{G} = [\mathbf{g_1}, \mathbf{g_2}, \ldots, \mathbf{g_n}]$ is $N \times K$. In LT code, codes are generated and transmitted continuously, until the sender gets the acknowledge information by the receiver. The encoding process can be shown through Tanner graph [15] as in Fig. 1.

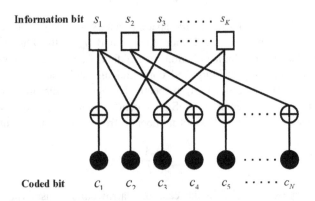

Fig. 1. Tanner graph of LT code

Every column of the generating matrix $\mathbf{G}$ is chosen randomly based on Degree distribution function $\rho(d)$. In Block code, degree depicts the number of the information bits involved in the encoding process, while Degree distribution function $\rho(d)$ describes the proportion of different degrees d in the process of encoding. The proportion of the node where $d = t$ is given by $\rho(d) = n_t/n$, in which n_t is the number of the nodes where $d = t$, and n is the total number of the nodes. While encoding, the number of the information bits chosen randomly is determined by the Polynomial of degree distribution of the check node decoder (CND) as

$$h(x) = \sum_{t=1}^{h_{\max}} h_t x^t, \tag{7}$$

where the coefficient h_t is the proportion of the CND with a degree of t, and it meets $\sum_{t=1}^{h_{\max}} h_t = 1, 0 \le h_t \le 1$, where $h_{\max}$ is the max check node degree. Because of the fact that the information bits are determined by CND in random and variable node decoder (VND) obeys Poisson distribution, the Polynomial of degree distribution of VND can be nearly expressed as

$$v(x) = \sum_{t=1}^{v_{\max}} v_t x^t, \tag{8}$$

where the coefficient v_t is the proportion of the VND with a degree of t, and it meets $v_t = \frac{e^{-\mu}\mu^t}{t!}$, where $v_{\max}$ is the max variable node degree. The coefficient μ of Poisson distribution is given by

$$\mu = h_{avg}\frac{N}{K} \tag{9}$$

where h_{avg} is the Degree distribution of average VND. For the sake of improving the BER performance of fountain codes, VND with lower Degree distribution need to be as less as possible. A degree query table [16] recording Degree trajectory of the Variable nodes can be built up to provide adjacent degrees for all VND. This kind of degree distribution can bring a better system performance.

In deep space channels, signals are influenced by Channel fading and noise during transmission period, resulting in the uncertainty of the correct start of the decoding. Belief propagation (BP) algorithm [17] is introduced to solve this problem. Making use of the received soft information, BP algorithm does Iterative operation between CND and VND. The soft information being delivered is the Log Likelihood Ratio of the received symbols. Under the given Channel estimation and receiving signal, we estimate the Posterior probability of every symbol of the Noisy sequence in every step of the iteration, and send the estimated Posterior probability to the next iteration. The soft information $L_{c_j \to v_i}$ [18] that the jth CND passes on to the ith VND can be written as

$$L_{c_j \to v_i} = 2\tanh^{-1}\left(\tanh\left(\frac{L_{ch}^j}{2}\right)\right) \times \prod_{i' \in \aleph(j)\backslash(i)} \tanh\left(\frac{L_{v_{i'} \to c_j}}{2}\right) \tag{10}$$

where $\aleph(j)\backslash(i)$ represents all VNDs that are linked to the jth CND except the ith one. On the other hand, the soft information $L_{v_i \to c_j}$ [18] that the ith VND passes on to the jth CND can be written as

$$L_{v_i \to c_j} = \sum_{j' \in \aleph(i)\backslash(j)} L_{c_j \to v_i} \tag{11}$$

where $\aleph(i)\backslash(j)$ represents all CNDs that are linked to the ith VND except the jth one. The decoded information bits $\hat{s}_i$ can be shown as

$$\hat{s}_i = \sum_{j \in \aleph(i)} L_{c_j \to v_i} \tag{12}$$

4   Simulation Results and Analyses

This paper focuses on the bit error rate (BER) of fountain codes, discusses the system performance of fountain code system based on photon counting under the conditions of different transmit power, transmission distance and encoding bit rates in the case of the downlink of deep space channels. The simulation parameters are set [12] as shown in Table 1:

Table 1. Symbols and simulation parameters

Variables and dimensions	Symbolic definition	Range of values
P [W]	Input power	$10^{-2} - 10^2$ W
fc [Hz]	Center frequency	220 THz
L [km]	Transmission distance	$10^8 - 10^{10}$ km
R [slot/s]	Symbol generation rate	10^{11} slot/s
At [m]	Transmitting antenna diameter	0.31 m
Ar [m]	Receiving antenna diameter	10 m

Figure 2 shows the BER performance of the system at different transmission distances when transmitting power P = 0.5 W, P = 1 W, and P = 10 W are simulated. It can be seen from the simulation results that, the performance of fountain codes based on photon counting is excellent. For the communication distance within 10^8 km, BER can be under 10^{-3} with the transmitting power P = 0.5 W, covering the area within Mars also known as the near field communication range; when the communication distance goes up to 1.6×10^8 km (Mars), transmission power needs to be increased to P = 1 W to achieve a relatively low BER; furthermore, when the communication distance is 6×10^8 km (Jupiter), transmission power needs to be further increased to P = 10 W to achieve a BER of 10^{-2}. As depicted from the graph, for fixed transmit power, the performance of the system increases with the increase of transmitting distance, and the performance of point to point far field communication is pretty poor.

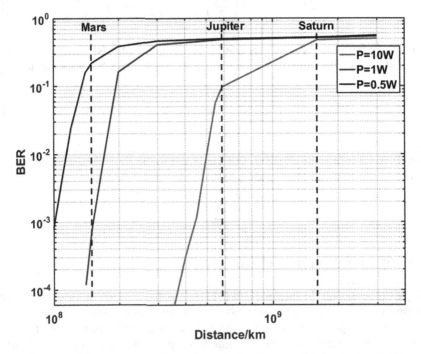

Fig. 2. BER of the system at different transmission distance with fixed transmit power

Figure 3 discusses the system error performance at different transmit powers for Mars, Jupiter, and Saturn. According to the simulation results, the increase of the communication distance imposes relatively big influence on the performance of fountain code system based on photon counting. When the transmission distance is 1.6×10^8 km (Mars), 6×10^8 km (Jupiter) and 1.5×10^9 km (Saturn), systems whose transmitting power are P = 1 W, P = 10 W and P = 100 W can achieve BER under 10^{-3}. It can be seen that as the communication distance increases, the attenuation of the signal in the deep space channel is becoming more and more serious, and the power of the transmitted signal needs to be improved to compensate for the attenuation of the channel.

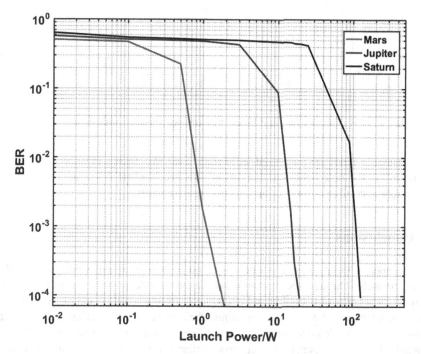

Fig. 3. BER of the system at different transmit power with fixed transmission distance

According to the analysis about the principle of fountain code, the matrix generated by the receiver based on the received encoding packages is random and does not have full rank. In order to ensure the performance of decoding, encoding can adopt longer code length, depending on the law of large numbers to ensure the stable decoding performance. Nevertheless, too long code length means more decoding complexity and more storage space. Figure 4 discusses the variation of system error performance with changing transmission distance at different code lengths. The simulation results show that, the larger the information encoding length K is, the lower BER can be approached at the same transmission distance. However, the extent of this reduction is becoming smaller and smaller, and with the increase of the transmission distance, the system

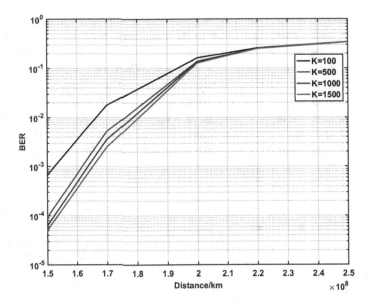

Fig. 4. BER of the system at different transmission distance with fixed code length

performance cannot be increased efficiently even by increasing the code length. Therefore, in the near field communication, it is necessary to select the coding length reasonably according to the communication requirements.

5 Conclusions

In this paper, a fountain code system based on photon counting is designed for deep space channels. Through the modeling and analysis of deep space channel, this paper designs the scheme of encoding and decoding of fountain codes, and deduces the Log Likelihood Ratio of the received signal and the soft value information of the Variable nodes and the Check nodes in the process of iterative decoding based on the Poisson channel. Also in this paper, the bit error performance of the system under different transmission power, different transmission distance and different coding rate are simulated, and the influence of transmission power, transmission distance and coding rate on the system is discussed. The simulation results show that the error probability of the proposed system can approach 10^{-3} for the transmit distance of 1.5×10^8 km, with a transmit power of 1 W and coding rate of 1/3, thereby meeting the demand of deep space communications. For deep space channels, a good design of Error correcting code can bring more reliability for the system, and improve the performance of the system with an obvious effect.

Acknowledgments. This work was supported by the National Natural Science Foundation of China under Grant No. 61571135, Shanghai Sailing Program 17YF1429100 and State Key Laboratory of Intense Pulsed Radiation Simulation and Effect Funding.

References

1. Sofia, J.J., Jayakumari, J.: Application of LT code technology in deep space communication. In: Global Conference on Communication Technologies, Thuckalay, pp. 458–463, 23–24 April 2015
2. Shokrollahi, A.: Raptor codes. IEEE Trans. Inf. Theor. **52**(6), 2551–2567 (2006)
3. Mitzenmacher, M.: Digital fountains: a survey and look forward. In: IEEE Information Theory Workshop, San Antonio, pp. 271–276, 24–29 October 2004
4. Yao, W., Chen, L., Li, H., et al.: Research on fountain codes in deep space communication. In: Congress on Image and Signal Processing, Sanya, pp. 219–224, 27–30 May 2008
5. Hashmi, A.J., Eftikhar, A., Adibi, A., et al.: Optimization of an optical array receiver for deep-space optical communication during earth-mars conjunction phase. In: IEEE Photonics Global Conference, Singapore, pp. 1–5, 13–16 December 2012
6. Giancristofaro, D.: Modems for deep space optical communications: from RF to optical deep space, the European contribution. In: Italian National Conference on Photonic Technologies, Rome, pp. 2–6, 6–8 June 2016
7. Edwards, B.L., Israel, D.J.: A geosynchronous orbit optical communications relay architecture. In: IEEE Aerospace Conference, Big Sky, pp. 1–7, 1–8 March 2014
8. Wang, L., Wornell, G.W.: A refined analysis of the Poisson channel in the high-photon-efficiency regime. IEEE Trans. Inf. Theor. **60**(7), 4299–4311 (2014)
9. Dolinar, S., Erkmen, B., Moision, B., et al.: The ultimate limits of optical communication efficiency with photon-counting receivers. In: IEEE International Symposium on Information Theory Proceedings, Cambridge, pp. 541–545, 1–6 July 2012
10. Matuz, B., Toscano, G., Liva, G., et al.: A robust pulse position coded modulation scheme for the Poisson channel. In: IEEE International Conference on Communications, Sydney, pp. 2118–2123, 10–14 June 2014
11. Zhu, X., Kahn, J.M.: Free-space optical communication through atmospheric turbulence channels. IEEE Trans. Commun. **50**(8), 1293–1300 (2002)
12. Waseda, A., Sasaki, M., Takeoka, M., et al.: Numerical evaluation of coherent signals for deep-space links. In: International Conference on Space Optical Systems and Applications, Santa Monica, pp. 334–342, 11–13 May 2011
13. Atkin, G.E., Fung, K.S.L.: Coded multipulse modulation in optical communication systems. IEEE Trans. Commun. **42**(234), 574–582 (1994)
14. Guha, S.: Classical capacity of the free-space quantum-optical channel. Massachusetts Institute of Technology (2004)
15. Yao, W.D., Li, H., Chen, L.J., et al.: Study on the fountain codes in deep space communications. Syst. Eng. Electron. **31**(1), 40–44 (2009)
16. Etesami, O., Shokrollahi, A.: Raptor codes on binary memoryless symmetric channels. IEEE Trans. Inf. Theor. **52**(5), 2033–2051 (2006)
17. Hussain, I., Xiao, M., Rasmussen, L.K.: Error floor analysis of LT codes over the additive white Gaussian noise channel. In: IEEE Global Telecommunications Conference, Kathmandu, pp. 1–5, 5–9 December 2011
18. Jenkac, H., Mayer, T., Stockhammer, T., et al.: Soft decoding of LT-codes for wireless broadcast. Proc. IST Mob. Summit **9**(1), 262–264 (2005)
19. Waseda, A., Sasaki, M., Takeoka, M., et al.: Numerical evaluation of PPM for deep-space links. J. Opt. Commun. Netw. **3**(6), 514–521 (2011)

Research on Cooperative Caching Strategy in 5G-Satellite Backhaul Network

Yuanxin Feng[1,2(✉)], Weidong Wang[1,2], Shuaijun Liu[1,2],
Gaofeng Cui[1,2], and Yinghai Zhang[1,2]

[1] Key Laboratory of Universal Wireless Communications,
Ministry of Education, Beijing, China
[2] Information & Electronics Technology Lab,
Beijing University of Posts and Telecommunications, Beijing, China
fengyuanxin@bupt.edu.cn

Abstract. With the advantage of stable communication links and broadcast coverage, satellites play an irreplaceable role in terrestrial-satellite integrated system nowadays. However, when taking consideration of satellite transmission in backhaul link, it will cost a long time due to its high altitude. As we know, 5G network will be deployed in 2020 with the requirements of higher capacity and lower latency. Thus, how to reduce the delay of transmission in 5G-satellite backhaul link after users' request is the research we discussed. Caching is considered an efficient and time-saving technique in terrestrial communication networks. Based on this reference, a cooperative caching strategy is proposed in this paper where caches can be placed at macro-micro cells deployed on the ground as well as satellite. Our target is to minimize the average latency of users during the requested files transmitting between satellite and ground. Then, we formulate the cooperative caching optimization problem as a NP-Hard problem. Furthermore, to avoid meeting premature convergence, the proposed optimized cooperative caching strategy is based on simulated annealing algorithm to carry out the caching allocation efficiently. The simulation results demonstrate that the proposed caching strategy can improve the performance of users' QoS.

Keywords: 5G-satellite networks · Cooperative caching
Heterogeneous network · Heuristic algorithm

1 Introduction

In recent years, due to the abundant multimedia services and the development of mobile internet, mobile data traffic is increasing explosively [1, 2]. With the upcoming deployment and completion of the use of the 5G network in 2020, people will enjoy a more efficient and convenient network life. However, we should notice that the existing communication facilities are network deployed on the ground. Once experienced natural disasters, such as earthquake, or suffered social unrest, like war, ground infrastructure is easily damaged. This will affect the efficiency of network even cause communication interruption.

© Springer Nature Singapore Pte Ltd. 2018
Q. Yu (Ed.): SINC 2017, CCIS 803, pp. 236–248, 2018.
https://doi.org/10.1007/978-981-10-7877-4_21

Therefore, it is necessary to introduce satellite as the data forwarding in 5G-backhaul link. Satellites have the characteristics of wide coverage and little influenced by the change of the external environment. By taking advantages of them, we can construct a stable and efficient communication network.

5G network should have the ability of loading much larger traffic than current network, and providing users with less than 1 ms access delay over the ratio access network (RAN) [3]. In brief, 5G requires higher capacity and lower latency. In this paper, we assume the macro-micro cell deployed on the ground network to increase the capacity of system. However, when taking consideration of satellite transmission, it will cost a long time due to its high altitude. In this paper, we propose a cooperative caching strategy between 5G network and satellite, which can effectively reduce the unnecessary consumption of backhaul link delay.

Caching is considered an efficient and time-saving technique in terrestrial communication networks. To make effective use of caching, an informative decision has to be made as to which documents are to be evicted from the cache in case of cache saturation. In fact, caching can be applied to the environment of 5G-satellite backhaul network, and there are some related research previously. This is particularly important in a wireless network, where the size of the client cache at the satellite terminal is small [4]. [4] researches the problem of joint transport cluster, and the strategy to reduce the backhaul link data traffic when consider caching at the base stations. [5] takes latency into consideration, which focus on cooperative caching for multicast to improve caching hit ratio, thus to enhance QoS of users. [6] formulates femtocell-like BS called helpers to make up a wireless dispersed topology and to study caching strategy in them. However, these studies did not consider the introduction of satellite caching. [7] takes the situation that satellite works as data relay and storage module to cache files in terrestrial-satellite backhaul link. However, it neglects considering that each user should requests for particular files instead of requests' probability, which is not accurate. In addition, the genetic algorithm proposed in that optimization process will fall into local convergence.

In this paper, we combine satellite with terrestrial 5G network as backhaul link to transmit data files. Under this situation, a cooperative caching strategy is proposed where caches can be placed at macro-micro cells as well as satellite. Contents for caching are set according to files popularity and the cooperation of each node. The probability for caching the same file is different. This kind of cooperative caching strategy could arrange the cache content more reasonable, and could remarkably reduce the average latency of users.

The contribution of this paper is three-fold:

(1) We propose a novel network architecture, which obtains terrestrial macro-micro cell and satellite to storage and delivery content efficiently. The satellite could receive the file requests from ground stations during **the collection interval**, and then send files back to the ground through the broadcast. This practical scenario can be applied to future 5G networks.

(2) We analyze the cooperative relationship of each node, and make the optimized cache strategy. Then formalize the problem of 5G-satellite cooperative caching and show that finding the optimal placement is NP-hard.

(3) To avoid meeting local optimal solution, we propose an optimized caching strategy based on the simulated annealing algorithm. By using the mechanism of slow cooling and Metropolis criterion, the optimal solution can be obtained.

The rest sections of the article are arranged as follows. In Sect. 2, We model the applicative scenario of 5G-satellite backhaul network, and analyze its cooperative caching model. Then, In Sect. 3, we formulate the problem of caching and propose an optimized caching strategy based on the simulated annealing algorithm. In addition, the simulation result is showed in Sect. 4. Finally, the conclusions we gained are drawn in Sect. 5.

2   System Model and Analyze

In this section, we firstly formulate a caching model of 5G-satellite network. Then we model the service procedure of content delivery based on the network. In particular, the process of file caching and delivery on satellite is discussed. In addition, we analyze the 5G-satellite caching problem and propose a cooperative caching model between each nodes. Finally, the delay calculation is analyzed that will be implemented in this paper.

2.1   Terrestrial-Satellite Caching Topology

We formulate the terrestrial-satellite model in Fig. 1. It can be seen that satellite as a node in 5G return link, plays the role of data relay in the process of content delivery. A geostationary satellite could transmit the requested data from a remote server to local earth stations over its broadcasting property.

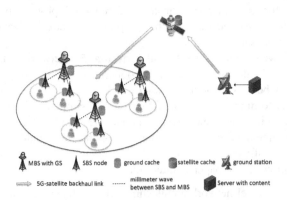

Fig. 1. 5G-satellite caching model in backhaul link

To achieve the target of dense access and high system capacity in 5G networks, a heterogeneous network with joint distribution of the macro-cell and small-cell is constructed on the ground. Each macro-cell base station (MBS) distributed dispersedly with its coverage ranges from 1 km to 25 km. Through the configuration of the ground station (GS) facilities, MBS can communicate with the satellite. We place small-cell base stations (SBSs), such as pico-cell and femto-cell [9], connected to MBS by millimeter wave. Users are randomly distributed within the broadcast and directly connected to SBSs.

In the proposed terrestrial-satellite system, caches are deployed on satellite and all MBSs and SBSs, under the different limitation of storage capacity. We assume that cached content should be in the form of files, which attracts people, like hotpot-multimedia. The caches in SBSs can be denoted by set $\mathbf{C}_1$, and we have

$$\mathbf{C}_1 = \left\{\mathbf{x_{s_1}}, \mathbf{x_{s_2}}\ldots\mathbf{x_{s_{N1}}}\right\}^T, \ \mathbf{x_{s_n}} = \left\{x_{s_n,1}, x_{s_n,2}\ldots x_{s_n,I}\right\} \tag{1}$$

where N_1 is the amount of SBSs. similarly, caches in MBS can be:

$$\mathbf{C}_2 = \left\{\mathbf{x_{m_1}}, \mathbf{x_{m_2}}\ldots\mathbf{x_{m_{N2}}}\right\}^T, \mathbf{x_{s_m}} = \left\{x_{s_m,1}, x_{s_m,2}\ldots x_{s_m,I}\right\} \tag{2}$$

and the satellite caching is set as $\mathbf{x_0}$ which could be denoted as

$$\mathbf{x_0} = \left\{x_{0,1}, x_{0,2}\ldots x_{0,I}\right\} \tag{3}$$

All cached file state values {0, 1}. In addition, the cache capacity of each SBS is V_1, and V_2, V_0 denote the size of MBS and satellite.

Moreover, to make full use of the characteristic of broadcast, we present a **collection interval** τ for satellite to receive file requests from ground stations. Though the cache capacity on satellite is limited, it can reduce the consumption of satellite radio resources and improve the QoS of users.

2.2 Service Procedure

The service of content delivery procedure can be described as follows. Users request for the target file to affiliated SBS in the probability of file popularity. If the local SBS cached the file, then user receives it directly. Otherwise, the request will go upward to MBS node as well as the adjacent SBS node until the target file is found. Once the file is not cached within the user's searchable range, the request will be sent to satellite.

The satellite could receive the file requests from ground stations during τ. If satellite cached the files, then send them back to the ground through the broadcast. If not, it continue to request to the remote server. Finally, the file will be delivered through satellite to the ground station (MBS) in backhaul link.

In our formulation, we make the following assumptions:

(1) The optimal caching placement in satellite and the terrestrial nodes has been accomplished in advance due to proposed optimized cooperative caching strategy.
(2) In our problem, we focus on multimedia files to cache, like video. We consider that the popularity of these contents update slowly, which follow Zipf distribution. The popularity of the i-th file [8] can be denoted as

$$P_i = \frac{\Omega}{r_i^z} \qquad (4)$$

where $\Omega = (\sum_i^I r_i^{-z})^{-1}$, and r_i represents the ranking of popularity of the i-th file in all files. z is a random number between [0, 1].

(3) In our system, all users send file requests at the same time, and we consider files with same size to simplify the calculation.

(4) The delay of transmission between users and terrestrial nodes can be ignored compared with the satellite-terrestrial backhaul link. Therefore, in this paper, we do not consider the time delay in ground transport.

2.3   Cooperative Model

Formulating a cooperative relationship between nodes to cache more reasonable is what we concerned. In this paper, we present a factor to reflect the probability between adjacent nodes caching the same file. The order of the nodes has been arranged in advance and the probability of caching the same file in two adjacent node should be different. When one node closer to user has cached the file i, the probability of the next node caching the same file could be represented as

$$h_{n+1,i} = \frac{\alpha}{1 - (-1)^{C_{n,i}} h_{n,i}} = \begin{cases} \frac{\alpha}{1 - h_{n,i}} & x_{n,i} = 1 \\ \frac{\alpha}{1 + h_{n,i}} & x_{n,i} = 0 \end{cases} \qquad (5)$$

where $h_{n,i}$ denotes the probability of closer node caching the file i, which could be considered the popularity of file i. $x_{n,i} \in \{0, 1\}$ represent the caching desicion in n-th node. α is a constant values between [0, 1], which could be considered the degree of collaboration between two nodes. In accordance with the cooperation between nodes, it can improve the utilization ratio of nodes and ensure the diversity of cache content.

2.4   Delay Calculation Model

In this paper, we optimize the cache scheme to reduce the average delay after user requests. As we consider delivery of multimedia files which users are not sensitive, we do not set a specific threshold. When files needs to be relayed or downloaded from satellite, the transmission will create a consumption of delay. We set $t_d = 270$ ms to represent delay once by the satellite-ground link if target file is cached on satellite. Else, the delay becomes $2t_d$. The results will be shown in the following experiments compared with previous algorithms.

3   Problem Formulation and Solution

In this section, we construct the optimization problem of caching in the proposed 5G-satellite caching model. Through the formulation, we conclude that this is a NP-Hard problem. Therefore, we propose a cooperative caching strategy based on the simulated annealing (SA) algorithm to get the optimal scheme. The symbols used in this problem are summarized in Table 1.

Table 1. Parameter descriptions

Symbol	Description
C_1	Cache in SBS shown in (1)
C_2	Cache in MBS shown in (2)
C_0	Cache in satellite
$\mathbf{x_s}$	Caching result in s-th SBS
$\mathbf{x_m}$	Caching result in m-th MBS
$\mathbf{x_0}$	Caching result of in satellite
V_1	Cache size of SBS
V_2	Cache size of MBS
V_0	Cache size of satellite
s_i	The size of file i
r_k	The request of user k
$h_{n,i}$	A factor to reflect the cooperation between adjacent nodes
S_k	The set of SBS that attached to user k
M_k	The set of MBS that attached to user k
$q_{m,k}$	Search result arriving at MBS attached to user k
$q_{0,k}$	Search result arriving on satellite attached to user k
λ	The average arrival rate on satellite
p_0	The average arrival number on satellite
τ	Collection interval that satellite receives request from ground
t_d	Time delay of propagation from satellite to ground

3.1 Problem Formulation

We assume $\mathbf{r_k} = [0,1,0,\ldots 0]_{1 \times I}$ as the request of user k which is subjected to Eq. (3), and 1 represents the demand file. According to the system model, the request first arrives the belonged SBS to search the cache. We set $q_{m,k}$ as the search result arriving at affiliated MBS, which could be denoted:

$$q_{m,k} = \| \mathbf{r}_k * \mathbf{x}_s \|_{s \in S_k} \tag{6}$$

where $\mathbf{x}_s = \{x_{s,1}, x_{s,2} \ldots x_{s,I}\}$, $s \in S_k$ represents the cache state in s-th SBS belonged to user k, and the operation here is Hadamard product. The $q_{m,k}$ values 0 or 1, which indicates if the search should be carried out in MBS or not. Similarly, the search result arriving at satellite could be expressed as:

$$q_{0,k} = \| \mathbf{r}_k * \mathbf{x_m} \|_{m \in M_k} (1 - q_{m,k}) \tag{7}$$

where $\mathbf{x_m}$, $m \in M_k$ represents cache in m-th MBS that user k could connect. In this paper, we consider that the amount of request arrives at satellite follows Poisson distribution with the average arrival rate λ. Obviously, the arrival number on satellite could be concluded by:

$$p_0 = 1 - e^{-\lambda \tau} \qquad (8)$$

Thus, in our formulation, time delay during the transmission of the whole backhaul link can be split into two sections: $q_{0,k}p_0 \parallel \mathbf{r_k} * \mathbf{x_0} \parallel t_d$ (when satellite cached the file), and $q_{0,k}p_0(1- \parallel \mathbf{r_k} * \mathbf{x_0} \parallel)2t_d$ (when satellite just relay the file from remote server).

Therefore, we can deduce our objective function:

$$\min \frac{1}{K} (\sum_{k \in K} q_{0,k}p_0 \parallel \mathbf{r_k} * \mathbf{x_0} \parallel t_d + \sum_{k \in K} q_{0,k}p_0(1- \parallel \mathbf{r_k} * \mathbf{x_0} \parallel)2t_d) \qquad (9)$$

subject to:

$$h_{n+1,i} = \frac{\alpha}{1 - (-1)^{C_{n,i}} h_{n,i}} \qquad (10)$$

$$s_i \parallel \mathbf{x_s} \parallel \ \leq V_1 \qquad (11)$$

$$s_i \parallel \mathbf{x_m} \parallel \ \leq V_2 \qquad (12)$$

$$s_i \parallel \mathbf{x_0} \parallel \ \leq V_0 \qquad (13)$$

$$x_{s,i} \in \{0,1\} \qquad s \in S_k, i \in I \qquad (14)$$

$$x_{m,i} \in \{0,1\} \qquad m \in M_k, i \in I \qquad (15)$$

$$x_{0,i} \in \{0,1\} \qquad i \in I \qquad (16)$$

Constraints (10) guarantees the cooperative caching relationship between adjacent nodes. (11), (12) and (13) emphasize that caches at SBS, MBS, and satellite node should not exceed their respective capacity sizes. Finally, the set of constraints (14), (15) and (16) explain the 0–1 range of the cache variable.

It is obvious that this optimal problem is a NP-Hard problem with high complexity. In order to find an optimal solution of Eq. (8), we adopt the simulated annealing algorithm to solve this cooperative caching problem.

3.2   Solution

After the discussion of the objective function, we can conclude that problem in Eq. (8) is a NP-Hard problem since it contains both continuous variables and 0–1 variables, and existing multilayer iterations. Therefore, we decide assuming a heuristic algorithm to solve the problem. As a prevalent algorithm, Simulated Annealing (SA) is generally applied in global optimization problems [9]. It overcomes the defects of local minimum and the dependence on initial value. In the process of cooling, the particles tend to be orderly, and finally the inner energy reduce to the minimum, that is, in our problem, the optimal caching results can be obtained.

In our optimization strategy, we consider C_1, C_2, C_0 as particle state. In the case of given initial temperature T_0 and attenuation parameter K, the system begin to cool down. The state of particles at each iteration can be expressed as

$$C_1^n = \{x_{s1}, x_{s2} \cdots x_{sN_1}\}^T = \{x_{s_1,1}, x_{s_1,2} \cdots x_{s_1,l}, x_{s_2 1} \cdots x_{sN_1,l}\}$$

$$C_2^n = \{x_{m1}, x_{m2} \cdots x_{mN_2}\}^T = \{x_{m_1,1}, x_{m_1,2} \cdots x_{m_1,l}, x_{s_2 1} \cdots x_{mN_2,l}\} \quad (17)$$

$$C_0^n = \{x_{0,1}, x_{0,2} \cdots x_{0,l}\}$$

which represent cache decision in SBS, MBS and satellite nodes. The iteration number L is set at each temperature T, and a new set of solutions is generated in each iteration according to the Metropolis criterion. The current optimal solution is outputted until the termination condition is satisfied. The simulated annealing processes is shown in Algorithm 1, the functions within are explained in the latter:

Initialization:

The initial solution space $\{C_1^1, C_2^1, C_0^1\}$ is randomly decided before algorithm implementation.

Update Criterion:

According to the criteria formulated in the Eq. (5), at each iteration of the same temperature, we find nodes that has the possibility of optimization, then randomly select some of them to adjust according to cooperation. By means of balancing random and cooperation, the system can achieve quasi equilibrium when iteration finished at current temperature.

Metropolis Criterion:

We set $\Delta f = f(\widehat{C}_1^{n+1}, \widehat{C}_2^{n+1}, \widehat{C}_0^{n+1}) - f(C_1^n, C_2^n, C_0^n)$. When meet $\Delta f < 0$, the new states $\{\widehat{C}_1^{n+1}, \widehat{C}_2^{n+1}, \widehat{C}_0^{n+1}\}$ is always accepted. If not, we implement Metropolis Criterion as follows:

$$\{C_1^{n+1}, C_2^{n+1}, C_0^{n+1}\} = \begin{cases} \{\widehat{C}_1^{n+1}, \widehat{C}_2^{n+1}, \widehat{C}_0^{n+1}\} & if \ \exp(-\Delta f/t) > r \\ \{C_1^n, C_2^n, C_0^n\} & else \end{cases} \quad (18)$$

where r is an uniform random number in [0,1]. Through the formula, the worse solution can be retained with a certain probability.

Termination Criterion:

In our algorithm, we set the criteria for termination when target value maintains stable, that is, the function converges, and then finishes the iteration cycle with the optimal values $\widetilde{F}$. In the following simulation, we can prove that the final solution $\{\widetilde{C}_1, \widetilde{C}_2, \widetilde{C}_0\}$ is the global optimum.

Algorithm 1 *SA Algorithm*

Input

T_0 : initial temperature; T_{stop} :terminal temperature; K :attenuation parameter;

L : iteration times; *Update* :criterion for update the solution set in each iteration

process; L_{stop} :iterative stopping condition; f : objective function.

Output

$\{\widetilde{C}_1, \widetilde{C}_2, \widetilde{C}_0\}$: optimal solution space;

$\widetilde{F}$: optimal objective function.

Process

1: $\{C_1^1, C_2^1, C_0^1\}$ = Initialization (); $t = T_0$

2: while ~termination criterion:
     $t = t * K$

3:   for L=0, L_{stop}, L++ do
       $\{\widetilde{C}_1^{n+1}, \widetilde{C}_2^{n+1}, \widetilde{C}_0^{n+1}\}$ = Update(C_1^n, C_2^n, C_0^n)
       $\{C_1^{n+1}, C_2^{n+1}, C_0^{n+1}\}$ = Metropolis criterion();
     end
   end

4: $\widetilde{F} = f(\widetilde{C}_1, \widetilde{C}_2, \widetilde{C}_0)$

---

4   Simulation Results

To verify the cache efficiency of our proposed algorithm, we compare it with the genetic algorithm proposed in [3], as well as random cache strategy. Genetic algorithm is one of the heuristic algorithms to find approximate optimal solution, but is easy to converge prematurely. The results of the experiments show that our algorithm based on cooperation can avoid this problem. We assume that SBSs are uniformly assigned to MBS and each base station cover all users within the satellite beam range. The parameters we adopt in simulation could be listed in Table 2.

4.1   Influence of Satellite-Caching Capacity on Delay

From Fig. 2, we can see that, with the increase in satellite cache capacity, the average latency of users through different strategies are all of a downward trend. This is because that link consumption could be saved between remote server and satellite when satellite-caching capacity gradually increases. It is obvious that delay of the random cache strategy is the longest, for storing duplicate files, resulting in low utilization efficiency.

The results obtained by the genetic algorithm are basically consistent with the algorithm we proposed, but at some points, the results it worked out are relatively

Table 2. Typical parameters for simulation

Symbol	Description	Values
N_1	The number of SBSs	40
N_2	The number of MBSs	10
s_i	The size of files	1
I	The number of files	10000
V_1	The capacity of SBS	100
V_2	The capacity of MBS	200
V_0	The capacity of satellite	Variable or 200
τ	Collection interval of satellite broadcast	Variable or 5
T_0	Initial temperature	100
K	Attenuation parameter	0.998
L	Iteration in each temperature	50

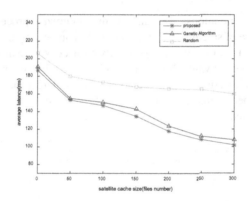

Fig. 2. The influence of satellite cache size on average delay ($\tau = 5$)

higher. This represents they do not reach the global optimum. When satellite capacity increases, the complexity of the algorithm becomes larger, and is easier to get the local optimal solution. In contrast, the strategy we proposed achieves the better performance. The proposed algorithm can select the solution with relatively poor performance at a certain probability in each iteration. As the temperature drops slowly, the system search and filter adequately and finally get the optimal solution.

4.2 Influence of Collection Interval of Satellite Broadcast

From Fig. 3 we can obtain that when τ increases, results of random cache decreased obviously whereas others' are smooth with no further improvement in average delay. This is because that the results obtained by the heuristic algorithm are already close to the optimal allocation that can be optimized. The effect of satellite broadcast duration is little. At the same time, it can also be verified that the performance of our proposed algorithm is better than the former algorithm.

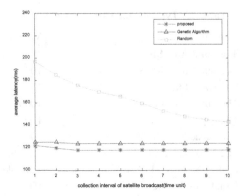

Fig. 3. The influence of collection interval of satellite broadcast on delay ($V_0 = 200$)

4.3   The Tendency of Delay

With the increase of iterations, we can see the optimized process of target value through SA when size of satellite is 200 in Fig. 4. As can be seen from the graph, in the process of annealing, the target value is gradually reduced, and finally tends to be stable and converges to a specific value. It is worth noting that, when the number of iterations is about 10 and 20, the system selects the point which is larger than current target. We can infer that the metropolis is carried out in this iteration, and the value of poor performance is selected.

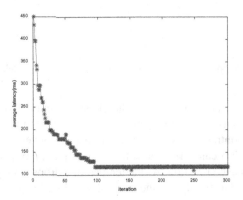

Fig. 4. Tendency of the average latency ($\tau = 5$, $V_0 = 200$)

To better reflect the role of collaboration, we observe the impact of different schemes on performance by changing the number of nodes. As we can see in Fig. 5, the average delay decline in each scenario. It is worth mentioning that the result of SA algorithm is very close to other schemes when the amount of cooperative nodes is very little or even zero. As the number of nodes increases, the complexity of content distribution increases as well, and the result of simulated annealing algorithm decreases

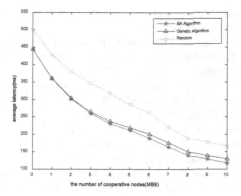

Fig. 5. The influence of the number of cooperative nodes on average delay ($\tau = 5$, $V_0 = 200$)

rapidly and finally reaches the minimum. In contrast, the genetic algorithm can also achieve relatively good results accompanied by weaker performance; the effect of random allocation is obviously unsatisfactory.

According to the existence of a certain probability to select the solution with poor performance, we can finally obtain the best performance of users in the terrestrial-satellite cooperative caching scenario.

5   Conclusion

In this paper, we propose a novel network architecture, which obtaining terrestrial macro-micro cell and satellite to storage and delivery content in backhaul link efficiently. To minimize the average delay of content delivery, we formalize the optimal problem and propose an optimized caching strategy based on the simulated annealing algorithm. The proposed caching strategy can obtain the global optimal solution, and has better performance than the previous algorithm to improve the QoS for users.

Acknowledgment. This work was supported by the National Natural Science Foundation of China (No. 91438114).

References

1. Fenech, H., Tomatis, A., Amos, S., Soumpholphakdy, V., Serrano-Velarde, D.: Future high throughput satellite systems. In: IEEE First AESS European Conference on Satellite Telecommunications (ESTEL), Rome, pp. 1–7, October 2012
2. Botta, A., Pescape, A.: New generation satellite broadband internet services: should ADSL and 3G worry? In: IEEE Proceedings of International Conference on Computer Communications (INFOCOM), Turin, pp. 3279–3284, April 2013
3. Nakamura, T., Benjebbour, A., Kishiyama, Y., et al.: 5G radio access: requirements, concept and experimental trials. IEICE Trans. Commun. **E98.B**(8), 1397–1406 (2015)

4. Balamash, A., Krunz, M.: An overview of web caching replacement algorithms. IEEE Commun. Surv. Tutor. **6**(2), 44–56 (2004)
5. Yu, Y.J., Tsai, W.C., Pang, A.C.: Backhaul traffic minimization under cache-enabled CoMP transmissions over 5G cellular systems. In: 2016 IEEE Global Communications Conference (GLOBECOM), Washington, DC, pp. 1–7 (2016)
6. Huang, X., Zhao, Z., Zhang, H.: Latency analysis of cooperative caching with multicast for 5G wireless networks. In: 2016 IEEE/ACM 9th International Conference on Utility and Cloud Computing (UCC), Shanghai, pp. 316–320 (2016)
7. Golrezaei, N., Shanmugam, K., Dimakis, A.G., Molisch, A.F., Caire, G.: FemtoCaching: wireless video content delivery through distributed caching helpers. In: 2012 Proceedings of the IEEE INFOCOM, Orlando, FL, pp. 1107–1115 (2012)
8. Wu, H., Li, J., Lu, H., Hong, P.: A two-layer caching model for content delivery services in satellite-terrestrial networks. In: 2016 IEEE Global Communications Conference (GLOBECOM), Washington, DC, pp. 1–6 (2016)
9. Web Caching and Zipf-like Distributions: Evidence and Implications
10. Askarzadeh, A., dos Santos Coelho, L., Klein, C.E., Mariani, V.C.: A population-based simulated annealing algorithm for global optimization. In: 2016 IEEE International Conference on Systems, Man, and Cybernetics (SMC), Budapest, pp. 004626–004633 (2016)

Task Flow Based Spatial Information Network Resource Scheduling

Fei Sun, Lin Gui[✉], and Haopeng Chen

Shanghai Jiao Tong University, Shanghai 200240, China
{sf19912010,guilin,chen-hp}@sjtu.edu.cn

Abstract. Spatial information network (SIN) acting as an important infrastructure for real-time access, transmission and processing of spatial information is of great significance to the development of the country. Considering the current situation of the uneven distribution of the overall satellite resources in China's space application system, the inefficient use of resources and single system. Based on the study of spatial missions and resources, in this paper, we propose a task flow based spatial network resource scheduling mechanism. Particularly, we formulated it into an integer programming problem. A heuristic algorithm is applied to solve this problem. Finally, simulation results demonstrate that the proposed resource scheduling mechanism can effectively achieve multi-user, multi-task optimized access control and resource mapping.

Keywords: Spatial information network · Resource scheduling
Task flow · Integer programming · Heuristic algorithm

1 Introduction

Spatial information network (SIN) is a network system based on space platforms (e.g. synchronous satellite or medium and low orbit satellites, stratospheric balloons and unmanned aircraft) as the carrier, and serves for real-time access, transmission and processing of spatial information [1]. As an important national infrastructure, SIN can serve a large number of major applications such as ocean navigation, emergency rescue, navigation and positioning, air transportation, aerospace monitoring and control. With the continuous improvement of China's comprehensive national strength, the scope of national interests has expanded from the territory to the global and even space. Additionally, with the advance of the "the Belt and Road Initiatives" policy, the influence of China further expands in the global interests. Therefore, we must also consider the burst of spatial missions in some special areas. Consequently, these large and sudden resource demands further propose higher information transmission requirements to the SIN. However, the current satellite systems in China are divided into different departments. The scattered construction of satellite and the self-contained system make the utilization of space fragmented. On the other hand, the heterogeneous diversification of satellites and inter-satellite links, the differentiation

© Springer Nature Singapore Pte Ltd. 2018
Q. Yu (Ed.): SINC 2017, CCIS 803, pp. 249–258, 2018.
https://doi.org/10.1007/978-981-10-7877-4_22

of satellite ability, the differentiation of the technical management system and protocol and the decentralized pattern of autonomy have resulted in the passive situation of the uneven distribution of the overall satellite resources and the inefficient use of resources and single systems in China's current space application system [2]. At present, there are about 10 users of relay satellite service in China. It is estimated that by 2020, the number of users will increase by 10 times, and the demand of user missions will increase dramatically. In the case that the platform resources are generally limited, the sudden changes of the number of users and spatial missions will make the contradiction between the limited resources and users' demands more intensified. In this case, how to realize the optimization of access control and resource mapping of the multi-user and multi-task, to achieve the efficient use of resources, is a major problem needed to be solved. Different from traditional networks on ground, SIN has the characteristics of dynamically changing network topology, various types of nodes and users and a wide range of services. And the spatial link has the characteristics of long delay, discontinuity, asymmetry of the data transfer rate and high error rate [3,4]. On the other hand, the types of resources in SIN are complex, including information collection resources (e.g. sensors, cameras), communication resources (e.g. spectrum, power), storage resources, and computing resources (e.g. CPU, DSP). In term of SIN missions, most of the spatial missions are described by natural language (e.g. to detect a certain area at a certain time), which is different from the single transmission task on the ground. Spatial missions generally need a variety of task combinations to complete, and there is a certain coupling between the tasks, which leads to some difficulties in resource scheduling. Therefore, it is necessary to describe the task flow of spatial missions as a reference for resource scheduling. However, there is little detailed analysis of the flow of spatial tasks in the existing resource scheduling research in SIN. Most of the researches are focused on single constraint target [5–8]. Therefore, we propose a task flow based resource scheduling mechanism in SIN, and further investigate the impact of the task flow on result of the resource allocation in SIN. With the analysis of the resources requirement and the existing empirical task flows of the missions in SIN, we propose a task flow based resource scheduling mechanism in SIN. Considering the restriction of SIN resources and the mission demands, the proposed mechanism divides and reschedules the task flows of the missions, so as to meet the demands of more spatial missions. And this is a multi-task scheduling problem, i.e. a multi-attribute decision-making problem. There exists lots of multi-attribute decision-making problems in engineering design, economy, management, military and many other areas. However, in SIN, there are few researches on multi-task planning, while most of the existing researches mainly focus on the selection of existing decision-making methods. Similar researches have been done in multidimensional planning of space and unmanned aerial vehicle coordination [9,10].

2   Task Flow Based Resource Scheduling

First of all, according to the characteristics and empirical data of traditional spatial missions, we describe the task flow set of spatial missions (e.g. line, tree or mesh). Secondly, considering the task flow sets of the SIN missions, we divide and reschedule the task flows according to the QoS demands and resource status in SIN. Then the optimal resource mapping and assignment are carried out. Finally, we can acquire the optimal planning paths of the SIN missions and the corresponding resource allocation status. Here, the rescheduling task flow of a certain mission needs to conform to the logical relationship in the task flow set, however, can be integrated into multiple logical processes according to the network status.

2.1   Task Flow Description

Different from the traditional ground task, spatial missions are mostly described by natural language. In order to carry out resource scheduling, artificial decomposition is necessary. However, this kind of system is of low efficiency and has long response time. Therefore, in his paper, the decomposition of SIN missions are based on the existing empirical data, i.e. the missions are described as a collection of a variety of task flows. In this way, resource scheduling in SIN can be achieved in a more intelligent way, and the system efficiency can be improved. As shown in Fig. 1, we take a remote sensing satellite reconnaissance mission as an example. This kind of mission can be divided into a collection of multiple task flows. According to the network resources and mission conditions, we can intelligently choose the optimal logic process of tasks to improve system efficiency. As shown in Fig. 1, assuming an imaging mission for an area of 500 km * 500 km. The maximum width of single star in the constellation is 300 km. If single star

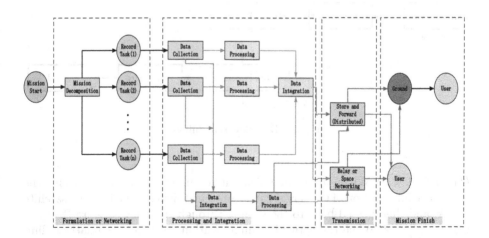

Fig. 1. SIN mission task flow modeling

cannot meet the imaging needs, satellites formation or networking can be used to record the target data. Data processing includes packaging or subcontracting, compression, deletion and extraction. The processing and integration need to be carried out according to the integrated considerations of the SIN resources and mission status. Additionally, the former processes will also impact the part of storage. According to the different width of the single image, the image size can vary from several GBs to tens of GBs, the storage resource of satellite are then constrained. Finally, the playback task of target data can be achieved by store and forward, relay satellite or space networking. The choice of specific task flow is related to the status of network resources and mission's QoS requirement.

2.2   Task Flow Scheduling

The ultimate goal of SIN resource scheduling is to achieve multi-task paths scheduling. According to the QoS requirements of the missions and the status of the network resources, we analyze and calculate the optimal task flow of each spatial mission, as well as the resource allocation status of each satellite on the scheduled path. Then, as shown in Fig. 2, for a single imaging mission, there may be multiple paths in case of different network and mission conditions.

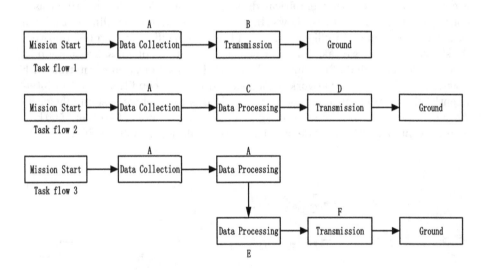

Fig. 2. Task flow scheduling

(1) Task flow 1: When the communication resources in SIN is sufficient, the image information of the target can be obtained through the imaging satellite A, and then passed back to the ground through the relay satellite B.
(2) Task flow 2: When the network communication resources are relatively limited, the image can be initially processed on satellite C, and then be passed back to the ground through satellite D.

(3) Task flow 3: When the network communication resources and the processing ability of C are limited, the image can be initially compressed on C and then spread to the E for further processing, and finally back to the ground through F. In summary, the final scheduling path of the spatial mission changes according to the different network conditions, however, the task path must meet the logic of the task process set in order to ensure the completion of the mission.

3 Problem Formulation

According to the description and analysis above, in this paper, we take the computation intensive mission as an example to model and analyze the task flow based resource scheduling in SIN.

3.1 Network Modeling

First of all, we divide the satellite nodes in SIN into user satellites and server satellites. The set of user is denoted by $U = \{u_1, u_2, \ldots u_K\}$, while the set of servers is represented by $C = \{c_1, c_2, \ldots c_L\}$. The processing frequency of the server satellite is assumed to be the same, represented by f_c, and the processing frequency of the user is f_u. And we use the Markov random channel to simulate the interstellar link, which includes only two cases of channel conditions (i.e. good or bad). The channel gain of the interstellar link is $g_t = \{g_G, g_B\}$, which corresponds to two different transmission rates.

$$r_t = \begin{cases} r_g, & g_t = g_G \\ r_b, & g_t = g_B \end{cases} \tag{1}$$

The transition probability matrix is,

$$P = \begin{vmatrix} p_{GG} & p_{GB} \\ p_{BG} & p_{BB} \end{vmatrix} \tag{2}$$

It is assumed that the transmission rate of the channel remains fixed during single unit time slot.

3.2 Task Modeling

The set of SIN mission is denoted by $A = \{a_1, \ldots a_K\}$, which corresponds to the set of the user satellite. We assume that all of the user's satellite missions can be decomposed into discrete tasks that can be transmitted. Each task can be processed on any of the server satellites in the network. As shown in the Fig. 3, each of the three spatial missions is divided into five tasks, respectively, where mission 1 is linear logic, mission 2 is tree logic and mission 3 conforms to mesh logic. Linear and tree logic missions are single input structures with strong logical relationship between tasks. While the relationship in the mission of mesh

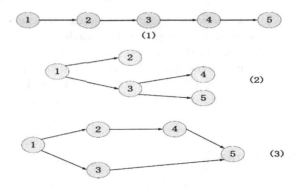

Fig. 3. Task modeling

logic is weaker compared to the former two logic models. However, the form of multiple input will lead to a higher computing complexity. We use matrixes to describe the logical structures of the SIN missions above, where each row of the matrix represents the input required to complete the task (i.e. the task set that needs to be completed in the previous session).

With the analysis above, single task is denoted by a ternary set $\phi_k = (\omega_k, \alpha_k, \beta_k)$, where ω_k represents the load of computation, α_k and β_k represent the amount of input and output data. In the linear logic shown in Fig. 3, there exists $\beta_k = \alpha_{k+1}$, while in the mesh logic $\alpha_5 = \beta_4 + \beta_3$, which means that task 5 must be completed with completion of task 3 and 4. In this way, the logical relationship between the tasks will directly affect the results of resource scheduling.

In order to calculate the response time of the SIN missions, we need to model the response time of each task first. The response time of each task is composed of queuing time, communication time and processing time. The processing time of task on satellite is represented as $p_{i,j} = \omega_i / f_j$ $(f_j = f_c \, or \, f_u)$. Due to the existence of multiple input, the task transmission delay need to take the logical matrix of the task into consideration. Then communication time of task on satellite is,

$$d_{i,j,k} = \max \left\{ \frac{\beta_l}{r_k} I_{i,l} \mid l < i, l \in N^* \right\} \tag{3}$$

where r_k represents the data transmission rate during the assigned time slot, $r_k = r_g, r_b, \infty$. $I_{i,l} = \{0, 1\}$ represents the input relationship of the former tasks. The unit slot for resource scheduling is defined as,

$$t = \frac{\min [d_{i,j} + p_{i,j}] + \max [d_{i,j} + p_{i,j}]}{2} \tag{4}$$

where

$$\min [d_{i,j} + p_{i,j}] = \frac{\min \{\omega_i\}}{f_c} \tag{5}$$

$$\max\left[d_{i,j} + p_{i,j}\right] = \max\left\{d_{i,j}\right\} + \frac{\max\left\{w_i\right\}}{f_u} \tag{6}$$

The queueing time for task can be denoted by,

$$q_{i,j,k} = \begin{cases} k - 1 - bt_i, & i = 1 \\ \{k - 1 - \max\left\{y * I_{i,l} * x_{l,*,y} \,\middle|\, l < i, y \le h, \right\}\} t, & i > 1 \end{cases} \tag{7}$$

where $q_{i,j,k}$ is the queueing time of task i on satellite j, bt_i $(i = 1)$ represents the birth time of task 1, i.e. the generate time of the whole mission. With the analysis above, the response time interval of task i can be defined as,

$$\tau_{i,j,k} = ((k-1)t - q_{i,j,k}, \quad kt] \tag{8}$$

And the response time of the spatial mission is the interval length of all the task response intervals.

3.3 Problem Formulation

With the analysis above, the task flow based resource scheduling in SIN can be modeled as follows

$$\min \quad \frac{1}{K} \sum_{l=1}^{K} \left| \bigcup_{\substack{i \le |a_l| \\ j \le n, k \le h}} \tau_{i,j,k} * x_{i,j,k} \right| \tag{9}$$

$$s.t. \quad \sum_{j=1}^{n} \sum_{k=1}^{h} x_{i,j,k} = 1 \tag{10}$$

$$x_{i,j,k} = 0 \ if \ t < d_{i,j,k} + p_{i,j} \tag{11}$$

$$q_{i,j,k} \ge 0 \tag{12}$$

$$x_{i,j,k} = \{0, 1\} \tag{13}$$

where n is the number of the satellites in SIN, h is the maximum amount of time required to complete all tasks. The target of the formulation is to minimize the average response time (9). Constraint (10) ensures that each task is only processed once. Constraint (11) ensures the rationality of the time slot arrangement. Constraint (12) guarantees the logical relationship of the spatial missions. Constraint (13) means that the problem is an integer programming problem.

According to the analysis, the proposed task flow based resource scheduling in SIN can be formulated into an integer programming problem, which is an NP-hard problem. It can be solved by search algorithms such as breadth-first search, depth-first search, Dijktra algorithm, Bellman-Ford algorithm and other deterministic graph search algorithm, branch and delimitation search algorithm, genetic algorithm (GA), particle swarm optimization (PSO) and so on.

4   Simulation Result

According to the above analysis, the task flow based resource scheduling can be formulated as 0–1 integer programming problem, which is an NP-hard problem. In particular, genetic algorithm is suitable for this kind of problem. Therefore, we apply a genetic algorithm to solve the above-mentioned integer programming problem, and acquire some preliminary simulation results. Specific simulation process is given as follows:

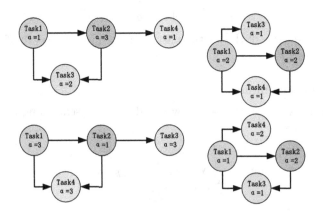

Fig. 4. Simulation task flow

First, we assume that there are 20 satellite nodes in the network, including 4 user nodes and 16 server nodes. The simulation time domain has a total of 30 time slots. And there are four missions randomly generated in the network. Each mission can be divided into 4 tasks. The logical flow of these tasks is shown in Fig. 4. The 4 spatial missions are generated in the 23rd, 22nd, 14th and 3rd time slot. According to the generate time of different missions, computation load of each task, logic flow and network resources status in the network, the final task allocation results are shown as follows. As shown in Fig. 5, so as to achieve the minimal response time of spatial missions, tasks belonging to a certain mission are allocated adjacently. The generate time and logical relationship between tasks impact the final results of resource assignment.

Additionally, in order to prove the efficiency of the proposed resource mechanism, we compare the genetic algorithm and greedy algorithm in the same simulation condition. Corresponding simulation results are shown in Fig. 6. As shown in Fig. 6, the average response time achieved by the genetic algorithm is 12.5 units, while the result of the greedy algorithm is 15 units. And it is observed that, the genetic algorithm can acquire better simulation results in about 100 iterations. In the simulations, the greedy algorithm only focuses on the minimization of the response time of a single mission. While the genetic algorithm concentrates on the minimization of the average response time of all the spatial missions. From

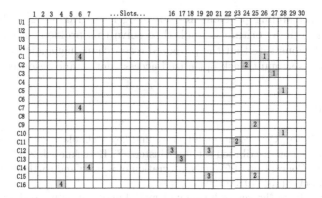

Fig. 5. Task time slot and satellite allocation

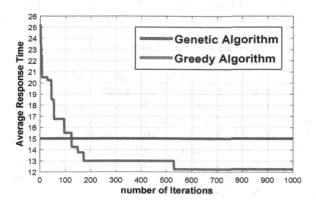

Fig. 6. Average response time

the simulation results we can see that, the genetic algorithm is better than greedy algorithm. Considering the dichotomy used in the genetic algorithm, the computational complexity of each iteration is $O(T) * [O(NH) + O\log(NH)]$, where T is the population of the task set. N and H denote the satellite and time set respectively. Therefore, the computational complexity of the genetic algorithm is $O(G) * O(T) * O(NH) = O(GTHN)$, where G is the number of iterations.

5 Conclusion and Future Work

Spatial information network (SIN) acting as an important infrastructure for real-time access, transmission and processing of spatial information is of great significance to the development of the country. Considering the current situation of the uneven distribution of the overall satellite resources in China's space application system, the inefficient use of resources and the single system. With the study of spatial missions and resources, in this paper, we propose a task flow based spatial network resource scheduling mechanism in SIN. In particular, we formulated the resource scheduling problem into an integer programming problem. Then a heuristic genetic algorithm is applied to solve this problem. Finally, simulation results demonstrate that the proposed resource management can effectively achieve multi-user, multi-task optimized access control and resource mapping.

References

1. Wang, J.C., Yu, Q.: System architecture and key technology of space information network based on distributed satellite clusters. ZTE Technol. J. **22**(4), 9–13 (2016)
2. Shen, R.J.: Conception of China's integration of heaven and earth aerospace Internet. Eng. Sci. **8**(10), 19–30 (2006)
3. Liu, F.: Study on the key technology of spatial information network resource management. Tsinghua University (2013)
4. Feng, Y.: Research and implementation of congestion control algorithms for the resource restricted space network. National University of Defense Technology (2013)
5. Cui, Z.X.: Research on relay satellite mission scheduling method. National University of Defense Technology (2009)
6. Dai, S.W., Sun, H.X.: Intelligent planning and scheduling system for spacecraft operations. Control Decis. **18**(02), 203–206 (2003)
7. Chen, K.: Research on distributed task planning model and algorithm for remote sensing satellite. National University of Defense Technology (2011)
8. Yin, L.: Multi-load earth observation satellite target access calculation and task scheduling method. National University of Defense Technology (2012)
9. Peng, Z.L., Zhang, Q., Li, Z.R., et al.: Improved maximizing deviation decision-making model and its application in multi-mission planning of near space system. Syst. Eng. Theory Pract. **34**(2), 421–427 (2014)
10. Deng, Q.B.: Research on multi-UAV collaborative mission planning technology. Beijing University of Science and Technology (2014)

Vortex Wave Generation Based on Tensor Holographic Artificial Impedance Surface

Xiao Shaoqiu[(⊠)] and Zhang Zongtang

Institute of Applied Physics,
University of Electronic Science and Technology of China,
Chengdu 610054, China
xiaoshaoqiu@uestc.edu.cn

Abstract. In this paper, a holographic vortex wave antenna with a modulated tensor artificial impedance surface is presented for the first time. This antenna consists of an array of sub-wavelength metallic patch with periodically varying gaps printed on a grounded dielectric substrate. The holographic impedance modulation technique is used to design the tensor impedance surface to generate vortex wave in a desired direction. A holographic antenna is designed as an example and simulated results are presented.

Keywords: Vortex wave · Orbital angular momentum
Holographic artificial impedance surface

1 Introduction

Nowadays, full control of electromagnetic (EM) wave has been a research hotspot in EM field. Many works have been done to extend our understanding of full control of EM wave, including manipulating amplitude, phase, polarization and orbital angular momentum (OAM).

The OAM was first recognized in 1992 [1], which was carried by a helical transverse phase structure of $\exp(il\varphi)$ and independent of the polarization state. Here l is an unbounded integer (the OAM state number, also called topological charge number), indicating the number of twists of the wavefront within one wavelength. Because OAM has infinite orthogonal states in theory and different OAM states are mutually orthogonal, OAM has much potential in communications [2]. For example, one can establish a well-defined line-of-sight link for which each OAM beam at the same carrier frequency can carry an independent data stream, thereby increasing the capacity and spectral efficiency by a factor equal to the number of OAM states.

Till now, various methods have been proposed to generate vortex wave in radio and millimeter-wave frequencies, such as spiral phase plate [3], spiral parabolic antenna, circularly polarized patch antenna, antenna array, etc. In this paper, we reported a holographic vortex wave antenna based on holographic impedance modulation technique for the first time.

© Springer Nature Singapore Pte Ltd. 2018
Q. Yu (Ed.): SINC 2017, CCIS 803, pp. 259–263, 2018.
https://doi.org/10.1007/978-981-10-7877-4_23

2   Brief Review of HAIS

Like the concept of optical holography, microwave holograms are created in a similar way. The holographic artificial impedance surface (HAIS) is designed by generating the interference pattern between a reference wave and an objective wave. The basic concept of HAIS is based on Oliner's work on leaky waves propagation along a sinusoidally modulated reactance surface [4]. Then, the HAIS has developed to control radiation direction, polarization, beamwidth, etc. There are two kinds of HAIS, the scalar HAIS and the tensor HAIS. Normally, the scalar HAIS only can be used to control radiation direction and beamwidth. In order to control orbital angular momentum through a holographic vortex wave antenna, the tensor HAIS is chosen in our work.

The overall design process of HAIS is shown in Fig. 1, as fully illustrated and explained in [5]. For the sake of brevity, the details of each step are not given here.

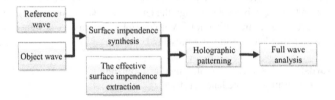

Fig. 1.   Block diagram of the overall design process

3   Holographic Vortex Wave Antenna

3.1   Design Process

As a simple example, the holographic vortex wave antenna that carrying $l = 1$ OAM state is designed using the holographic impedance modulation technique mentioned above. In order to generate the circularly polarized vortex wave that carrying $l = 1$ OAM state, the object wave are represented by

$$E_{\text{rad}} = (j \cos \theta, 1, -j \sin \theta)e^{-jk'r}e^{j\varphi} \tag{1}$$

where $k' = k(\sin \theta \cos \varphi, \sin \theta \sin \varphi, \cos \theta)$ and θ is radiation direction. The monopole is selected to feed the holographic vortex wave antenna and the surface current is given by

$$J_{\text{surf}} = \frac{(x, y, 0)}{r}e^{-jknr} \tag{2}$$

where n is the refractive index. According to the relationship between the desired electric field and surface current

$$\begin{pmatrix} E_x \\ E_y \end{pmatrix} = \begin{pmatrix} Z_{xx} & Z_{xy} \\ Z_{yx} & Z_{yy} \end{pmatrix} \begin{pmatrix} J_x \\ J_y \end{pmatrix} \qquad (3)$$

where $Z_{xy} = Z_{yx}$ [5]. The tensor impedances are calculated as follows

$$Z_{xx} = X + M \frac{x}{r} \cos \theta \cos \gamma'$$

$$Z_{xy} = Z_{yx} = \frac{M}{2} (\frac{y}{r} \cos \theta \cos \gamma' - \frac{x}{r} \sin \gamma'') \qquad (4)$$

$$Z_{yy} = X - M \frac{x}{r} \sin \gamma''$$

$$\gamma' = \mathrm{krsin}\theta\cos\varphi - \mathrm{knr} - \varphi$$
$$\gamma'' = \mathrm{krsin}\theta\sin\varphi - \mathrm{knr} - \varphi \qquad (5)$$

where X is the average reactance and M is the reactance modulation depth. The calculated tensor impedance components are shown in Fig. 2. Then, using the holographic patterning technology in [5], we solve the inverse problem, and then numerically obtain the desired tensor HAIS.

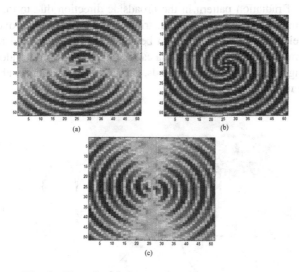

(a)

(b)

(c)

Fig. 2. The calculated tensor impedance components

3.2 Numerical Results

The unit cell used for tensor impedance surface in our design is composed of a circular metal patch with slice and a dielectric layer with a PEC ground, as shown in Fig. 3(a). The substrate was 1.27 mm thick Taconic RF-60, with a dielectric constant of 6.15, and the lattice constant is 3 mm. The generated tensor HAIS is shown in Fig. 3(b) and (c). The size of the entire structure is 153 mm × 153 mm. A simple monopole on the HAIS center is used as a feeder. The proposed antenna is designed to work at 15 GHz.

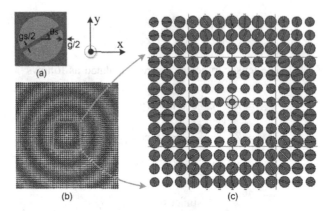

Fig. 3. (a) Unit cell used for tensor impedance surface. (b) The generated tensor holographic impedance surface structure. (c) A part of the whole tensor holographic impedance surface

The simulated radiation pattern and near field phase structure at 15 GHz are shown in Figs. 4 and 5. All simulation results are based on full wave analysis performed using Computer Simulation Technology (CST) studio suite Microwave Studio. There is an amplitude null of radiation pattern in the broadside direction due to the helical phase profile. The simulated near field phase distribution is at 105 mm above the antenna, about five wavelengths in 15 GHz. It can be seen from the simulated results that the designed holographic vortex wave antenna carries $l = 1$ OAM order indeed. Compared with the existing OAM generation methods, the proposed method is able to generate arbitrary OAM mode vortex wave.

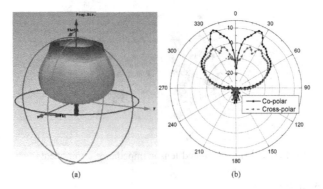

Fig. 4. (a) Simulated 3-D radiation pattern at 15 GHz. (b) Simulated radiation pattern at 15 GHz.

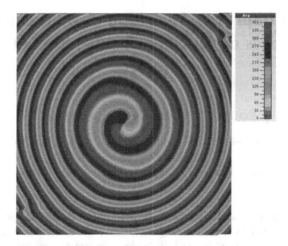

Fig. 5. Simulated Ex phase structure at 15 GHz.

4 Conclusion and Future Work

A vortex wave generation method based on tensor holographic modulated artificial impedance surface is introduced. As a simple example, a holographic vortex wave antenna that carrying $l = 1$ OAM state is presented, and the simulated results show that we can manipulate OAM by holographic impedance modulation technique.

References

1. Allen, L., Beijersbergen, M.W., Spreeuw, R.J., et al.: Orbital angular momentum of light and the transformation of Laguerre-Gaussian laser modes. Phys. Rev. A **45**, 8185–8189 (1992)
2. Yan, Y., Xie, G., Lavery, M.P.J., et al.: High-capacity millimetre-wave communications with orbital angular momentum multiplexing. Nat. Commun. **5**(4876), 1–9 (2014)
3. Uchida, M., Tonomura, A.: Generation of electron beams carrying orbital angular momentum. Nature **464**(7289), 737–739 (2010)
4. Oliner, A., Hessel, A.: Guided waves on sinusoidally-modulated reactance surfaces. IRE Trans. Antennas Propag. **7**, 201–208 (1959)
5. Fong, B.H., Colburn, J.S., Ottusch, J.J., et al.: Scalar and tensor holographic artificial impedance surfaces. IEEE Trans. Antennas Propag. **58**, 3212–3221 (2010)

An Improved Algorithm of Differential Services on Satellite Channel S-ALOHA Protocol

Xin He[1(✉)], Hanwen Sun[2], and Hao Yin[1]

[1] China Electronics System and Engineering Company, Beijing, China
hexin214@163.com
[2] China Academy of Space Technology, Xian, China

Abstract. Based on the performance analysis of S-ALOHA protocol, a Multi-Copy ALOHA scheme is designed to deliver the differentiated services in random access satellite channel which divides users into different priority groups and enables high priority users sending multiple packets to decrease the channel collision probability according to their access latency requirements. The simulation results suggest that Multi-Copy ALOHA scheme has high throughput and limited access latency features and can effectively deliver the differentiated services for different requirements in S-ALOHA channel.

Keywords: Multi-Copy S-ALOHA · Random access satellite channel Differentiated services

1 Symbol Table

λ	User business arrival rate	X	Random variable of retransmission interval
Λ	System business arrival rate	p_n	Probability of an successful transmission after n retransmissions
T	S-ALOHA time slot width	$\overline{M}$	Average number of times for an successful transmission
$P(n)$	Probability of sending n packets in one time slot	K	Number of consecutive packets sent at once
T_R	Transmission time between satellite and user	S	System packet throughput
T_P	Onboard processing time for user packet	D	Mean user access delay

Q. Yu (Ed.): SINC 2017, CCIS 803, pp. 264–274, 2018.
https://doi.org/10.1007/978-981-10-7877-4_24

2   Introduction

S-ALOHA is a random access protocol based on time synchronization, the user can send a packet at the beginning of each time slot regardless of whether other users are using the same time slot. The protocol is flexible for networking and easy to implement. At present, S-ALOHA are widely used in many kinds of satellite communication systems for network resource allocation and service access. For example, in GEO satellite communication systems (such as the Inmarsat series, AEHF series), users' signals for service access and resource allocation are mainly using S-ALOHA protocol to access the uplink RACH channel; in some low-orbit constellation communication systems (such as OBCOMM), narrow-band burst M2M services are mainly using S-ALOHA protocol to access the satellite uplink traffic channel.

By using S-ALOHA protocol, when two or more users send packets in the same time slot, the signal collision which leads to packet lost and retransmission will happen in that time slot. Because users' traffic throughput is mainly determined by collision probability and retransmission time interval, lowering collision probability and shortening the retransmission time interval can effectively improve the channel access efficiency.

Usually packet collision can be determined by whether the correct response has been received within a specified time. Since the user can only begin packet retransmission after realizing the packet collision, the retransmission time interval is at least twice of the end-to-end transmission delay. Especially in satellite communication scenario which the transmission delay is larger than 100 ms, the user access time delay is usually several seconds in consideration of retransmission time interval. Due to the large end-to-end transmission delay, the retransmission time interval cannot be shortened to a significantly level. The user access efficiency will be significantly reduced caused by the large and undiminished retransmission time interval. As a result, improving the user access efficiency of satellite communication system must start with the reduction of the probability of packet collision.

At present, parameters of S-ALOHA access protocol (such as the probability density function of retransmission time interval) in majority satellite communication systems remain unchanged, and cannot be adjusted dynamically, resulting incapability for differentiated services for different users. In this paper, an improved S-ALOHA access protocol that supports differentiated services is proposed. This protocol allows some high-priority users to send multiple identical packets to reduce collision probability and to decrease the access delay.

3   The S-ALOHA Protocol

In S-ALOHA protocol, timeline is divided into several time slots and each time slot carry one packet. Users are keeping in time synchronization state and send packets at the beginning of each slot. If only one packet arrives (including newly arrived packets and retransmitted packets) within a time slot, the packet transmission is successful. If two or more packets arrive within a certain time slot, a packet collision event occurs and the retransmission process will start after a random time interval (Fig. 1).

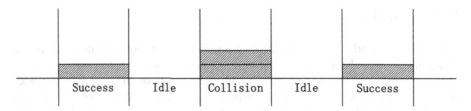

| Success | Idle | Collision | Idle | Success |

Fig. 1. S-ALOHA successful and collision transmission

In the satellite communication, user access process usually includes several independent signal interaction with satellite network controller. The time required for user access which requires n times signal exchange is the time for one signal interaction multiplied by n. Generally, we assume that the user in the access process only need one successfully signal interaction. The specific access procedure is as follows:

1. The user uses S-ALOHA protocol to send access request;
2. The satellite processes the access request and sends an access confirmation message to the user;
3. The user receives the confirmation message and reaches the completion of the access process.

If the number of users in the satellite communication network is, assuming that the arrival process of each user is independent Poisson random process. The total arrival rate (including new arrivals and retransmissions) of the user is and the total arrival rate of the whole network is $\Lambda = \sum_{i=1}^{N} \lambda_i$. The probability of sending packets within the time interval is (Fig. 2)

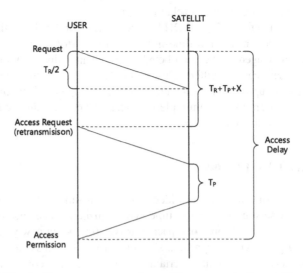

Fig. 2. User access process in satellite communication system

$$P(n) = \frac{(\Lambda t)^n e^{-\Lambda t}}{n!} \tag{1}$$

Assuming that the slot width of S-ALOHA is and the number of packets arriving within a time slot follows the Poisson random process with the parameter which is the average number of packets sent in one time slot. The probability of no packet to be sent from other users is $P(0) = e^{-\Lambda T}$. As only one user sends packet in a time slot can result a successful transmission, the probability of success is $P(0) = e^{-\Lambda T}$. It can be induced that the throughput of the S-ALOHA protocol is $S = \Lambda T e^{-\Lambda T}$ which gets the maximum value 0.368 when $\Lambda T = 1$.

After sending the access request packet, if the user receives the access permission it can be considered as a successful access process, however if the user does not receive the access permission, the access process fails and the user can retransmit the access request packet after a random time interval.

If T_R represents the satellite-to-user link transmission delay. T_P represents the onboard processing time for user packet. $P(0) = e^{-\Lambda T}$ represents the probability of successful access process, using random variable X to represent the retransmission time interval, Without link errors, the probability of a successful transmission and $n - 1$ retransmissions is

$$p_n = (1 - P(0))^{n-1} P(0) \tag{2}$$

The total time spent is

$$t_n = n(T_R + T_p) + \sum_{j=1}^{n-1} x_j \tag{3}$$

The average delay for user access is

$$
\begin{aligned}
E(T) &= \sum_{n=1}^{\infty} t_n (1-p)^{n-1} p_n \\
&= \sum_{n=1}^{\infty} [(n-1)(T_R + T_P + E(X)) + T_R + T_P](1 - P(0))^{n-1} P(0) \\
&= \frac{1}{P(0)}(T_R + T_P) + \frac{1 - P(0)}{P(0)} E(X)
\end{aligned} \tag{4}
$$

From the above, the user access delay is composed of two parts, the first part is caused by the channel transmission delay, and the second part is caused by retransmission. Given that the large transmission delay within the satellite channel, further reducing the retransmission time interval is not practical. As a result, the reduction of user access delay should mainly depend on the decreasing of collision probability.

The time interval at which the user sends two adjacent packets (either retransmitted or newly arrived) is $T_R + T_P + X$, where the random variables X represents the traffic arrival distribution for different users. If the retransmission time interval $\theta = T_R + T_P + X$ has exponential distribution, the distribution of user packet arrival follows Poisson process with the parameter $\lambda = \frac{1}{\theta} = \frac{1}{T_R + T_P + E(X)}$. In order to simplify the analysis, it can be assumed that the time interval between two adjacent packets follows the exponential distribution and the similar analytical methods can be applied to other distributions.

For arrival of new packets, the probability of successful transmission with only once access is $P(0)$, the probability of successful transmission with twice access is $(1 - P(0))P(0)$, the probability of successful transmission with n times access is $(1 - P(0))^{n-1}P(0)$, resulting the average number of attempts to a successful transmission is:

$$\overline{M} = \sum_{n=1}^{\infty} n(1 - P(0))^{n-1}P(0) = \frac{1}{P(0)} \tag{5}$$

If total arrival rate (including the newly arrived packet and retransmission packet) is λ, It can be concluded that the proportion of new arrivals is $P(0)$ and the arrival rate is $P(0)\lambda$.

4 Differential Access Policy

As above, reducing the collision rate would shorten the user access delay. In order to increase the success probability of once transition attempt, Multi-Copy strategy which increase the success transmission rate by repeating the packet before receiving the permission. For high-priority users are usually with high repetition factor. In the condition with the same collision rate, using Multi-Copy strategy can significantly reduce the access delay.

Assume that the user's repetition factor is K, which means user can send consecutively K packets before the reception of acknowledgement. If the successful rate of one time slot is $P(0) = e^{-\Lambda T}$, the probability of at least one packet successfully received is $1 - [1 - P(0)]^K$. This probability is decreasing by the increment of repetition factor K.

In S-ALOHA, the throughput is the product of the total traffic arrival rate and the time slot collision probability. When the retransmission time interval remains unchanged, the user access delay is determined by the time slot collision probability, while the time slot collision probability is determined by all users' total traffic arrival rate which is determined by the probability of collision and the rate of newly arrival packets. As a result, the feedback exists between the time slot collision probability and the total traffic arrival rate. When the Multi-Copy strategy is adopted, the increase of the total service arrival rate leads to the decrease of single time slot successful transmission probability. It is necessary to adjust the back off time to avoid collision and control the total service arrival rate so that the probability of single time slot successful transmission $P(0)$ remains the same (Fig. 3).

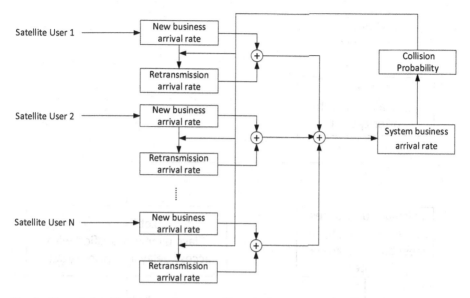

Fig. 3. The relationship between the new traffic arrival rate, the total traffic arrival rate, and the probability of collision

In order to realize the differential access service, all users should be divided into n different priorities. User who is at the priority i will has the repetition factor i and can send consecutive i packets before the reception of acknowledgement. Suppose that the overall arrival rate of users at priority i is λ_i, the total arrival rate of entire system is $\Lambda = \sum_{i=1}^{n} \lambda_i$, and the average repetition factor is $N = \Lambda^{-1} \sum_{i=1}^{n} i\lambda_i$. As a result, the probability of one time slot successful transmission is $P(0) = e^{-N\Lambda T}$, and the probability of user which belongs to priority i successful access is $P_i(0) = 1 - (1 - e^{-N\Lambda T})^i$ and the system throughput is

$$S = \sum_{i=1}^{n} \lambda_i P_i = \sum_{i=1}^{n} \lambda_i (1 - (1 - e^{-N\Lambda T})^i) \tag{6}$$

Compared with the traditional S-ALOHA access protocol, the Multi-Copy ALOHA strategy can significantly shorten the high priority user access delay, but the success rate of single transmission and system throughput is reduced.

Based on the improved differentiated service of S-ALOHA, to meet the traffic arrival rate and access delay requirements for each user, each user should get a reasonable priority level. Let's divide total M users into N disjoint subsets where different users belonging to the same subset has the same access priority level. Use U to represent the collection of all users, and use U_i $(1 \le i \le N)$ to represent the users belonging to the subset i, the relation between U_i and U is $U = \bigcup_{i=1}^{N} U_i$, $|U| = M$. The overall arrival rate of users at priority i can be calculated as follows:

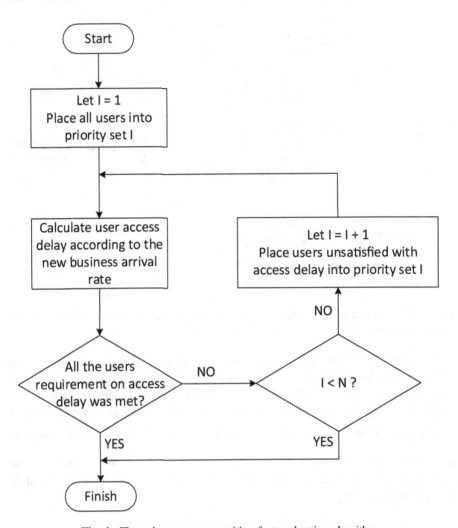

Fig. 4. Flow char on user repetition factor planning algorithm

$$\Lambda_i = \sum_{k=1}^{|U_i|} \lambda_k \bigg|_{k \in U_i} \tag{7}$$

Assume that the successful transmission probability in one time slot is $P(0)$, the total traffic arrival rate is

$$\Lambda = \frac{1}{P(0)} \sum_{i=1}^{N} i\Lambda_i \tag{8}$$

The average access delay of users at priority i can be solved by substitute $P(0) = e^{-N\Lambda T}$ into Eq. (4).

$$D_i = \frac{1}{1 - [1 - P(0)]^N}(T_R + T_P) + \frac{[1 - P(0)]^N}{1 - [1 - P(0)]^N}E(X) \tag{9}$$

In summary, for some scenarios of satellite communication, channel access delay is main factor of QoS. Based on the Multi-Copy strategy, the S-ALOHA protocol can be used to improve the high priority user's access efficiency. It is crucial to determine the user's service level and the corresponding access policy. The specific process is shown below.

There are two conditions for the algorithm termination: one is the normal exit, which means all the user access delay requirements have been met; the other one is abnormal exit which means not all users could reach delay requirements. In that case, the user access delay requirements or the users traffic arrival rate should be decreased before repeat until the requirements are met. When the algorithm exits abnormally, different adjustment strategies should be used according to different application scenarios and traffic requirements. For example, for high-capacity GEO satellite communication system, reduction on the service level of some users should be used to meet the access requirements of users with high priority; for low-orbit constellation system, increasing the retransmission time interval due to collision can be applied to limit the total traffic which will compensate for additional access overload of high priority users brought by Multi-Copy repetition.

5 Performance Simulation

5.1 S-ALOHA Protocol

Suppose each user's new traffic arrival rate be the same λ_0 and the number of users is M, and the probability of successful transmission in single time slot is $P(0)$, and the total traffic arrival rate is Λ, take the time slot length as a unit, $P(0)$ can be solved by the Eq. (10). The average attempt number of a successful transmission is $1/P(0)$.

$$\begin{cases} \Lambda = \dfrac{M\lambda_0}{P(0)} \\ P(0) = e^{-\Lambda} \end{cases} \Rightarrow P(0)\ln P(0) = -M\lambda_0 \tag{10}$$

5.2 Multi-Copy ALOHA 区分服务策略

M users are divided into N subsets which map to the N priority levels each. Users in the priority subset i can transmit i packets consecutively. $P(0)$ can be solved by the Eq. (11). The average number of attempt transmissions is $1/\left[1 - (1 - P(0))^i\right]$.

$$\begin{cases} \lambda_i = |U_i|\lambda_0 \\ N = \dfrac{\sum\limits_{i=1}^{n} i\lambda_i}{M\lambda_0} \Rightarrow P(0)\ln P(0) = -MN\lambda_0 \\ \Lambda = \dfrac{MN\lambda_0}{P(0)} \\ P(0) = e^{-\Lambda} \end{cases} \tag{11}$$

5.3   Simulation Result

When S-ALOHA protocol is adopted, the relationship between the traffic arrival rate and the system throughput is shown in the following figure. The simulation results show that the maximum throughput of the S-ALOHA is 0.384. When the traffic arrival rate is 1, the throughput of the system is of the maximum (Fig. 5).

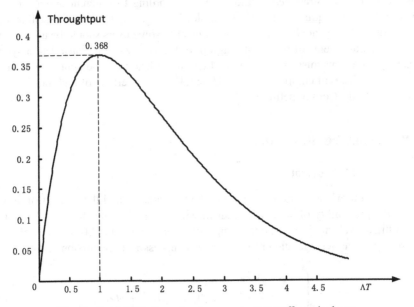

Fig. 5. S-ALOHA throughput versus system traffic arrival rate

When S-ALOHA protocol is adopted, the successful transmission probability in one time slot is the ratio of the system throughput to the total traffic arrival rate. If probability of success in one time slot remains unchanged, the relation between Multi-Copy repetition factor K and the average number of attempt is shown in the following figure. The simulation results show that the average number of attempts is reduced rapidly as the factor K increasing. The larger K means the more effort paid to decrease the average number of attempts which indicates the value of K is not always the bigger the better (Fig. 6).

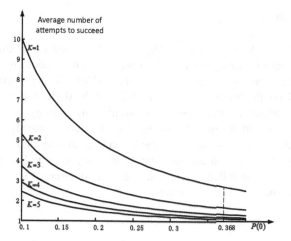

Fig. 6. The relation between average number of attempts and the one time slot successful transmission probability

Assuming that there are 10 users, the arrival rate of each new packet is the same. According to the S-ALOHA, the average number of attempts at different traffic arrival rates can be calculated and listed on the following Fig. 7.

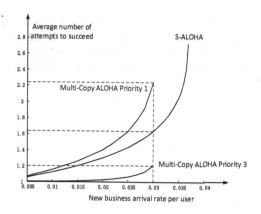

Fig. 7. Comparison between S-ALOHA protocol and Multi-Copy ALOHA on differential service strategy

When the traffic arrival rate is 0.03, the average number of attempts is 1.61313. If a user requires the average number of attempts is not higher than 1.2, running result of algorithm described on Fig. 4 is to set the user to priority level 3, and the other users to priority level 1. It can be seen that the average number of attempts reduces to 1.2 for high-priority users which result in access delay increasing for low priority users.

6 Conclusion

At present, S-ALOHA protocol is widely used in satellite communication system, especially in terms of user access and short burst communication. Its performance is determined by the access delay and service quality, which affects the service experience of users. Based on the analysis of access delay of S-ALOHA protocol, this paper proposes a differentiated service based on Multi-Copy strategy, which reduces the access delay by transmitting multiple identical packets consecutively at once attempt, and verify the algorithm by simulation. The theoretical analysis and simulation results show that the S-ALOHA protocol based on Multi-Copy strategy has features on both high throughput and controlled access delay, and the differential service capability of S-ALOHA could be effectively improved.

References

1. Abramson, N.: The ALOHA system-another alternative for computer communications. In: Fall Joint Computer Conference, pp. 281–285 (1970)
2. Abramson, N.: The throughput of packet broadcasting channels. IEEE Trans. Commun. **25**, 117–128 (1977)
3. Rom, R., Sidi, M.: Multiple Access Protocols Performance and Analysis. Springer, New York (1989). https://doi.org/10.1007/978-1-4612-3402-9
4. Li, J., Sheng, M., Li, H.: The Introduction to Communication System, 2nd edn. Higher Education Press (2011)
5. Li, J., Guo, T., Wu, G.: Mobile Communication, 4th edn. Xidian University Press
6. Wang, S., Sun, D., Zhang, Y.: Performance analysis for ALOHA protocol of underwater acoustic networks with a serial route. J. Harbin Eng. Univ. **37**(3), 360–367 (2016)
7. Wang, F., Zhang, W.: Grouping of dynamic frame-slotted ALOHA algorithm. Appl. Comput. Syst. **22**(7), 77–80 (2013)

LS-SVM Based Large Capacity Random Access Control Scheme in Satellite Network

Yali Feng and Guangliang Ren[(✉)]

State Key Laboratory of Integrated Service Networks, Xidian University,
No. 2 South Taibai Road, Xi'an 710071, China
glren@mail.xidian.edu.cn

Abstract. Massive number of the uncoordinated machine-type communication (MTC) terminals accessing the satellite hub overloads the CDMA slotted Aloha (SA) random access system with a large capacity, whose performance is drastically reduced, and introduce a long service time for the activated terminals. To improve the performance of the random access scheme, we propose a Least Squares Support Vector Machines (LS-SVM) regression based random access control scheme with a sliding window. By using one step and multistep LS-SVM predicting algorithm, satellite hub predicts the channel loads of the future slots, and computes the access probability, then broadcasts to all MTC devices. Simulation results show that the proposed scheme approaches to the perfect control scheme, and the throughput is more than 2.5 times, and the total service time for all the activated terminals is less than 0.4 times that of the available EKF based control scheme in the satellite network.

Keywords: LS-SVM regression · Sliding window · Large capacity MTC
Bursty traffic · Access probability

1 Introduction

Satellite Internet of Things (IoT) has become one of the most important parts of the IoT, since a large number of machine-type communication (MTC) terminals distributed in the remote and vast areas in the IoT [1] can collect a great amount of information for various monitoring application scenarios including the disaster relief, rescue, target tracking and so on. The traffic of the MTC terminals (nodes) [2] is the burst with a low duty cycle and low energy consumption, and needs unprecedented access and exchange of information. Due to the remote and large area, the MTC terminals are outside the coverage of the terrestrial network or the regions where the terrestrial network collapses due to the disaster, and can be served by the satellite communication system [3].

In the large coverage of a spot beam of the satellite IoT, there may be distributed more than tens of thousands of MTC terminals, which introduces a great access challenge for the satellite network. In the current random access schemes, such as, the

This work was supported in part by National Natural Science Foundation of China (grant No. 91538105) and the National Basic Research Program of China (973 Program 2014CB340206).

Q. Yu (Ed.): SINC 2017, CCIS 803, pp. 275–287, 2018.
https://doi.org/10.1007/978-981-10-7877-4_25

traditional slot MAC protocols like slot Aloha, cannot handle such a huge number of the burst random access requests of the large number of MTC terminals due to the collisions of the overlapping packets on the slots, and this leads to the traffic congestion, which consequently lowers the system throughput as well as costs much more time to provide the service.

The effective method to resolve multiple concurrent overlapping packets transmission is the ALOHA-type CDMA random access with the multiple packet reception (MPR) for uncoordinated MTC terminals in wireless network environment [4, 5]. However, the throughput declines much sharply if the channel load exceeds the critical point. To maintain the high throughput under the high offered load, one technique for the CDMA slotted ALOHA (SA) system is the packets access control at the MTC terminals, which limits the number of simultaneous transmissions less than or equal to the maximum number of the overlapping packets which the satellite receiver can successfully decoded. The optimal accessing probability can be computed by the knowledge of the number of the "uncertain" nodes which tend to transmit, but it is unpractical to know the perfect information of on-going transmissions beforehand at the transmitter. Some literatures have proposed many methods to collect the available imperfect information to predict the offered load, and by which the optimal access factor can be computed. For example, literature [6] models the burst traffic as the aggregate of on/off Markov sources, utilizes the feedback from the receiver and the prior information about the traffic characteristics to predict the system state. Due to the shortcoming of the prediction method, it performs well for the constant channel load, but badly for the varying load. Literature [7] adopts the extended Kalman filter (EKF) to keep track of the traffic being offered to the access channel, and predicts the number of the active nodes in following slot, however, the precision of the predicted load is low when the channel load is heavy, and the prediction time is too short, and cannot be suitable for the satellite network with the large propagation delay, such as the Round Trip Time (RTT) can be as large as 500 ms for GEO and 11 ms for LEO. Literature [8] considers the effect of RTT when sensing channel load, the hub in which predicts offered load based on the number of packets received successfully during several slots, apparently it only adapts to the steady offered load, cannot be used for the time varying load of the MTC traffic.

To improve the performance of the satellite IoT system with a large capacity of MTC terminals, we propose an LS-SVM [9, 10] based channel load prediction algorithm to estimate the channel load with a large RTT, and compute the optimal accessing probability for the MTC terminals. The proposed LS-SVM based random access control scheme can effectively solve the overload problem of the ALOHA-type CDMA random access system with MPR.

In the paper, Sect. 2 gives the model of the packet transmission system with the completely uncoordinated nodes. Section 3 presents the LS-SVM regression based prediction method to estimate the number of the activated nodes in the future slots. Section 4 describes the investigation of the proposed scheme in the satellite network by the computer simulation.

2 System Model

The MTC terminals accessing system with a single satellite hub in the satellite IoT is shown in Fig. 1. The GEO or LEO with the multi-beam provides the ubiquitous coverage and offers the continuous service to a very large population of MTC devices which are low cost and energy-constrained. Nodes in system can sense surrounded events, if none of events trigger in the environment, they generally are in a state of sleep or non-activated for keeping energy. If some events trigger, some of them are waked or activated to access network. After the on-board processing at the satellite hub, all the data collected in the remote area are transmitted to the ground station, then through the internet to the data center for the further use. In this paper, for simplicity, we only consider nodes in the single beam.

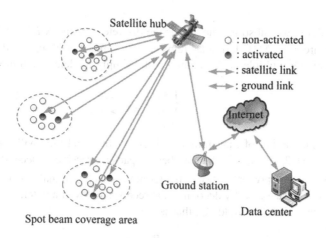

Fig. 1. Architecture of the satellite IoT accessing system

The CDMA SA protocol and the slot with the duration of T_{slot} are considered for the random access. It is also assumed that the active nodes are synchronized before its transmission. The propagation delay in the satellite accessing system is depicted in Fig. 2. The satellite hub and nodes can transmit data packets simultaneously in two channels (i.e. uplink and downlink channel). Acknowledge (ACK, binary feedback flags whether packets received in the slot correctly or not) or the accessing probability can be broadcasted to all nodes through the satellite downlink broadcasting channel. Let T_R be the single hop propagation delay, $T_R = h_{sat}/v_c$, where h_{sat} is the height of satellite, and v_c is the velocity of light. Let T_p be the processing delay on-board. So the accessing time delay $T_D = 2T_R + T_p$, where T_p is so small and can be ignored. The normalized access time delay D is defined as $D = T_D/T_{slot}$. This means it has past $D/2$ slots before transmitted packets reach to satellite hub, and past D slots before nodes receive feedback to know whether the packets they transmitted are received correctly or not.

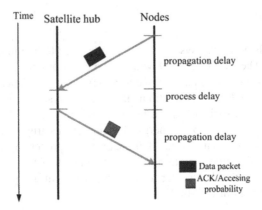

Fig. 2. Propagation delay in the satellite accessing system

For simplicity, we substitute the slot as the discrete time index $i(i = 1, 2, \ldots)$, and assume there are N^{total} MTC terminals registered. The receiver is supposed to have the ability of receiving multiple packets, and can be simply modeled by follows:

$$N^{rx}_{i+D/2} = \begin{cases} N^{tx}_i & N^{tx}_i \leq K \\ 0 & N^{tx}_i > K \end{cases} \tag{1}$$

where N^{tx}_i is the number of transmitted packets in slot i, and they will reach satellite hub in slot $i + D/2$, $N^{rx}_{i+D/2}$ is the number of packets received successfully in slot $i + D/2$. If we assume power control at the terminals, each terminal reaches to hub has equal power P. For successfully decoding, the received *SINR* of any terminal should be equal or greater than a threshold θ_{th}, that is

$$SINR = \frac{P}{\sigma^2 + \frac{K-1}{\kappa}P} \geq \theta_{th} \tag{2}$$

where σ^2 is Gaussian noise power, κ is spreading gain. Therefore the maximum processing limit K of receiver is

$$K := \left\lfloor \kappa \left(\frac{1}{\theta_{th}} - \frac{1}{P/\sigma^2} \right) \right\rfloor + 1 \tag{3}$$

where $\lfloor \bullet \rfloor$ denotes the flooring function. If we only concern the packet-level behavior of multiuser detector, the model in (1) can be simply interpreted as that if the total number of transmitted packets is less than K, all the packets in the slot can be retrieved; else all the packets are lost because of large interference.

Due to the propagation delay, the received packets in current slot $i(i > D/2)$ are transmitted by nodes in the slot $i - D/2$, ACK or accessing probability will reach to nodes in the slot $i + D/2$, since nodes could not know transmitting packets are received correctly or not until they get the feedback, so they are not permitted to send packets

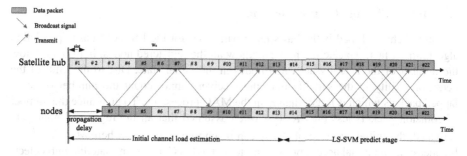

Fig. 3. CDMA slotted ALOHA with MPR $(D = 4, W_a = 3)$

from slot $i - D/2 + 1$ to slot $i + D/2 - 1$ if they have transmitted a packet in the slot $i - D/2$, as shown in Fig. 3.

Suppose the total attempted accessing nodes in slot i is $M(M \leq N^{total})$, in order to maximize throughput, it is hoped that M is equal to or less than K. When M is larger than K, it is necessary to limit the number of nodes by using the access probability p_i at the nodes. Since the p_i takes effect in all nodes, every nodes has the equal probability p_i (or $1 - p_i$) transmitting (or not transmitting) a packet in the slot i, which follows the binomial distribution $B(M, p_i)$, the optimal probability should be selected as follows

$$
\begin{aligned}
p_i^*(M) &= \arg\max_{0 < p_i \leq 1} \sum_{n=1}^{K} n \Pr\{N^{tx} = n\} \\
&= \arg\max_{0 < p_i \leq 1} \sum_{n=1}^{K} n \binom{M}{n} p_i^n (1 - p_i)^{M-n}
\end{aligned}
\tag{4}
$$

Each activated node (wants to transmit packet) generates a random p_i' at the local, and compares it with p_i^*, if it is passing the check, that is $p_i' < p_i^*$, the packet is allowed to be transmitted. If not, it attempts at the next slot until it is passing the check.

The optimal access probability p_i^* can be computed by the knowledge of the channel load (the number of the activated nodes) in the future slots, which introduces a great challenge for the prediction algorithm due to the large propagation delay in the satellite network.

3   SVM Based Prediction Algorithm

To satisfy the requirement of the long time prediction in the optimal access probability computation, the LS-SVM regression based prediction algorithm is proposed for the estimation of the channel load, i.e., the number of active nodes in the future slot in the CDMA SA random access scheme. The proposed algorithm contains two steps. The first step is the initial estimation of the channel load, and the second step is to predict the channel load for the next slots by the LS-SVM algorithm with a sliding window.

3.1   Initial Channel Load Estimation

The initial channel load is the basis input parameter for the LS-SVM based prediction algorithm. In fact, the satellite hub can know all the registered nodes, but do not know the number of the actually activated nodes in the initial state. Due to the limit of the detection ability in the satellite hub, the receiver cannot count the number of over-lapped packets which is larger than K in the MAC processing. To guarantee the number of collision packets less than K, it is often assumed that all the registered nodes are activated, the initial access probability can be chosen as $p^*(\hat{M})$, where $\hat{M} = N^{total}$. By broadcasting the initial access probability to all the MTC nodes, the satellite hub detects the numbers of overlapped packets in the average window W_a, which is shown in Fig. 3. If the detected number of the packets is $N^{rx}(W_a)$, the initial channel load in slot i can be estimated as

$$\hat{x}_i = \left\lceil \frac{N^{rx}(W_a)}{W_a p^*(\hat{M})} \right\rceil \tag{5}$$

where $\lceil \bullet \rceil$ denotes the ceiling function. If the number of the activated is much less than N^{total}, for the small value of $p^*(\hat{M})$, $N^{rx}(W_a)$ may be zero. For this case, the satellite hub increases the $p^*(\hat{M})$ by two times, and repeats until the $N^{rx}(W_a)$ is not zero and the value of $p^*(\hat{M})$ is less than 1.

3.2   LS-SVM Based Prediction Algorithm with Sliding Window

LS-SVM transforms the quadratic programming problem into a linear equations, simplifying the computational complexity as well as improving computation speed. Its basic operation is to map the data into a high dimensional space by a nonlinear mapping and do the linear regression in the mapped space. The prediction algorithm based on the SVM contains three stages. The first is the training stage, the second is one step prediction stage, and the third stage is multi-step prediction with sliding window.

The first stage is to solve the regression problem, which is to find the function by minimizing the structural risk with the training data set. It is often assumed that the training data set can be represented as $\{(\mathbf{x}_i, y_i) | i = k, k+1, k+2, \ldots, k+L-1, k \in N\}$, L represents the number of training data pair, where the input data $\mathbf{x}_i \in R^m$, and m is input data dimension, that is $\mathbf{x}_i = (\hat{x}_{i-m+1}, \hat{x}_{i-m}, \ldots, \hat{x}_i)$, and the desired value $y_i = \hat{x}_{i+1}$, $y_i \in R$. For the training data set, there are $L+m$ available $\hat{x}_i$ assemble to L training data pairs, as shown in the Fig. 4. The initial training data can be obtained by the initial channel load estimation, and the following $\hat{x}_i$ can be obtained by

$$\hat{x}_i = \begin{cases} \lceil (\frac{N_i^{rx}}{p_{i-D/2}} + \sum\limits_{j=1}^{W_a-1} \hat{x}_{i-j})/W_a \rceil & N_i^{rx} \le K \\ \lceil \eta \cdot \hat{x}_{i-1} \rceil & N_i^{rx} > K \end{cases} \tag{6}$$

where $p_{i-D/2}$ is the access probability in slot $i - D/2$. If the number of the received packets is out of the detection ability of the satellite hub, the estimation of the number

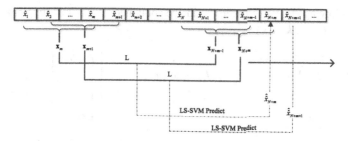

Fig. 4. Sliding window of the training data set

of activated nodes can be replaced by η times the value of the last estimation $\hat{x}_{i-1}$, W_a and η is defined by the simulation in advance.

With the prepared training data, the desired linear model in the high space is expressed as

$$f(\mathbf{x}) = \boldsymbol{\omega} \bullet \phi(\mathbf{x}) + b \tag{7}$$

where $\boldsymbol{\omega}$ is the weight vector, b is the bias, $\phi(\mathbf{x})$ is the nonlinear transformation, and the construct function should make the total fitting deviation between all data points and the object function be minimal, that is

$$\min_{\omega,b,\xi_i} J(\boldsymbol{\omega}, b, \xi_i) = \frac{1}{2}\boldsymbol{\omega}^T\boldsymbol{\omega} + C\sum_{i=k}^{k+L-1} \xi_i^2$$
$$s.t. \quad y_i = \boldsymbol{\omega}^T\phi(\mathbf{x}_i) + b + \xi_i \quad i = k, k+1, \ldots, k+L-1, k \in N \tag{8}$$

where $\xi_i (i = k, k+1, \ldots, k+L-1, k \in N)$ are error variables, which is the distance between each training data and the regression function. The first term in the above formula makes the fitting function more flat, thereby enhances the generalization capability; and the second term ensures the deviation of samples is minimum. C is used to adjust training model avoiding overfitting or underfitting and can be set manually. It is often that the Lagrangian is used to solve the formula (8), as follows

$$L_{LS-SVM} = \frac{1}{2}\|\boldsymbol{\omega}\|^2 + C\sum_{i=k}^{k+L-1} \xi_i^2 - \sum_{i=k}^{k+L-1} \alpha_i(\boldsymbol{\omega}^T\phi(\mathbf{x}_i) + b + \xi_i - y_i) \tag{9}$$

where $\alpha_i (i = k, k+1, \ldots, k+L-1, k \in N)$ are the Lagrange multipliers. Based on KKT optimization condition obtains following [10].

$$\begin{cases} \frac{\partial L_{LS-SVM}}{\partial \boldsymbol{\omega}} = 0 \rightarrow \boldsymbol{\omega} = \sum_{i=k}^{k+L-1} \alpha_i\phi(\mathbf{x}_i) \\ \frac{\partial L_{LS-SVM}}{\partial b} = 0 \rightarrow \sum_{i=k}^{k+L-1} \alpha_i = 0 \\ \frac{\partial L_{LS-SVM}}{\partial \xi_i} = 0 \rightarrow \alpha_i = C\xi_i \\ \frac{\partial L_{LS-SVM}}{\partial \alpha_i} = 0 \rightarrow \langle \boldsymbol{\omega}, \phi(\mathbf{x}_i)\rangle + b - \xi_i - y_i = 0 \end{cases} \tag{10}$$

The following linear equation can be obtained by eliminating ω, $\xi_i(i = k,$
$k+1,\ldots,k+L-1, k \in N)$.

$$
\begin{bmatrix}
0 & 1 & \cdots & 1 \\
1 & K(\mathbf{x}_k, \mathbf{x}_k) + 1/C & \cdots & K(\mathbf{x}_k, \mathbf{x}_{k+L-1}) \\
\vdots & \vdots & \ddots & \vdots \\
1 & K(\mathbf{x}_{k+L-1}, \mathbf{x}_k) & \cdots & K(\mathbf{x}_{k+L-1}, \mathbf{x}_{k+L-1}) + 1/C
\end{bmatrix}
\begin{bmatrix}
b \\
\alpha_k \\
\vdots \\
\alpha_{k+L-1}
\end{bmatrix}
=
\begin{bmatrix}
0 \\
y_k \\
\vdots \\
y_{k+L-1}
\end{bmatrix}
\quad (11)
$$

where $K(x, z) = <\phi(x), \phi(z)>$ is defined as kernel function, which helps in taking
the dot product of two vectors in the feature space without having to calculate the
mapping results explicitly, avoids the complicated calculation in the high-dimension
and solves the nonlinear problems of the training data in the original space. α_i and b can
be figured out by solving Eq. (11), Substitute them into (7), then the model is converted
as follows

$$
f(x) = \sum_{i=k}^{k+L-1} \alpha_i y_i K(\mathbf{x}_i, \mathbf{x}) + b \quad (12)
$$

For the nonlinear model, Gaussian RBF Kernel $K(x_1, x_2) = \exp(-\gamma\|x_1 - x_2\|^2)$, $\gamma > 0$ is the most suitable choice, where γ is a tunable parameter which has an
effect on the complexity level of the model.

When the RBF Kernel is defined in advance, the choice of parameters L, C and γ
have an effect on the regression performance directly, where L is used to determine the
number of useful samples for the training stage. If L is too large, it will increase training
time, else it will cause that the model is not trained sufficiently. The choice of L can be
found by the simulation test. C and γ can be defined by the cross validation, and their
detail operations are as follows:

(1) Fix C, change γ, find γ_{opt} by minimizing the prediction error.
(2) Fix γ_{opt}, change γ, find γ_{opt} by minimizing the prediction error.
(3) Fix $C = C_{opt}$, change γ, repeat step (1), verify whether $\gamma = \gamma_{opt}$ is the optimal
    value or not.
(4) If (C_{opt}, γ_{opt}) in step (3) are the optimal values, choose (C_{opt}, γ_{opt}) for following
    use.
(5) If (C_{opt}, γ_{opt}) in step (3) are not the optimal values, go back to step (1).

The second stage is to predict the number of the activated nodes in next slot.
Suppose the current slot index is i, $\hat{y}_i = \hat{x}_{i+1}$ is the prediction value in slot $i+1$, the
SVM model has been well-trained with the past training data pair $(\mathbf{x}_{i-L}, y_{i-L})$,
$(\mathbf{x}_{i-L+1}, y_{i-L+1}), \ldots, (\mathbf{x}_{i-1}, y_{i-1})$, and parameters α and b in formula (12) are known
already, so the predicted value can be estimated as

$$
\hat{y}_i = \sum_{k=i-L}^{i-1} \alpha_k y_k K(\mathbf{x}_k, \mathbf{x}_i) + b \quad (13)
$$

The third stage proceeds with the help of sliding window. By regarding the predicted value as the true value in the training data set, the two stages above are iteratively to obtain the multi-step prediction values, which can be described as follows. Suppose current slot index is i, and the number of the activated nodes $\hat{\hat{x}}_{i+D}$ in the slot $i+D$ is desired to estimate. With the well-trained model, one-step prediction $\hat{y}_i = \hat{\hat{x}}_{i+1}$ can be obtained, then add the predicted value $\hat{\hat{x}}_{i+1}$ to the available training data set, discard the old data $\hat{x}_{i-L-m+1}$, as shown in Fig. 4. That is the sliding window moving forward one step, and the training data pair is updated to $(\mathbf{x}_{i-L+1}, y_{i-L+1})$ $(\mathbf{x}_{i-L+2}, y_{i-L+2}), \ldots, (\mathbf{x}_{i-1}, y_{i-1}), (\mathbf{x}_i, \hat{y}_i)$. The SVM model is re-trained and one-step prediction is conducted to get the predicted value $\hat{y}_{i+1} = \hat{\hat{x}}_{i+2}$. By repeating the above steps D times, one can obtain the desired prediction value $\hat{\hat{x}}_{i+D}$ in the slot $i+D$.

4 Simulation Result

The CDMA SA satellite packet communication system with the proposed SVM based random access control scheme is investigated by computer simulation. In the system, the data rate is 9.6 kbps, the packet size is 1000 bit, the duration of the slot T_{slot} approximately equals to 105 ms, the normalized access timing delay $D = 1$ under the LEO environment, and D approximately equals to 5 under the GEO environment, as those in [8]. The other fixed parameters in the algorithm are set as follows: $C = 0.05$, $\gamma = 0.05$, $m = 2$, $\eta = 1.5$, $W_a = 2$, where C and γ are defined by the cross validation between the section [0.001, 1000], m, η and W_a defined by the section are [1, 10], (1, 5] and [1, 10] respectively, the five parameters are optimally selected by the simulations. The burst traffic model is considered for the MTC terminals. That is, N^{total} MTC nodes are supposed to require accessing the satellite hub in a random slot simultaneously, and it is also assumed that each node needs to be served exactly once, and the node, which has not been served, will keep on trying to access network until it is served in a random access slot. The performance metrics, the normalized throughput (the successful packets per slot at satellite hub, and normalized by the value of K), total service time (the total number of access slots required to serve N^{total} nodes) are tested in the simulation. Two benchmark schemes are also conducted for comparing with the proposed method, the first benchmark is the perfect random access control scheme (Perfect), which knows in advance the number of attempting nodes and can always choose the optimal p^* before accessing. The second benchmark is the EKF based random access control scheme, which is given in literature [7].

Figure 5 shows the effect of the sliding window length L on the performance of the normalized throughput and the total service time when $N^{total} = 20000$, $K = 10$. It can be seen the normalized throughput first increases with L and reaches the peak at $L = 50$, then starts declining. The total service time first declines with L and reaches the minimum at $L = 50$, then starts increasing. It is found that the optimum length of the sliding window L is 50.

Figures 6 and 7 show the normalized throughput and the total service time with different number of MTC devices which are all activated simultaneously, where $L = 30$, $D = 5$. In Fig. 6, it can be seen that the proposed SVM control scheme

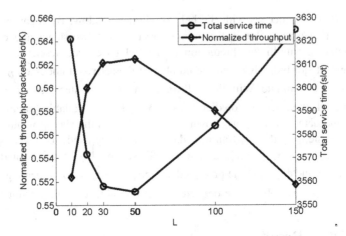

Fig. 5. Throughput, total service time vs. the length of training data pair

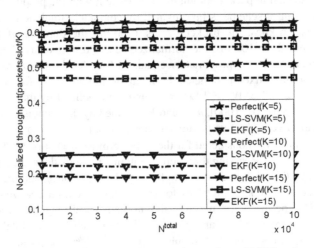

Fig. 6. Normalized throughput vs. the number of MTC nodes

(LS-SVM) can keep a constant throughput for each of K, and get more and more closer to perfect scheme when K becomes larger. We can also find the normalized throughput is higher about 2.5-times than that of the EKF for each of K. In Fig. 7, the total service time of the proposed SVM based control scheme increases linearly as the number of nodes increases, and is about the same as that of the perfect control scheme, and is less than 0.4-times that of the EKF based control scheme for each of K.

Figure 8 shows normalized throughput and the total service time with different propagation delay, and Fig. 9 shows normalized mean square error (NMSE) with different propagation delay, both use same parameters: $N^{total} = 50000$, $L = 30$, $K = 10$. In Fig. 8, It can be seen the normalized throughput and the total service time of SVM are almost about the same as that of the perfect control scheme. While for the

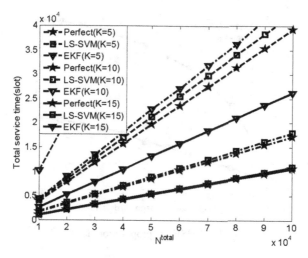

Fig. 7. Total service time vs. the number of MTC nodes

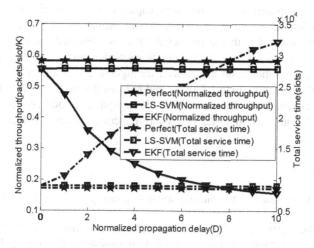

Fig. 8. Normalized throughput, total service time vs. propagation delay

EKF based control scheme, the throughput decreases and the total service time increases as the propagation delay increases. This can be explained with Fig. 9, the prediction error of the proposed algorithm still remains at 10^{-2} order of magnitudes even propagation delay increases, while the prediction error of the EKF algorithm increases sharply and almost approach to 1 as the propagation delay increases.

In addition, the throughput by the proposed SVM based scheme is about 1.2-times for the LEO environment (that is $D = 1$), and 2.5-times for the GEO environment (that is $D = 5$) more than that by the EKF based control scheme. The total service time by the proposed scheme is about less than 0.8 times for the LEO, and 0.4 times for the GEO, that by the EKF based control scheme.

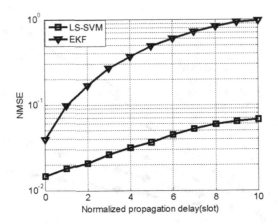

Fig. 9. NMSE vs. propagation delay

5 Conclusion

To satisfy the requirement of the large-capacity MTC terminals accessing the satellite-based Internet of thing, the prediction algorithm based on LS-SVM and the optimum access control with the predicted value is presented for the ALOHA-type CDMA random access scheme in the satellite network with a long propagation delay. For the LEO environment, the normalized throughput and total service time performance of SVM loads more than 1.2-times and reduces 0.8-times less than that of EKF. For the GEO environment, the normalized throughput and total service time performance of SVM loads more than 2.5-times and reduces 0.4-times less than that of EKF.

References

1. Li, S., Xu, L.D., Zhao, S.: The internet of things: a survey. Inf. Syst. Front. **17**(2), 243–259 (2015)
2. Borges, L.M., Velez, F.J., Lebres, A.S.: Survey on the characterization and classification of wireless sensor network applications. IEEE Commun. Surv. Tutorials **16**(4), 1860–1890 (2014)
3. Sanctis, M.D., Cianca, E., Araniti, G., et al.: Satellite communications supporting internet of remote things. IEEE Internet Things J. **3**(1), 113–123 (2016)
4. Schlegel, C., Kempter, R., Kota, P.: A novel random wireless packet multiple access method using CDMA. IEEE Trans. Wirel. Commun. **5**(6), 1362–1370 (2006)
5. Meloni, A., Murroni, M.: Interference calculation in asynchronous random access protocols using diversity. Telecommun. Syst. **63**(1), 45–53 (2016)
6. Ghanbarinejad, M., Schlegel, C.: Distributed probabilistic medium access with multipacket reception and Markovian traffic. Telecommun. Syst. **56**(2), 311–321 (2014)
7. Ghanbarinejad, M., Schlegel, C., Khabbazian, M.: Random access with multipacket reception and adaptive filtering. In: Global Communications Conference, pp. 4215–4220. IEEE (2014)

8. Saito, M., Okada, H., Sato, T., et al.: Throughput improvement of CDMA slotted ALOHA system by modified channel load sensing protocol. In: IEEE International Symposium on Personal, Indoor and Mobile Radio Communications, pp. 103–107, vol. 1. IEEE (2002)
9. Chang, C.C., Lin, C.J.: LIBSVM: a library for support vector machines. In: ACM (2011)
10. Wang, H., Hu, D.: Comparison of SVM and LS-SVM for regression. In: International Conference on Neural Networks and Brain, ICNN&B, pp. 279–283. IEEE (2005)

Beam Coverage Dynamic Adjustment Scheme Based on Maximizing System Capacity for Multi-beam Satellite Communication System

Bao Wenqian[⊠], Wang Weidong, Liu Shuaijun, and Cui Gaofeng

Information and Electronic Technology Lab,
Beijing University of Posts and Telecommunications, Beijing, China
baowenqian@bupt.edu.cn

Abstract. Multi-beam technique has been widely applied in modern satellite communication systems. However, the satellite power and bandwidth resources are scarce and expensive due to the limitation of satellite platform. Thus it is urgent to utilize the resources efficiently. Meanwhile, due to the disequilibrium of the non-uniform distribution of traffic request and the uniform coverage of satellite beams, the capacity of the overloaded beams may decrease since the lack of resources, while the resource utilization of the under-loaded beams will be insufficient. In order to increase the capacity of the multi-beam satellite communication system and improve the load balancing performance of the system, a beam coverage dynamic adjustment scheme based on maximizing system capacity is proposed in this paper. Theoretical analysis and simulation results demonstrate the correctness and effectiveness of the proposed scheme.

Keywords: Multi-beam satellite communication system
Beam coverage dynamic adjustment · Resource allocation
System capacity · Load balancing

1 Introduction

In recent years, the multi-spot-beam technique has played an important role in the satellite communication systems, as it can not only supply higher power density to a particular spot beam but also construct flexible service networks [1]. However, the satellite resources are scarce and expensive due to the limitation of satellite platform, thus it is urgent to improve the resources utilization.

Meanwhile, the current uniform coverage of spot beams and the fixed equal allocation algorithm over satellite downlinks cannot match the non-uniform distribution of traffic demands. The capacity of the overloaded beam may decrease since the lack of resources while the resource utilization of the under-loaded beams will be insufficient. And the load imbalance over beams will affect the performance of the multi-beam satellite communication system.

To increase the resource utilization and the system capacity, many related works have been proposed. In [2], the water-filling approach is introduced, which can achieve

Q. Yu (Ed.): SINC 2017, CCIS 803, pp. 288–298, 2018.
https://doi.org/10.1007/978-981-10-7877-4_26

the maximum total capacity through power allocation according to channel conditions. In [3], the author proposes a frequency reuse method to increase the system capacity, and add the interference mitigation approach to reduce the inter-beam interference. As for dynamic resource allocation algorithms, researches in [4, 5] respectively allocate the power and the bandwidth resource according to the traffic demand of each user, and model the problem as an optimization problem with restricted conditions. Combine power and bandwidth allocation, the work in [6] proposes a joint power and bandwidth optimal algorithm, and the problem solving is similar to [4, 5]. To improve the load balancing performance, the work in [7] proposes an access scheme in which the new traffic request chooses the under-loaded beam to access, that is, the channels of the under-loaded beam are allocated to the new traffic request. In [8, 9], the authors propose that the resource of under-loaded beams could be used by overloaded beams in order to achieve load balancing. The existing researches mainly increase the capacity and improve the load balancing performance of the multi-beam satellite system through allocating the power and bandwidth resources, overlooking that for satellite, its antenna radiation pattern and beam coverage are also adjustable resources. In this paper, we utilize the beam coverage with resource allocation to increase the capacity and improve the load balancing performance.

The main contribution of this work is the beam coverage dynamic adjustment scheme for multi-beam satellite communication system. The coverage of beams is adjusted dynamically based on the distribution of traffic requests, then the power and bandwidth resources are allocated according to the traffic distribution after the beam coverage adjustment.

The rest of this paper is organized as follows. Section 2 describes the system model and the problem formulation. We propose the optimal scheme for the mentioned problem in Sect. 3. Section 4 presents the simulation results of the proposed scheme. Section 5 concludes the whole paper.

2   Problem Formulation

2.1   System Model

Figure 1 shows the system configuration of a multi-beam satellite communication system, in which the traffic requests of mobile terminals are non-uniform distributed. Assuming there are 7 spot beams in this system, 1 center beam and 6 peripheral beams. The center beam is heavy-loaded and the peripheral beams are light-loaded. It is assumed that the system consists of N mobile earth stations (MES) and each MES has a traffic request represented as T_{ij}. These MESs can be represented as MES_{ij}, which means the jth MES in the ith beam.

2.2   Problem Model

In practice, due to the non-uniform geographical distribution of the traffic sources and the periodic satellite motion, the traffic among beams has a non-uniform distribution. The load of each beam is different, the capacity of the overloaded beam may decrease

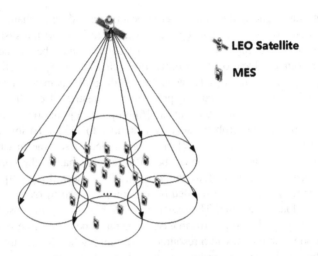

Fig. 1. System model

since the lack of resources while the resource utilization of the under-loaded beams will be insufficient.

To solve the problem mentioned above, the Beam Coverage Dynamic Adjustment (BCDA) Scheme Based on Maximizing System Capacity is proposed in this paper. In this study, the objective is to maximize the system capacity, taking account of the beam coverage area and the available channel and power resources of each beam. Therefore, the optimization problem is formulated as follows:

$$\max \sum_{ij} C_{ij} = \sum_{ij} B_{ij} \log_2 \left(1 + \frac{P_T G_T(\theta_{ij}) G_R(0) \left(\frac{\lambda}{4\pi d_{ij}}\right)^2}{kTB_{ij}}\right) \qquad (1)$$

Subject to

$$S_{Center\ Beam} + S_{Peripheral\ Beam} \geq S_{Area} \qquad (2)$$

$$\sum_j B_{ij} = B_{i\_avail} \qquad (3)$$

$$\sum_j P_{ij} = P_{i\_avail} \qquad (4)$$

Where:
C_{ij} is the capacity of MES_{ij},
B_{ij} is the number of channels allocated to MES_{ij},
P_{ij} is the power allocated to MES_{ij},
P_T is the transmit power of the LEO satellite antenna,
G_T is the gain of transmit antenna at the LEO satellite,

θ_{ij} is the off-axis angle of the LEO satellite transmit antenna main lobe in the direction of MES_{ij},

G_R is the gain of receive antenna at MES, since the use of omnidirectional antenna, the gain of receive antenna at MES can always be $G_R(0)$,

d_{ij} is the distance between the LEO satellite and MES_{ij},

$S_{Center\,Beam}$ is the area of the center beam coverage,

$S_{Peripheral\,Beam}$ is the area of the peripheral beams coverage,

S_{Area} is the area of the target coverage region,

B_{i_avail} is the number of available channels of beam i,

P_{i_avail} is the available power of beam i.

The objective function (1) represents the main purpose in this work. We aim to maximize the system capacity of the multi-beam satellite system. In theory, the capacity of a single MES is related to the channel and power resources allocated to it, the transmit antenna gain in the direction of it, and the distance between the LEO satellite and it.

The constraint (2) indicates the target coverage region should be full covered as the initial state after the beam coverage dynamic adjustment. Condition (3) and (4) imply the channel and power resources allocated to MESs in one beam should be equal to the available channel and power resources of that beam.

3   Proposed Beam Coverage Dynamic Adjustment Scheme

From the analysis above, when the allocated channel and power is fixed, the capacity of a single MES is only associated with the gain of the LEO satellite transmit antenna. And due to the characteristic of the satellite transmit antenna, the gain is negatively correlated with the off-axis angle. The smaller the off-axis angle is, that is, the closer the distance between beam center and MES is, the greater the transmit antenna gain will be. And the capacity of that single MES will be increased.

When this single-user conclusion is extended to multi-user scenario, then when more users are close to their service beam center, the capacity of the system will be increased, and vice versa. The proposed BCDA scheme is designed based on this conclusion, and achieves the optimization objective through adjusting the beam coverage according to the distribution of MESs. The beam coverage depends on the projection range of the satellite beam on the ground, which can be achieved by adjusting the antenna radiation angle. Considering the peer-to-peer relationship among MESs, that is, there is no difference in traffic demands and priorities among MESs. The procedure of the proposed BCDA scheme is given as follows:

The initial beam coverage state: The target coverage region is covered by 7 beams with the same radius D, and the center beam is heavy-loaded and the peripheral beams are light-loaded.

Step 1: According to the initial coverage of beams, calculate the allocated channel and power resources for each MES_{ij}. Since the peer-to-peer relationship among

MESs, the satellite resources are allocated to each beam with equal amount, and the resources of one beam are allocated to the MESs within this beam with equal amount.

Step 2: Calculate the capacity C_{ij} of each MES, then calculate the system capacity $\sum\limits_{i,j} C_{ij}$.

Step 3: Set the center beam to beam 1, calculate the capacity C_{1j} of each MES in the center hot beam. Sort C_{1j} in descending order, record the capacity ranking at 95% as C_{th}. And record the corresponding location of that MES, set the distance between the center of the hot beam and that MES to d.

Step 4: Adjust the antenna radiation angle, change the coverage of each beam. The radius of the center beam is reduced to R, $R = d$. In order to achieve the full coverage of the target region, the radius of the peripheral beams is increased to r, $r = \sqrt{(3D^2 - 3DR + R^2)}$ according to the geometric relationship.

Step 5: According to the coverage of beams and the distribution of MESs, recalculate the allocated channel and power resources for each MES_{ij}.

Step 6: Recalculate the capacity C'_{ij} of each MES, then calculate the system capacity $\sum\limits_{i,j} C_{ij}'$.

Step 7: Compare $\sum\limits_{i,j} C_{ij}'$ with $\sum\limits_{i,j} C_{ij}$, if $\sum\limits_{i,j} C_{ij}' > \sum\limits_{i,j} C_{ij}$, return to step 3. Else, terminate the algorithm, and the value obtained in the last round is the optimal value.

The algorithm flowchart is shown in Fig. 2.

In step 1 and 2, the channel and power resources are allocated to each MES and the system capacity is calculated in the initial state, this is, the target coverage region is covered by 7 beams with the same radius.

In step 3, the capacity of each MES in the center hot beam is calculated and sorted. Here the concept of the cell edge users is introduced. Edge users are the users whose capacity is ranking at the last 5% of the capacity statistics of one beam. The performance of the edge users is poor since the lack of communication resources. To solve this problem, these edge users can be serviced by the peripheral light-loaded beams rather than the center hot beam.

In step 4, the coverage of each beam is changed. The radius of the center beam is reduced based on the result obtained in step 3, and because of this, the edge users in center beam is now covered by peripheral beams and serviced by them. In this way, the burden of communication in the over-loaded center beam is reduced and the resources utilization in the peripheral beams is improved. Meanwhile, the change in beam coverage should meet the requirement for full coverage of the target region, and now the target region is covered by 7 beams with different radius.

In step 5 and 6, the resources are reallocated to each MES and the system capacity is calculated after the beam coverage dynamic adjustment.

In step 7, the system capacity after beam coverage dynamic adjustment is compared with that of the last iteration, and performance an iterative search for the optimal solution until the constraint condition $\sum\limits_{i,j} C_{ij}' > \sum\limits_{i,j} C_{ij}$ is not satisfied.

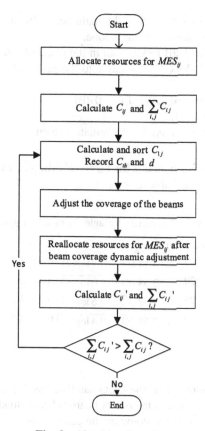

Fig. 2. Algorithm flowchart

4   Simulation Results

4.1   Antenna Radiation Pattern

According to [10], the antenna radiation pattern of LEO satellite which is used to express antenna gain in different direction is as follows:

$$
\begin{aligned}
G(\psi) &= G_m - 3(\psi/\psi_b)^\alpha \text{ dBi for } 0 < \psi \le a\psi_b \\
G(\psi) &= G_m + L_N + 20\log(z) \text{ dBi for } a\psi_b < \psi \le 0.5b\psi_b \\
G(\psi) &= G_m + L_N \text{ dBi for } 0.5b\psi_b < \psi \le b\psi_b \\
G(\psi) &= X - 25\log(\psi) \text{ dBi for } b\psi_b < \psi \le Y \\
G(\psi) &= L_F \text{ dBi for } Y < \psi \le 90° \\
G(\psi) &= L_B \text{ dBi for } 90° < \psi \le 180°
\end{aligned}
\tag{5}
$$

Where:

$$X = G_m + L_N + 25\log(b\psi_b) \text{ and } Y = b\psi_b 10^{0.04(G_m + L_N - L_F)},$$

$G(\psi)$ is the gain at the angle ψ from the main beam direction,

G_m is the maximum gain in the main lobe,

ψ_b is the one-half the 3 dB beamwidth in the plane of interest (3 dB below Gm),

L_N is the near-in-side-lobe level relative to the peak gain required by the system design,

L_F is the far-out side-lobe level, $L_F = 0\,\mathrm{dBi}$,

L_B is the back-lobe level,

z is (major axis/minor axis) for the radiated beam.

The numeric values of a, b, and α for L_N = –15 dB, –20 dB, –25 dB, and –30 dB side-lobe levels are given in Table 1.

Table 1. Parameters for antenna radiation pattern

L_N (dB)	a	b	α
−15	$2.58\sqrt{1 - 0.4\log(z)}$	6.32	1.5
−20	$2.58\sqrt{1 - 1.0\log(z)}$	6.32	1.5
−25	$2.58\sqrt{1 - 0.6\log(z)}$	6.32	1.5
−30	$2.58\sqrt{1 - 0.4\log(z)}$	6.32	1.5

4.2   System Parameters

In the simulation, we assume that the GEO satellite has 7 beams, including 1 center beam and 6 peripheral beams, and the center beam is heavy-loaded while the peripheral beams are light-loaded. In order to compare the performance of our proposed algorithm to other algorithms, we set satellite transmit power and spectrum utilization efficiency as the x-axis. We set the transmit power P_T from 10 w to 100 w and the spectrum utilization ρ from 5 bps/Hz to 15 bps/Hz according to LEO system. More detailed parameters are illustrated in Table 2.

Table 2. Parameters setting

Para.	Value	Description
H	1000 km	The height of LEO satellite
D	400 km	The initial radius of beams
CH_total	100	The total number of channels
G_m	41.6 dBi	The maximum gain of the satellite antenna
f	2185 MHz	The downlink transmission carrier frequency band
N	30	The number of MESs
T	290 K	The noise temperature
L_N	−25	The parameters of the satellite transmit antenna
a	$2.58\sqrt{1 - 0.6\log(z)}$	
b	6.32	
α	1.5	

4.3   Simulation Results

The proposed scheme is compared with the conventional resources allocation scheme and the Beam Coverage Static Adjustment (BCSA) scheme [11]. In the conventional resources allocation scheme, the satellite resources are allocated to each beam with equal amount, and the resources of one beam are allocated to the MESs within this beam with equal amount, without considering the non-uniform distribution of MESs and the load imbalancing among beams. In BCSA, the beam coverage is adjusted considering the distribution of traffic, however, the beam coverage mode is switched between two fixed coverage modes: 1. equal beam size coverage; 2. the radius of the center beam is reduced to $0.62D$ and the radius of the peripheral beams is increased to $1.18D$ for full coverage of the target region.

Figures 3 and 4 show the ground coverage topology before and after the beam coverage dynamic adjustment scheme. The solid circles represent the satellite beam and the dotted circle represents the target coverage region. The radius of the center beam is reduced and the radius of the peripheral beams is increased. The load balancing performance of the system is improved visually in the comparison of these two figures. Meanwhile, we can intuitively see that more users are close to their service beam center, which can improve the system capacity in the previous analysis, and the numerical demonstration will be shown and discussion later.

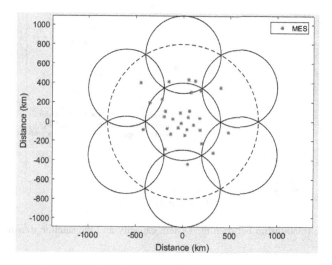

Fig. 3. The ground coverage topology before BCDA scheme

Figure 5 shows the relationship between the system capacity and the satellite transmit power of the three algorithms. According to the function (1), the system capacity of each scheme is becoming lager as the transmit power becomes larger. The conventional resources allocation scheme has the worst performance in terms of the system capacity. The BCSA scheme is better than conventional resources allocation scheme due to the consideration of traffic demand, but it still worse than the proposed

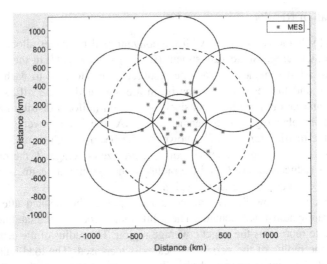

Fig. 4. The ground coverage topology after BCDA scheme

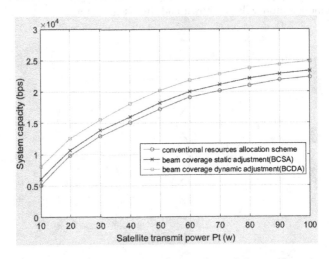

Fig. 5. The relationship between the system capacity and the satellite transmit power

BCDA algorithm since the lack of dynamic adjustment of the beam coverage. In BCDA scheme, the non-uniform distribution of MESs is considered in terms of the resources allocation, and the beam coverage is dynamically adjusted along with resources reallocation according to the traffic demand, then utilize the iterative search algorithm to obtain the optimal solution. This scheme increase the system capacity effectively.

Figure 6 shows the relationship between the maximum transmission time and the spectrum efficiency of the three algorithms. The system maximum transmission time can be used as a measurement for the load balancing performance of the system, the shorter the maximum transmission time is, the better the load balancing performance will be. The transmission time can be represented as

$$t_{ij} = \frac{T_{ij}}{B_{ij}\rho} \tag{6}$$

where t_{ij} is the transmission time of MES_{ij}. From Fig. 6, the maximum transmission time of each scheme is becoming shorter as the spectrum utilization becomes larger, which is consistent with the function (6). The BCDA scheme improves the load balancing performance of the system comparing to the conventional resources allocation scheme and the BCSA scheme.

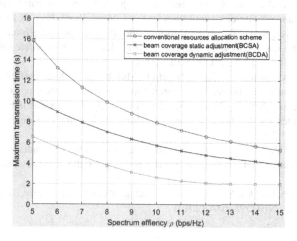

Fig. 6. The relationship between the maximum transmission time and the spectrum efficiency

5 Conclusion

To achieve maximum system capacity and improve the load balancing performance of the multi-beam satellite communication system, a beam coverage dynamic adjustment scheme (BCDA) based on maximizing system capacity is proposed in this work. The proposed algorithm consider the non-uniform distribution of MESs, and the beam coverage is dynamically adjusted along with resources reallocation according to the traffic demand, then utilize the iterative search algorithm to obtain the optimal solution. Theoretical analysis and simulation results indicate the proposed scheme has significant advantages over the conventional resources allocation scheme and the beam coverage static adjustment (BCSA) scheme.

Acknowledgement. This work was supported by the National Natural Science Foundation of China (No. 91438114).

References

1. Roddy, D.: Satellite Communication. McGraw-Hill, New York (2001)
2. Park, U., Kim, H.W., Oh, D.S., et al.: Optimum selective beam allocation scheme for satellite network with multi-spot beams, pp. 78–81 (2012)
3. Nakahira, K., Kobayashi, K., Ueba, M.: Capacity and quality enhancement using an adaptive resource allocation for multi-beam mobile satellite communication systems. In: Wireless Communications and NETWORKING Conference, WCNC 2006. IEEE Xplore, pp. 153–158 (2006)
4. Wang, H., Liu, A., Pan, X., et al.: Optimization of power allocation for multiusers in multi-spot-beam satellite communication systems. Math. Probl. Eng. **2014**(2), 1–10 (2014)
5. Wang, H., Liu, A., Pan, X., et al.: Optimal bandwidth allocation for multi-spot-beam satellite communication systems. In: International Conference on Mechatronic Sciences, Electric Engineering and Computer, pp. 2794–2798 (2013)
6. Wang, H., Liu, A., Pan, X.: Optimization of joint power and bandwidth allocation in multi-spot-beam satellite communication systems. Math. Probl. Eng. **2014**(6), 1–9 (2014)
7. Tzeng, C.W., Ke, K.W., Wu, H.T.: Resource allocation and adaptive routing in multimedia low Earth orbit satellite mobile networks. In: IEEE International Conference on Multimedia and Expo, pp. 1795–1798, vol. 3. IEEE (2004)
8. Lizarraga, J., Angeletti, P., Alagha, N., et al.: Multibeam satellites performance analysis in non-uniform traffic conditions. In: Vacuum Electronics Conference, pp. 1–2. IEEE (2013)
9. Lizarraga, J., Angeletti, P., Alagha, N., et al.: Flexibility performance in advanced Ka-band multibeam satellites. In: IEEE International Vacuum Electronics Conference, pp. 45–46. IEEE (2014)
10. RECOMMENDATION ITU-R S.1528. Satellite antenna radiation patterns for non-geostationary orbit satellite antennas operating in the fixed-satellite service below 30 GHz
11. Zhang, S., Qian, C., Qin, X., et al.: Beam coverage Adjustment Scheme Based on the Traffic Demand. CN, CN103595463A (2014)

Quasi-Cyclic LDPC Codes Constructed Based on Row-Column Constrained Matrices

Hengzhou Xu[1(✉)], Baoming Bai[2], Hai Zhu[1], Mengmeng Xu[1], and Bo Zhang[1]

[1] School of Network Engineering, Zhoukou Normal University,
Zhoukou 466001, China
hzxu@zknu.edu.cn
[2] State Key Laboratory of Integrated Services Networks, Xidian University,
Xi'an 710071, China

Abstract. Row-column (RC) constraint structure plays an important role in the design of LDPC codes. In this paper, we study the construction of quasi-cyclic (QC) LDPC codes based on RC-constrained matrices. We first analyze the relation between the cycles and the exponent matrix of a QC LDPC code, and present a method to design the exponent matrices for a given degree distribution and an expansion factor k. By dispersing every element of the exponent matrix into circulant permutation matrix (CPM) or zero matrix (ZM) of size $k \times k$, a QC LDPC code is obtained. Numerical simulation results show that our constructed QC LDPC codes have fast convergence of iterative decoding and good performance over the AWGN channel.

Keywords: LDPC code · Quasi-cyclic · Row-column (RC) constraint
Girth · Dispersion

1 Introduction

Low-density parity-check (LDPC) codes, invented by Gallager in 1962 [1], are a class of error-correction codes which can approach Shannon capacity limits. Recently, numerical results show that LDPC codes constructed from partial geometries do not have error floor over the additive white Gaussian noise (AWGN) channel at the bit error rate (BER) down to 10^{-15} [2]. This makes LDPC codes much attractive for applications requiring very low error floor, such as data storage systems, optical communications, and space communications. In particular, for both near-earth and deep-space communications, LDPC codes had been accepted as the standard codes of Consultative Committee for Space Data Systems (CCSDS) [3].

As a special type of LDPC codes, quasi-cyclic (QC) LDPC codes [4] have the following advantages: (1) their encoder and decoder can be easily implemented in hardware by using the linear shift register [5–7]; (2) they have a fast rate of iterative decoding convergence [8]; (3) they have good performance in the waterfall and error-floor regions [9]. Construction of QC LDPC codes has two important ingredients including *exponent matrices* and *matrix-dispersion*. Actually, matrix-dispersion is an expansion process, i.e., replacing every element of an exponent matrix with a circulant

© Springer Nature Singapore Pte Ltd. 2018
Q. Yu (Ed.): SINC 2017, CCIS 803, pp. 299–306, 2018.
https://doi.org/10.1007/978-981-10-7877-4_27

permutation matrix (CPM) or a zero matrix (ZM) of size $k \times k$. Note that k is usually called expansion factor (or lifting degree) [10]. In general, QC LDPC codes are mainly constructed based on graph theory and algebraic or combinatorial tools, such as protograph [11], balanced incomplete block design (BIBD) [12], group divisible design (GDD) [13], finite geometry [14], and finite field [15]. But the expansion factor is not flexible in these construction methods. Moreover, in [16], Bocharova *et al.* found that QC LDPC codes with large-size exponent matrices would have better performance under iterative decoding.

Short cycles, especially cycles of length 4, will degrade the performance of an LDPC code when decoded with the iterative algorithm based on belief propagation [17]. A constraint imposed on the parity-check matrix of the LDPC code can effectively avoid the cycles of length 4 in the Tanner graph [18]. This is the well-known row-column (RC) constraint: no two columns (or two rows) have more than one nonzero element in the same position. If a matrix or an array of CPMs and/or ZMs satisfies the RC-constraint, we say this matrix or this array is RC-constrained. It is ensured that the RC-constrained matrix or array of CPMs and/or ZMs results in LDPC codes with girth at least 6.

In this paper, we construct a class of QC LDPC codes with large-size exponent matrices based on the RC-constrained matrices. We first analyze the cycle structure of QC LDPC codes and then propose an algorithm to design the exponent matrix for a given degree distribution and expansion factor k. By dispersing each element of the exponent matrix into a CPM or ZM of size $k \times k$, a QC LDPC code is obtained. Numerical results show that our proposed codes perform well over the AWGN channel.

2   QC LDPC Codes and Cycles in Their Tanner Graphs

A QC LDPC code is defined by the null space of the following $J \times L$ array $\mathbf{H}$ of CPMs and/or ZMs:

$$\mathbf{H} = \begin{bmatrix} I(p_{1,1}) & I(p_{1,2}) & \cdots & I(p_{1,L}) \\ I(p_{2,1}) & I(p_{2,2}) & \cdots & I(p_{2,L}) \\ \vdots & \vdots & \ddots & \vdots \\ I(p_{J,1}) & I(p_{J,2}) & \cdots & I(p_{J,L}) \end{bmatrix},$$

where, for $1 \leq i \leq J$, $1 \leq j \leq L$, $p_{i,j} \in \{\{-1\} \cup Z_k\}$, and for $p_{i,j} \in Z_k$, $I(p_{i,j})$ is a CPM of size $k \times k$ obtained by shifting $p_{i,j}$ positions of each row of the identity matrix $\mathbf{I}$ of size $k \times k$ to the right, and $I(-1)$ stands for a $k \times k$ ZM. We can see that the positions of nonzero elements in $\mathbf{H}$ are exactly determined by the following matrix:

$$\mathbf{P} = \begin{bmatrix} p_{1,1} & p_{1,2} & \cdots & p_{1,L} \\ p_{2,1} & p_{2,2} & \cdots & p_{2,L} \\ \vdots & \vdots & \ddots & \vdots \\ p_{J,1} & p_{J,2} & \cdots & p_{J,L} \end{bmatrix}.$$

This matrix $\mathbf{P}$ is called *exponent matrix*. It can be observed that there is a one-to-one correspondence between $\mathbf{H}$ and $\mathbf{P}$. If $\mathbf{H}$ has constant column weight γ and row weight ρ, then the resulting QC LDPC code is (γ, ρ)-regular; otherwise, it is irregular.

Consider a QC LDPC code C defined by the null space of $\mathbf{H}$, and use g and $\mathbf{P}$ to denote its girth and exponent matrix, respectively. The cycles in the Tanner graph of C can be represented by the ordered series of CPMs [4]. Without loss of generality, a cycle of length $2i$, denoted by $2i$-cycle, corresponds to the following ordered CPMs in $\mathbf{H}$:

$$I\left(p_{j_1,l_1}\right), I\left(p_{j_2,l_1}\right), I\left(p_{j_2,l_2}\right), I\left(p_{j_3,l_2}\right), I\left(p_{j_3,l_3}\right), \ldots,$$
$$I\left(p_{j_{i-1},l_{i-1}}\right), I\left(p_{j_i,l_{i-1}}\right), I\left(p_{j_i,l_i}\right), I\left(p_{j_1,l_i}\right), I\left(p_{j_1,l_1}\right),$$

where $j_{i+1} = j_1, l_{i+1} = l_1, j_m \neq j_{m+1}, l_m \neq l_{m+1}, 1 \leq j_m \leq J$ and $1 \leq l_m \leq L$ for $1 \leq m \leq i$. According to Eq. (2) in [19], the necessary and sufficient condition for the existence of such a $2i$-cycle is

$$\sum_{m=1}^{i} \left(p_{j_m,l_m} - p_{j_{m+1},l_m}\right) = 0 \pmod{k}, \tag{1}$$

where $g \leq 2i \leq 2g - 2$. It can be proved that Eq. (1) is only the necessary condition for the existence of a $2i$-cycle when $2i \geq 2g$. Hence, Eq. (4) in [4] and Eq. (3) in [20] are only suitable for the cycle with length smaller than $2g$. Notice that the above $p_{j,l}$ takes values in the set Z_k for $1 \leq j \leq J, 1 \leq l \leq L$. If one of $p_{j,l}$ in Eq. (1) is equal to -1, the corresponding cycles will not exist. In other words, the numbers of cycles in a QC LDPC code are associated with the values of $p_{j,l}$ in its exponent matrix $\mathbf{P}$. Therefore, from the perspective of cycle distribution, the construction of QC LDPC codes is equivalent to the design of the exponent matrix $\mathbf{P}$. Generally, the exponent matrix $\mathbf{P}$ can be obtained by the following two parts: (1) the position selection of the elements which do not belong to Z_k, i.e., the position selection of -1's; (2) the optimization of the elements which are not equal to -1. In fact, the first part can be viewed as the design of the masking matrix [21]. In order to avoid the 4-cycles in the constructed QC LDPC codes, we employ the RC-constrained matrices as the masking matrices in this paper.

3 Construction of QC LDPC Codes from RC-Constrained Matrices

In this section, we construct QC LDPC codes based on RC-constrained matrices for a given degree distribution and expansion factor. Notice that RC-constrained matrices can be obtained on the basis of algebraic or combinatorial tools, such as finite fields and finite geometries. It is well-known that the progressive-edge-growth (PEG) algorithm [22] is a greedy algorithm to construct a Tanner graph with large girth. Hence, we employ the PEG algorithm to construct the RC-constrained matrices. Therefore, to design an exponent matrix $\mathbf{P}$, we only need to optimize the elements in $\mathbf{P}$ which are not equal to -1.

Based on Eq. (1), we can see that if the Eq. (1) is not satisfied, the corresponding $2i$-cycles will not exist for $g \leq 2i \leq 2g - 2$. Hence, we can optimize the elements in the exponent matrix $\mathbf{P}$ which do not equal -1 by checking if Eq. (1) is satisfied. By jointly optimizing the girth values and the number of the shortest cycles in the constructed QC LDPC codes, the following algorithm, i.e., Algorithm 1, is proposed. In Algorithm 1, $\mathbf{M}$ is the RC-constrained matrix constructed from the PEG algorithm. Notice that $\mathbf{M}$ is a matrix of size $J \times L$ and its elements take values in $\{0, 1\}$.

Algorithm 1. *Element optimization of the exponent matrix* $\boldsymbol{P}$

Input:	RC-constrained matrix $\mathbf{M}$, expansion factor k
Step 1:	Replace 0 and 1 in $\mathbf{M}$ with -1 and 0, respectively,
	and obtain a new matrix $\mathbf{B}$;
Step 2:	Optimize the elements of $\mathbf{B}$ which are not equal to
	-1 one by one; (Optimization rule: enlarge the girth
	value and reduce the number of shortest cycles)
Step 3:	Denote the resulting matrix in the above step as the
	exponent matrix $\mathbf{P}$;
Output:	Exponent matrix $\mathbf{P}$

For a given degree distribution and an arbitrary expansion factor k, we can easily obtain an exponent matrix $\mathbf{P}$ based on the PEG algorithm and Algorithm 1. By dispersing the elements in $\mathbf{P}$ into the corresponding CPMs or ZMs of size $k \times k$, the required QC LDPC codes are constructed.

4   Simulation Results

To show the effectiveness of Algorithm 1 and the good performance of the proposed QC LDPC codes, the following example is given.

Example 1. Consider a (4,31)-regular QC LDPC code with code length 9920 and expansion factor 64. We can see that the size of the exponent matrix of this code is 20×155. It is easy to construct a RC-constrained matrix $\mathbf{M}$ of size 20×155 based on the PEG algorithm. Notice that the cycle distribution of the Tanner graph of $\mathbf{M}$ is $0x^4 + 121788x^6 + 7377873x^8 + \dots$. By employing Algorithm 1, we can obtain the designed exponent matrix $\mathbf{P}$. Finally, we disperse the elements of $\mathbf{P}$ into CPMs/ZMs of size 64×64 and a matrix $\mathbf{H}$ of size 1280×9920 is constructed. Notice that the rank of $\mathbf{H}$ is 1279 and the cycle distribution of the Tanner graph of $\mathbf{H}$ is $0x^4 + 101824x^6 + 8316704x^8 + \dots$. The null space of $\mathbf{H}$ gives a (9920,8641) QC LDPC code with rate 0.871. The performance of this code over the AWGN channel decoded with the sum–product algorithm (SPA) (10 and 50 iterations) is shown in Fig. 1. At a bit error rate (BER) of 10^{-8}, the proposed code performs about 1 dB from the Shannon limit when decoded with the SPA (50 iterations). Furthermore, this code has fast decoding convergence, since the performance gap between 10 iterations and 50 iterations is less than 0.3 dB at the BER of 2×10^{-7}. As shown in Fig. 2, to verify the good performance of our proposed QC LDPC code, we also plot the performance curves of two comparable LDPC codes, i.e., (4,32)-regular (8160,7159) QC LDPC code in [22] and (4,31)-regular (9920,8641) LDPC code constructed based on the PEG algorithm [23]. We assume that transmission is over the AWGN channel with BPSK modulation and the decoding algorithm is the SPA with 50 iterations. We can see from Fig. 2 that at the BER of 10^{-8}, our proposed (9920,8641) QC LDPC code outperforms the (8160,7159) QC LDPC code in [22] by about 0.1 dB, but our code is 1760 bits longer than the (8160,7159) QC LDPC code. Furthermore, our proposed (9920,8641) QC LDPC code achieves a coding gain of 0.03 dB over the (9920,8641) PEG-LDPC code at the BER of 10^{-7}.

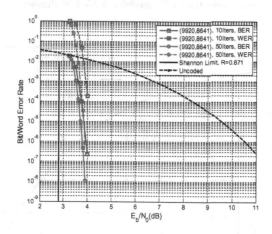

Fig. 1. The error performances of the proposed (9920,8641) QC LDPC code given in Example 1.

In order to find the error floor of the proposed (9920,8641) QC LDPC code, we employ the hard reliability-based iterative majority-logic decoding (*HRBI-MLGD*) algorithm in [24] to decode the received codewords. Since this decoding algorithm is a low-complexity decoding algorithm, we can easily obtain the performance of the proposed (9920,8641) QC LDPC code at the BER of about 10^{-10} by using C++ on a PC with 3.3 GHz CPU and 8 GB RAM. Figure 3 shows the error performance of the proposed (9920,8641) QC LDPC code decoded with the *HRBI-MLGD* algorithm (50 iterations) over the BPSK modulated AWGN channel. It can be observed that the proposed (9920,8641) QC LDPC code has no visible error floor down to BER $\sim 10^{-12}$.

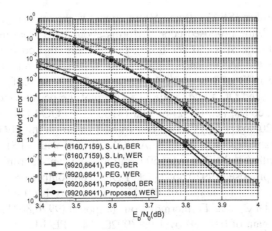

Fig. 2. The error performances of the proposed (9920,8641) QC LDPC code, (8160,7159) QC LDPC code in [22], and the (9920,8640) PEG-LDPC code [23] when decoded with the SPA (50 iterations). Transmission over the BPSK modulated AWGN channel is assumed.

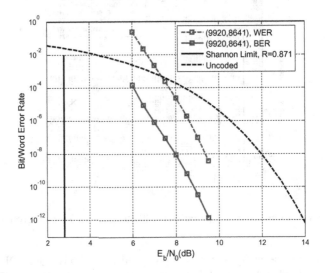

Fig. 3. The error performance of the proposed (9920,8641) QC LDPC code when decoded with the hard reliability-based iterative majority-logic decoding algorithm (50 iterations) in [24]. Transmission over the BPSK modulated AWGN channel is assumed.

5   Conclusion and Future Work

In this paper, we analyzed the cycle structure of QC LDPC codes and presented a method to construct the exponent matrices of QC LDPC codes based on RC-constrained matrices for a given degree distribution and an expansion factor k. Notice that the expansion factor can be an arbitrary positive integer. By dispersing all elements of the resulting exponent into circulant permutation matrices or zero matrices of size $k \times k$, a QC LDPC code is constructed. Experimental results show that the constructed QC LDPC codes perform well over the AWGN channel and converge fast under iterative decoding. Moreover, there is no visible error floor observed down to BER $\sim 10^{-12}$.

Girth and cycles in the Tanner graph affect the error performance of QC LDPC codes decoded with the iterative algorithms. For a QC LDPC code with a given degree distribution and an expansion factor, girth and cycles are determined by its exponent matrix. Hence, in the future, we focus on the optimization of the elements in the exponent matrices of QC LDPC codes which have the better performance under iterative decoding.

Acknowledgements. This work was supported in part by National Natural Science Foundation of China under Grants 61372074, 91438101, 61771364, 61103143, U1404622, and U1504601, Key Scientific and Technological Project of Henan under Grants 162102310589 and 172102310124, Key Scientific Research Projects of Henan Educational Committee under Grants 16A520105 and 18B510022, and School-Based Program of Zhoukou Normal University under Grant ZKNUB2201705.

References

1. Gallager, R.G.: Low-density parity-check codes. IRE Trans. Inf. Theory **8**(1), 21–28 (1962)
2. Diao, Q., Li, J., Lin, S., Blake, I.F.: New classes of partial geometries and their associated LDPC codes. IEEE Trans. Inf. Theory **62**(6), 2947–2965 (2016)
3. CCSDS 231.1-O-1. Short Block Length LDPC Codes for TC Synchronization and Channel Coding. Washington DC (2015)
4. Fossorier, M.P.C.: Quasi-cyclic low-density parity-check codes from circulant permutation matrices. IEEE Trans. Inf. Theory **50**(8), 1788–1794 (2004)
5. Khodaiemehr, H., Kiani, D.: Construction and encoding of QC-LDPC codes using group rings. IEEE Trans. Inf. Theory **63**(4), 2039–2060 (2017)
6. Li, Z., Chen, Z.L., Lin, S., Fong, W.H.: Efficient encoding of quasi-cyclic low-density parity-check codes. IEEE Trans. Commun. **54**(1), 71–81 (2006)
7. Huang, Q., Diao, Q., Lin, S., Abdel-Ghaffar, K.: Cyclic and quasi-cyclic LDPC codes on constrained parity-check matrices and their trapping sets. IEEE Trans. Inf. Theory **58**(5), 2648–2671 (2012)
8. Zhang, L., Lin, S., Abdel-Ghaffar, K., Zhou, B.: Circulant arrays: Rank analysis and construction of quasi-cyclic LDPC codes. In: IEEE International Symposium on Information Theory 2010, pp. 814–818 (2010)
9. Li, J., Liu, K., Lin, S., Abdel-Ghaffar, K.: Quasi-cyclic LDPC codes on two arbitrary sets of a finite field. In: IEEE International Symposium on Information Theory 2014, pp. 2454–2458 (2014)
10. Li, J., Liu, K., Lin, S., Abdel-Ghaffar, K., Ryan, W.: An unnoticed strong connection between algebraic-based and protograph-based LDPC codes, Part I: binary case and interpretation. In: Information Theory and Applications Workshop (ITA) 2015, pp. 36–45 (2015)
11. Mitchell, D.G.M., Smarandache, R., Costello, D.J.: Quasi-cyclic LDPC codes based on pre-lifted protographs. IEEE Trans. Inf. Theory **60**(10), 5856–5874 (2014)

12. Lan, L., Tai, Y., Lin, S., Memari, B., Honary, B.: New constructions of quasi-cyclic LDPC codes based on special classes of BIBD's for the AWGN and binary erasure channels channels. IEEE Trans. Commun. **56**(1), 39–48 (2008)
13. Xu, H., Feng, D., Sun, C., Bai, B.: Construction of LDPC codes based on resolvable group divisible designs. IEEE International Workshop on High Mobility Wireless Communications **2015**, 111–115 (2015)
14. Diao, Q., Tai, Y., Lin, S., Abdel-Ghaffar, K.: LDPC codes on partial geometries: Construction, trapping set structure, and puncturing. IEEE Trans. Inf. Theory **59**(12), 7898–7914 (2013)
15. Song, S., Zhou, B., Lin, S., Abdel-Ghaffar, K.: A unified approach to the construction of binary and nonbinary quasi-cyclic LDPC codes based on finite fields. IEEE Trans. Commun. **57**(1), 84–93 (2009)
16. Bocharova, I., Kudryashov, B., Johannesson, R.: Searching for binary and nonbinary block and convolutional LDPC codes. IEEE Trans. Inf. Theory **62**(1), 163–183 (2016)
17. Mackay, D.J.C.: Good error-correcting codes based on very sparse matrices. IEEE Trans. Inf. Theory **45**(2), 399–431 (1999)
18. Tanner, R.M.: A recursive approach to low complexity codes. IEEE Trans. Inf. Theory **27**(5), 533–547 (1981)
19. Xu, H., Feng, D., Luo, R., Bai, B.: Construction of quasi-cyclic LDPC codes via masking with successive cycle elimination. IEEE Commun. Lett. **20**(12), 2370–2373 (2016)
20. Tasdighi, A., Banihashemi, A.H., Sadeghi, M.: Efficient search of girth-optimal QC-LDPC codes. IEEE Trans. Inf. Theory **62**(4), 1552–1564 (2016)
21. Liu, Y., Li, Y.: Design of masking matrix for QC-LDPC codes. In: IEEE Information Theory Workshop (ITW) 2013, pp. 1–5 (2013)
22. Ryan, W.E., Lin, S.: Channel codes: Classical and Modern, pp. 452–453. Cambridge University Press, USA (2009)
23. Hu, Y., Eleftheriou, E., Arnold, D.M.: Regular and irregular progressive edge growth Tanner graphs. IEEE Trans. Inf. Theory **51**(1), 386–398 (2005)
24. Huang, Q., Kang, J., Zhang, L., Lin, S., Abdel-Ghaffar, K.: Two reliability-based iterative majority-logic decoding algorithms for LDPC codes. IEEE Trans. Commun. **57**(12), 3597–3606 (2009)

Research on Deep Space Optical Quantum OFDM System Based on Positive Operator Valued Measurement Detection

Xiao Zhao, Xiaolin Zhou$^{(\boxtimes)}$, Chongbin Xu, and Xin Wang

Key Laboratory of EMW Information,
Fudan University, Shanghai 200433, China
zhouxiaolin@fudan.edu.cn

Abstract. The current deep space communication is still based on traditional radio communication. However, features like long distance, weak signal, large unstable delay and high volume data make it increasingly difficult for traditional ways to meet the requirements of deep space communication. In order to improve the efficiency and speed of communication system, reduce the communication cost of aircrafts, accelerate the practical process of deep space optical quantum communication network, an optical quantum communication system based on the all-optical OFDM model is proposed. Meanwhile, based on the expansion in the Fock space, a well-performing algorithm of positive operator valued measurement called least square root quantum detection is presented, aiming at the non-orthogonality of the sending quantum symbol set. Also, several simulations of the system performance and possible influential factors are carried out. The results show that the proposed optical quantum OFDM system has a better performance with the usage of least square root quantum detection. In addition, some influential factors are analyzed and possible solutions are proposed.

Keywords: Deep space communication · Optical quantum communication
OFDM · POVM

1 Introduction

In the exploration of deep space, it is the communication system that undertakes missions such as transmitting telemetry information, tracking navigation and scientific data transmission, which makes it the magnitude guarantee of the whole deep space exploration mission. Deep space communication generally refers to the communication between different types of aircrafts away from earth orbit or between aircrafts and ground control center [1]. Unlike traditional ground communication and near-earth satellite communication, deep space communication distinguishes itself with characteristics such as long distance, weak signal, large and unstable time delay and huge data quantity [2]. Although traditional optical communication has advantages like large information capacity, small equipment size and low energy consumption, it still encountered difficulties in security, weak signal detection and unstable time delay [3]. Quantum communication, which combines quantum mechanics and communication

Q. Yu (Ed.): SINC 2017, CCIS 803, pp. 307–317, 2018.
https://doi.org/10.1007/978-981-10-7877-4_28

technology, is an important branch of quantum information. Based on principles of quantum mechanics, through analyzing and applying physical characteristics of micro field to communication technology, quantum communication, with its unparalleled superiorities over traditional communication, has become one of the research hot points in communication field [4]. Except for all the advantages of traditional optical communication, quantum communication also has very high security, great anti-interference performance and so forth. Since IBM proposed the BB84 quantum communication scheme in 1984 [5], quantum communication has made a great progress with its unique superiorities. There has been plenty of ground-based quantum communication network systems built in different regions of Europe, the United States and Japan [6, 7]. Meanwhile, China is also leading the way in developing quantum communication technology: the world first quantum communication satellite was launched delivered successfully in 2016; the long distance quantum communication backbone network, which linked Beijing and Shanghai, ran through this year [9]. Ground-based quantum communication has entered the period of large scale commercial application currently. Furthermore, due to a series of unique characteristics of photon such as extremely low loss in outer space, weak de-coherence effect and multiple optical windows, quantum communication is promising to replace wireless communication and traditional optical communication as the best way for deep space communication [10].

Considering that in deep space exploration mission, aircrafts need to transmit scientific data including images, audio and video. Therefore, high data rate is required in deep space communication systems. It will bring improvements on communication rate and channel capacity to a large extent, if we are able to transmit multiple optical signals with different wavelengths in multiple channels, also known as Wavelength Division Multiplexing (WDM). Hence quantum channel multiplexing is the inevitable choice for future deep space quantum communication and practical quantum information network.

Orthogonal Frequency Division Multiplexing (OFDM), with its high frequency utilization rate, well bandwidth expandability and mature achievement scheme, has become one of the most promising scheme among all the classical multiplexing technologies. OFDM has a rather high fitness for optical pulses with different wavelengths and independent frequencies. Currently, research teams from HUST and UESTC had achieved 8–40 Gbits [11] and 8–112 Gbits [12] classical all-optical OFDM transmission systems over optical fiber.

In most cases, quantum states in all-optical OFDM system are non-orthogonal, which makes the Positive Operator Valued Measure (POVM) necessary [14]. Based on different criteria, there are several POVM operator formation algorithms such as the Best Bayes Detection and the Photon Counting Detection. In this paper, we adopt the algorithm called Square Root Measurement (SRM) to form POVM operators based on signal states for detection. This algorithm matches the requirement for deep space aircrafts to reducing processing cost due to its low complexity. Meanwhile, the advantage of low optical power makes this algorithm suitable for long and weak deep space communication signals.

We studied the characteristics of deep space environment, all-optical OFDM communication system based on Mach-Zehnder Interferometer (MZI) and SRM algorithm for quantum phase signal. In Sect. 2, the procedure and realization of all-optical OFDM system are introduced. In Sect. 3, the POVM detection and the SRM algorithm are illustrated. In Sect. 4, the performance of this quantum OFDM system based on POVM detection is studied based on simulation results. Also, through the comparison with traditional detection, factors which could affect the system performance are analyzed.

2 The Quantum OFDM System Based on MZI

The main idea of OFDM is to divide the channel into several sub-channels in frequency domain and then modulate all the subcarriers separately for parallel transmission. The OFDM system based on MZI, which is achievable in optical domain completely, meets the demands of quantum communication.

At the transmitter, in order to ensure the frequency interval between subcarriers, Optical Comb Generator (OCG) generates eight optical subcarriers, which have same frequency interval and are orthogonal in frequency domain. Then through the usage of MZI, these orthogonal optical subcarriers are modulated by quantum phase signals. As shown in Fig. 1, an optical pulse with a duration of T ($T = 1/\Delta f$, where Δf is subcarrier interval) is sent into a MZI with pre-established phase difference to generate two non-overlapped pulses, denoted by r and s. These two successive optical pulses have the same duration as the original pulse, while each only has half intensity. Their phase difference Φ represents the classical information, as depicted in Fig. 1.

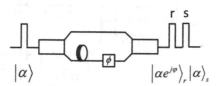

Fig. 1. Quantum phase modulator

After the modulation of subcarriers, n-path optical signals form a single path through optical coupler, generating the OFDM symbols that carries quantum information. And all these OFDM symbols will be transmitted in deep space environment (Fig. 2).

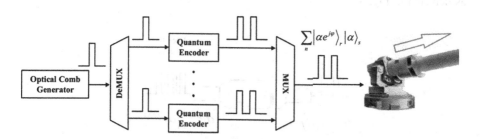

Fig. 2. All-optical quantum OFDM system transmitter

At the receiver, all the received optical quantum OFDM signals will be demodulated after through a series of MZDIs. Each MZDI consists of two couplers, a phase shifter and a delay line. The time delay and differential phase are denoted as (τ, θ) while the central frequency is denoted as f. Thus the transmission function is given by:

$$T(f, \tau, \theta) = \frac{1}{2} \begin{pmatrix} 1 & j \\ j & 1 \end{pmatrix} \begin{pmatrix} e^{-j2\pi f\tau} & 0 \\ 0 & 1 \end{pmatrix} \begin{pmatrix} e^{j\theta} & 0 \\ 0 & 1 \end{pmatrix} \begin{pmatrix} 1 & j \\ j & 1 \end{pmatrix} \qquad (1)$$

Once the OFDM signals enter the receiver, they will be delayed and shifted by MZDIs of each level. After the time delay of MZDI of three levels, quantum OFDM signals will be divided into eight paths respectively, as shown in Fig. 3.

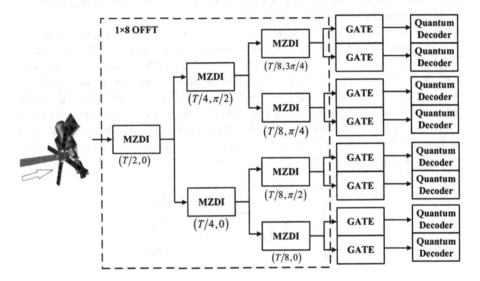

Fig. 3. All-optical quantum OFDM system receiver

Once the r and s pulses are obtained from each optical subcarrier, they will be sent into pre-established MZI. Through the function of detective gate, it is feasible to get the intermediate optical pulse which carries the phase difference Φ. With the help of appropriate measurement, classical information can be extracted from quantum signal, as depicted in Fig. 4.

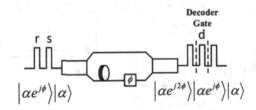

Fig. 4. Quantum phase demodulator

The phase of original optical pulse is arbitrary since the information is carried by relative phase of two optical pulses. Meanwhile, during the transmission, any possible phase interferences would affect both pulses simultaneously, rather than their phase difference. Hence the whole system is particularly resistant to phase noise.

3 Quantum POVM Detection and SRM Measurement

3.1 Quantum Coherent State

There are several commonly used forms of quantum state, including squeezed state, Gaussian state, coherent state, etc. Coherent state is adopted in this paper. Coherent state refers to the quantum optic field which is completely coherent. In optical domain, supported by microscopic particle system and driven by classical source, electromagnetic field generates coherent states optical field through quantum resonance effect. Therefore, laser is coherent state. Coherent state set is capable of constructing a non-orthogonal and over-complete representation since coherent state is the eigenstate of non-Hermitian operator [15]. In the optical quantum OFDM system, when mapping classical information to quantum state, the resulting quantum states are normally non-orthogonal, namely:

$$\left\langle \alpha e^{jk\frac{\pi}{4}} \mid \alpha e^{jm\frac{\pi}{4}} \right\rangle \neq 0, k = 1, 3, 5, 7, m = 1, 3, 5, 7 \tag{2}$$

The photon-number representational form of coherent state is given by [16]:

$$|\alpha\rangle = e^{-\frac{1}{2}|\alpha|^2} \sum_{n=0}^{\infty} \frac{\alpha^n}{\sqrt{(n!)}} |n\rangle \tag{3}$$

where $|\alpha|$ denotes its amplitude, $|n\rangle$ denotes photon-number state and $\langle n \rangle = \langle \alpha | a^\dagger a | \alpha \rangle = |\alpha|^2$ denotes the average photon number. Moreover, $|\alpha|^2$ also represents average optical power. It should be noted that quantum states are transmitted during quantum communication compared with traditional optical communication and quantum effect won't manifest itself unless the photon number is at a low level. Fortunately, this feature just suits the deep space environment in which the received signals are normally very weak.

3.2 Quantum POVM Measurement

In order to obtain classical information from received quantum states, an appropriate measurement operator set $\{M_m\}$ is necessary. It should be note that this measurement operator set $\{M_m\}$ must satisfy completeness equation:

$$\sum_m M_m^\dagger M_m = I \tag{4}$$

where m denotes the possible measurement result. These operators act on the system state space. If the state of quantum system before measurement is $|\varphi\rangle$, then the probability of getting the result as m is given by:

$$p(m) = \langle\varphi|M_m^\dagger M_m|\varphi\rangle \tag{5}$$

System state after measurement is given by:

$$\frac{M_m|\varphi\rangle}{\sqrt{\langle\varphi|M_m^\dagger M_m|\varphi\rangle}} \tag{6}$$

Obviously, completeness equation is equivalent to a one sum for all the possible results. Hence, the above measurement is called general measurement.

Positive operator valued measure is an extension of von Neumann orthogonal projective measurement from closed system to open system, also an extension from complete measurement system to incomplete measurement system [17]. During the practical quantum communication, we care about measurement results instead of the system state after measurement. Hence, based on general measurement, we define $E_m = M_m^\dagger M_m$. It is easy to infer that E_m is a positive operator, which satisfies $\sum_m E_m = I$ and $p(m) = \langle\varphi|M_m|\varphi\rangle$. Such operator E_m is called POVM operator and the operator set $\{E_m\}$ is called a POVM measurement. Based on different criteria, there are different POVM operators designed for different POVM measurement methods.

3.3 SRM Measurement

It is unable to completely determine transmitted quantum states via complete orthogonal measurement methods such as Von Neumann measurement because quantum states of OFDM system are normally non-orthogonal. Therefore, it is necessary to find a measurement basis to minimize error probability of measuring non-orthogonal states, namely, minimize Bayes cost [18]. Quantum square root measurement, the best measurement under the least square root condition, is a well-performed algorithm among all the POVM method. Furthermore, it's also the best method when quantum states in the system have a certain type of geometric symmetry [19]. The basis of SRM method can be obtained directly from a given set of quantum states with a really concise procedure. Expand the transmitted state set under the n-dimensional photon-number state representation and we get the set $\{|\varphi_i\rangle\}$, in which all the vectors $|\varphi_i\rangle$ are linearly independent. Matrix $\Phi = [|\varphi_1\rangle, \ldots, |\varphi_n\rangle]$, formed by all the vectors $|\varphi_i\rangle$, is obviously nonsingular. Then, through the singular value decomposition, namely $\Phi = U\sum V^*$, the relationship between measurement matrix M and Φ can be written as:

$$M = UV^* = \Phi(\Phi^*\Phi)^{-1/2} = \left((\Phi\Phi^*)^{1/2}\right)^\dagger\Phi \tag{7}$$

Extracting the column vectors of matrix M, denoted as $\{|\mu_i\rangle\}$, it is the optimal measurement set. Meanwhile, the POVM operators are given by:

$$\prod_i = |\mu_i\rangle\langle\mu_i| \tag{8}$$

3.4 Measurement Error Analysis

Unlike classical communication, because of the quantum no-cloning theorem, at the receive end, it is impossible to duplicate received signals and detect them separately like classical receivers. However, it is feasible to minimize the detection error probability through appropriate detective methods. Denote $|e_i\rangle = |\varphi_i\rangle - |\mu_i\rangle$ as error vector, then form POVM operators to minimize mean square error:

$$E = Tr((\Phi - M)(\Phi - M)^*) = Tr(U^*(\Phi - M)(\Phi - M)^*U) = \sum_i \langle e_i \mid e_i \rangle \tag{9}$$

As for the SRM detection method with a symbol set which contains a total number of K quantum states, under the condition of equal quantum states input probability, the bit error rate of for detection is given by:

$$P_e = 1 - \frac{1}{K}\sum_{i=1}^{K} \langle\phi_i \mid \mu_i\rangle \tag{10}$$

Then, it can be deduced that it needs infinite photon number states overlapping to represent a coherent state through the analysis of the photon number representational form of coherent states. Hence, theoretically, it takes infinite dimensional vectors to represent coherent states. Obviously, this is unacceptable in practical situation. By carefully observing the coefficient $e^{-\frac{1}{2}|\alpha|^2}\sum_{n=0}^{\infty}\frac{\alpha^n}{\sqrt{(n!)}}$ of photon number state $|n\rangle$, it is easy to find that the bigger the amplitude $|\alpha|$ is, the bigger the coherent state's dimensional number is, thus the more accurate the representation is. Although with the increase of accuracy, it is inevitable of computing complexity to increase accordingly. However, when the coherent state's dimensional number reaches a certain level, the coefficient is close to zero, which means that the following increment of dimensional number almost won't contribute to accuracy any more. Therefore, it's reasonable to choose an appropriate n according to $|\alpha|$, instead of an infinite number.

Taking a further analysis of the expressions of error vector and detection error, it can be found that the amplitude $|\alpha|$ of the coherent state may also affect the detection performance besides of the dimensional number n. Thus, with the increase of the amplitude of coherent state, it will become easier to distinguish different states. Apart from the average photon number of the transmitter, this paper also takes a consideration of the effect upon system performance, which is due to optical power changes caused by time delay and background optical noise.

Among all the three pulses at the receiver, it is only necessary to extract the intermediate one which carries the phase information [22]. During the procedure of extraction, because of the influence of time delay and quantum channel, it is likely that the intermediate pulse won't fall into the extract gate entirely. This may not only affect the optical power, but also introduce background noise in the blank section [23]. The power of background noise can be written as following:

$$P_b = H_b\Omega b_f \tag{11}$$

where H_b denotes unit radiance, Ω denotes the performance coefficient of optical receiver and b_f denotes the range of background noise. Although background noise won't affect the coherent states directly, it will mix with optical signals. This may make the receiver difficult to distinguish noise photons from signal photons, thus affecting system performance and communication quality indirectly.

4   Simulation Results and Analysis

In order to test the performance of the proposed optical quantum OFDM system, some relevant simulations were carried out. First of all, based on the SRM detection method, without the influence of thermal noise, three frequently used quantum phase modulations (Q-BPSK, Q-QPSK, Q-8PSK) were simulated, when the coherent state dimensional number $n = 30$, optical subcarrier number $N = 8$. Compared with classical photon counting detection, the simulation result is as follows (Fig. 5):

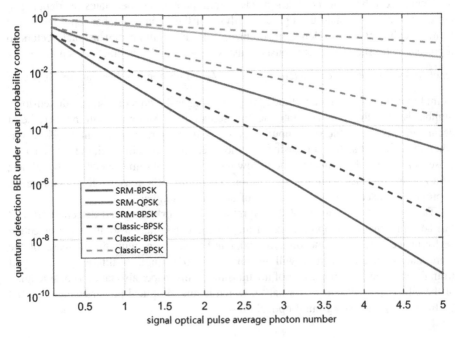

Fig. 5. Three types of quantum phase modulations based on SRM method compared with classical detection

From the simulation result, SRM detection method has better BER performance compared with classical photon counting detection method. Meanwhile, with the increase of average photon number, detection BER keeps reducing, thus it's easier to distinguish different quantum states. Besides, with the increase of modulation order, the discrimination of quantum expansions becomes lower, thus degrading the BER performance.

Then, another simulation was carried out on the time delay issue mentioned before, when the average photon number $n = 5$. The horizontal axis represents the ratio $E(|\tau|)/T_{gate}$ between the absolute expectation $E(|\tau|)$ of time misalignment τ and the optical extracting gate width T_{gate}. The vertical axis represents detection BER, the simulation result is as follows (Fig. 6):

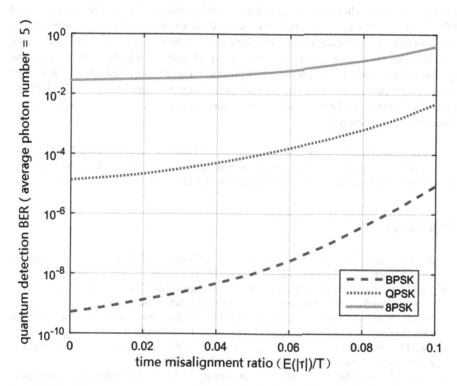

Fig. 6. Quantum measurement affected by optical pulse time misalignment ratio

As the result shown, when the time misalignment is relatively small, the system BER performance is less affected. However, with the time misalignment ratio increasing, not only the optical power in the extracting gate is lower, but also more background noise is introduced, both caused the degradation of detection performance. Hence, in practical situation, receivers are supposed to adjust the range of extract gate adaptively based on the first optical pulse, thus increase the accuracy and robustness of detection. It has been mentioned before that several domestic teams had already realized classical all-optical OFDM systems based on MZI. By changing the modulation carrier into quantum state, these existing practical all-optical systems are still usable, thus providing the physical feasibility and achievability. Also, more research and realistic simulation are needed for the reason that transmission medium is vacuum rather than optical fiber. This is also the further research objective and direction.

5 Conclusions

In this paper, through the analysis of the characteristics of deep space communication and the all-optical OFDM system based on MZI, combined with quantum phase modulation, we proposed an optical quantum OFDM system suitable for deep space exploration. Meanwhile, according to the non-orthogonality of the transmitted quantum OFDM signal states, we proposed a scheme of expanding quantum states under photon-number representation and measuring the received states with SRM detection method. The simulation result shows that it's performance is better than the classical quantum detection method. Moreover, another simulation was carried out to show how the average photon number and optical pulse time misalignment would affect the system performance. These effects were summarized and some possible optimization measures were discussed.

Acknowledgments. This work was supported by the National Natural Science Foundation of China under Grant No. 61571135, Shanghai Sailing Program 17YF1429100 and State Key Laboratory of Intense Pulsed Radiation Simulation and Effect Funding.

References

1. An, J.P., Jin, S., Xu, J., et al.: Development and outlook of deep space communication network protocol. J. Commun. **37**(7), 50–61 (2016)
2. Ye, P.J., Yang, M.F., Peng, J., et al.: Review and prospect of atmospheric entry and earth reentry technology of China deep space exploration. Sci. Sinica **45**(3), 229 (2015)
3. Bai, S., Wang, J.Y., Zhang, L., et al.: Development progress and trends of space optical communications. Laser Optoelectron. Prog. **52**(7), 1–14 (2015)
4. Lai, J.S., Wu, B.B., Tang, R., et al.: Analysis on the application and development of quantum communication. Telecommun. Sci. **32**(3) (2016)
5. Shor, P.W., Preskill, J.: Simple proof of security of the BB84 quantum key distribution protocol. Phys. Rev. Lett. **85**(2), 441 (2000)
6. Peev, M., Langer, T., Lorunser, T., et al.: The SECOQC quantum-key-distribution network in Vienna. In: Conference on Optical Fiber Communication - Includes Post Deadline Papers, OFC 2009. IEEE (2009). OThL2
7. Sasaki, M., Fujiwara, M., Ishizuka, H., et al.: Field test of quantum key distribution in the Tokyo QKD network. In: Quantum Electronics Conference and Lasers and Electro-Optics, pp. 507–509. IEEE (2011)
8. Wang, K.Y.: The research of the development of quantum communication and facing problems. Telecom World **1**, 110–111 (2017)
9. Zhang, G.L.: The "Beijing-Shanghai Line" of quantum secrecy communication opened at the end of the year. Dual Use Technol. Prod. **13**, 21 (2016)

10. Diao, W.T., Song, X.R., Duan, C.D.: The development of quantum secret communication between the ground and satellite. Space Electron. Technol. **13**(1), 83–88 (2016)
11. Zhou, Z.H., Liu, X.Y., Mei, Y., et al.: Study on transmission performances of 8 × 40 Gbits/s all optical OFDM systems. Study Opt. Commun. (6), 21–24 (2012)
12. Zhang, H.B., Gao, X., Zhang, J., et al.: 8 × 122 Gbits all optical OFDM fiber transmission system based on optical FFT. J. Optoelectron. Laser (3), 493–499 (2013)
13. Hillerkuss, D., Winter, M., Teschke, M., et al.: Simple all-optical FFT scheme enabling Tbit/s real-time signal processing. Opt. Express **18**(9), 9324–9340 (2010)
14. Brandt, H.E.: Positive operator valued measure in quantum information processing. Am. J. Phys. **67**(67), 434–439 (1998)
15. Bouwmeester, D., Zeilinger, A.: The physics of quantum information: basic concepts. Stud. Hist. Philos. Sci. Part B Stud. Hist. Philos. Mod. Phys. **34**(2), 331–334 (2000)
16. Sanders, B.C., Bartlett, S.D., Rudolph, T., et al.: Photon-number superselection and the entangled coherent-state representation. Phys. Rev. A **68**(4), 4343–4349 (2003)
17. Pei, C.X., Han, B.B., Zhao, N., et al.: QBER modeling and simulation of QKD in optical fiber with force. Guangzi Xuebao/Acta Photonica Sinica **38**(2), 422–424 (2009)
18. Song, H., Dai, K., Wang, Z.Y., Pan, L.: A quantum algorithm for finding minimum. Comput. Eng. Appl. (14), 37–39 (2003)
19. Hausladen, P., Jozsa, R., Schumacher, B., et al.: Classical information capacity of a quantum channel. Phys. Rev. A **54**(3), 1869–1876 (1996)
20. Eldar, Y.C., Forney, G.D.: On quantum detection and the square-root measurement. IEEE Trans. Inf. Theory **47**(3), 858–872 (2000)
21. Zhao, S.M., Wang, C.L., Zheng, B.Y.: Research on quantum multi-user detection based on SRM algorithm. Sig. Process. **23**(3), 365–369 (2007)
22. Bahrani, S., Razavi, M., Salehi, J.A.: Orthogonal frequency-division multiplexed quantum key distribution. J. Lightwave Technol. **33**(23), 4687–4698 (2015)
23. Yu, Z.Y., Li, M., Lu, P.F.: Photon polarizations in free-space quantum communication. J. Beijing Univ. Posts Telecommun. **36**(2), 1–9 (2013)

Space Representation and Fusion Processing

Overview of Terahertz Radar Cooperation in Space Based Information Networks

Yuan Gao[1,3(✉)], Su Hu[2], Wanbin Tang[2], Dan Huang[2],
Xiangyang Li[1], and Shaochi Cheng[1]

[1] China Defense Science and Technology Information Center,
Beijing 100142, China
yuangao08@tsinghua.edu.cn
[2] University of Electronic Science and Technology of China,
Sichuan 610054, China
[3] State Key Laboratory on Microwave and Digital Communications,
National Laboratory for Information Science and Technology,
Tsinghua University, Beijing 100084, China

Abstract. The development of anti-stealth technologies become popular recently, especially the method to tackle the 5th combat aircraft such as F-22 from the US Air Force. Terahertz Radar has become one effective and promising way to detect stealth unit, and the characteristic of frequency makes it effective to discover the 5th stealth unit. However, the result is relying on many uncontrollable influence factors such as climate, temperature, speed, etc. In this work, we discuss the cooperation strategy to enhance the effect of Terahertz Radar systems, through the cooperation using space based information networks, the terahertz radar and traditional microwave radar could work together through the high-speed communication link, the speed and the accuracy of the detection could be improved significantly.

Keywords: Terahertz radar · Radar cooperation
Space based information network · Hybrid cooperation
Heterogeneous network

1 Introduction

Terahertz radar is one of the most promising radar technology [1–3], the radar wave work between the microwave and infrared band. As a new radar for the United States F-22 and other stealth aircraft to detect, and thus become a stealth weapon The F-22 stealth aircraft, whether based on the shape of stealth or radar absorbing paint stealth, or even based on plasma stealth. Terahertz radar can make it appear prototype, which is currently the majority of conventional radar can not do [4].

In the US military participation in the war in Afghanistan, the US Air Force fighter use infrared precision guided weapons, in the sand environment hit rate as low as 10%. When the dust is blown by the wind, even if the pilot to try dangerous low-altitude bombs, most of the time it is difficult to use infrared guidance way hit the target. If there is a terahertz radar, the situation is not the same, it can be in the dust and tanks, armored vehicles to release the heavy smoke screen to accurately identify the target and guide the precision guided bomb hit the target [5]. Due to fear of dust, clouds, terahertz-imaging radar can be used to detect enemy concealed weapons, camouflage ambush of armed personnel.

Terahertz radar can work around the clock, thereby enhancing the performance of synthetic aperture radar. Its imaging is more widely used than the currently widely used C-band and X-band synthetic aperture radar resolution [6], can improve the accuracy of the map for military reconnaissance, surveillance tasks to provide higher quality information. Terahertz radar penetration characteristics can be used to detect deep targets on the ground, such as the enemy underground command post [7], is a strategic strike weapon.

However, the development of terahertz radar is limited by the equipment and electronic components [8–10]. The range and the effect of detection are not satisfied due to the imperfect condition. Therefore, terahertz cooperation through space based information networks becomes one possible solution to current status of anti-stealth radar [11]. In this work, we summarize the advantages and shortages of heterogeneous terahertz cooperation by using the terahertz radar and traditional microwave radar in heterogeneous networks. The rest of the paper is organized as follows. In part 2, we propose the system model, in part 3, we describe the advantages and shortages of the cooperation, in part 4, we present the simulation based on system level simulation platform. Conclusion and acknowledgement are listed at the end of the work.

2 System Model

As we all know, the radar mainly by receiving the target reflection signal to find the target. If the target surface can make the radar wave is absorbed or scattered, can greatly reduce the probability of discovery, to achieve the purpose of stealth. Therefore, the commonly mentioned stealth technology is mainly by the shape [12], absorbing coating, the formation of plasma cloud absorption or change the direction of the radar wave to achieve stealth.

After the application of stealth technology, the conventional narrow-band micro-wave radar in the detection of radar cross-section of small stealth weapons often appear "powerless." Therefore, for a long time [13], people are talking about "hidden" dis-coloration. Nevertheless, the current stealth technology is impeccable; they can only be a very specific band to play a role, beyond this specific range will be powerless.

On the one hand, the wavelength of terahertz radar is very short, about 30 um– 3 mm range [14], much smaller than the wavelength of microwave and millimeter waves, which can be used to detect smaller targets and more accurate positioning. It also contains the rich frequency, has a very wide bandwidth, can be thousands of kinds of frequencies [15] to launch nanosecond and even picosecond pulse, much more than the scope of the existing stealth technology. The United States is the first country to introduce the concept of terahertz radar, and has carried out 0.2 THz, 1.56 THz, 0.6 THz [16] and other high-resolution radar experiments to verify the feasibility of ter-ahertz radar, Terahertz radar as a future high-precision, anti-stealth radar one of the direction of development in the military will have a broad application prospects.

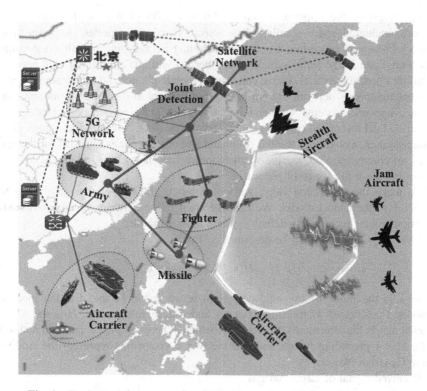

Fig. 1. Terahertz radar cooperation through space based information networks

In Fig. 1, we present the system model of terahertz radar through space based information networks [17]. To enhance the detection, the traditional radar and terahertz radar could be deployed in heterogeneous way, that means, the terahertz radar could be installed on the ground [18], in the plane (Airborne Warning And Control System) or in the space (satellite based radar). To reduce the influence of the shortage, traditional microwave radar is also deployed and could cooperate with the terahertz radar. The cooperation could obtain gain from both heterogeneous and space (degree of freedom [19]). First, the gain from heterogeneous deployment is obtained through different types of radars, that means the gain from terahertz radar and traditional microwave radar will be retrieved [20]. Then the gain from geographical distributed deployment. The cooperative link such as microwave, visible light communication, laser communication, etc. could provide high-speed transmission link without suffering from severe interference of the counterwork environment.

3 Analysis of the Terahertz Radar Cooperation Through Space Based Information Networks

Integration of heaven and earth network to satellite network as the backbone, by the deep space network, adjacent space network, ground network together. The satellite backbone network is generally referred to as the space-based network, including the various levels of the implementation of different tasks of the satellite, deep space network, including space shuttle, Mars detectors and other nodes. Adjacent space network known as space-based network, including aircraft, hot air balloon Airships, helicopters, unmanned aerial vehicles and other low-altitude aircraft. Ground network, including ships, submarines, trains, cars, tanks, mobile phones and other ground nodes. This heterogeneous network system breaks the barriers to data sharing among independent network systems and can effectively integrate resources (including rail resources, load resources, communications resources, etc.). Not only for combat of the reconnaissance, navigation, combat command and other services, but also for the sea - land - air communication, marine weather forecasting, navigation, emergency rescue, etc. to provide a full range of support.

To make the discussion clear, we will compute the cooperative gain using the following mathematical model. We take the cooperation between two terahertz radar (traditional radar included as default) system as an example:

The receiving vector can be described as follows:

$$r(k, l) = H(k, l) U s(k, l) + n(k, l) \tag{1}$$

where k is the index of transmit symbol in resource blocks and l is the index of symbols. Considering M transmit antennas and N receive antennas, H is the $N \times M$ channel matrix that represents the channel coefficient between the cooperation nodes, U is the $M \times 1$ precoding matrix and n is the $N \times 1$ vector that represent the Additive White Gaussian Noise.

Received signal of target radar is:

$$r(k, l) = (H_0(k, l)\, H_1(k, l)) \begin{pmatrix} U_0 \\ U_1 \end{pmatrix} s(k, l) + n(k, l) \tag{2}$$

After the MMSE detector, the central unit could predict the received signal as:

$$\hat{r}(k, l) = W(k, l) \times (H_0(k, l)\, H_1(k, l)) \begin{pmatrix} U_0 \\ U_1 \end{pmatrix} \\ \times s(k, l) + W(k, l) \times n(k, l) \tag{3}$$

The MMSE detector $W(k, l)$ is calculated using the equation below:

$$W(k, l) = \begin{pmatrix} U_0 \\ U_1 \end{pmatrix}^H (H_0(k, l)\, H_1(k, l))^H (k, l)$$

$$\times \left\{ \begin{matrix} (H_0(k, l)\, H_1(k, l))(k, l) \begin{pmatrix} U_0 \\ U_1 \end{pmatrix} \begin{pmatrix} U_0 \\ U_1 \end{pmatrix}^H \\ (H_0(k, l)\, H_1(k, l))^H (k, l) \\ + \dfrac{R_n}{\sigma^2} \end{matrix} \right\}^{-1} \tag{4}$$

The Signal to Interface plus Noise Ratio (SINR) of the received cooperative signal is listed below:

$$SINR(k,l) = \frac{\sigma^2 |W(k,l)(H_0(k,l)\,H_1(k,l))\begin{pmatrix} U_0 \\ U_1 \end{pmatrix}|^2}{W(k,l)R_n W^H(k,l)} \tag{5}$$

Expanded to multi-radar cooperation scenario, radars of different types are transmitting required information to each other and enhance the detection, so the received signal can be described as:

$$\begin{aligned}
\hat{r}_i(k,l) &= W_{i,0,1}(k,l) \\
&\times [(\,H_{i,0}(k,l) \quad H_{i,1}(k,l)\,) \times \begin{pmatrix} U_{0,0} \\ U_{0,1} \end{pmatrix} \times s_0(k,l) \\
&+ (\,H_{i,0}(k,l) \quad H_{i,1}(k,l)\,) \times \begin{pmatrix} U_{1,0} \\ U_{1,1} \end{pmatrix} \times s_1(k,l) + n(k,l)]
\end{aligned} \tag{6}$$

4 Simulation and Analysis

In this part, we simulate the effect of cooperation in terahertz radar systems using the system level simulation platform. To make the simulation simple and clear, we use the Rayleigh fading channel as channel model, the typical scenario is the free space transmission. We have established three-terahertz radar and three microwave radar as typical cooperative nodes.

In Fig. 2, we present the comparison of different deployment strategy using the system level simulation. We compare three indicators to represent the system performance.

Note that all the values are normalized, the reference value are terahertz method. Target Identify Rate means the rate to successfully detection of the target, target SINR means the recovered SINR using the cooperative link, and the detection range means the maximum range to detect required target. The deployment strategies are the combination of traditional radar and terahertz radar in different positions, where space and heterogeneous gain are obtained through different combinations. The space-ground deployment means the deployment of single type of radar (microwave or terahertz) are distributed located on the ground and in the air (using plane or low orbit satellite), and heterogeneous space-ground deployment means the traditional radar and terahertz radar are deployed together. By analyzing the data in this figure, we have the following conclusions:

1. The detection rage of terahertz radar is the smallest, for the limitation of the bandwidth, by using the hybrid heterogeneous cooperation; the detection rage could be significantly increased;
2. The terahertz radar could enhance the detection rate of the radar, for the spectrum characteristic to detect stealth target, so traditional radar may become weak when working alone;
3. The target SINR of the cooperation will be increased through the cooperation by adopting the fusion gain.

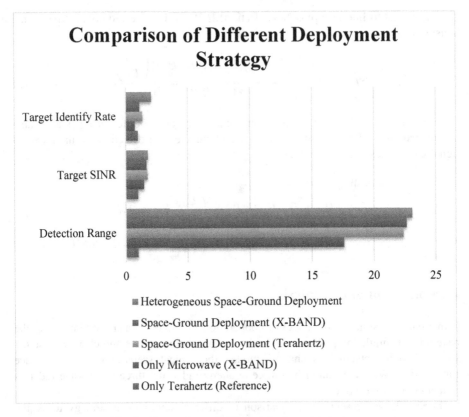

Fig. 2. Comparison of different deployment strategy

5   Conclusion and Future Work

In this paper, we discussed the terahertz radar cooperation in space based information networks. From theoretical point of view, the cooperation is very important to status of the terahertz radar, for the limitation of the electronic component and the technological process. Based on the status, we discuss the advantages and shortages of the terahertz radar cooperation, through cooperation and heterogeneous fusion, the performance of both range and SINR of the terahertz radar are improved up to 37%, which is a significant improvement using this method. However, we do not consider the complex environment, e.g. the channel model, delay, and we will discuss this in the future.

Acknowledgement. This work is funded by China's 973 project under grant of 2012CB316002 and China's 863 project under grant of 2013AA013603, National Natural Science Foundation of China (61701503), International Science and Technology Cooperation Program (2012DF G12010); National S & T Major Project (2013ZX03001024-004), Operation Agreement between Tsinghua University and Ericsson, Qualcomm Innovation Fellowship. The work of Su Hu was jointly supported by the MOST Program of International S&T Cooperation (Grant No. 2016YFE 0123200), National Natural Science Foundation of China (Grant No. 61471100/61101090/

61571082), Science and Technology on Electronic Information Control Laboratory (Grant No. 6142105040103) and Fundamental Research Funds for the Central Universities (Grant No. ZYGX2015J012/ZYGX2014Z005). We would like to thank all the reviewers for their kind suggestions to this work.

References

1. Murano, K., et al.: Demonstration of short-range terahertz radar using high-gain leaky-wave antenna. In: 2016 41st International Conference on Infrared, Millimeter, and Terahertz waves (IRMMW-THz), Copenhagen, pp. 1–2 (2016)
2. Jiang, Y., Deng, B., Wang, H., Qin, Y., Liu, K.: An effective nonlinear phase compensation method for FMCW terahertz radar. IEEE Photonics Technol. Lett. **28**(15), 1684–1687 (2016)
3. Jasteh, D., Hoare, E.G., Cherniakov, M., Gashinova, M.: Experimental low-terahertz radar image analysis for automotive terrain sensing. IEEE Geosci. Remote Sens. Lett. **13**(4), 490–494 (2016)
4. Liang, D., et al.: Broadband time-domain terahertz radar: cross section measurement and imaging. In: 2015 40th International Conference on Infrared, Millimeter, and Terahertz waves (IRMMW-THz), Hong Kong, pp. 1–2 (2015)
5. Lui, H.S., et al.: Terahertz radar cross-section characterisation using laser feedback interferometry with quantum cascade laser. Electron. Lett. **51**(22), 1774–1776 (2015)
6. Bian, M., Dong, X., Guo, A., Lu, Z., Cui, K., Wang, S.: Design and implementation of spaceborne terahertz cloud radar. In: 2016 European Radar Conference (EuRAD), London, pp. 354–357 (2016)
7. Dzwonkowski, P., Samczynski, P., Kulpa, K., Drozdowicz, J., Gromek, D., Krysik, P.: Towards a mobile low-terahertz SAR imaging radar — limitations and prospects. In: 2015 Signal Processing Symposium (SPSympo), Debe, pp. 1–5 (2015)
8. Cao, K., et al.: Simulation research of terahertz coded-aperture imaging technology with high resolution. In: 2016 Progress in Electromagnetic Research Symposium (PIERS), Shanghai, pp. 3414–3418 (2016)
9. Wang, R., Deng, B., Qin, Y., Wang, H.: Bistatic terahertz radar azimuth-elevation imaging based on compressed sensing. IEEE Trans. Terahertz Sci. Technol. **4**(6), 702–713 (2014)
10. Liu, F., Cui, W., Zhu, Z., Dong, S., Shang, S., Yao, Z.: The spaceborne terahertz remote sensing techniques. In: IET International Radar Conference 2013, Xi'an, pp. 1–5 (2013)
11. Siegel, P.H.: THz for space: the golden age. In: 2010 IEEE MTT-S International Microwave Symposium, Anaheim, pp. 816–819 (2010)
12. Lu, Z., Liu, X., Pan, Y., Huang, S., Chen, L., Wang, H.: Application of terahertz technology in cooperative detection of space targets. In: 2016 IEEE 9th UK-Europe-China Workshop on Millimetre Waves and Terahertz Technologies (UCMMT), Qingdao, pp. 202–205 (2016)
13. Du, J., Jiang, C., Wang, J., Ren, Y., Yu, S., Han, Z.: Resource allocation in space multiaccess systems. IEEE Trans. Aerosp. Electron. Syst. **53**(2), 598–618 (2017)
14. Wang, S., He, J., Huang, Y., Wang, A.: Cooperative task assignment of uninhabited combat air vehicles based on improved MOSFLA algorithm. In: 2016 3rd International Conference on Systems and Informatics (ICSAI), Shanghai, pp. 427–432 (2016)
15. Wang, Y., et al.: A capture method based on series-parallel manipulator for satellite on-orbit service. In: 2016 35th Chinese Control Conference (CCC), Chengdu, pp. 6284–6289 (2016)
16. Campbell, M.E., Ahmed, N.R.: Distributed data fusion: neighbors, rumors, and the art of collective knowledge. IEEE Control Syst. **36**(4), 83–109 (2016)

17. Du, J., Jiang, C., Guo, Q., Guizani, M., Ren, Y.: Cooperative earth observation through complex space information networks. IEEE Wirel. Commun. **23**(2), 136–144 (2016)
18. Gelli, S., Bacci, A., Martorella, M., Berizzi, F.: Space-Doppler processing with adaptive compensation for bistatic multichannel ISAR imaging of non-cooperative targets. In: 2015 European Radar Conference (EuRAD), Paris, pp. 13–16 (2015)
19. Wang, P., Sun, Z., Tan, J., Huang, Z., Zhu, Q., Zhao, W.: Development and evaluation of cooperative adaptive cruise controllers. In: 2015 IEEE International Conference on Mechatronics and Automation (ICMA), Beijing, pp. 1607–1612 (2015)
20. Yang, H., Jin, M., Xie, Z., Zhang, Y., Sun, K., Zhao, X.: Ground micro-gravity verification of free-floating non-cooperative satellite docking. In: 2015 IEEE International Conference on Advanced Intelligent Mechatronics (AIM), Busan, pp. 1253–1258 (2015)

Remote Sensing Image Intelligent Interpretation Based on Knowledge Graph

Bitao Jiang[1], Lei Ma[2(✉)], and Lin Cai[1]

[1] Beijing Institute of Remote Sensing Information, Beijing 100192, China
[2] Institute of Automation, Chinese Academy of Sciences, Beijing 100190, China
lei.ma@ia.ac.cn

Abstract. Recently more and more observation sensors carried by different platforms make people be able to obtain massive multi-source data, this kind of explosive increase of information extraction brings great challenge. However, remote sensing image interpretation depends on the knowledge from experience of the experts, there are also few available knowledge graphs for the intelligent interpretation of multi-source remote sensing big data. In this article, we provide a survey of such knowledge graph and propose the framework to auxiliary interpreters.

Keywords: Knowledge graph · Remote sensing · Intelligent interpretation
Image fusion

1 Introduction

With the rapid development of remote sensor technologies, human observation of the earth has risen to the level that has never been reached. The various sensors, different bands and resolution of the satellite load make the remote sensing data increasingly, the amount of remote sensing data is also significantly increased. Therefore, the remote sensing data show "big data" features obviously [1].

In the process of traditional interpreting remote sensing images, it is necessary to rely on the knowledge and experience of experts he field of remote sensing. At the same time, a large amount of information can be obtained to support for the interpretation, the workload is large and the efficiency is very low. So the accumulation, expression and use of expert knowledge, and build a knowledge-based system, auxiliary interpreters faster and more effective solution to the interpretation of the work is a very meaningful work. In addition, many satellites around the world form a large amount of remote sensing information, how to provide a highly efficient data management, information extraction, semantic analysis and other technologies and methods, integrated satellite remote sensing data, ground observation data and simulation

---

This work was supported by National Defense Science and Technology Innovation Fund of the Chinese Academy of Sciences (CXJJ-16M109).

Q. Yu (Ed.): SINC 2017, CCIS 803, pp. 329–338, 2018.
https://doi.org/10.1007/978-981-10-7877-4_30

models and other multi-source, heterogeneous data, become the current urgent problem. A platform or knowledge organization on the a priori information can support remote sensing big data expression, information semantic integration, collaborative management, and ultimately to achieve mass spectrometry data services, semantic integration and interoperability, sharing platform construction [2].

Knowledge Graph [3, 6] is a network that links different semantic concepts, entities, and attributes in a way that conforms to human cognition. Semantic concepts, entities and attributes constitute the nodes of the network, and its semantic relations constitute the edges of the network. The concept of Knowledge Graph was proposed by Google in May 2012, then many user-friendly products were launched. Its purpose is to improve the ability of search engine's to enhance the user's search quality and search experience, to provide users with faster and easier access to information and knowledge of efficient tools. Because Knowledge Graph can organize data efficiently at the knowledge level, it can greatly drive the development of technologies and applications such as intelligent search, intelligent Q&A, and personalized recommendation.

The contribution of this article is to review current knowledge graph techniques, and present some perspectives on construction for remote sensing intelligent interpretation. This article is organized as follows: Sect. 1 gives an overview of the big data of remote sensing and value of Knowledge Graph; Sect. 2 introduce the framework of Knowledge Graph for Remote Sensing Interpretation; Sect. 3 review the building of Knowledge Graph; Sects. 4 and 5 addresses and highlights inference and visualization of Knowledge Graph and finally Sect. 6 presents some conclusions and comments.

2 Framework of Knowledge Graph for Remote Sensing Interpretation

The framework of Knowledge Graph is shown as Fig. 1. Firstly, the data include structed data, unstructed data and semi-structed data. The unstructed data is also acquired from multi-source imagery, such as panchromatic, multispectral, hyperspectral, SAR, infrared images, LiDAR, GIS. Of course, the data need to be preprocessed before knowledge extraction. Data cleaning can remove the noise, then object recognition and data filtering are applied to extract the object and import information from the unstructed data. The ontology library need to be constructed according to the domain knowledge of the expert and the unsupervised learning algorithm. Secondly, knowledge extraction includes entity extraction, relation extraction, attribute extraction and other extraction. A very good mathematical description is built to represent the entity and the relation, with a very efficient vector in space. According to the effective vector representation, a new deep neural network is applied to solve the specific modeling problems in the process of Knowledge Graph construction, including identification, classification and so on. Thirdly, knowledge fusion can merge the same or very similar entity by entity disambiguation and similarity computation. Inference is also applied to information fusion. Finally, knowledge graph can be constructed after knowledge fusion. As the remote sensing data is updated very quickly, the Knowledge Graph must have self-learning ability to update its knowledge structure. In order to

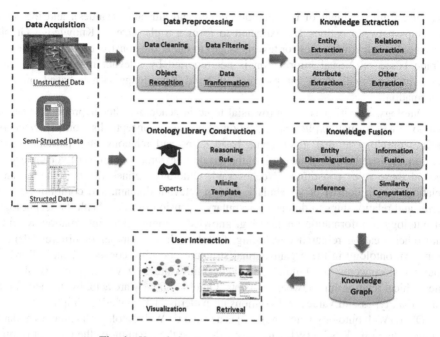

Fig. 1. Knowledge graph construction framework

adapt to the retrieval needs of all kinds of people, the retrieval algorithm also has certain intelligence characteristics, which adapt to the needs of personalized retrieval. The visualization will greatly improve the efficiency of the use of Knowledge Graph, but also for non-professional critics to facilitate the use of Knowledge Graph.

3   Knowledge Graph Building

3.1   Ontology Library

Knowledge Graph is essentially a semantic network of knowledge. The semantic network is constituted by an ontology library with a set of triples. Ontology defines the concept of a series of $C = \{c,c,...,c\}$, entity, $E = \{e,e,...,e\}$, attribute, $A = \{a,a,..., a\}$ and the values for each attribute $Va = \{Va,Va,...,Va\}$, and so on. Knowledge Graph is a collection triples, which includes entities 1, relationships, entity 2 and concepts, attributes, attribute values, entities are the most basic elements of Knowledge Graph, there are different relationships between different entities. Concept mainly refers to the collection, classification, object types, classes of things, such as characters and geography; property referring to objects may have properties, features, characteristics, features and parameters; the property value mainly refers to that the object is specified in the value property.

From the composition of Knowledge Graph, it can be seen above, to construct a Knowledge Graph, you firstly need to construct an ontology library and get the concept, from the input of information entities and attributes (values), and the relationships between entities are extracted to form a triple. Due to Knowledge Graph based only on text messages (or text message) to build, the construction of Knowledge Graph based on Visual information is not reported by relevant researches, so this following part will focus on progress of build Knowledge Graph based on text information.

Ontology definition is a controversial topic in academia. Studer proposed that an ontology is a formal, explicit specification of a shared conceptualisation [4]. Nechers defines ontology as that given some basic terms and relations of a particular collar domain vocabulary and take use of the terminology and definitions of vocabulary to extend these rules constitutes. Neches said, Ontology defines the basic terms and relations which consist of vocabulary field of relevant domain, and combining these terms and relationships to define a vocabulary extension of rules. With the technology of ontology in information engineering, knowledge engineering, information systems and other areas of research developing, Ontology has a number of different definitions. An ontology in the organizational structure generally consists of the following four parts: concepts, attributes, entity and entities attribute value. There is often a hierarchical relationship between concepts. Ontology library are actually defined in the basic data types and values and relationship patterns of Knowledge Graph.

OWL (Web ontology language) [10] is a semantic Web ontology language standard recommended by W3C. OWL can clearly describe the meaning of the concept of and the relationships between concepts, it follows the object-oriented thought, describe structure contained domain knowledge in the form of the classes and properties, OWL language also has a logical description and calculation of reasoning ability. Method of constructing Chinese Knowledge Graph based on multiple data sources is generally divided into three kinds: artificial construction, automatic and semi-automatic constructing method.

With the development of semantic Web and knowledge engineering, the ontology technique has received wider researching interests because of its superiority in field knowledge expression and knowledge reuse. Ontology can be used as a concrete formalization of the conceptual model in a specific field which helps for knowledge sharing. But for direct application on remote sensing information processing and interpretation, there are still some problems need to be solved. Among them, the greatest issues are the bottlenecks in large-scale ontology storage and inference performances. Up till now some practical solutions such as LAS, IS, DLDB and Seasame have been proposed by native and foreign researchers, which are based on the combination of RDBMS technique and ontology inference. Constrained OWL Lite model is used to describe the knowledge derived from remote sensing image interpretation, thus the polynomial processing time length can be promised. Based on an existing ontology mapping model, an improved mixed version OOM/OIIM is proposed to map the ontology interpreted from the remote sensing image to relational database. Then according to the semantic and inference rules of OWL Lite and OWL Lite- models, inference rules for interpreting TBox and ABox ontologies can be extracted, which are passed to the inference procedure for illustrating the usage of these rules.

3.2   Recognition and Alignment of Entities

The aim of entity recognition is to extract containing entities from the input source data (which refers to text here). Techniques for entity recognition can be categorized into dictionary based methods, supervised learning based methods, active learning based methods and clustering based methods etc. Here are some brief descriptions on these methods in below:

(1) Dictionary based methods: the recognition of dictionary based methods largely depends on the feature dictionary being constructed, generally performed by different kinds of string searching algorithms used for entry matching in the dictionary being constructed. Performance of the dictionary based entity gene naming recognition is mainly dependent on the quality of the matching method and the dictionary being built. For the matching methods, which include the fuzzy and exact versions, they determine the similarity between the dictionary entries and the text content to be processed; while the compactness of the dictionary decides the accuracy and recall-rate of recognition of gene-named entities.

(2) Rule based methods are built on manually designed rule-set, where biologically named entity cognition rules are devised from analysis of the entity vocabulary and phrasing habits. The explicit benefits of this method include the flexibility of definition and the extendibility of the rule set; yet when the definition of such amount of rules requires specific expertise knowledge, which makes them expensive in acquisition time and hard for extension into other fields. Narayanaswamy etc. [5] manually built a set of rule through a selected quantity of keywords, English grammar and contextual information. Given these information, a number of abbreviations are extracted via pattern recognition algorithms, which are useful for picking out the core terms and functional terms expressed by each word. Finally, the multi-word entities are recognized by the connection and extension rules defined with these abbreviations.

(3) Supervised classification based methods: the supervised method divides the original input information into semantic blocks (e.g. to get a word sequence by the segmentation of a given statement), then assign these blocks with labels manually. The assigned categorical label of an entity semantic block is the entity itself, while all other non-entity semantic blocks are usually uniformly categorized by an extra label. Given an appointed number of training data with such {semantic block sequence, label} format, common machine learning methods can be adopted to train an entity recognition model. Machine learning based methods are currently the most widely used means for recognizing biomedical named entities, which mainly include Maximum Entropy (ME) [7], Hidden Markov Model (HMM) [8], Conditional Random Field (CRF) [9] etc. For the most commonly used CRF methods, its starting point is that the labeling of a single semantic block not only depends on its own feature, but also the blocks around it in context. CRF has shown a considerable capability in multiple entity naming tasks, it provides a feature oriented, globally optimized entity naming framework. On the JNLPBA2004 task, Settles et al. [11] firstly used the CRF model, with only traditional features plus some extra new ones, it reached a F score close to 70%.

Recently, due to the fast development and high performance of deep learning methods, their appliance on the entity recognition has also been inspected. At present, it has been employed for extracting the deep representation of the semantic blocks. Collobert et al. [12] used the neighboring vocabulary of a word as context and devised a companying feed-forward neural network to recognize the entity. In [13], Chiu and Nichols showed by experiments that the usage of Character embedding and Word embedding as the descriptive features for semantic block can significantly raise the entity recognition accuracy. Huang et al. [14] introduced a bi-directional Long-Short Term Memory (LSTM) network to model the contextual relationship between different semantic blocks, and managed to further raise the recognition rate with traditional manual features. Limsopatham and Collier [15] considered orthographic features, and used them as the input of the deep neural network.

(4) Entity alignment: normal entity recognition involves classifying candidate semantic blocks into major categories (such as locations, names of persons etc.), while the entity alignment involves further correlating semantic blocks with specific entities based on recognition results. Standard entity alignment consisted of matching and disambiguation. For the first matching step, the selected semantic block is matched with the entities in the existing entity ontology library, where one or several candidate entities are chosen. For the second step, when there are conflicting entities, especially the case where a single entity name is matched with numerous entities, one most possible entity is picked by the disambiguation technique. Dai et al. [16] performed entity alignment by a Markov Logical Network modeling the relational constraints between entities. Liu et al. [17] used a graph model to synthesize the entity recognition and entity alignment processes for simultaneous recognition and alignment. Li and Liu [18] proposed an unsupervised entity alignment method. This method firstly used word embedding for to measure the similarity between entities, then re-arrange similar candidate entities with sorting algorithm at the level of words and phrases to get the aligned entities. Chen et al. [20] had utilized multiple features to capture the semantic information from diverse aspects, and also introduced a learning based sorting framework for the alignment procedure.

3.3 Relation Extraction

What relation extraction means is to decide the relationship between two entities according to a raw input (e.g. a piece of sentence) and two appointed entities. Relation extraction is one of the most closely watched topics in natural language processing. Most early relation extraction algorithms require a large quantity of very detailed labeling information. Mintz et al. [21] proposed a fuzzy supervised method, which assigned all the sentences picked from the dataset including the two entities with the same label. But such method would introduce the problem of erroneous labeling. To address this issue, Riedel et al. [22] introduced multi-instance single label learning concept to categorize relationships thus the samples with negative instances also became valid. Surdeanu et al. [23] further introduced multi-label multi-instance learning concept to enhance the relation extraction involving multi-class relationships. Recently, deep learning based methods have also been applied onto the relation extraction problem. Socker et al. [24] utilized a Recursive neural network for the relation extraction, which abstracted a sentence as a conceptual tree with word embeddings as its nodes. In another research report, Zeng et al. [25] made use of the Convolutional neural network widely used in the image processing for constructing an end-to-end relation extraction algorithm, in which, distances between the pair of entities and the vocabularies exterior of the ontology are made as the input of the network. Xie et al. [26] had considered the use of a wider range of textual information as the auxiliary feature for feature extraction. As the attention mechanism proved to be effective for natural language processing task, Lin et al. had tried to introduce it into the relation extraction in [27].

4   Inference of Knowledge Graph

Inference of Knowledge Graph involves two aspects mainly: one is the inference of knowledge chain based on rules; the other is graph packing. Introductions are as follows.

(1)   Inference of Knowledge Chain Based on Rules

Path ranking is a representative knowledge chain inference algorithm, which uses the link route between two entities to forecast the relationship of them. The technique was first proposed by Lao and Cohen [28], which uses random walk as a basis. Path ranking contains three main steps. First, path extraction using random walk; Second, figure up the features of every route respectively, including relationships of multiple routes; Third, classification on the basis of the first two steps. Wang et al. [29] moved forward to culster relationships through routes, and shared context routes in multiple relations through multi-task learning. They then have done the inference work with paths ordering algorithms. Pujara et al. [30] proposed a probable soft-logic method to do the derivation of knowledge chain.

(2)   Graph Packing

Graph packing depends on feature interpretation of entites and relations, also known as Embedding-based method. Current approaches can be devided into two classes, one is Tensor factorization based, the other is Neural network based. Tensor factorization based method [31] visualize knowledge graph as a three-dimensional close-neighbor tensor, in which two dimensions are entities, the third one is the relation between entities. For every relation, through tensor decomposition, we can build up a latent-component representation matrix and a matrix describing the interactions between components and class k. We can do the packing to the original tensor through these two matrices. Furthermore, Nickel and Tresp [32] analyzed the generalization performance of the tensor. Neural network based methods [33] typically construct a scoring function to describe a triple (two entities and a relation between them) in which entities and relations are represented as embedded vectors and tensors respectively. The scoring function is modeled on a neural network. Using existing samples to train it, we can classify new entities. Socher et al. [34] proposed a neural tensor networks to do the graph packing, the net could allow entities to combine with each other, generating new entities. Due to the face that neural net based methods are very dependent on the effectiveness of the vectorization of entities, Guo et al. [35] considered the geometric structure inside the embedded space of entities and proposed a semantic smoothing embedding approach. Ji et al. [36] drew sparsity into the modelling of embedded space.

5   Visualization of Knowledge Graph

Information visualization is first mentioned explicitly in 1989 by Stuart Cade, York McKinley and George Robertson [37], which is an interactive visualization of abstract data through computer to enhance our cognition to non-physical information. Due to the youth of knowledge graph, there's a lack of research on visualization about it. Cao et al. [38] designed the Facet Atlas system to demonstrate the biomedicine knowledge graph (disease-therapy-medication) visually, which supported simple switches of global demonstration and local demonstration. Lohmann et al. [39] researched on user-oriented visualization, especially, an easy-understanding visual interaction language was proposed. Lohmann et al. [40] did researches on visualization algorithm of uncertain networks, which decomposed uncertain networks into certain instances using Monte Carlo process. [41] developed a visualization platform to support knowledge graph editing.

6   Conclusion and Future Work

This paper puts forward the technical framework of establishing the Knowledge Graph of remote sensing image interpretation, and summarizes the key technologies. The Knowledge Graph construction framework for remote sensing application is proposed, including remote sensing data acquisition, data preprocessing, ontology library construction, knowledge extraction, knowledge fusion, the visualization and retrieval. In the future, the type and quantity of remote sensing data will grow rapidly, and the breadth and depth of ground observation will be developed rapidly. It is urgent to carry out research on remote sensing data. In the face of mass and multi-source data, it is a bottleneck to restrict the application of remote sensing data by relying on experienced interpreters. In order to improve the ability of knowledge graph which applied to remote sensing interpretation, complexity will be also analyzed. How to construct the knowledge structure of expert knowledge and realize the intelligent retrieval and intelligent reasoning of remote sensing data not only has very important academic value, but also has important practical significance.

References

1. Deren, L., Liangpei, Z., Guisong, X.: Automatic analysis and mining of remote sensing big data. Acta Geodaetica Cartogr. Sin. **43**(12), 1211–1216 (2014)
2. Xie, R., Luo, Z.W., Wang, Y.C., Chen, W.: Key techniques for establishing domain specific large scale knowledge graph. Radio Eng. **47**(04), 1–6 (2017)

3. Bashar, M.A., Li, Y., Gao, Y.: A framework for automatic personalised ontology learning. In: IEEE International Conference on Web Intelligence, pp. 105–112 (2016)
4. Studer, R., Benjamins, V.R., Fensel, D.: Knowledge engineering: principles and methods. Data Knowl. Eng. **25**, 161–197 (1998)
5. Narayanaswamy, M., Ravikumar, K.E., Vijay-shanker, K.: A biological named entity recognizer. In: Proceedings of Pacific Symposium on Biocomputing, p. 427 (2003)
6. Bordes, A., Gabrilovich, E.: Constructing and mining web-scale knowledge graphs. In: Proceedings of the 20th ACM SIGKDD International Conference on Knowledge Discovery and Data Mining, New York, pp. 1967–1967. ACM (2014)
7. Wang, J.: Chinese named body recognition based on maximum entropy model. Nanjing University of Science and Technology (2005)
8. Yu, H., Zhang, H., Liu, Q., Lv, X., Shi, S.: Chinese named entity recognition based on cascaded hidden Markov model. J. Commun. **27**, 86–93 (2006)
9. Sun, X., Sun, Z., Ren, F.: Biomedical named entity recognition based on deep conditional random field. Pattern Recogn. Artif. Intell. **29**(11), 997–1008 (2016)
10. Knublauch, H., Oberle, D., Tetlow, P., Wallace, E.: A semantic web primer for object-oriented software developers. W3C. Accessed 30 July 2008
11. Settles, B.: Biomedical named entity recognition using conditional random fields and rich feature sets. In: Proceedings of the International Joint Workshop on Natural Language Processing in Biomedicine and its Applications, pp. 104–107 (2004)
12. Collobert, R., Weston, J., Bottou, L., Karlen, M., Kavukcuoglu, K., Kuksa, P.: Natural language processing (almost) from scratch. J. Mach. Learn. Res. **12**, 2493–2537 (2011)
13. Chiu, J.P.C., Nichols, E.: Named entity recognition with bidirectional LSTM-CNN. TACL, vol. 4, pp. 357–370 (2016)
14. Huang, Z., Xu, W., Yu, K.: Bidirectional LSTM-CRF models for sequence tagging. CoRR abs/1508.01991 (2015)
15. Limsopatham, N., Collier, N.: Learning orthographic features in bi-directional lstm for biomedical named entity recognition. In: Proceedings of the 2016 Biennial Workshops on Building and Evaluating Resources for Biomedical Text Mining. Association for Computational Linguistics (2016)
16. Dai, H.-J., Tsai, R.T.-H., Hsu, W.-L.: Entity disambiguation using a markov logic network. In: Proceedings of 5th International Joint Conference on Natural Language Processing, pp. 846–855 (2011)
17. Liu, X., Zhou, M., Wei, F., Fu, Z., Zhou, X.: Joint inference of named entity recognition and normalization for tweets. In: Proceedings of the 50th Annual Meeting of the Association for Computational Linguistics: Long Papers (ACL 2012), vol. 1, pp. 526–535. Association for Computational Linguistics, Stroudsburg, PA, USA (2012)
18. Li, C., Liu, Y.: Improving text normalization via unsupervised model and discriminative reranking. In: ACL (2014)
19. Sproat, R., Jaitly, N.: RNN approaches to text normalization: a challenge (2016)
20. Chen, Y., He, S., Liu, K., Zhao, J., Lv, X.: Entity linking based on multiple feature. J. Chin. Inf. Process. **30**(4), 176–183 (2016)
21. Mintz, M., Bills, S., Snow, R., Jurafsky, D.: Distant supervision for relation extraction without labeled data. In: Proceedings of ACLIJCNLP, pp. 1003–1011 (2009)
22. Riedel, S., Yao, L., McCallum, A.: Modeling relations and their mentions without labeled text. In: Proceedings of ECML-PKDD, pp. 148–163 (2010)
23. Surdeanu, M., Tibshirani, J., Nallapati, R., Manning, C.D.: Multi-instance multi-label learning for relation extraction. In: Proceedings of EMNLP, pp. 455–465 (2012)
24. Socher, R., Bauer, J., Manning, C.D., Ng, N.Y.: Parsing with compositional vector grammars. In: Proceedings of ACL (2013)

25. Zeng, D., Liu, K., Lai, S., Zhou, G., Zhao, J.: Relation classification via convolutional deep neural network. In: Proceedings of COLING, pp. 2335–2344 (2014)
26. Xie, R., Liu, Z., Jia, J., Luan, H., Sun, M.: Representation learning of knowledge graphs with entity descriptions. In: Proceedings of the Twenty-Fifth International Joint Conference on Artificial Intelligence (2016)
27. Lin, Y., Shen, S., Liu, Z., Luan, H., Sun, M.: Neural relation extraction with selective attention over instances. In: Meeting of the Association for Computational Linguistics, pp. 2124–2133 (2016)
28. Lao, N., Cohen, W.W.: Relational retrieval using a combination of path-constrained random walks. Mach. Learn. 81(1), 53–67 (2010)
29. Wang, Q., Liu, J., Luo, Y., Wang, B., Lin, C.-Y.: Knowledge base completion via coupled path ranking. In: Meeting of the Association for Computational Linguistics (ACL), pp. 1308–1318 (2016)
30. Pujara, J., Miao, H., Getoor, L., Cohen, W.: Knowledge graph identification. In: Proceedings of the 11th International Semantic Web Conference, pp. 542–557 (2013)
31. Nickel, M., Tresp, V., Kriegel, H.P.: A three-way model for collective learning on multi-relational data. In: International Conference on Machine Learning, ICML 2011, Bellevue, Washington, USA, 28 June–July DBLP, pp. 809–816 (2011)
32. Nickel, M., Tresp, V.: An analysis of tensor models for learning on structured data. In: Blockeel, H., Kersting, K., Nijssen, S., Železný, F. (eds.) ECML PKDD 2013. LNCS (LNAI), vol. 8189, pp. 272–287. Springer, Heidelberg (2013). https://doi.org/10.1007/978-3-642-40991-2_18
33. Bordes, A., Weston, J., Collobert, R., Bengio, Y.: Learning structured embeddings of knowledge bases. In: Conference on Artificial Intelligence, number EPFL-CONF-192344 (2011)
34. Socher, R., Chen, D., Manning, C.D., Ng, A.: Reasoning with neural tensor networks for knowledge base completion. In: Advances in Neural Information Processing Systems, pp. 926–934 (2013)
35. Guo, S., Wang, Q., Wang, B., Wang, L., Guo, L.: Semantically smooth knowledge graph embedding. In: Proceedings of ACL, pp. 84–94 (2015)
36. Ji, G., Liu, K., He, S., Zhao, J.: Knowledge graph completion with adaptive sparse transfer matrix. In: Proceedings of the Thirtieth AAAI Conference on Artificial Intelligence (AAAI 2016), pp. 985–991 (2016)
37. Goh, K.I., Kahng, B., Kim, D.: Universal behavior of load distribution in scale-free networks. Phys. Rev. Lett. 87(27), 278701 (2001)
38. Cao, N., Sun, J., Lin, Y.-R., Gotz, D., Liu, S., Qu, H.: FacetAtlas: multifaceted visualization for rich text corpora. IEEE Trans. Vis. Comput. Graph. 16(6): 1172–1181 (2010)
39. Lohmann, S., Negru, S., Haag, F., Ertl, T.: VOWL2: user-oriented visualization of ontologies. In: Janowicz, K., Schlobach, S., Lambrix, P., Hyvönen, E. (eds.) EKAW 2014. LNCS (LNAI), vol. 8876, pp. 266–281. Springer, Cham (2014). https://doi.org/10.1007/978-3-319-13704-9_21
40. Lohmann, S., Negru, S., Bold, D.: The ProtégéVOWL plugin: ontology visualization for everyone. In: Presutti, V., Blomqvist, E., Troncy, R., Sack, H., Papadakis, I., Tordai, A. (eds.) ESWC 2014. LNCS, vol. 8798, pp. 395–400. Springer, Cham (2014). https://doi.org/10.1007/978-3-319-11955-7_55

Author Index

Printed in the United States
By Bookmasters